Antifeminism in American Thought

an annotated bibliography

G. K. Hall

WOMEN'S STUDIES

Publications

Barbara Haber
Editor

Antifeminism in American Thought

an annotated bibliography

CYNTHIA D. KINNARD

G.K.HALL &CO.

70 LINCOLN STREET, BOSTON, MASS.

Library of Congress Cataloging-in-Publication Data

Kinnard, Cynthia D.
  Antifeminism in American Thought.

  (A reference publication in women's studies)
  Includes index.
  1. Feminism—United States—Bibliography. 2. Women's rights—United
States—Bibliography. 3. Women—United States—Bibliography. I. Title.
II. Title: Antifeminism in American Thought. III. Series.
Z7964.U49K56   1986   016.3054'2'0973   86-19525
[HQ1426]
ISBN 0-8161-8122-5

This publication is printed on permanent/durable acid-free paper
MANUFACTURED IN THE UNITED STATES OF AMERICA

Contents

The Author

Cynthia D. Kinnard, an associate professor of English, directs
the Graduate Program in American Studies and also teaches in the
American Studies and Women's Studies Programs at Indiana University.
She has written articles on Mariana Griswold Van Rensselaer and
coauthored articles on teaching introductory women's studies courses
(with Jean Robinson) and on teaching women's studies in a women's
prison (with Martha Vicinus), both of which appeared in Radical
Teacher. She was a senior Fulbright lecturer in Yugoslavia in 1984–
85. She is presently at work on a biography of Rebecca Harding
Davis. Born and reared in New Jersey, she holds a B.A. from
Dickinson College, an M.A. from Shippensburg State College, and a
Ph.D. from Johns Hopkins University, where she held Danforth and
Woodrow Wilson fellowships.

Preface

This bibliography is divided topically into eight sections, within each of which the items are listed chronologically, books appearing first (in alphabetical order) in each year's entry, then articles, which are arranged by month (with those with month only followed by those dated by day within the month: thus, an article for May precedes one for 6 May). Within each month or day of the month, entries are alphabetical. Items are numbered consecutively. Topics are arranged starting with general discussions and moving to more narrow and specific statements. Each section begins with a compressed overview that notes trends, peaks in activity, and shifts in argument. The researcher is also referred to other sections where overlapping material may be found.

The first section is concerned with women's rights and feminism, an all-inclusive category in which can be found material opposing more than one specific reform and, indeed, opposing the very idea of women's rights. This topic predates all the others. The next section deals with woman suffrage, not only the most specific category but also the largest because antifeminists expended so much energy and so many resources in trying to prevent the extension of suffrage to women. This second topic could be considered a subcategory of the first, and indeed suffrage is attacked by writers listed in the women's rights section as well. The distinction is that items in the woman suffrage category are devoted exclusively to fighting woman suffrage. This section concludes with entries for six antisuffrage periodicals, of which The True Woman is quite rare and not included in the History of Women microfilm collection. Articles in these periodicals have not been separately annotated, but many of them appeared earlier in periodicals and pamphlets.

A survey of domesticity, femininity, and motherhood follows--the main message of which is that women belong in the home as wives and mothers. Here will be found articles upholding the doctrine of the spheres and the cult of true womanhood. It may seem less vehemently antifeminist than the first two categories, but it should be seen as a milder way of still opposing women's rights and woman suffrage.

Then come two areas that focus on women's minds and their training: first, the fairly specific subject of education; second,
women's intellect and character, where will be found articles dis-
cussing women's limited intellectual capacity and deformed character.
These two sections complement each other. The next section, on
women's work, is also highly focused and includes material dealing
with the kinds of work women should and could do outside the home, as
well as articles examining whether women are equally creative as men.
This does not mean to imply that women did not work in the home, of
course; that material is found in section 3. The final sections deal
with two extremely significant topics, namely, on woman's role in the
church and on women's bodies; this final survey includes material on
women's anatomy, physiology, physical activity, and apparel.

Assignment of material to these categories had to be somewhat
arbitrary, as many of the contributions might easily have been included in two or more sections. The user of this bibliography should
consult all the categories: she will find guidance for overlaps in
this introduction, in the brief headnotes to each section, and in the
index, which includes references both to people mentioned in the
annotations and to authors themselves.

I have avoided editorializing in the annotations and instead
attempted to present the tone and voice of the various authors. The
user of this bibliography should always hear the author of the article or book, not the compiler, in these entries. Accordingly, I have
quoted extensively to give the reader the flavor of the piece. This
has meant that I have often felt that I was absorbing, and at the
same time neutralizing, a great deal of antifeminist hostility (perhaps that is why I suffer from a colicky gall bladder). The critical
analysis may now begin.

Acknowledgements

I wish to thank Indiana University for awarding me two grants in aid of research and a summer faculty fellowship for work on this project. The staffs at the Boston Public Library, the New York Public Library, the Enoch Pratt in Baltimore, the Library of Congress, the Indianapolis Public Library, and the University of Wisconsin at Madison assisted me at various stages in my research. Special thanks go to Anthony Shipps, Steven Sowards, and Debbie Long at the Indiana University Library. Andy Lewis of Ursa Systems provided valuable computer assistance, as did the Indiana University Computing Center. Barbara Haber's editorial suggestions were greatly appreciated. My late husband Jack R. Kinnard was my mainstay throughout this project.

Introduction

When I began this project more than six years ago, I had a
limited idea of the scope it would finally reach. I had become
interested in opposition to woman suffrage while writing a disserta-
tion on Mariana Griswold Van Rensselaer, an important nineteenth-
century American art critic who was also a pamphleteering antisuffragist. I was puzzled that an independent and pioneering woman like
Van Rensselaer would oppose the extension of suffrage to women (see
her pamphlet, 467). In coming to grips with Van Rensselaer, I was
drawn into further reading of the antisuffragist literature. Even-
tually, I presented a paper on antisuffrage at the Berkshire Confer-
ence in 1976. When Barbara Haber proposed that I do a bibliography
on antifeminism in America, I jumped at the chance to pursue thor-
oughly what was becoming an obsession. Now, many libraries, dusty
books, and obscure periodicals later, I have begun to outline the
scope of antifeminism in America, a movement brought here from native
countries and with us still, a movement that reached its peak with
antisuffrage but which is by no means limited to it. And it has not
gone away.

Let us begin with definitions. Antifeminism implies, indeed
requires, feminism. It does not exist in a vacuum, as does misogyny.
As the root of the word implies, misogynists hate and fear women.
The stimulus for misogyny is simply the presence of women in the
world. I read misogynist pieces, sheer gratuitous nastiness about
women, which did not make their way into the bibliography. Sometimes
the misogyny is blatant, sometimes covert, but the undertone is one
of detestation of women (perhaps we need distinctions here as those
who study satire distinguish between juvenalian and horatian satire).
Two inconsequential books by Gelett Burgess will help to make my
point. The first, with a long and supposedly humorous title, The
Maxims of Methuselah: Being the Advice Given by the Patriarch in His
Nine Hundred Sixty and Ninth Year to His Great Grandson at Shem's
Coming of Age, in Regard to Women (1907), is misogynistic but not
antifeminist. Methuselah repeats all the familiar complaints about
women: women are deceitful, dishonest, vain, shameless, and incon-
sistent. All women are alike and hate other women. He never mentions feminists, woman suffragists, or women's rightists. Four years

later, in a similar book, similarly titled--The Maxims of Noah,
Delivered from his Experience with Women Both Before and After the
Flood as Given in Counsel to His Son Japhet (1911; see item 285)--
Burgess takes swings at suffragists and supporters of women's rights
and now, in my lexicon, he "advances" himself into the ranks of the
antifeminists.

This is a roundabout way of getting at a crucial definition of
antifeminism. But first we still need to define feminism, what the
antis were reacting against. Feminists perceive inequalities between
men and women in their treatment, prospects, education, opportunities
for employment, roles in the family, etc. Feminists write and speak
about these inequalities, seek to explain them, and work to remove
them. Anyone, then, who opposes any of these activities--speaking or
writing about women's situation, exposing inequalities, seeking to
change and improve the lives of women--is by definition antifeminist.
Books and articles that were not explicit in opposing feminists'
activities have been omitted. Often authors specifically mentioned
women's rightists, suffragists, dress reformers in their text--Gelett
Burgess's second book is an example--or even named feminists by name.
To be included in this bibliography they had to oppose or attack a
desired change, not the female sex in general.

This also means that books and articles must be taken in their
historical context. It is not antifeminist in the first half of the
nineteenth century for a sermonizer to state that woman's place is in
the home and that she should be educated for the home. He is just
maintaining the status quo. When he attacks movements or theories to
the contrary, when he refers to an infidel woman's rights campaign or
mocks notions that women could possibly sit in legislatures or be
judges or study physics, only then does he become antifeminist.

I am aware that the term "antifeminism" is an anachronism when
applied to material written before about 1900, for "feminism," which
derives from the French, was not then in use. If the term was not in
use, however, the social phenomenon of antifeminism was, and it has
been convenient to use it instead of some clumsier term like anti-
women's rights, although I do use antisuffrage as a subcategory of
antifeminism.

There was feminist activity in America as early as the 1790s:
Judith Sargent Murray published an essay on the equality of the sexes
in 1790, and Mary Wollstonecraft's Vindication of the Rights of Woman
went through two American editions in 1792. But it was not until
after 1798, when William Godwin's candid memoirs of Wollstonecraft
were published, that there was significant American notice of women's
rights demands. Wollstonecraft remained a bogey to drag out whenever
women demanded "rights"; she remained someone to point to with scorn.
Later, feminists like Harriet Martineau and Margaret Fuller, although
sympathetic, felt obliged to distance or dissociate themselves from
her; only later did feminists like Stanton and Anthony claim her as a
forerunner.

Introduction

Frances Wright provided new stimulus for antifeminists in the late 1820s when she lectured and published a paper that demanded improvements in woman's condition, including better education, legal rights, and more liberal divorce laws. She was quickly linked with Wollstonecraft as a practitioner of "free love" and an infidel (see index for many citations of Wollstonecraft and Wright).

Close on the heels of this scandal Harriet Martineau provoked a new antifeminist response with her call in Society in America (1837) for political rights for women. Martineau was more of a feminist theorist than Wright. For instance, she anticipated objections that women would not have enough time for political duties: let women decide, she said. She also mocked the notion of woman's influence and continued to uphold the principle of equal rights.

All this shows the existence of some notable feminist activism, and explains the presence of antifeminism, even before the first women's rights convention in 1848. Each convention, each demand, whether for better education, legal rights, improved work conditions and equal pay, equality in marriage, or more accessible divorce, brought new complaints from the antis, which grew in intensity during the late nineteenth century and reached regular peaks with each new suffrage campaign. We notice a decided falling off of antifeminism in the teens of the twentieth century, due partly to the distraction of the war but also a partial consequence of the growing certainty that woman suffrage would come. But antifeminists still opposed women's education; they criticized both women's colleges and coeducation, and opposed women's working outside the home as well as woman suffrage.

This brief introduction is not the place to discuss all the material included in this bibliography, but to indicate through the extremely compressed history of antifeminism in America above, how the antifeminist argument developed, and to perceive a pattern. Education will serve as an example. People make proposals, which increase in intensity until they become demands that women be better educated, that they study what men study. Antifeminists then assert that women are incapable of the intellectual rigors of male education. Feminists persist: they found schools, run colleges, and force the admission of women on an equal basis with men in medical and law schools. A number of prominent women prove that they are capable of equality in educational achievement. In fact, they win all the prizes. The antis then assert that women are good pupils but not original. Genius (male) is brilliant, active; it does not win prizes. Therefore, women are not equal. Or it is alleged that women are ruining their health by attempting to acquire a male education. Edward Clarke was the foremost proponent of this opinion (see the section on the education of girls and women for demonstration of his pervasive influence). This charge forces feminists to assert and prove that the health of young women is not being destroyed by equal education. They administer questionnaires and gather data. No sooner is that objection answered—actually, it recurs regularly:

see 1091--than the antifeminists allege that women's higher education is causing sterility in women, harming them physically, and making them psychologically unfit to be or undesirous of becoming mothers.

The argument, then, is constantly shifting. Feminists must answer antifeminist charges, even changing their own program to do so. When M. Carey Thomas expressed pleasure in the failure of Bryn Mawr women to marry, because of their commitment to intellectual careers, she was attacked roundly in the press.

Dress reform provides another example of the feminist/ antifeminist tussle. Almost everyone who cared to address the topic insisted that women's dress needed to be modified, tight lacing stopped, excessive cloth reduced, and weight lessened. But when feminists like Elizabeth Smith Miller and Amelia Jenks Bloomer actually modified their dress, they were mocked, attacked, and pil- loried, so that they finally had to discontinue wearing the reform dress. People agreed that women's dress should be modified to pre- vent women from harming, or even being prevented from bearing, future generations but would not agree that women's dress should be changed to provide them wider movement.

Every advance proposed by the feminists was opposed, blocked, mocked, and ridiculed. They persisted, but sometimes were forced to modify or even abandon one change--for instance, dress reform--in order not to lose a more significant and larger improvement like higher education or suffrage for women. The image that unpleasantly comes to mind is one of battle, with forces massed on one side moving into the enemy's territory, blocked, repulsed, and redeploying their troops for a side flank or distraction to allow others to advance. Each victory was contested, each gain hard-won. No conquest was ever safe. That is why even after suffrage was won by women, someone could write in the Weekly Review that woman suffrage would "impair to disastrous extent those distinctive attributes of women which are so unspeakably precious an element of human life" (see 797). That is why woman's right to higher education was never secure. That is why ground has been lost whenever feminists let up their guard. It is not that they were complaisant but rather that the foe was so vigor- ous, protean, and persistent.

I have come away from this research with intense admiration for the long struggle by women like Stanton, Anthony, Catt, Addams, and Gilman. They were not always admirable in every pronouncement-- Stanton's racism comes to mind immediately--but they persisted in spite of vicious personal attacks, scrutiny of their chosen lives (especially of Gilman's, who divorced her husband and "abandoned" her child, and whose writings on the restructuring of the home and family could therefore be and were attacked on personal grounds), and pre- cious few victories in their lifetimes. Until now interest and research have concentrated on the positive side of their struggle: their slow advances, their strategies, their theories. We have been relatively unaware of their opponents. This bibliography provides the essential negative side to understanding feminism as it developed in the first women's movement.

My sources for the bibliography have been books and periodical articles published in America from colonial times through woman suffrage. Foreign material is included only if reprinted in the United States, so that we can be sure that at least a portion of Americans saw it. Volume, date, and place of publication are given wherever these could be found. I have excluded as too limited in readership and too ephemeral all newspaper articles unless reprinted in more permanent form. With only a few exceptions I have excluded literature: I have included a poem, a short play, and some narratives that were clearly journalistic rather than creative in intention.

Suffrage provided a convenient stopping point for my purposes, since if antifeminism did not cease at that point, it did slow down dramatically in the first twenty years of this century and seem to come to a pause. Furthermore, the story of antifeminism in the twentieth century, most notably the anti-ERA movement, is quite well known and much more accessible to the researcher than the materials I have assembled.

To amass these more than nine hundred periodical articles and four hundred books and pamphlets, I have examined three thousand books and almost six thousand periodical articles in 240 periodicals. The History of Women microfilm collection, drawing largely on the Schlesinger Library, was a rich source for books and pamphlets, but there are many other books included in the bibliography. In addition to the Indiana University, the New York Public Library, the Boston Public Library, and the Library of Congress were important resources.

The breakdown by sex of author was nearly equal with books and pamphlets, men writing 53 percent and women 47 percent. With articles there is a decided preponderance of male authors 67 to 33 percent female. Four periodicals had a notable number of articles: the Ladies' Home Journal, whose editor, Edward Bok, was a vigorous antifeminist, often having an editorial a month opposing some feminist effort, had sixty-six. Outlook, edited by a staunch antisuffragist, Lyman Abbott, had fifty-seven articles. Godey's Lady's Book had fifty-two. Its long-time editor, Sarah Josepha Hale, is an interesting study, for she supported many of the feminists' goals but stopped short of suffrage, dress reform, coeducation, and many kinds of employment. Finally, North American Review (cited in text as North American) had forty-three articles. These and others like the Popular Science Monthly deserve closer study by women's studies scholars. Religious publications also merit further attention.

The clergy form one of the largest groups to fight feminism in the years leading up to suffrage. There are many sermons reprinted in pamphlet form as well as articles, advice books, and other books by clergymen in the bibliography. One Roman Catholic archbishop asked his priests to urge their female parishioners to sign antisuffrage petitions and campaign against woman suffrage (see 754). Cardinal James Gibbons was particularly active in speaking and writing against woman suffrage. Other professional groups are also represented among the antifeminists: male and female doctors argued that higher education incapacitated women for motherhood, for instance; lawyers denied that women had any remaining legal disabilities, or they wrote against the legal advisability of giving women the vote. Academics also entered the fray: President Charles W. Eliot of Harvard; President G. Stanley Hall of Clark; the presidents of Bowdoin, Williams, Wellesley; the dean of Radcliffe; professors from the University of Chicago, Harvard, and Hamline University in Red Wing, Minnesota--all wrote against feminist advances. Names of famous people jump off the page: Henry James, Sr., Horace Mann, Ida Tarbell, Havelock Ellis, Jane Swisshelm, Catharine Beecher; authors Rebecca Harding Davis, Rose Terry Cooke, Lydia Sigourney, Octave Thanet, Margaret Deland, Kate Douglas Wiggin, Mary Wilkins, John R. Dos Passos (the author's father). Richard Watson Gilder, poet and editor of Century, was joined in his opposition to woman suffrage by his wife, Helena, and his sister Jeannette, editor of the Critic. Several wives worked with husbands, although the husbands tended to be more active: Mr. and Mrs. Lyman Abbott, Mr. and Mrs. John Martin, Mr. and Mrs. Francis M. Scott. Wives of former presidents Harrison and Cleveland and the sister of former president Roosevelt--all wrote against woman suffrage.

The fear, hatred, and loathing of women revealed by this bibliography is astonishing. I will not repeat all the argumens, all the nastiness, all the wrongheaded notions. Each reader will have her own favorite horrors. Rather, I want to try to offer an explanation for this strong current of antifeminism in American culture. What flows through it all is the insistence that men and women are different. This has rewards for men, of course, as Simone de Beauvoir pointed out long ago in The Second Sex. But, as I have demonstrated, women took an almost equal part in writing against various aspects of the first women's movement. This would have to mean that they too gained something from being different, something so necessary that they did not mind being inferior, lesser, weaker.

Sex is the last difference. It transcends race, class, and religion. Furthermore, the earlier forms of gaining status--being from the city, having a larger farm or a cow, being from a famous family, having money--had lost significance by the nineteenth century. In America, so the myth went, everybody was equal. This had advantages, but it was also unsettling. In America there were no remnants of feudalism, with its neat, rigid, and reassuring hierarchy. So the differences stressed were sex differences. This meant not only an insistence on separate spheres but also different bodies, different brains, different nervous systems, encased by different clothing, nourished by different food and intellectual materials, and with different abilities and roles. Writer after writer worried that

woman would unsex herself if she voted or studied with men or spoke
on a platform or worked outside the home. She would then find herself in a kind of gender limbo, neither male nor female. We want
womanly women and manly men. Again and again writers mocked mannish
women, effeminate men, as <u>lusus</u> <u>naturae</u>—jokes of nature. Mannish
women were sterile. Mannish women were causing the birth rate to go
down. Scientists pompously proclaimed that the higher the civilization, the greater the differences between the two sexes. Education
was supposed to foster these differences, not erase them.

Of course, oppression of women and imputation of sex differences
are not exclusive to American culture and certainly not confined to
the nineteenth century. As we do more research in women's studies,
we are realizing the universality of misogyny. On the basis of a
limited sample, mainly those British materials reprinted in American
publications, I would suggest that in England antifeminism was even
more intense than in the United States. American antifeminists are
almost mild in comparison. What is distinctive about American antifeminism is its reliance on sex as the final difference, after all
others, fostered by the culture's almost pathological need to have a
basis of differentiation and yet to avoid class definitions.

We cannot estimate the damage that American antifeminists did:
the young women who ceased to exercise in the fear that they would
damage their unborn children, or who curbed their intellectual appe-
tites because doctors like Edward Clarke and S. Weir Mitchell told
them their reproductive organs would atrophy and they would become
unwomanly; artists, musicians, and writers who underestimated their
talents, or ceased to create altogether, because of articles telling
them of women's inherent intellectual and creative inferiority. We
do know that even so self-assured a writer as Willa Cather wrote in a
newspaper column in 1895 that "it is a very grave question whether
women have any place in poetry at all. Certainly they have only been
successful in poetry of the most highly subjective nature. If a
woman writes any poetry at all worth reading it must be emotional in
the extreme, self-centered, self-absorbed, centrifugal." Cather was
forty before she made a name for herself in literature. Now we have
a chance to see what kinds of things she was reading in the popular
magazines and books of the time to fill her with this distrust of
female authorship.

Women's Rights and Feminism

The earliest books and articles in this section use words like "absurd," "disagreeable," "ridiculous," and "revolting" to attack the general notion of women's rights and equality. As the nineteenth century proceeds, women's abolition activities are criticized and complaints increase about women's public speaking. Antifeminists oppose the demands of women who seek better education and professional training. In response to early women's rights conventions, there is an abrupt increase in the number of items in 1850 and throughout the 1850s. Antifeminist writings subside during the Civil War, only to pick up dramatically in the late 1860s as suffragists worked to achieve woman suffrage with black suffrage.

The antifeminist tempo slows noticeably in the 1880s but increases again in the mid and late 1890s, with intensified agitation for woman suffrage and the publication of Stanton's Woman's Bible. Feminism now enters the vocabulary and is attacked specifically. The number of items remains steady until the mid-teens, then dramatically falls off as America enters World War I and woman suffrage appears certain.

Researchers interested in specific reforms advocated by the women's rights movement such as woman suffrage, education, work, and so forth, should also consult those sections.

1766

1 KNOX, JOHN. The First Blast of the Trumpet against the Monstrous Regimen of Women; to Which Is Added the Contents of the Second Blast, and a Letter from John Knox to the People of Edinburgh, Anno 1571. Reprint. Philadelphia: Andrew Steuart, 64 pp.
    Famous opening: "To promote a woman to bear rule, superiority, dominion, or empire, above any realm, nation, or city, is repugnant to nature, contumely to God, a thing most contrarious to his revealed will and approved ordinances; and, finally, the subversion of good order, of all equity and justice." Says

1

injustice, disorder, and confusion will result if women bear
authority. The outlines of Knox's polemic are well known. Of
interest is its reprinting in the colonies.

1799

2   MORE, HANNAH. The Works of Hannah More. Vol. 5, Strictures
     on the Modern System of Female Education. Philadelphia:
     Edward Earle, 356 pp.
         Insists that woman's great talent is influence. Finds
     female warriors and politicians disgusting and unnatural.
     Opposes women's rights, their intellectual and political pre-
     tensions, as intending "not only to rekindle in the minds of
     women a presumptuous vanity dishonorable to their sex, but pro-
     duced with a view to excite in their hearts an impious discontent
     with the post which God has assigned them in the world." Women's
     rights would actually depreciate woman's real value. Urges women
     to remain contentedly in the path marked by Providence "rather
     than to stray awkwardly, unbecomingly, and unsuccessfully, in a
     forbidden path." Asserts that it is "her zeal for [women's] true
     interests which lead her to oppose their imaginary rights."

1802

3   KNAPP, SAMUEL LORENZO. Letters of Shehcoolen [pseud.], a
     Hindu Philosopher, Residing in Philadelphia; to His Friend El
     Hassan, an Inhabitant of Delhi. Boston: Russell & Cutler,
     152 pp.
         In the form of letters, the first part on the "new philoso-
     phy," one of whose grand objects is "a total renovation of the
     female character, and a destination in society, totally new."
     Alleges that Wollstonecraft, having had lovers, showed herself
     inconsistent, since she supposedly held reason so high but fell
     to pleasures of the senses. She wished to strip women of every-
     thing feminine "and to assimilate them, as fast as possible, to
     the masculine character." Calls her a "female lunatic." As if
     adopting masculine habits and ideas is not bad enough, she wants
     to introduce women into government and military. Blames her for
     a transparent, clinging dress adopted in America and for female
     profanities.

1808

4   MILLER, SAMUEL. A Sermon, Preached 13 March 1808, for the
     Benefit of the Society Instituted in the City of New York, for
     the Relief of Poor Widows with Small Children. New York:
     Hopkins & Seymour, 31 pp.
         Upholds the doctrine of the spheres; women should not have
     the same employments as men. Recalls that "there was a time,

indeed, when a very different doctrine had many adv
appeared to be growing popular:--viz. that in conducting
tion, and in selecting employments, all distinctions of sex ought
to be forgotten and confounded; and that females are as well
fitted to fill the academic Chair, to shine in the Senate, to
adorn the Bench of justice, and even to lead the train of War, as
the more hardy sex." Fortunately, this "delusion" has been
discarded. God has raised barriers against "such wild and mis-
chievous speculations."

1810

5   AIKIN, LUCY. Epistles on Women, Exemplifying their Character
     and Condition in Various Ages and Nations. Boston: Wells &
     Wait, 154 pp.
        In the introduction, disclaims entirely "the absurd idea
     that the two sexes ever can be, or ever ought to be, placed in
     all respects on a footing of equality." Urges women to content
     themselves with becoming noble women rather than "aspiring to be
     inferior men." Epistles are in verse form.

1818

6   CROCKER, HANNAH MATHER. Observations on the Rights of Women,
     with Their Appropriate Duties, Agreeable to Scripture, Reason
     and Common Sense. Boston: Printed for the author, 92 pp.
        Believes that even though women may be equal to men in
     judgment and powers of mind, "it would be morally improper, and
     physically very incorrect, for the female character to claim the
     stateman's berth, or ascend the rostrum to gain the loud applause
     of men." For the same reasons, woman should not plead at the bar
     of justice, as "no law can give her the right of deviating from
     the strictest rules of rectitude and decorum." Describes Mary
     Wollstonecraft as "a woman of great energy and a very independent
     mind" and commends her Rights of Woman as "replete with fine
     sentiments, though we do not coincide with her opinion respecting
     the total independence of the female sex," but finds her theories
     "unfit for practice."

1823

7   MORTON, Mrs. SARAH WENTWORTH. My Mind and Its Thoughts, in
     Sketches, Fragments, and Essays. Boston: Wells & Lilly,
     295 pp.
        In an essay entitled "Rights and Wrongs," castigates Mary
     Wolstoncroft [sic], who, "by her pernicious precepts, and still
     more pernicious practice, has, in proclaiming 'the rights of
     women,' involved the sex in more real wrongs, and been the occa-
     sion of greater restraints upon their intellectual character,

3

than the whole host of masculine revilers." Calls her a "pre-
sumptuous woman" who "vainly rejected the good, in weak prefer-
ence of evil, not only by personal error, but by profligate
opinion, wandering from the straight path, with endeavours to
seduce the innocent and mislead the unwary." Says she got what
she deserved, ending in "misery, ignominy, and destitution."
Warns women against trying to enter man's occupations.

1824

8   BINGHAM, PEREGRINE. The Law of Infancy and Coverture.
     Exeter, N.H.: George Lamson, 367 pp.
         After explaining the law of coverture, warns that "they
     who, from some ill-defined notion of justice or generosity, would
     extend to women an absolute equality, only hold out to them a
     dangerous snare." Once women were released from the obligation
     to please, men would become antagonistic toward them. Says men
     are superior because they are stronger. In man's hands "the
     power allotted to him at once supports itself without external
     interference; give but the legal authority to the wife, and every
     moment would produce a revolt on the part of the husband, only to
     be quelled by assistance from without."

1826

9   The Ladies' Companion, Containing First, Politeness of Manners
     and Behaviour, Second, Fenelon on Education, Third, Miss
     More's Essays, etc. Carefully Selected and Revised by a
     Lady in the County of Worcester, Massachusetts. 2d ed.
     Brookfield, Mass.: Printed for the proprietor, 156 pp.
         More insists on completely separate spheres and qualities
     for women and men and counsels that it is far better for women to
     succeed as women than to fail as men, "to be good originals,
     rather than bad imitations . . . excellent women, rather than
     indifferent men."

1828

10   CARY, Mrs. VIRGINIA. Letters on Female Character, Addressed
     to a Young Lady, on the Death of Her Mother. Richmond, Va.:
     A. Works, 199 pp.
         Worries that "some aspiring females are not content to
     retain any vestige of subordination to the anointed lords of the
     creation. They aim at equality of rights." Blames woman that
     man was banished from his home of bliss. She must now make up
     for it by sweet and contented subordination. Holds up French
     women before the revolution as dire examples. Says Frances
     Wright is "a disgrace to the name of woman" but not as dangerous
     as "poor Mary Wolstonecraft" [sic], who "could only explain and

4

expose difficulties, without removing them." Wollstonecraft's
book made a "great noise" about twenty-five years ago and "some
unfortunate young women were destroyed by the literal adoption of
her tenets," but most women saw the danger and avoided it.

11   "Sketches of American Character. No. V. The Village School-
      mistress." Ladies' Magazine 1 (May):202-19.
         Preface to this sketch argues that "it is idle to talk of
      the 'Rights of Woman'" if they would put her in a station against
      the intentions of Providence. It is "absurd" for woman to com-
      plain that her sphere is less honorable than man's or to imagine
      herself commanding armies or speaking in legislatures. Wants the
      profession of schoolteaching appropriated to women.

                              1829

12   HALE, SARAH J. "An Authoress--II." Ladies' Magazine 2
      (March):130-34.
         Asserts that no one who wishes woman well would want to
      place her "in the lecture room of a physician--in the forum--the
      desk--or the halls of legislation." Says that "the attempts to
      inspire women with an ambition to appear like men, is [sic] too
      absurd to merit discussion." Women have more important things to
      do than involve themselves in political strife. Wants women
      employed as schoolteachers.

                              1830

13   SIGOURNEY, LYDIA. "The Two Sexes." [Godey's] Lady's Book 1
      (November):276.
         Believes that the two sexes are constructed and intended
      for different spheres. Man may enter woman's and woman man's,
      but "revoltings of the soul would attend this violence to nature;
      this abuse of physical and intellectual energy; while the beauty
      of the social order would be defaced, and the fountains of
      earth's felicity broken up." Reprinted in 14.

                              1831

14   SIGOURNEY, LYDIA. "The Two Sexes." [Godey's] Lady's Book 3
      (November):272.
         Reprint of 13.

                              1832

15   JAMESON, ANNA BROWNELL. Memoirs of Celebrated Female Sov-
      ereigns. 2 vols. New York: J. & J. Harper, 493 pp.

In her preface to a study of female sovereigns, observes
that "women, in possession of power, are so sensible of their
inherent weakness, that they are always in extremes. Hence,
among the most arbitrary governments recorded are those of
women." Women must substitute will for men's superior physical
and mental strength. "On the whole, it seems indisputable that
the experiments hitherto made in the way of female government
have been signally unfortunate; and that women called to empire
have been, in most cases, conspicuously unhappy or criminal."
Her chapter on Queen Christina is notable for its critique of her
rule and life.

16   HALE, SARAH J. "A Chapter from Our Book of Thoughts."
      Ladies' Magazine 5 (February):86-87.
      Does not want woman to go out of her sphere to have her
influence felt. Considers "every attempt to induce women to
think they have a just right to participate in the public duties
of government as injurious to their best interests and derogatory
to their character."

                              1834

17   A., W.A. "Should Females Be Employed in Cookery?" American
      Ladies' Magazine 7 (November):481-87.
      Recounts that a friend stated that females were not in-
tended by the Creator for anything so menial as cooking. Recalls
that Wolstonecraft [sic] and Wright also had elevated notions of
woman's sphere. Wright would mount the rostrum and "figure away
largely on female rights and the importance of female elevation
and independence" and the audience would gape and stare. Asserts
that it is good to have "such a monster in creation . . . rise
up, once in an age, and show us the value of plain, practical
common sense," so Wright and Wollstonecraft have done some good.
Likens them to a hurricane or volcano. Favors "emancipation" but
would have women involved in cookery to make sure their children
are well nourished.

                              1835

18   "On the Characteristic Differences between the Sexes, and on
      the Position and Influence of Woman in Society." Southern
      Literary Messenger 1 (May):493-512; (July):621-32;
      (August):672-91.
      Quotes Voltaire on the differences between the sexes and
says that, contrary to Wollstonecraft, the difference in occupation between the sexes is due principally to difference in physical organization. Woman could never be a physician, lawyer, or
statesman because "to succeed at all, she would be obliged to
desert the station and defeat the ends for which nature intended

her." Woman should not preach or be active in the church. And she can never make a good politician, for she is too emotional. She is an unsafe depository of power and an unequal administrator of justice.

1836

19   GORE, CATHERINE GRACE FRANCES. The Diary of a Désennuyé. Philadelphia: E.L. Carey & A. Hart, 216 pp.
      A chatty diary, not precisely dated, with a few criticisms of women. Asserts that "the most able of female politicians makes herself as disagreeable as ridiculous." Mocks contemporary literary women: "What an ocean of milk and water! False sentiment, tawdry style, and a total absence of either sense or sensibility!"

1837

20   BEECHER, CATHARINE E. Essay on Slavery and Abolitionism, with Reference to the Duty of American Females. Philadelphia: H. Perkins, 152 pp.
      Opposes activities of women in abolition movement if those activities throw them into the public sphere, cause them to take a coercive role, draw them out of the domestic sphere, and make them "expose themselves to the ungoverned violence of mobs, and to sneers and ridicule in public places." Doubts even that petitions from women in behalf of slaves are within the sphere of female duty. Would have women properly educated but not claim male prerogatives. Attacks Fanny Wright and Robert Owen as atheists and says that since Wright came upon the stage and exposed herself to public criticism, it is right to express disgust at her and make her appear odious to others. Counsels women to be mediators and peacemakers, not advocates of causes.

21   "Miss Martineau on America." American Quarterly Review 22 (September):21-53.
      Calumniates feminists: the clamor for more female autonomy is absurd. "Excepting it be Fanny Wright or Harriet Martineau, there is not a sane woman in the world, much less in the United States, who has a desire to enlarge her sphere of action beyond the limits of her domestic home." Wonders what more Miss Martineau wants, what more range for her sex than that she herself exercised in America. Does not like Martineau criticizing American treatment of women.

1838

22   SIGOURNEY, LYDIA H. Letters to Mothers. Hartford, Conn.: Hudson & Skinner, 240 pp.

Asserts that mothers have a special duty--to teach obedience. They also serve the state but not directly. "The admix-
ture of the female mind in the ferment of political ambition,
would be neither safe if it were permitted, nor to be desired if
it were safe." The patriotism of women is "not to thunder in
senates, or to usurp dominion, or to seek the clarion-burst of
fame, but faithfully to teach by precept and example, that wisdom, integrity and peace, which are the glory of a nation."

23   WINSLOW, Rev. HUBBARD. Woman as She Should Be. Boston: T.H.
      Carter, 81 pp.
         Is appalled that woman would raise "her delicate voice" to
declaim on political affairs about which she is nearly as ignorant as a child. Expresses shock that woman would speak against
churches and ministers who dissent from her views. "What a sad
wreck of female loveliness she is then! She can hardly conceive
how ridiculous she appears in the eyes of all sober, discreet,
judicious Christian men, or how great the reproach she brings
upon her sex." Opposes women as public teachers or lecturers,
women traveling and giving talks, women's societies that propose
to judge others, conventions, petitions, all of which lead to
"boldness, arrogance, rudeness, indelicacy, and the spirit of
denunciation." The world has had enough of Fanny Wrights."
Reprinted in 1854 as The Lady's Manual of Moral and Intellectual
Culture. See 70.

24   HALE, SARAH JOSEPHA. "Editor's [sic] Table." Godey's Lady's
      Book 16 (March):143-44.
         Quotes a letter from Adelaide Mongolfier, editor of the
French monthly La Ruche, with whose opinions on the duties of
women the editor of Godey's concurs. Says "it is better to
suffer wrong than to do wrong." Enlightened women should not
plead for their rights but rather should "only ask for light and
knowledge that they may be able to fulfil their duties as wives,
mothers and members of society." Mlle Mongolfier deplores the
"ridiculous and disgusting ideas" advanced by so-called apostles
of women. Feels that women's duties should be strongly marked
out and enforced and women should adhere to them rather than
follow the "miserable and ephemeral writings which have of late
appeared on the 'Rights of Women.'"

1839

25   COXE, MARGARET. The Young Lady's Companion. Columbus, Ohio:
      I.N. Whiting, 342 pp.
         Asserts that "a female politician is only less disgusting
than a female infidel." Woman's domestic role is far more honorable than any public role would be. Assigns woman to a completely different sphere of duty than man. Warns woman against
"seeking hopelessly, and in direct opposition to the delicacy of

her sex, to obtain for her political privileges," against competing with man in the public arena.

1840

26   SEDGWICK, CATHARINE MARIA. Means and Ends; or, Self-Training.
     4th ed. Boston: Marsh, Capen, Lyon, & Webb, 264 pp.
        Attempts to take a moderate approach to the issue of
     women's rights. Urges her young readers to improve their edu-
     cation and act like rational, responsible human beings. But
     antifeminist sentiment creeps in: "My dear young friends, noth-
     ing is further from my intention than to make you the bold as-
     sertors of your own rights, and the noisy proclaimers of your own
     powers." Thinks women were never intended to "lead armies,
     harangue in halls of legislation, bustle up to the ballot-boxes,
     or sit on judicial tribunals."

27   "On the Legal Rights of Woman." Christian Review 5
     (June):269-89.
        Examines women's condition in other nations, both ancient
     and modern. Finds American women enjoying equal political rights
     except for electing and being elected to political office. Says
     woman is excluded from suffrage to preserve social peace and as
     part of the division of labor. But she is also exempted from
     defending her country. It is not law but public opinion that
     rebukes her if she violates the proprieties of her station by
     becoming a public lecturer or "engaging with masculine energy in
     the distracting controversies of the day." Defends the legal
     nullity of married women by saying that it preserves domestic
     union and harmony. Describes a wife's inability to bind herself
     by contract as a privilege. Warns against agitators.

28   "Influence of Mothers." Christian Review 5 (September):
     442-50.
        Regrets there are individuals in the land who are trying to
     make women dissatisfied with their present position in society.
     Alleges that these reformers "are generally those who are stran-
     gers to maternal feelings" and do not know the pleasures of the
     home, woman's proper sphere. "She was never intended by Provi-
     dence for the bar, the Senate chamber, or the pulpit. Those who
     would elevate her, by pushing her into the arena of public life,
     are not aware of the gulf of misery and degradation into which
     they would plunge her." Woman's rights would be a blight over
     the morals of the nation. "Bereft of her own native modesty, she
     would associate with the vile, and become the victim of the
     lowest impulses and passions."

9

1842

29   COXE, MARGARET. Claims of the Country on American Females. 2
      vols. Columbus, Ohio: Isaac N. Whiting, 486 pp.
           States that woman's station has been providentially ap-
      pointed. Blasts "ultra reformers" who try to subvert the best
      interests of the human race with their ingenious arguments.
      "Alas! minds thus perverted in judgment, and blinded by preju-
      dice, evince an inability to detect the finely marked, but ex-
      pressive lines, which give grace and personality to woman's
      nature, when regenerated and sanctified by the grace of God."

30   MUZZEY, ARTEMAS BOWERS. The Young Maiden. Boston: Crosby &
      Co., 264 pp.
           Asserts that women differ from men in physical, intellec-
      tual, and moral constitution. "It is not the province of woman
      to enter into Political life. . . . How unfeminine were it in
      her to raise her gentle voice amid the storm of debate, or to
      rush into the heat and strife of partizan politics! Let such
      scenes never be coveted save by the Wolstonecrafts [sic] and the
      Wrights who have madly unsexed themselves." Objects to women
      being seen and heard at public meetings, saying that "man becomes
      effeminate by intermeddling with the province of woman. She also
      becomes coarse and masculine, when she enters his sphere." Con-
      tention, violence, and passion are unladylike.

31   SANBORN, E.D. "The Progress of Society as Indicated by the
      Condition of Women." American Biblical Repository, 2d ser., 8
      (July):91-115.
           Says woman has the right to be thoroughly educated but
      argues for separation of duties and rights of woman and man.
      Woman's "most important duties . . . must be domestic, connected
      with the home of her children. She cannot engage in those public
      duties which require long absence from home, much less in those
      long, protracted investigations which belong to the secluded
      scholar."

1843

32   GRAVES, Mrs. A.J. Woman in America: Being an Examination
      into the Moral and Intellectual Condition of American Female
      Society. New York: Harper & Brothers, 262 pp.
           Laments the "erratic course of many of our female reform-
      ers." Believes that "they have inflicted deep injury where they
      intended good, by drawing woman away from her true and allotted
      sphere--domestic life." Alleges that if women had the same
      political rights and privileges as men, this would bring "the
      total disorganization of the family institution, . . . dissolve
      the domestic ties, and destroy all that makes woman efficient as
      a moral helpmate of man."

33   K., J. "Lady Morgan's First and Last Work." Godey's Lady's
      Book 27 (September):128-33.
           Starts out as a review but quickly turns to an examination
      of woman's position in society. Finds some unjust laws but no
      malice on the part of men. Addresses the question of woman
      suffrage as proposed by Harriet Martineau and asserts that "suf-
      frage is in itself a great evil" endured only because it guards
      and defends against still greater evils, tyranny and misgovern-
      ment. Denies that women are oppressed and subjected. Points out
      "all the effort and argument which have been expended, from the
      days of Mary Wolstonecraft [sic] to our own, have utterly failed
      in awakening the party oppressed to a consciousness of its
      misery--a most unaccountable fact, if that misery really exists."

1844

34   SPRAGUE, WILLIAM BUELL. An Address Delivered at the Close of
      the Annual Examination of the Young Ladies' Institute,
      Pittsfield, Massachusetts, 28 September 1844. Pittsfield:
      E.P. Little, 32 pp.
           Opposes women speaking in public and engaging in reform
      activities, women "who make a desperate effort to climb up where
      they may be seen; who flatter themselves that they have a mission
      to harangue the multitude; and, with this impression, sail about
      the world to do men's work, under the banner of an imaginary
      philanthropy." Abhors this feature of the times. Prefers that
      his daughter join a nunnery "than that she was going up and down
      the world haranguing promiscuous assemblies."

35   BENJAMIN, PARK. "The True Rights of Woman." Godey's Lady's
      Book 28 (June):271-74.
           Worries that too much attention has been paid to educating
      the head and not enough to the heart. Feels that woman's best
      right is that of cultivating the affections and spreading peace
      and contentment. Opposes woman's entry into the literary arena
      or intellectual competition with men. "The most truly sensible
      women do not contend for a mental equality," for women are and
      always have been intellectually inferior to men. This is proved
      by the absence of women of genius in poetry, prose, painting, and
      music. Women may shine in their proper sphere, but they would
      forfeit men's courtesy and deference by trying to enter the
      political arena. Abjures young women to be happy at home and
      amiable rather than smart or suave of disposition.

1846

36   M., A.G. "The Condition of Woman." Southern Quarterly Review
      10 (July):148-73.

Takes exception to Margaret Fuller's wishing "every arbitrary barrier thrown down." Is relieved that "all women are not
innoculated with this ambitious spirit," for considering how
excitable and enthusiastic they are, men should long ago have
lost their supremacy. Evokes all the stereotypes: women are
nervous, excitable, passive, emotional, dominated by imagination,
sympathetic, weaker, timid, dependent on men. When woman mingles
with man in pursuit of knowledge, she is no longer a woman but
becomes "unsexed." Asserts that "woman as a sex, is not and
never has been learned." Prefers that she keep out of "the rough
and rugged paths of life," tumultuous assemblies, politics, public
office, or the legislative hall.

37   "Letters of Royal and Illustrious Ladies." Eclectic Magazine
     8 (August):82-95.
        In discussing these letters, shows no sympathy with "those
     who, in their new-fledged zeal for the 'rights of women,' would
     fain have her plunged into the rough business cares and ostensi-
     ble political strifes, which form the every-day life of men."
     There is an essential difference between the minds of woman and
     man. Hints that such agitation has blown in from the far west.
     Reprinted from British Quarterly Review (London) 3 (May):416-38.

                              1847

38   CURTIS, HARRIOT F. S.S.S. Philosophy. Lowell, Mass.:
     Merrill & Heywood, 160 pp.
        A series of paragraphs on topical and inspirational sub-
     jects. Of interest is one on Female Reformers: "When a woman,
     from disappointment, want of attraction, or otherwise, gives up
     all hopes or forswears matrimony, she has gained a diploma to use
     up her surplus sympathies on public objects." The pages on
     woman's rights were missing from the copy I examined.

39   TUTHILL, LOUISA CAROLINE. The Young Lady's Home. Boston:
     William J. Reynolds & Co., 332 pp.
        Observes that some "bold and daring innovators" are not
     contented with their sphere but doubts that they have had an
     impact. "Has Miss Martineau aided in persuading American women
     that they are not allowed the rights of free citizens?" Doubts
     that women will be "persuaded out of our best and truest inter-
     ests by these masculine marauders." Mingling in public affairs
     and hankering for applause are unbecoming to the dignity and
     delicacy of women. Deplores women taking part in debate socie-
     ties with men, saying they have loud voices. "Where will these
     bold innovators stop?" Says the majority of women appreciate
     their "right to move in the calm sequestered sphere which Heaven
     . . . ordained them." Cautions against satanic temptations.
     Reprinted in 110.

                              12

<u>1848</u>

40   ARTHUR, TIMOTHY SHAY. <u>Advice to Young Ladies in Their Duties</u>
      <u>and Conduct in Life</u>. Boston: Phillips & Sampson, 204 pp.
          In a chapter entitled "Equality of the Sexes," criticizes
      the bold intellectual ladies who contend for equality of the
      sexes and who long to see woman competing with man "in the camp,
      on the bench, at the bar, in the pulpit, in the dissecting-room,
      or hospital, with the operator's knife in her hand,--in fact,
      wherever strong nerve, powerful intellect, decision, and firmness
      are required." Is revolted by their "pernicious doctrines."
      Insists that woman's and man's brains are different, with man
      having a larger upper brain, woman a larger lower. Says this can
      be demonstrated by comparing sizes of heads--men's are higher and
      fuller in front, women's broader and larger behind. Taking woman
      out of her sphere is absurd and revolting.

41   CHAPIN, Rev. EDWIN HUBBELL. <u>Duties of Young Women</u>. Boston:
      G.W. Briggs, 218 pp.
          Argues that although woman has accomplished great work in
      literature, "we cannot in justice say that thus far she has
      attained to the same intellectual eminence as man." Would allow
      her to go out into the political arena but believes that no true
      woman "who feels the true dignity and mission of her womanhood"
      would wish to mingle among "the troubled elements of commercial,
      legislative, and political life." Worries that "if woman ne-
      glects the work which has been given her to do, there is no one
      to perform it." Paints pictures of gloomy home, neglected chil-
      dren, abandoned husband, no one to nurse. "Shall woman's heart
      become cold, and callous, and world-hardened?" No--she knows
      the place her Creator has appointed for her.

<u>1849</u>

42   DALL, CAROLINE WELLS. <u>Essays and Sketches</u>. Boston: S.G.
      Simpkins, 116 pp.
          In a chapter on reform, the author asserts that she takes
      no interest in women's rights. Argues that "the business of our
      country and our age . . . is to organize the rights of man. One
      of the holiest of his rights is to find woman in her proper
      place." Man is robbed if woman steps out of her proper sphere.
      Doubts that Providence intended woman to share in the political
      duties of man. "We feel that this is utterly incompatible with
      the more precious and positive duties of the nursery and the
      fireside."

<u>1850</u>

43   BEECHER, CATHARINE E. <u>A Treatise on Domestic Economy for the</u>
      <u>Use of Young Ladies at Home and at School</u>. Rev. ed. New
      York: Harper & Brothers, 369 pp.

Wishes that "those who are bewailing themselves over the fancied wrongs and injuries of women in this Nation" could see things as they are. They would then discover that if there are any elements of woman's condition in need of remedy, women should merely use their influence and men will make the required changes.

44   GANNETT, EZRA S. An Address Delivered at the Fourth Conven-
        tion of the Graduates and Members of the West Newton State
        Normal School, 24 July 1850. Boston: Charles C.P. Moody,
        24 pp.
        Opposes women's rights if they lead women out of their proper sphere. Objects to "masculine women" and "effeminate men." Says "woman's proper position can never give her any other influence than that which, in its most direct action and largest extent, shall leave her in possession of the delicacy and sensibility which belong to her sex." Reprinted in 50.

45   MC INTOSH, MARIA JANE. Woman in America, Her Work and Her
        Reward. New York: D. Appleton, 155 pp.
        God has ordained inequality, including political inequality. "Let those who would destroy this inequality, pause ere they attempt to abrogate a law which emanated from the all-perfect Mind." There needs to be force behind laws, which women cannot give.

46   HALE, SARAH JOSEPHA. "Editors' Table." Godey's Lady's Book
        40 (January):75.
        Favors cultivating woman's intellect but not woman's rights. Glories in the improvement in woman's education since Godey's began publishing. Twenty years ago a few had "foolishly and clamorously urged" woman's rights and would indiscreetly "have broken down the barriers of true modesty, and destroyed the retiring graces of woman's nature." Godey's work has rather been gently to unfold the flower of womanhood "as the sun's rays in the spring warm and expand the rose till its beauty is seen and its sweet incense induces the admirer to preserve it for its virtues as well as its loveliness."

47   BRAINERD, Rev. "Editors' Table." Godey's Lady's Book 40
        (June):416-17.
        Extract from an address before the Literary Institute in Pittsfield, Massachusetts. Says the real rights of women, of which we hear so much, are, "like their blessed New England mothers, to be released from strolling over the country as public lecturers, from wasting their time in street gossip and novel reading, and to make their homes tidy and happy."

48   HALE, SARAH JOSEPHA. "Editors' Table." Godey's Lady's Book
        41 (July):58-59.
        Announces that she has a new work in preparation that will show women their true sphere. Disagrees with claims by "enterprising women" of equality with men. Objects to placing women in

male professions and offices. "We consider this a very low aim,
and acknowledge we have no penchant for man's work." Women,
holding the moral power of the world, have higher and holier
duties than men.

49   NEVIN, JOHN W. "The Moral Order of Sex." Mercersburg Review
      2 (November):549-73.
           Upholds the doctrine of the spheres and warns that when
      woman steps out of her sphere, she becomes "weak, and forfeits
      her title to respect." Insists that "the popular platform, the
      rostrum, the pulpit, are interdicted to her nature, no less than
      the battle field and crowded exchange. All public primacy is
      unsuited to her sex." Calls it unnatural and immoral "to be
      unsexly, in costume, habit, spirit or occupation." Opposes
      socialists and Fourierites who call for the emancipation of
      women, calling this doctrine "most mischievous and false," a
      perversion, disastrous to woman. "Such an 'emancipation' . . .
      would involve the overthrow ultimately of all taste and refine-
      ment, the downfall of all morality and civilization."

                              1851

50   PINCKNEY, CHARLES COTESWORTH. The Young Woman's Gift of
      Literature, Science, and Morality. Boston: J. Buffam,
      192 pp.
           Warns against those "who prate of 'woman's rights,' and
      talk of domestic love as of some insipid thing for which they
      have no relish, and which they would madly barter in order 'to do
      something for society'--that is, to usurp the dominion of the
      other sex, and seek gain, renown, perhaps, in the senate or the
      court house!" Includes an extract from a sermon by the Reverend
      Dr. Thatcher entitled "The Duties of Woman" and an extract by
      Ezra Gannett (see 44).

51   SPRAGUE, WILLIAM B., D.D. The Excellent Woman as Described in
      the Book of Proverbs. Anne Pratt, compiler. Boston: Gould &
      Lincoln, 249 pp.
           In his introduction, regrets that woman has not always been
      happy to stay within the bounds set by Providence. "She has
      sometimes forgotten her native modesty, and thrust herself into
      the rough and tumultuous scenes of life, where her voice has been
      heard, not to allay, but to swell the tempest. She has talked
      extravagantly and violently of her own rights--mistaking a fren-
      zied ambition to be known and heard and talked about, for an
      honest desire to reform and purify society." Even when she has
      stopped short of this impropriety, she often raises her voice
      where it should not be heard, talking of subjects about which she
      knows nothing. Urges women to remember their place.

52   WISE, DANIEL. The Young Lady's Counselor; or, The Sphere, the
     Duties, and the Dangers of Young Women. Cincinnati:
     Hitchcock & Walden, 160 pp.
          Contrasts repugnant Joan of Arc, with her masculine charac-
     ter, to admirable Hannah More, who was also patriotic but not
     public about it. Asserts that no one can love "the masculine
     energy of that really strong-minded woman, Queen Elizabeth."
     Woman must stay in her sphere, where she is noble and lovable.
     Brings up the question of woman's sphere because of the modern
     agitators who are clamoring for "woman's rights." Says they
     demand "the ballot-box, the hustings, the bar, the halls of
     legislation, the offices of state, the pulpit." Warns young
     ladies that they would have woman be an Amazon. Says if woman
     steps out of "the calm of home," her own sex will dispise her,
     she will meet unhappiness, and men will be unable to love her.

53   AGNEW, Professor J.H. "Woman's Offices and Influence."
     Harper's Magazine 3 (October):654-57.
          Insists that women's place is in the home. Their office is
     "to soften political asperities in the other sex, and themselves
     to shun political publicity." Influence is better than power.
     Save us from the "woman's rights" women. Woman "has no right to
     be a man."

54   "Kavanagh's Woman in France." Southern Quarterly Review 20
     (October):433-58.
          Says the influence of woman in France during the last
     century, when she sought emancipation, was for evil. She usurped
     man's place and rendered bad worse. A cautionary tale.

                              1852

55   The Lady's Companion; or, Sketches of Life, Manners, and
     Morals, at the Present Day. Edited by a Lady. Philadelphia:
     H.C. Peck & Theo. Bliss, 222 pp.
          Wants woman to stay in her proper sphere; out of it she is
     powerless. Observes that none can deny "that there have been
     women whose minds have been equal to any human undertaking," but
     fortunately, "these giants of their kind are rare." Insists that
     woman's duty is to direct, not to govern, but that "her moral
     influence, in the humblest grade, is as powerful as the influence
     of one of her sex who rules a nation or occupies a throne."

56   HALE, SARAH JOSEPHA. "Editors' Table." Godey's Lady's Book 44
     (January):88-89.
          Worries about the attempt to take woman out of the home and
     make her a rival of man. Marvels that any American woman would
     be willing to give up her heavenly privileges; doubts that lead-
     ers of the movement have considered its consequences. Urges
     women to follow the Bible, the "Magna Charta of woman's rights."

                              16

57   "Dr. Dewey on Woman's Rights." Democratic Review 30
     (February):180-82.
          Apparently Dr. Dewey had lectured that St. Paul was out of
     date. Author objects, finding woman's rights agitation leading
     to leveling, disorganizing tendencies. Says that Christian dogma
     puts Christ at the head of every man, man at the head of every
     woman; destroy the integrity of the Christian marriage and you
     destroy the church. Protests against "the degradation of woman
     by false position and by teachings at war with God's laws."
     Wants woman to stay in "the graceful orbit of duty." "Must we
     have women brazening the stare of the mob, in Bloomer costumes?
     meeting in public rooms to declare their contempt of Christian
     obligations, and their fitness for masculine advocations?" Woman
     can never be man.

58   FELTON, C.C. "Rights and Wrongs of Women." Christian
     Examiner 52 (March):194-215.
          A review essay, approving of Beecher's The True Remedy for
     the Wrongs of Woman (810), disapproving of The Proceedings of the
     Women's Rights Convention of 1850. Worries that the women's
     rightists have connected themselves with radical views on other
     subjects, which aim "to destroy all the sacred privacy of domes-
     tic life." We must make the family more permanent, not less, and
     surround and guard it with every support of science, art, and
     literature.

59   "Female Politicians." Democratic Review 30 (April):355-59.
          Says the safety, honor, permanence, power of the state
     depend on the virtues of the women. Wishes to see no class of
     female politicians in our country--"patriots, not politicians;
     angels, not agitators." Woman in ordinary life simply cannot
     have the time and rarely the strength of mind to form decisions
     on public matters. Either her opinions are the same as her
     husband's or else she tries to overtop him and thereby degrades
     him in the world's eyes and lowers his self-esteem. Wherever
     women are politically ambitious, they show "a radical defect of
     mental and moral organization." Apparently, women were active in
     the Harrison campaign, carrying banners, making speeches, etc.
     Fathers and husbands are warned to look to their duties.

60   M., L.S. "Woman and Her Needs." DeBow's Review 13
     (September):267-91.
          Essay stimulated by Elizabeth Oakes Smith's book of the
     same title. Criticizes woman's rightists: "Woman was made for
     duty, not for fame." If she throws herself from her position,
     seeking notoriety, she debases herself. She achieves in litera-
     ture only if she does not strive after fame. "It is this same
     misguided love for notoriety, which now misleads women to insist
     upon political rights . . . to strip themselves to the strife and
     wrestle in the public arena." Woman is the cause of all her
     degradation. Nature made woman to persuade and not to combat, to

but not to force. "Woman's task is to make herself the
ed woman, not the counterfeit man."

61 WOODBURY, HENRY E. "Woman in Her Social Relations." Godey's
Lady's Book 45 (October):333-37.
Praises woman as sister, wife, and mother. Acknowledges
woman's mental powers. But opposes introducing woman into a
sphere which does not belong to her or having her become en-
grossed in political excitements. Believes that if those advocating woman's rights had been properly educated, they would see
"the inconsistency and folly of the schemes they vindicate."

1853

62 ABELL, Mrs. L.G. Woman in Her Various Relations: Containing
Practical Rules for American Females. New York: R.T. Young,
319 pp.
Believes women have as many rights as they can possibly
need if they just use them properly. Particularly opposes the
Turkish or Bloomer costume. No rightly educated, true-minded,
delicate, modest women would ever dress in clothing of the oppo-
site sex or do anything to provoke vulgar remarks or notoriety.
The Bible forbids women to wear men's garments. Alleges that
nothing but "a perverted education, a familiarity with the indel-
icate dress, attitudes, and performances of the stage" would ever
have induced a woman to adopt such a dress. Other harsh remarks
against Miss Weber and Fanny Kemble.

63 JAMES, JOHN ANGELL. Female Piety: Or, The Young Woman's
Friend and Guide Through Life to Immortality. New York:
R. Carter & Brothers, 450 pp.
Insists that woman is excluded by reason and by Christianity from the professor's chair, the bar, the pulpit, "from the
corruption of the camp, the debates of the senate, and the plead-
ings of the forum." Cautions woman against listening to "the
doctrines of effeminate debaters," modern reformers, or fashionable journalists. Warns against having her speak in popular
assembly or in the church. Asks, "who, but a few wild vision-
aries, and rash speculatists, and mistaken advocates of woman's
rights, would take her from the home of her husband, her children, and her own heart, to wear out her strength, to consume her
time, and to destroy her feminine excellence in committee-rooms,
on platforms, and in mechanics' or philosophical institutions?"

64 MANN, HORACE. A Few Thoughts of the Power and Duties of
Woman, Two Lectures. Syracuse: Hall, Mills, & Co., 141 pp.
Calls the desire of a few women for suffrage and office-
holding "grotesque and unwomanly." Favors improved employment
and full education but opposes woman suffrage. Calls those who
propose woman's rights "an epicene school" and has particularly

harsh words for dress reformers. Insists on the need for distinction in dress "to prevent society at large from becoming
Sodom at large." Women's clothes guard them from trouble. Any
woman who discards womanly dress "is traitorous to the virtue of
both sexes. Is revolted at "the idea of our wives and sisters
mingling promiscuously with men in the varied affairs of life,
industrial, social and political."

65   MATHEWS, JOSEPH MC DOWELL. Letters to School Girls.
     Cincinnati: Swormstedt & Poe, 247 pp.
     This principal of the Oakland Female Seminary favors a good
education for women and denies that it will make them more masculine. Likens "those females who deliver public harangues, and
desire to be heard in legislative halls and political contests"
to "meteors that blaze across the sky, and disappear." Says they
are "unsubstantial vapor" and cannot hurt God's system. Woman
was made for domestic duties, and her nature would have to be
very much perverted before she would cease to love those duties.
Then she would become a monster.

66   [JAMES, H.]. "Woman and the 'Woman's Movement.'" Putnam's 1
     (March):279-88.
     Feels that "the immediate aims of the ladies who manage the
[woman's] movement and give it character, are ludicrously unworthy." It proves women's incapacity for political activity.
Woman is excluded from civil and political life so that she may
occupy a higher sphere. Learning and wisdom do not become her.
Would exclude her from all professions. Calls it "a scandalous
conception of womanhood" to suggest that woman is capable of
entering into rivalry with man. "Woman is by nature inferior to
man"--in passion, in intellect, in physical strength. She should
cultivate her own special attributes.

67   E. "Woman's True Mission; or 'The Noble Ladies of England.'"
     Southern Literary Messenger 19 (May):303-6.
     Prefers woman to walk in her own peculiar path. "Alas for
these days of Bloomerism and Woman's Rights." Criticizes the
ladies of England for being moved by Stowe's Uncle Tom's Cabin,
"the most pernicious book that ever disgraced female authorship."
Condemns Stowe and supports benevolent slavery.

68   SEARS, BARNAS, D.D. "Characteristics, Duties and Culture of
     Woman." Bibliotheca Sacra 10 (July):433-47.
     Argues that men and women are different physically and
mentally. Education should therefore be different. Women must
be trained for domestic life and the companionship of man. As
for employment, it must be distinct and appropriate to each sex.
Finds "much sublime nonsense" uttered about the equality of the
sexes and rights of women. Opposes having women involved in
political life or holding public office.

69   "Editor's Table: Woman's Rights." Harper's Magazine 7
      (November):838-41.
          Finds "a strange affinity" binding together woman's rights
      with all the other "radical and infidel movements of the day,"
      all grounded in the fallacy of individual right. Woman's rights
      is opposed to nature, to proprieties, to revelation--even more
      infidel and antibiblical than the other reforms. Upholds the
      doctrine of the inner and outer spheres. Warns that the woman's
      rights movement would reduce marriage to a contract, revocable at
      any time. Opposes changes in laws to create separate property
      for husband and wife. Opposes woman suffrage--woman votes
      through her husband. Denies that St. Paul subjugated women;
      rather, he counseled against "unnatural mixture" of habits, em-
      ployments, and dress, that would bring on degradation.

                                1854

70   WINSLOW, Rev. HUBBARD. The Lady's Manual of Moral and Intel-
      lectual Culture. New York: Leavitt & Allen, 81 pp.
          Reprint of 23.

71   Woman's Influence and Woman's Mission. Philadelphia: W.P.
      Hazard, 159 pp.
          Says woman's equality is a matter "too ludicrous to be
      treated anywhere but in a professed satire." Men and women
      should never become rivals. Nor should women leave their duties
      for men to perform.

72   CLAPP, Mrs. L.A.C. [Shirley]. "The Equality of the Sexes."
      Pioneer 1 (February):85-88.
          Regrets that hundreds of lovely women are spoiling their
      complexions and wasting their time demanding their "Rights."
      Asserts that it is God, not man, who has set her in her proper
      orbit. Addresses "Dear Lucy Stone and Co." and asks them to
      redress wrongs but cease to demand rights which they will never
      obtain. "Is it dignified, is it womanly, is it well done to
      crowd yourselves into a sphere, where your presence cannot be
      useful, because it will always be unwelcome?" Warns them that
      their "shrill assertions" are making them unattractive. Insists
      that men and women are so entirely different that the two cannot
      be compared.

73   "Rights and Wrongs of Women." Harper's Magazine 9 (June):
      76-78.
          Editorial warning reformers that "a woman such as ye would
      make her--teaching, preaching, voting, judging, commanding a man-
      of-war, and charging at the head of a battalion--would be simply
      an amorphous monster." Would allow women to be "doctoresses" but
      prefers them as medical assistants. Suggests that a female
      doctor would be dangerous for male patients. Predicts neglected

children and deserted homes if the woman's righters have their
way. Deplores giving women public functions, thus destroying
their influence and moral nature. Any woman who would prefer the
public to the private life is not a woman, she is a "natural
blunder."

74   "Human Nature in Chunks. Chunk No. 1--Woman's Rights."
      Democratic Review 34 (November):434-40.
         A mocking description of a woman's rights convention, con-
      taining women in bloomers, taking snuff, denouncing men, sounding
      silly. Bloomer costume is especially criticized.

                              1855

75   FOLIO, FRED [pseud.]. A Book for the Times. Lucy Boston; or,
      Woman's Rights and Spiritualism. Auburn & Rochester, N.Y.:
      Alden & Beardsley, 406 pp.
         In his introduction, lumps together woman's rights and
      spiritualism as "fanatical and splenetic . . . prejudiced or
      malicious." Calls them "the two greatest humbugs of modern
      times." The rest is in the form of a novel.

76   HALE, SARAH JOSEPHA. Woman's Record; or, Sketches of All
      Distinguished Women from the Creation to A.D. 1854. 2d ed.
      New York: Harper & Bros., 912 pp.
         Has no intention to controvert the husband's authority or
      the right of men to make laws and govern. Has "no sympathy with
      those who are wrangling for 'woman's rights'; nor with those who
      are foolishly urging my sex to strive for equality and competi-
      tion with men." Maintains the biblical doctrine of woman as
      moral teacher and inspirer of man. "The Bible does not uphold
      the equality of the sexes." Has compiled the Woman's Record to
      show that woman has been God's agent in the moral progress of
      mankind. Woman will never be able to enter the arena of business
      and public life equal with man because she "cannot put off the
      moral delicacy of her nature."

77   HOWITT, ANNA MARY. "Editors' Table: Youth and Genius on the
      Side of Truth." Godey's Lady's Book 50 (May):465-66.
         Expresses a great lack of sympathy with women who wish to
      be men. God has given women just as many benefits as men. "Let
      us never sigh after their lower so-called privileges."

78   "Woman in the Nineteenth Century." Living Age 46
      (1 September):550-52.
         Reviews of Fuller's book from various British sources.
      "The Press" felt that she exhibited such "innate grossness of
      mind [and] utter laxity of principle as should exclude the volume
      from every decent house in the kingdom."

79   HUNTINGTON, F.D. "Woman's Position." Monthly Religious
     Magazine 14 (November):241-51.
          Says Christianity offers the only true relief for woman's
     present social and civil condition. Women and men were not
     intended for the same activities. Some women are not satisfied
     because they do not value the heart and wish to copy men's func-
     tions and enter his sphere. Calls the whole controversy "a
     monstrous absurdity, conceived in a miserable jealousy, prose-
     cuted by an insane insurrection against good manners, and sure to
     end in nothing but a profane putting asunder of what God has
     married together." Wants women to stay away from "separatist
     conventions," platforms, "novel schemes of political economy or
     social reorganization."

80   PERKINS, PATIENCE PRICE. "My Baby." Godey's Lady's Book 51
     (November):404-7.
          Formerly an advocate of woman's rights, now has married a
     widower with ten children and had her own child and finds that a
     woman who has a baby needs nothing else. Of course she could
     leave the baby with a hireling, but then she would have to super-
     vise the servant. "Something is wrong somewhere. Either the
     Woman's Rights doctrine is a mistake, or the order of nature is
     at fault." Believes the only way for women to be equal with men
     is to have no husband or children. Obviously, a baby is better.
     Women can rule through their husbands.

                              1856

81   PENDLETON, Mrs. HESTER. The Parent's Guide for the Transmis-
     sion of Desired Qualities to Offspring, and Childbirth Made
     Easy. New York: Fowler & Wells, 212 pp.
          Asserts that one cannot overlook the laws of nature and try
     to assign to woman political privileges which are "totally dis-
     cordant to her nature, her habits, or her inclinations."

82   AN OLD GENTLEMAN. "My Wife's Portrait." Godey's Lady's Book
     52 (January):56-59.
          Contrasts his wonderful wife with feminists. Complains
     that the latter are not content with absolute dominion but "now
     insist upon the impudent and world-wide proclamation of it.
     'Woman's rights,' is the cry, forsooth!" Insists that women have
     been spoiled. Men should revolt. His wife, Fidelia, knows best
     and saves him from such a ruinous venture.

83   CECILIA. "Tennyson's Portraiture of Woman." Southern
     Literary Messenger 22 (February):97-100.
          Praises Tennyson for giving the true idea of woman's duty
     and mission. Says we need him especially "in these days, when
     there is so much fanaticism in regard to 'woman's rights.'"
     Recommends the closing pages of "The Princess" for "a just and

beautiful exposition of her nature and her relatio
Agrees with Tennyson that woman should withdraw "fr
light glare and open combat" if she would fulfill her
tiny. Her influence should be silent and soft, soothin
male cares.

1857

84   EDDY, DANIEL CLARKE. The Young Woman's Friend; or, The
      Duties, Trials, Loves, and Hopes of Woman. Boston: Wentworth
      & Co., 250 pp.
          Says woman's sphere is not the field or army, not the
      forum, public debate, legislative assembly, not public speaking,
      not the pulpit. "God has not granted to woman those natural
      faculties which will render her fitted for a public office in the
      debates of men. . . . When she thrusts herself forward as an
      orator or a declaimer, she has mistaken her calling, and departed
      from her Heaven-appointed sphere." Points out that literary
      women are usually plain: "Somehow, God seems to have denied to
      most literary women extraordinary grace of person. He has made
      plainness to be a companion to intellect."

85   HOPKINS, JOHN HENRY. The American Citizen: His Rights and
      Duties, According to the Spirit of the Constitution of the
      United States. New York: Pudney & Russell, 459 pp.
          Says we feel "instinctive disgust . . . at the spectacle of
      an effeminate man, or a masculine woman." It is the voice of
      nature as well as the revealed word of God that determines the
      relative position of the sexes. Women's brains should not be
      taxed to learn mathematics, dead languages, physiology, chem-
      istry, geology, metaphysics, or logic. "The whole of this ambi-
      tious effort to place the minds of women on the same level as
      those of men must end in disappointment, because it is contrary
      to nature." Argues that nothing makes woman "more repulsive and
      disagreeable" than "masculine learning." Objects to public ex-
      aminations because they give woman the mistaken notion that her
      sphere is to be public.

86   "Our Daughters." Harper's Magazine 16 (December):72-77.
          Editorial. Wants "our daughters" to marry and deplores the
      decreasing marriage rate. Opposes making woman a rival of man.
      Allows that woman should have a wider field for employment and be
      more self-reliant but does not want her trained "to imitate man
      either in speech, manner or costume." Says "the masculine school
      of woman's rights reformers" has hurt women by disparaging femi-
      nine qualities and favoring instead "a certain boldness and
      hardness" that yet fails to be masculine. Woman's true sphere is
      the home. "The mother silences the Amazon, and the Antoinette
      Browns and Lucy Stones of the pulpit and rostrum appear at the
      cradle very much as other women."

58

... *The Happy Home*. New York: Harper

1857

ns to man."
m the sun-
true des-
g away all

...xtreme position. Says the advo-
...ive women mixed up in all the
... it is obvious from their "bodily
...women to be the weaker vessel.
...oliticians, lawyers, soldiers.
... her physical unfitness for those
... within the domestic circle,
...er." Women who want a wider
...ezebels, Catharines de Medici, Mary
...corts [sic], or Fanny Wrights. They become unsexed,
and their principles and character go together to the bottom."

88   WILLSON, Mrs. ARABELLA M. <u>The Lives of Mrs. Ann H. Judson,</u>
     <u>Mrs. Sarah B. Judson, and Mrs. Emily C. Judson, Missionaries</u>
     <u>to Burmah</u>. New York: C.M. Saxton, 371 pp.
     In her preface argues that missionary work provides a field
for "the development of the highest excellence of female character." Contrasts the independence, energy, and intrepidity of
her subjects with the "weak and despicable" struggles of "many
misguided women in our day, who seek to gain a reluctant acknowl-
dgement of equality with the other sex, by a noisy assertion of
their rights, and in some instances, by an imitation of their
attire!" Would rather honor women who sacrifice themselves in
the field, sharing their husband's labor "in his errand of love
to the heathen" than those women who push themselves into the
law, the courthouse, at the bar.

89   HALE, SARAH JOSEPHA. "Editors' Table." <u>Godey's Lady's Book</u>
     57 (September):273-75.
     Has much praise for Craik's <u>A Woman's Thoughts about Women</u>
(see 95). Was relieved to find it free of "wild assertion,
extravagant declamation, claims impossible to be granted, privileges demanded" which so often characterize women's writings
these days. Confesses that she opens a work on this subject with
dread, hoping that the author has been true to her sex, anxious
lest she mar her argument by advancing an impractical scheme.

90   "Woman." <u>Living Age</u> 59 (13 November):483-99.
     Calls woman's rightists "modern Amazons who insist upon
setting up their sex as a separate class of beings, naturally at
enmity with man, and by him unjustly subjugated and ignorantly
tyrannized over." The female-rights vindicators are composed of
unmarried and unprotected women who may need more rights but
cannot be the standard for all women as they are "the least truly
women." Women in business exaggerate the defects of the busi-
nessman. Deplores sex antagonism. Finds women least fitted for

the functions of judge and legislator. Reprinted from <u>National</u> <u>Review</u> (London) 7 (October):333-61.

1859

91 THAYER, WILLIAM MAKEPEACE. <u>Poor Girl and True Woman; or,</u> <u>Elements of Woman's Success Drawn from the Life of Mary Lyon</u> <u>and Others</u>. Boston: Gould & Lincoln, 353 pp.
     Calls claims for women's rights "preposterous." Says Abby Kelley Foster "has unsexed herself clamoring for 'Women's Rights' on the public rostrum. Curiosity may induce many to listen once or more to her harangues, but few there are who can respect her on account of her unwomanly character." Contrasts feminists with Mary Lyon, "content to perform a woman's mission in the humblest walks of life." Castigates Mary Wolstencroft [<u>sic</u>] and Frances Wright for their impiety. "Popular opinion has branded them as a disgrace to their sex; the verdict of society has consigned them to merited shame." Says Wollstonecraft was rewarded for her unholy zeal by having her name become "a hissing and by-word in virtuous circles."

92 "Position, Influence, and Wishes of Women." <u>Eclectic Magazine</u> 46 (January):1-17.
     Reprinted from <u>National Review</u> (London) 7 (October 1858):333-61. Reprinted in 90.

93 SANDS, ALEXANDER H. "Intellectual Culture of Woman." <u>Southern Literary Messenger</u> 28 (May):321-32.
     Does not want to import into Virginia "this new-fangled system of Woman's Rights." Favors slavery and wants women to uphold it. Sees the connection, implicitly, between abolition and women's rights.

94 "Womanhood and Its Mission." <u>Eclectic Magazine</u> 47 (July):349-65; (August):492-505.
     Finds the most extreme expression of the rights of women in America, "the cradle of extreme tendencies," in bloomerism, "which flourished for a time to shock and amuse the world." Argues that men and women are interdependent and differ in kind, not in degree. Should woman attempt to be man, "she either sinks to a non-existence, or she becomes a deadly woe." Lady Macbeth is cited. Woman's mission is to be true to her womanhood. Reprinted from <u>Dublin University Magazine</u> 53:623ff and 696ff.

1861

95 CRAIK, DINAH M. <u>A Woman's Thoughts about Women</u>. Philadelphia: T.B. Peterson & Brothers, 309 pp.

Complains about derogation of women but calls "equally blasphemous, and perhaps even more harmful, . . . the outcry about 'the equality of the sexes'; the frantic attempt to force women, many of whom are either ignorant of or unequal for their own duties--into the position and duties of men." Exclaims, "A pretty state of matters would ensue!" Mocks women's committees, letters of business, bookkeeping, etc. "Equality of the sexes is not in the nature of things."

1863

96 "The Legal Rights of Married Women." New Englander 22
    (January):22-35.
        A long and generally favorable review of Caroline Dall's
    Women's Rights under the Law. But asserts that "men of learning
    and sound practical judgment" have refrained from supporting the
    women's rights movement because "it is made up of so much that is
    not only absurd and impracticable, but even subversive of domes-
    tic and social order, and positively hostile to the principles of
    Christianity." Also faults the movement for having among its
    supporters and leaders "individuals of the most chimerical no-
    tions and tendencies--scoffers at religion--nullifiers of all
    distinctions between the sexes--followers of Andrew Jackson
    Davis--worshipers at the shrine of free love."

1864

97 "Womanliness." Knickerbocker Magazine 63 (March):227-32.
        Defines manliness as active, womanliness as passive, a fact
    forgotten by "those dangerous extreme reformers (save the term)"
    shouting "Woman's Rights" who "would have women step from and
    exceed their sphere." If women wander from their established
    paths, calamity ensues. Worries about women in the gymnasium
    becoming muscular and broad.

98 SHERWOOD, Mrs. VIRGINIA. "American Women." Continental
    Monthly 6 (October):416-33.
        Believes that the woman's rights pioneers have done good
    work but that there have been some "ultraists" who make extrava-
    gant and unsuitable claims. Warns that "anything which tends in
    the least to unsex, to unsphere woman," produces in man and
    society "a gradual and dangerous deterioration." Woman must not
    demand anything that would introduce confusion and disorder among
    the social forces. The woman's rights advocates forget that
    there is sex of mind; mistakenly assume that men and women should
    occupy the same spheres; place men and women in antagonism; and
    believe that marriage makes slaves of women.

<u>1866</u>

99   "Something about Woman's Work." <u>Hours</u> <u>at</u> <u>Home</u> 2 (April):
      545-48.
         Declares that woman's rights advocates meet with little
      sympathy from the cultivated, refined, intelligent community.
      Calls them "fanatics" who would "drag [woman], Cassandra-like,
      from the home-altar, from her divinely appointed work, and under
      the plea of giving her certain invaluable rights would bring her
      into ridicule and disgrace." Alleges that instead of being
      "strong-minded," these deluded women are really weak, as shown by
      their attempts to copy men's clothing. Objects to female swag-
      gering. Asserts that woman cannot stand equal politically and
      mentally with man and still retain her feminine character.

<u>1867</u>

100   DOANE, WILLIAM CROSWELL. <u>A</u> <u>Sermon</u> <u>Preached</u> <u>at</u> <u>the</u> <u>Commence-</u>
      <u>ment</u> <u>of</u> <u>Cottage</u> <u>Hill</u> <u>Seminary</u> <u>for</u> <u>Ladies,</u> <u>Poughkeepsie,</u> <u>New</u>
      <u>York,</u> <u>19</u> <u>June</u> <u>1867.</u> Poughkeepsie: Telegraph Steam Presses,
      10 pp.
         Argues that woman must be educated for her Christian duty.
      Says that "of all horrible things, the progressive, popular
      assignment of woman's mission, in our day, to the platform and
      the pulpit and the polls, is the most offensive and unseemly."

101   TODD, Rev. JOHN. <u>Woman's</u> <u>Rights</u>. Boston: Lee & Shepard,
      27 pp.
         Insists that God never intended that women and men should
      occupy the same sphere. Women "cannot invent," "cannot compete
      with men in a long course of mental labor," cannot become
      artists. Women's real "rights" are to be protected by men and
      exempted from certain activities and drudgery. Opposes bloomer
      dress, which some women have put on in an attempt to become
      "semi-men," thereby losing all grace and mystery. Opposes woman
      suffrage as "unseemly." Opposes women displacing men in
      offices--"Every public employment diminishes woman's chance of
      marriage, and in proportion to its publicity." Opposes forcing a
      woman's mind to bear the rigors of a complete college course.

102   FROTHINGHAM, O.B. "Woman in Society." <u>Radical</u> 2 (June):
      598-610.
         Says woman reigns supreme in the home and in the world of
      fashion. Asserts that when "we give women their rights, we steal
      from them their prestige." Wants women to shine in society,
      dress beautifully, add culture and tone to the community, and
      thus control the opinions of men. They "would influence polit-
      ical measures more than by having themselves the ballot."

103   HALE, SARAH JOSEPHA.   "Editors' Table: How to Live and How to
       Love."   Godey's Lady's Book 75 (August):171.
              Men and women complement each other.   To confound these
       distinctions would be to break "Heaven's first law of order."
       Asserts that "God did not intend women to guide the plough, sail
       ships, invent machinery, build pyramids."   Women have more impor-
       tant work to do.

104   HEDGE, F.H., D.D.   "'Male and Female.'"   Monthly Religious
       Magazine 38 (October):241-51.
              Asserts that women are excluded from male occupations on
       grounds of fitness, of natural propriety, not willfully or wrong-
       fully.   Enlightened perception and refined feeling rather than
       blind prejudice are the determining factors.   As civilization
       advances, the distinctions become greater.   Would allow female
       physicians to administer to their own sex and engage in other
       employments that do not subvert the natural order.   If women
       wanted the vote, they should have it, but insists that the ma-
       trons of Massachusetts know that woman suffrage would be a "revo-
       lution . . . attended with great risk of domestic happiness, and
       with small advantage, if any, to the public good."   It would
       carry "the bitterness and broils of political life" into the
       family.

105   FROTHINGHAM, O.B.   "Women versus Women."   Nation 5
       (3 October):276-77.
              Says feminists alienate other women, are too radical, crit-
       ical, extreme.   Asserts that "woman's firmest and wisest cham-
       pions have been men."

                                   1868

106   "Women of the Middle Ages."   Eclectic Magazine 70 (March):
       299-308.
              Reflects on "woman's anxiety to unsex herself in the pres-
       ent age" and seeks to examine how women gained the advantages
       they presently possess, starting in the Middle Ages.   Reprinted
       from Blackwood's Edinburgh Magazine 102 (November 1867):613-34.

107   MORFORD, HENRY.   "Woman and Chivalry in America."
       Lippincott's 1 (April):417-21.
              Asserts that "chivalric devotion to womanhood has decayed
       from its height and glory among that large proportion of men
       which may be said to give tone to the whole mass."   Blames women
       who are asserting their right to make their way in the world.
       Womanhood used to give "tone" to society, especially in the
       larger cities of the East; lately it has been demanding too much
       and giving too little.

108   SHANKS, WILLIAM F.G.   "Woman's Work and Wages."   Harper's
       Magazine 37 (September):546-53.

In an otherwise prowoman article, cannot forebea...
at feminist activists who loudly and immodestly demande...
ical rights and "even claimed and exercised the privilege...
donning male attire." Finds that the "Bloomers" have inva...
been "the noisiest of the 'woman's rights' advocates" and wa...
that "this class has done much to prejudice the men against t...
real workers." Feels that it was premature for women to deman...
suffrage and ape men's dress.

1869

109 BROCKETT, LINUS PIERPONT, M.D. Woman: Her Rights, Wrongs,
Privileges, and Responsibilities. . . . Woman Suffrage, Its
Folly and Inexpediency. Hartford, Conn.: L. Stebbins,
447 pp.
Women are subordinate because that was decreed by God.
Favors equal education but prefers that women not occupy the
pulpit or give lectures to amuse or instruct. Will allow unmarried women to become physicians for women and children but finds
something "distasteful and unpleasant" about women in general
practice. Asserts that "women are not well adapted to the practice of surgery, and should never undertake it." Thinks true
women would find presiding over a court or arguing a case before
a jury to be "distasteful and unpleasant." Finds actresses
immoral. Opposes woman suffrage for the usual reasons.

110 TUTHILL, LOUISA CAROLINE. The Young Lady at Home and in
Society. New York: Allen Brothers, 330 pp.
Reprint of 39.

111 LOUGHBOROUGH, MARY W. "Women, and the Lives of Women." Land
We Love 6 (February):329-35.
Is shocked by the speech of a United States congressman
sneering at women. Paints a picture of woman's heroism and says
the congressman should try to have a noble influence over wayward
women. Believes that "few true women are anxious to appear at
the polls, and take part in public affairs." Most prefer to use
their influence. Finds few women "clamoring" for woman's rights
or wanting suffrage, so prominent men should not scorn all women
for the failures and shortcomings of a few.

112 BROWNSON, O.A. "The Woman Question." Catholic World 9
(May):145-57.
Denies that women have a natural right to suffrage. Uncon-
vinced by Frances Wright and Mary Wollstonecraft. Admits that
women have had some success in the arts but none have risen to
the front rank. Objects to woman suffrage because it would
render women and men mutually independent rather than interdepen-
dent. Denies that suffrage can cure or lessen social or moral
evils: it will produce discord and finally destroy the family.

r children and repress their maternal
d increase, and the human race would
on.   Once in the political sphere,
than men; Lady Macbeth is an example.
education.

'o Do!" <u>Eclectic</u> <u>Magazine</u> 72

per-class woman with nothing to do to "drop
social agitation, which alienate from her cause
pathetic and generous men," and work on improving women's
ucation so that women become fit to do their duty. Reprinted
from <u>Macmillan's</u> <u>Magazine</u> (London) 19 (March):451-54.

1869

114   WATKINS, B.U. "Mystical or Transcendental Skepticism and
      Woman's Rights." <u>Christian</u> <u>Quarterly</u> 1 (July):395-402.
         Bad women are worse than bad men and are closer to the
      devil. "Satan has never been so successful in corrupting the
      human race as when he undertakes to vitiate the faith and affec-
      tions of woman's heart." As it was with Eve, it is now with the
      woman's rightists--Satan is suggesting that the Gospel despoils
      woman of her rights. If she listens, she will become such a
      gorgon as helped introduce the French Revolution. The great
      movers for women's rights are shrewd schemers who want to rob the
      doctrine of Christ of its elevation of women. Opposes woman
      suffrage: to make woman an elector would be to allow her to rule
      over man, which her nature and God's plan do not allow.

115   "Woman's Rights Viewed Physiologically and Historically."
      <u>National</u> <u>Quarterly</u> <u>Review</u> 20 (December):79-101.
         Believes that the woman's rights movement is a discredit to
      our civilization. Savages and barbarians give women equal rights
      to work. Civilized nations protect women from rough work. Men
      do not want to marry unwomanly reformers. Alleges that woman's
      rights women and men become hermaphrodites, <u>lusus</u> <u>naturae</u>. That
      is why the greatest men and women oppose woman's rights. Uses
      Greek history to show what happened when women had "rights" and
      free love. Oppose having women work physically or intellectually
      with men because it degrades them. Does not want women to endan-
      ger their virtue by becoming physicians--attaining the training
      and education would blast their natural delicacy and modesty.

116   DENNETT, J.R. "A Hint to Our Female Agitators." <u>Nation</u> 9
      (2 December):479-80.
         Criticizes women's rights conventioners for dressing fash-
      ionably. Says men would never be taken seriously if modishly
      dressed.

117   "The Rights of Children." <u>Nation</u> 9 (9 December):503-4.
         Worries what will become of children if their mothers work,
      vote, etc.

1870

118   BLAKE, SILAS LEROY. Woman's Rights. A Fast-Day Sermon
       Preached in the South Congregational Church, Concord, New
       Hampshire, 7 April 1870. Concord, N.H.: B.W. Sanborn & Co.,
       32 pp.
           Says we must make distinctions between womanly and un-
       womanly employments. Harriet Hosmer has made some sculptures
       which "would and ought to make modest women blush." Worries that
       women's rightists will offend propriety, lose what power they
       already have. "The movement is fraught with vast evil." Calls
       the cry of oppression "simply puerile and pitiful." Alleges that
       those in the movement simply want office and notoriety. It is
       better for women to remain disinterested, not wading in "the mire
       that lies ankle-deep all over the arena of public strife." In-
       sists that some supporters have mocked and violated their mar-
       riage vows, and use vulgar and indecent language. Opposes woman
       suffrage.

119   DAVIS, REBECCA HARDING. Pro Aris et Focis: A Plea for Our
       Altars and Hearths. New York: Virtue & Yorston, 132 pp.
           Insists that woman's altar and hearth are one. She cannot
       wreck one without destroying the other. Argues that a woman
       becomes passionless by adopting a male profession. Finds woman's
       moral right to enter the medical profession questionable: she
       will find her refinement and modesty shocked on every side.
       Alleges that women who draw up in hostile ranks against men and
       claim political and social equality are frequently just trying to
       get men's attention and admiration. Wants women to stick to
       their high, grand work.

120   ELLIS, JOHN B. Free Love and Its Votaries; or, American
       Socialism Unmasked. New York: U.S. Publishing Co., 502 pp.
           Particularly attacks John Humphrey Noyes. Finds the women
       of the Oneida or Perfectionist community coarse, sensual, filthy
       in conversation, without modesty or shame. Says woman's rights
       advocates are antimarriage and have joined forces with the Free-
       Love party to strike blows against Christian marriage. Insists
       that "it will require but a cursory glance to find that the
       Woman-Suffrage party, the Free-Love party, the Spiritualist
       party, the Infidel party, are all one and the same organization.
       It is therefore a political and religious duty with every man to
       oppose any and all these organizations. The triumph of one means
       the triumph of all."

121   MAC CAIG, D. A Reply to John Stuart Mill on the Subjection of
       Women. Philadelphia: J.B. Lippincott, 242 pp.
           Accuses Mill of proceeding in an illogical and unphilosoph-
       ical manner. Opposes change in marriage laws, suffrage, woman's
       occupations. "The natural and logical consequences of Mr. Mill's
       doctrines would be to loosen all the bonds of society and the

extension of the franchise to woman is the first and most important step in bringing about this result." It would degrade and
unsex woman, and destroy family happiness. Woman's rights "at
best promises only a greater degree of restlessness and political
immorality and excitement to a people whose besetting sins carry
them already too far in this direction," without improving
woman's condition.

122   STRUTT, ELIZABETH. The Feminine Soul: Its Nature and
      Attributes. With Thoughts upon Marriage, and Friendly Hints
      upon Feminine Duties. Boston: H.H. & T.W. Carter, 199 pp.
         Presents all the standard notions of woman's role and
capacities. Argues against married women taking public roles,
including authorship, acting, singing, etc. "The same remarks
that apply to authorship in females may be extended to their
speaking in public, lecturing, and that most ridiculous of all
ideas that ever entered the brain of a theorist, taking their
places, with Men, as members of Parliament." Mocks such notions,
and denies that women can take men's roles. "But we wish not to
dwell on the thousand absurdities of a scheme which it is difficult to believe could ever have been seriously entertained and
promulgated, even by understandings as masculine as Miss
Martineau's or Miss Wright's."

123   WHITE, CARLOS. Ecce Femina: An Attempt to Solve the Woman
      Question. Hanover, N.H.: Privately published, 258 pp.
         Says women and men are different and intended by God for
different spheres. Demonstrates that minds correspond with
bodies. Men's bodies and minds are strong, coarse, slow; women's
are weaker, quicker, more rapid. "Woman's mind is not made to
grapple with hard, tough problems; but she can perform those
mental tasks that come within her sphere with celerity, accuracy,
ease, and grace." Demolishes Mill point by point, then turns to
the Innovators, who want to destroy the family and cause antagonism between the sexes. Says suffragists are queer, crazy man-
haters. Opposes women attorneys but will allow women physicians
if separately educated. Insists that women should earn less than
men so that men may continue to support families.

124   [NOBLE, L.G.]. "Notes on the Woman's Rights Agitation, By a
      Looker-On." Nation 10 (20 January):38-39; (10 February):88-
      89; (17 February):101-4.
         Criticizes woman's rights advocates for arguing from
special and accidental cases to universal rules and with trying
to redress life's most intimate and awful woes with civil law.
Says women can be just as miserable to live with as men. Worries
that the best women of the country will not be the ones seeking
public office.

125   HALE, SARAH JOSEPHA. "Editors' Table: Questions of Impor-
      tance." Godey's Lady's Book 80 (March):286.

Wants woman educated for her proper sphere
into the arena of politics and striving to gain
"through the rough machinery of suffrage."

126   MAYO, A.D.   "John Stuart Mill on Woman."   Monthly Religious
Magazine 43 (March):226-33.
Criticizes Anthony, Stanton, and Rose for their methods.
Says such "masculine assailants of woman's rights," such "sharp
and superficial ladies [as] now control the woman's conventions,"
will not be the ones to point out woman's true mission. Is most
critical of Mill for his liberalism and his philosophical defi-
ciencies. "Mill empties [woman] of all that inspires human
interest, and raises the question whether she have a soul at
all." Denies that woman has ever been subjected as Mill would
have it and says "every lofty souled woman will repudiate such a
champion of her rights."

127   L.   "The First Duty of Woman."   Monthly Religious Magazine 43
(May):514-15.
Quotes from and agrees with an article in the Boston
Journal on the duty of women to make themselves as fair as
possible. Both fear that "the reign of woman's rights is to be
fatal to the reign of her charms."

128   BIDDLE, CRAIG.   "The Coming Man."   Harper's Bazar 5
(June):651-54.
A mockery of the woman's rights movement. Argues iron-
ically that women should vote and rule--they always have, and are
eminently suited to politics, holding to their views with stub-
born obstinacy, devoted to a cause, resistant to cooperation.
Sarcastically calls it "a reproach to the civilization of the
nineteenth century" that women are wasting their time in domesticity and child-rearing when they might be serving the country
as policemen, aldermen, firemen, or members of the legislatures.
The population can be maintained more cheaply by immigration than
by child-bearing. Men will stay home and nurture the family,
keeping away from coarse and bold women.

129   WILDER, BURT G.   "Equal Yet Diverse."   Atlantic 26 (July):
30-40.
Man and woman are two halves of one, equal but diverse.
There is a real and fundamental distinction of sex. Women and
men are equal but not identical, diverse yet complementary.
Delves down into the animal kingdom to prove it. "The male is
best fitted to shine in public, the female in private. . . .
While both work together and equally well, the powers of the male
seem to flow from heart through the head, and those of the female
as instinctive perceptions of necessities from the head through
the heart, so as to fit her better for works of intimate care and
affection."

130   COOPER, SUSAN FENIMORE. "Female Suffrage: A Letter to the
       Christian Women of America." Harper's Magazine 41
       (August):438–46; (September):594–600.
           Maintains that women are naturally subordinate because of
       inferior physical strength, inferior intellect, and teachings of
       Christianity. We are now challenged in society, in print, and in
       legislatures to emancipate women by giving them suffrage. Denies
       that women are legally oppressed; to upset the traditional rela-
       tions of the sexes would be "formidable and dangerous." Women
       should ask men to correct any legal injustices. Refutes Mill.
       Degraded women will vote to excess, selling their vote more
       readily than the lowest class of men. Opposes allowing women to
       unsex themselves by entering male professions, although some
       separate higher education is acceptable.

131   GODKIN, E.L. "The Feud in the Woman's Rights Camp." Nation
       11 (24 November):346–47.
           Gloats over the separation into two groups, the Woman's
       Journal of Boston and the Revolution of New York. Says that
       people would really like to hear from the leading women of the
       movement on the pressing issues of the day.

                                  1871

132   LANDELS, WILLIAM, D.D. Woman: Her Position and Power.
       London and New York: Cassell, Petter, & Galpin, 288 pp.
           Complains that supporters of equal rights for women also
       want to have men worshipping at their feet. Insists that iden-
       tity with men is impossible and that "nothing but an overweening
       self-conceit would blind women to the consequences which must
       inevitably follow from cherishing incompatible desires." Finds
       the "feminine grumblers and agitators" to be inconsistent and
       blind to the fact that identical rights would destroy feminine
       precedence. Women belong in the home because they alone can
       perform domestic duties. Opposes woman suffrage because it would
       introduce dissension in the home.

133   SPENCER, Mrs. H.C. Problems on the Woman Question, Social,
       Political, and Scriptural. Washington, D.C., 17 pp.
           Lists 130 problems by number; questions woman's rights and
       suffrage with reference to St. Paul, the Sermon on the Mount, the
       Ten Commandments, and Genesis; and raises issues regarding labor-
       ing women, who do not support woman suffrage.

134   "The Two 'Movements' Among Women." Nation 12 (19 January):
       39–40.
           Says there are two movements going on among women today:
       one among farmers' daughters and working girls generally, who
       wish clean, indoor, and sedentary labor, who detest and abhor
       independence and want most to marry; the other, the woman's

rights movement, which wants not only suffrage but "admission on
equal terms with men to all employments and occupations" but
especially public professions not calling for women's work or
manual labor. The latter is having a pernicious influence upon
the young of both sexes.

135   M., W.P. "Woman's Rights in England." Lippincott's 7
      (February):221-24.
          Describes various cases--among them, a woman eloped with a
      blackleg (strikebreaker or scab) and charged so-called neces-
      saries to her husband, for which a jury found him liable--to
      demonstrate the folly of woman's rights. Denies that women are
      more moral than men.

136   DABNEY, Rev. R.L. "Women's Rights Women." Southern Magazine
      8 (March):322-34.
          Blames northerners and abolitionists for spawning the
      women's rights movement. Insists that they must support the
      latter radicalism if they supported the former. Predicts that
      this mad radicalism will destroy Christianity and civilization in
      America. Calls the theory of women's rights "sheer infidelity"
      and cites Scriptures in support. Quotes E.C. Stanton as calling
      for the abolition of permanent marriage ties. Expresses pity for
      the children.

137   GODKIN, E.L. "Sex in Politics." Nation 12 (20 April):270-72.
          Asserts that people distrust the woman's rights movement
      because its leaders persist in ignoring "the influence of the
      sexual passion on nearly every field of human activity."

138   BROWNE, JUNIUS HENRI. "Woman's Rights Aesthetically." Galaxy
      11 (May):725-30.
          Woman's true sphere is her heart. No womanly woman demands
      political and social rights. Women get more in the name of
      courtesy than by making demands. Warns that "men prefer love-
      liness to logic." The foundation and culmination of woman's
      rights is "loveliness and love."

139   PHELPS, Mrs. LINCOLN. "'Woman's Record.'" Godey's Lady's
      Book 83 (August):149.
          Ostensibly reviews Hale's Woman's Record (1853), "an anti-
      dote to the pernicious doctrines of the women suffragists";
      condemns feminists "who, leaving their domestic duties, wander
      about the country, to stir up the wives and mothers to discontent
      and rebellion against the laws, human and Divine."

140   LOWE, MARTHA PERRY. "Some Words about Women." Old and New 4
      (September):287-94.
          Says women must not put themselves in antagonism to men.
      They must not try to do men's coarse, rough work. Would open
      other work to them, improve education, but keep women out of the
      public arena of debate.

141   "The Mission of Woman." Southern Review, n.s. 9
       (October):923–42.
           Draws parallels between the fall of Rome as described in
       Lecky's History of Morals (1870) and the threat of the modern
       woman's movement. The root of the evil is the notion that woman
       is the equal of man. Women are better than man and so should
       keep out of politics. Quotes Scriptures. Women must obey.
       Cannot imagine that any "really beautiful and lovely woman will,
       in her right mind, actually join the ranks of the woman's rights
       movement." Predicts that the strong-minded women of the North
       will be its ruination. Congratulates women of the South for
       remaining pure.

                                    1872

142   Casca Llanna (Good News) [sic]: Love, Woman, Marriage: The
       Grand Secret! A Book for the Heartful. 4th ed. Boston:
       Randolph Publishing Co., 404 pp.
           Would allow woman her true and natural rights but "does
       object to, and make relentless war upon, that specious system of
       Woman's Rightsism, which proclaims free harlotage, the do-as-
       impulse-or-interest-promptsism and the right of murdering her
       unborn child, whether legitimate or not." No doubt alluding to
       Victoria Woodhull, objects to a "thrice-branded harlot" proposing
       to lead women to the promised land. Finds "intellectual amazons"
       a sad spectacle. Wants women to be gentle, sweet, emotional, not
       hard, sexless, cold. Alleges that woman's rightism has caused
       divorces to increase at least 500 percent.

143   DODGE, MARY ABIGAIL [Gail Hamilton]. Woman's Worth and
       Worthlessness. New York: Harper & Brothers, 291 pp.
           Begins with a narrative of a woman who attempts to learn to
       cook because her previous cooks have been unsatisfactory, tries
       to hire a starving needlewoman to be housekeeper, and then turns
       to reflections on woman's value. Asserts that woman was not made
       for physical toil, manual labor, or commercial industry. Rather,
       she is to nurture the race. The true woman's right is not to
       support herself at all. Describes women as ignorant, inexact,
       untrustworthy, shiftless, and unbusinesslike in men's work--they
       do not keep their word. Offers much advice for working women.
       Insists that women need qualities, not opportunities. As for
       woman suffrage, objects to the suffragists' methods. Believes
       women should be exempt from this duty.

144   MEEHAN, THOMAS. "Sexual Science." Old and New 5 (February):
       170–75.
           Using examples from plant and animal kingdoms, proves that
       nature divided humans into two sexes for two reasons--survival
       and reproduction. Woman has greater endurance and general vital-
       ity, man intellectual superiority and greater muscular strength.

Man was created to serve the woman's cause. Includes
in the list of "essential prerogatives of man." Says there will
always be aberrations from the general law--women who must support themselves--but society should not make laws to cover exceptions. Each sex should remain within its natural sphere.

145   PIKE, LUKE OWEN. "Woman and Political Power." Popular
      Science Monthly 1 (May):82-94.
         Explains woman's rights advocates by saying that they have
been unfortunate in their experience with men. Says that if
women "were to devote their whole energies to science or to
politics," it "would do violence to their physical organization,"
leading to "the abolition of motherhood." Says women with masculine intellects are even more rare than women with masculine
muscles. "There are few, if any, distinctively masculine pursuits in which any women have ever succeeded." Scientists know
that women's minds correspond to their bodies. Alleges that if
it could be proved that there exist no differences between the
minds of men and women, it would be the end of anthropology.
Totally opposes woman suffrage. Reprinted from Anthropological
Review (London).

146   "The Left Hand of Society." Penn Monthly 3 (June):283-99.
         Woman is the left hand of society. Woman and man are
profoundly unlike. Woman's work is to take care of people, man's
work principles. Would have medicine open to women but not
suffrage, because woman's gifts disqualify her to make fair and
just political decisions. Concludes that woman must be given a
chance to become even more a woman and more fit to do woman's
work, rather than made "mannish" or called to do things not in
her sphere.

                              1873

147   F. "On the Equality of the Sexes." Popular Science Monthly 2
      (March):552-60.
         Says men and women are not equals, and the laws that affect
their relations ought to recognize that fact. Totally opposes
John Stuart Mill. Reprinted from Pall Mall Budget (London).

148   MURPHY, B. "Marriage in the Nineteenth Century." Catholic
      World 16 (March):776-88.
         Calls the advocates of woman's rights "waifs of womanhood"
and faults them and others for promoting divorce. "The women of
a nation form the men; and, if marriage is to be reformed, it
must be done first through the women."

149   SHERWOOD, Mrs. M.E.W. "What Has America Done for Woman?"
      Scribner's Monthly 6 (July):300-303.
         Says unhappy women are a dangerous class. "We should save
those women from themselves, who, having no definite business in

life, go off into queer and unfit occupations." Particularly
wants to save them from "that dreadful abyss where struggle the
unhappy women who are trying to be men." Wants to "eradicate
that offensive weed known as woman's rights in this garden where
she has no wrongs, except those common to our common humanity."

150   BENSON, CARL. "'Woman's Rights' Again." Galaxy 16
       (August):196-98.
          Finds woman's rights agitation disorganizing and destruc-
       tive in setting women against men and in "making a man's foes
       emphatically those of his own household." Says the movement
       inevitably becomes "nagging" on a national scale. Insists that
       men are physically, mentally, and morally stronger and are
       "likely to remain so for some generations."

151   "Ownership in Women: Editorial." Scribner's Monthly 6
       (September):623-24.
          Argues that woman does belong to the man to whom she gives
       herself; the man then becomes her protector. Then their inter-
       ests are identified with each other. The reformers are trying to
       break up this identity of interests, to make women and men inde-
       pendent, women free to vote or trade or go to Congress. Argues
       that men are opposed to these latter-day doctrines and will
       protect true women from "the false philosophies and destructive
       policies of their few misguided sisters, who seek to turn the
       world upside down."

152   NOBLE, LULU GRAY. "Free Marriage." Scribner's Monthly 6
       (October):658-64.
          Blames some "new women" for vocally praising "temporary
       marriage." Says that the woman's movement is advocating "free
       marriage" as necessary for "the emancipation of the sex." Calls
       to the attention of "these wild dreamers . . . the fact that all
       such emancipation of woman tends directly to her slavery, a
       bondage, that, in a degree, would affect every member of the
       sex." Argues for the double standard of banishing immoral women
       but not men from society because it ensures that all women in
       society then can be assured decent, respectful treatment.

153   "The Woman Question." Brownson's Quarterly Review 22
       (October):508-29.
          Opposes woman suffrage. Says that because woman is phys-
       ically weaker than man, she is "less morally independent, less
       frank, open, and straightforward, and in a contest with man,
       compelled . . . to resort to art, artifice, intrigue, in which
       she alone can surpass him. Her accession to the political body
       could, therefore, only introduce an additional element of polit-
       ical and moral corruption." If woman becomes independent and
       ambitious, she becomes "a social anomaly, sometimes a hideous
       monster." Links woman suffrage to free love and says Stanton and
       Anthony "have become coarse and termagantish in comparison with

what they were in their youth, when we both knew and esteemed
them. They are no longer what they were."

1874

154   GLOVER, Rev. H.C. The Rights and Wrongs of Woman, a Poem.
      New York: J.W. Stoops, 72 pp.
           Woman's sphere is in the home--in monotonous iambic pen-
      tameter, rhyming couplets. Women should not be lawyers, judges,
      preachers, or doctors. Poem is on left side, advertisements on
      right side of book.

155   "Idle Women." Harper's Bazar 7 (28 March):202.
           Says that it is not that women lack opportunity as much as
      it is that they do not make the most of the opportunities they
      have. Any man who has ever lived at a New York boarding house
      has been impressed that "the chief occupation of the female mind
      is dawdling." Blames "false forms of life and emulative extrava-
      gance" for begetting in women "selfishness and idleness." Women
      who publicly bemoan the sorrows of the subject sex must "realize
      that the monster who is in the way of women's progress is not man
      so much as the idle women."

156   PHELPS, ALMIRA LINCOLN. "Woman's Duties and Rights."
      National Quarterly Review 29 (June):29-54.
           Says the lesson of Eve is full of instruction for woman--
      she is to be man's assistant, subordinate, and to beware tempta-
      tion. Recounts the sad and notorious life of Wollstonecraft and
      the infidel and immoral Wright, both of whom associated free love
      and infidelity with woman's rights. Describes the growth of the
      movement in America, the rise of the antis and the anti publica-
      tion The True Woman and some of its contributors and articles
      (see 799). Accuses woman's rights supporters of being "stimu-
      lated with false notions, and intoxicated with notoriety."
      Faults them for breaking away from their home duties "to lux-
      uriate in unrestrained freedom." Opposes Mill, who had spoken in
      favor of woman suffrage in Parliament. Insists on division of
      labor.

1876

157   HOPKINSON, Mrs. "Some Thoughts on the Completed Century."
      Godey's Lady's Book 92 (January):31-35.
           Praises women who have accomplished improvements in woman's
      condition over the past one hundred years, not as "hustling and
      pushing" woman's rightists, which would actually argue against
      their cause, but "with modesty and gentleness maintaining their
      places as helpers and companions of men, as examples and teachers
      of children."

158   "A Frenchman's View of It." Catholic World 23 (July):453-63.
       A description of and response to Claudio Jannet's Les
Etats-Unis Contemporains, ou les Moeurs, les Institutions et les
Idées depuis la Guerre de la Sécession (1876). Reviewer admits
that the woman's rights movement has had "a very unhappy influence upon the female mind, and a bad effect upon female education." The family relation has also been fearfully impaired,
with increase in divorce, prevalence of infanticide, "the growing
inability or unwillingness of American women to bear the burden of
maternity," breakup of homes, license allowed to the young of
both sexes, and more. Regrets the tendency of the times to
remove woman from the home and set her upon the platform.

                                1877

159   CLAPP, C.W. "Shall Womanhood Be Abolished?" New Englander 36
       (July):541-67.
          Condemns "this whole movement for the masculinization of
woman" for trying to make husband and wife separate and distinct
and for "profan[ing] the domestic altar into an arena of business
relations." Cites the New Testament to prove woman's inferior,
silent position. "Christ and the Apostles understood the value of
woman [and] . . . they never placed her in any public position."
Warns against thwarting nature's plans and confounding things she
intended to be distinct. Separate spheres are necessary to a
well-ordered system. Division of labor is the law of all human
activity. "No woman can play a man's part in life, and remain a
true woman."

                                1878

160   JOHNSTON, Rev. GEORGE H. "Woman, Wrong and Right."
       Mercersburg Review 25 (October):524-45.
          Says the woman's movement, begun "by fanatics and errorists
of both sexes, is founded in false premises, illogical and incon-
clusive in its reasonings, and damaging to [woman's] character in
proportion to its success." It causes rivalry between the sexes,
breeds discord in the family and home, sets husband and wife
against each other. Woman's rightists are insubordinate, strong-
minded, and impious, and reap a crop of "family feuds, coldness
and alienation of feeling and affection, divorces and lawsuits."
Opposes coeducation and cites Edward H. Clarke. Opposes dress
reform. Says if woman wants to vote, she should do so through her
brothers and father, later her husband.

161   "Biology and 'Woman's Rights.'" Popular Science Monthly 14
       (December):201-13.
          Like other female mammals, women are physically weaker by
nature, not because of subjugation. Men's brains are larger;
that is why they have attained superiority in the various arts

                                40

and sciences. The female intellectual, like the female athlete,
"is simply an anomaly, an exceptional being, holding a position
more or less intermediary between the two sexes," having under-
gone abnormal development. Warns that any attempt to alter the
present relations of the sexes is "a struggle against Nature."
Concludes: "'the woman's-rights' movement' is an attempt to
rear, by a process of 'unnatural selection,' a race of mon-
strosities--hostile alike to men, to normal women, to human
society. . . ." Reprinted from Quarterly Journal of Science
(London).

1879

162   GRAVES, ARTHUR PERCIVAL, D.D. Twenty-five Letters to a Young
      Lady. Chicago: Fairbanks, 135 pp.
          Written in the form of letters to his niece. He does not
      know why women of America and the world "are rocking with the
      agitated question of 'Woman's Rights.' Says they already have
      more rights than they can handle. "I would not lay a straw in
      the way of woman's filling the place for which God made her. . . .
      But when I am asked to endorse unreasonable positions and
      schemes of unmitigated sin, polygamy and the like, I stop, and
      enter protest with all my might." Objects to woman suffrage.
      "It would expose woman to vile associations where she never ought
      to be." Would have women do nothing that would interfere with
      their home duties. Says "freeloveism" is linked with the woman's
      rights movement.

163   PARKMAN, FRANCIS. "The Woman Question." North American 129
      (October):303-21; 130 (January 1880):16-30.
          Asserts that man is made for conflict, whereas woman is
      rounder and softer; reciprocity between the two halves of human
      nature prevails. Believes the differences of nature and function
      are so great that it is doubtful whether men and women can ever
      understand each other. Women can raise themselves and thus men,
      "but they will not do it by frothy declamations on platforms, or
      flooding the bookstalls with sensational stories, any more than
      by those other trivialities which professional reformers
      denounce."

1880

164   AMERICAN CHEMICAL SOCIETY. The Misogynist Dinner of Boston,
      27 August 1880. Photophonic Notes Arranged and Edited by
      Henry Morton, with the Assistance of a Special Correspondent
      of the New York Herald. New York: Russell Brothers, 16 pp.
          Toasts, songs, epigrams, poetry, all mocking women and
      marriage. Typical example:

```
            Though woman is a pest,
            Yet with her twice we're blest--
            Once when we marry her,
            Once when we bury her.
```


1882

165   GLADDEN, WASHINGTON. "The Increase of Divorce." Century 1
      (January):411-20.
            Blames agitation for woman suffrage and women's rights for
      developing female selfhood up to a point where women avoid the
      obligations of wifehood and maternity. The tendency of agitation
      for woman suffrage "has been to promote the theory that marriage
      is nothing but a contract, and to increase the facilities for its
      dissolution." Urges women unhappily wed to a coarse and selfish
      man to have a little patience and good will--"some of the finest
      characters are developed in common life under such conditions."

166   BACON, LEONARD WOOLSEY. "Polygamy in New England." Princeton
      Review, n.s. 10 (July):39-57.
            Deplores the increase in divorce in New England. Likens it
      to Mormon polygamy except that in New England it is consecutive,
      not simultaneous. Says that now that women like Anna Dickinson
      clamor for equal rights, they also want equal rights in divorce
      and remarriage. Gives the example of one prominent New England
      woman who had been married and divorced four times, with assis-
      tance from the Superior Court.

1883

167   DIX, MORGAN, D.D. Lectures on the Calling of a Christian
      Lady, and Her Training to Fulfill It. New York: D. Appleton,
      175 pp.
            A series of Lenten lectures. Finds the women's rights
      movement the most formidable of all movement against the order of
      God's world. Claims that it is "an organized attempt to disturb
      the true relations of men and women, and remove the woman from
      her proper place of work." Accuses supporters of being aligned
      with infidels and free-lovers, and says if they are able to carry
      out their schemes, the end of the world is not far off. Opposes
      coeducation as "mischievous. The sexes ought not to be educated
      together, unless all distinction between them be abolished."
      Says "nature herself forbids co-education and protests against
      it." Predicts that "the entrance of Athene" into our colleges
      will be closely followed by "the advent of Aphrodite."

1886

168   DEVAS, CHARLES S., M.A. Studies of Family Life: A Contri-
      bution to Social Science. New York: Catholic Publication
      Society, 296 pp.

Opposes emancipation of women which would result
assimilation of the two sexes in all things--this is "fo
mischief." The position and occupation of women and men
widely different in every society because of women's "ment
bodily peculiarities." It ought to be different because of
"Christian modesty and the subordination of women in the Chri
tian family." Opposes education of boys and girls in common a
detrimental to morals and says that "by giving both the same
training the girls run the risk of serious physical injury."

169 GIBBONS, Cardinal JAMES. "Relative Condition of Woman under
Pagan and Christian Civilization." American Catholic
Quarterly 11 (October):651-65.
Surveys degraded status of women in pagan times and shows
the elevation of women under Christianity. Reminds women that
equal rights are not synonymous with similar rights. "In the
minds of the Church . . . equal rights do not imply that both
sexes should engage promiscuously in the same pursuits, but
rather that each sex should discharge those duties which are
adapted to its physical constitution and sanctioned by the canons
of society." Opposes dress reform and fears that its spirit
still lives, to be channeled into the movement for woman suffrage. Closes with concern about the rising divorce rate, indirectly caused by women.

170 LINTON, E. LYNN. "The Future Supremacy of Women." Eclectic
Magazine 107 (November):697-706.
Warns that women are losing all their delicacy. Finds that
society is "demoralized" and becomes "hardened and coarsened"
when women act like men. Especially opposes woman suffrage.
"Publicity of life and action never has produced a race of vir-
tuous and estimable women." Reprinted from National Review
(London) 8:1ff.

171 "Women on the New York School Board." Science 8 (26 November):
470.
Editor favors women on school boards but opposes feminists.
Praises the mayor for avoiding appointing "any 'cranks' or any
professional agitators for 'woman's rights.'" Is sure such persons could have been found, but "their appointment would have
turned the whole movement into ridicule." Praises the two female
appointees as "of the highest standing, morally, intellectually,
and socially. They are neither agitators nor theorists, but
women of pure Christian character, great ability, and, what is
quite as essential to a commissioner of education, some common
sense."

172 JERSEY, Countess of. "Our Grandmothers." Living Age 171
(25 December):807-13.
Argues that things have not changed much. Whenever women
are immodest, express dislike of home occupations and the "desir

ete with men in ways unsuited to a woman's physical or
capacity," they are to be blamed, whether is in Queen
s or Queen Victoria's reign. Insists that woman who
lly understands what politics means will want a direct share
governing the state. Reprinted from National Review (London)
:408ff.

1887

173   Conversations on Home Education; or, A Mother's Advice to Her
Children. Translated from the French, by Lady Blanche Murphy.
New York: Benziger Brothers, 180 pp.
    Women and men have separate spheres. The girls gathered
around their mother laugh at the idea of women with "all the
rights of men in the administration of things, social and political." Asks the mother: "can you fancy a woman speaking in the
courts or the senate, hanging around the ballot-box on election
day, or sitting in judgment on a criminal?" Woman's duty is to
influence men, not compete with them.

174   "The Age of Woman." Eclectic Magazine 109 (November):643-46.
    Believes that woman's political emancipation would tend to
strengthen the revolutionary forces of the world. Warns that
"the true ballast of the world must always be kept by the man."
Women, because they are weak, are compassionate with the weak,
but vice dwells in weakness, and "they who are compassionate to
weakness are constantly tempted to be lenient to wrong." Worries
that men are in danger of losing power in this generation. Reprinted from Spectator (London) 60 (13 August):1084-86.

175   CRAIK, DINAH M. "Concerning Men." Eclectic Magazine 109
(December):738-44.
    Most of the article is about women because men and women
are inextricably mixed. Insists that absolute equality between
men and women is impossible. Nature is against it. Wants all
aspects of girls' education--mental, moral, and physical--to be
aimed at wifehood and motherhood, "the highest and happiest
destiny to which any woman can attain." Argues that woman's
powers are limited both physically and mentally. Condensed and
reprinted from Cornhill (London) 9 (October):368-77. See 860.

1888

176   PALMER, A.J. Divorce Abolished. 2d ed. New York: Baker &
Taylor, 85 pp.
    Opposes woman's rights. Believes it "would tend toward the
abolition of feminine gentleness and modesty." Blames the increase in marital unhappiness and divorce on mothers, who do not
educate their children properly.

177   REED, SAMUEL ROCKWELL. Offthoughts about Women and Other
       Things. Chicago: Belford, Clarke, 271 pp.
              Argues that the advanced thinkers of woman's elevation
       really want her to be a man—to enter man's professions and
       business, have man's freedom, wear man's clothing; except that
       woman is also supposed to be deferred to and preferred because
       she is a woman. Thinks, to the contrary, that putting women and
       men in mutual competition would be "mutual degradation." Be-
       lieves that the function of maternity is so absorbing to the mind
       that it appears to make woman incapable of statesmanship. Woman
       can not be both a mother and a voter. Mocks the beginning of the
       woman's movement, dress reform—says Stanton was truly heroic in
       wearing the costume since she looked hideous in it. Argues that
       men and women can never wear the same garments.

                                   1889

178   ALLEN, GRANT. "Woman's Place in Nature." Forum 7 (May):
       258-63.
              Points out that the higher the animal, the more superior
       and important the male. Finally with the highest animal of all,
       man, the relative importance of the male is so great that "almost
       all the practical life of the race is carried on by men alone,
       and most of all in the highest human communities." Finds women
       limited to the "merely reproductive" areas of the home, nursery,
       and schoolroom, whereas "all that is distinctively human is man—
       the field, the ship, the mine, the workshop." Warns that women
       unsex themselves when they follow male vocations.

179   COOKE, ROSE TERRY. "The Real Rights of Women." North
       American 149 (September):347-54.
              Lists woman's rights. Woman has the right to respect,
       especially as a mother; "to care and consideration on the score
       of their physical organization"; to her own religious opinions
       and preferences; to share in decisions about her children's
       education; to choose her own husband and her own physician; to
       have a home; to control and use her own money. Blames the "free-
       dom shriekers" who rant on platforms and usurp pulpits for the
       delay in the restoration of these God-given rights and privi-
       leges, true rights of women.

180   ALLEN, GRANT. "Plain Words on the Woman Question." Eclectic
       Magazine 113 (November):670-77.
              Complains that women's rights women are drawing the atten-
       tion of thinking women away from their real duties: to see that
       their education fits them for motherhood and to ensure that, "in
       consideration of the special burden they have to bear in connec-
       tion with reproduction, all the rest of life should be made as
       light and easy and free as possible." Modern women agitators
       instead hold up the ideal of an unsexed woman. States that "a
       woman ought to be ashamed to say she has no desire to become a

wife and mother." Such sexlessness is a "functional aberration."
He blames higher education for diverting woman from her true
function and making her "a dulled and spiritless epicene automa-
ton." Reprinted from Fortnightly (London) 52 (1 October):448-58.
Reprinted in 182.

181   BOYESEN, HJALMAR HJORTH. "Types of American Women." Forum 8
       (November):337-47.
            Allows that women's rights agitators may do good work but
       warns that they forfeit much of the charm which attracts men to
       them.

182   ALLEN, GRANT. "Plain Words on the Woman Question." Popular
       Science Monthly 36 (December):170-81.
            Reprinted from Fortnightly (London) 52 (1 October):448-58.
       Reprinted in 180.

                                   1890

183   COOPER, SAMUEL WILLIAMS. "The Present Legal Rights of Women."
       American 20 (20 September):448-49; 21 (25 October):27-28.
            Says woman already has many legal rights, has even "out-
       stripped the man, it would seem, and will soon stand with whip in
       hand, ready to pay him back for the alleged hardships and slavery
       of the past. . . . Perhaps the disinclination on the part of men
       to extend to her the right of suffrage is caused by the insatiable
       voracity that she displays." Women are invading all the profes-
       sions and higher education; "yet with all these privileges, 'the
       shrieking sisterhood' still cries for more. When universal suf-
       frage is granted to them by the legislatures, and society admits
       female trousers without jeers, will there still be something for
       the agitators to inflame over?" Blames female independence for
       family discord and increased divorces.

                                   1891

184   HARRISON, FREDERIC. "The Emancipation of Women." Eclectic
       Magazine 117 (December):748-58.
            Opposes woman suffrage because it would pulverize social
       groups, especially families, into individuals. Wants women's
       education improved but freed from the drudgery of specialization.
       Wants to free women from factory work but prevent them from
       public duties and privileges. Women's social function is based
       on biology. Women educate the world not by writing books or
       preaching sermons but by manifesting affection "hour by hour in
       each home by the magic of the voice, look, word, and all the
       incommunicable graces of woman's tenderness." Finally, women can
       either be women or "abortive men." Reprinted from Fortnightly
       (London) 56 (1 October):437-52.

1892

185   WARNER, ANNA BARTLETT. Up and Down the House. New York:
      A.D.F. Randolph & Co., 231 pp.
          Believes that in ball-rooms as well as mass meetings for
      woman's rights, "a woman shews more of her weakness than her
      strength." Woman's place is in the home.

186   The Woman's Place; Her Position in the Christian World. The
      Problem Considered under Four Grand Heads--Woman Outstripped
      by Man, Even in Domestic Handiwork. Richmond, Va. (?), 13 pp.
          Argues that it is clear from an anatomical and physiologi-
      cal inspection that women and men were created for different
      spheres. Women cannot compete with men, even in the domestic
      area; nor can they invent. They are also mentally and morally
      different. Men are mentally superior, women morally. Some of
      the New England women are in revolt, and the disease is spreading
      south, but Christian men will stamp it out. Reprinted from the
      Dispatch, 14 February 1892.

187   LINTON, E. LYNN. "The Partisans of the Wild Women." Eclectic
      Magazine 118 (April):540-46.
          Impugns the virility of male supporters of the women's
      movement. Such partisans are dupes at best, at worst lacking
      intellectual dignity, hysterical, emotional, mentally unsexed.
      It is only the unsexed woman who likes unsexed men: "Domineering
      women choose effeminate men whom they can rule at will." In
      turn, effeminate men need to fall back on "resolute and energetic
      women." Reprinted from Nineteenth Century (London) 31
      (March):455-64.

1893

188   CORBIN, CAROLINE F. A Woman's Philosophy of Love. Boston:
      Lee & Shepard, 302 pp.
          Urges women not to cease to be womanly by trying to vote or
      gain employment because we will see "a total obliteration of the
      lines of sexhood so far as nature will permit, a reduction of the
      entire race to an epicene condition which even the brutes would
      despise." Alleges that the feminists have failed. Says women
      are independent in the ideal home but slaves in industry. In her
      appendix discusses socialism and woman suffrage, opposing and
      linking both. Appendix was separately reprinted (see 506).

189   CREPAZ, ADELE. The Emancipation of Women and Its Probable
      Consequences. Translated from the German. New York:
      C. Scribner's Sons, 130 pp.
          Favors changes in woman's condition but opposes granting
      political rights. Asserts that man's physical and mental consti-
      tution is stronger, that woman is designed for the sphere of

feeling, man for that of reason. "Woman ever remains the guardian and natural educator of coming races, and this task alone excludes her from competing in other spheres with man." Wants woman to consider her natural vocation of motherhood, which "forms a powerful factor against the agitation for perfect equality between the two sexes." Opposes women physicians.

190   PHELPS, WILLIAM W. "Woman's Sphere Not in Politics."
       American Journal of Politics 2 (June):578-82.
       Contrasts womanly women with manly women; the latter seek "cheap notoriety . . . with ostentation and effrontery." Objects to strong-minded women: "The 'higher mental development of woman' is nothing but a highly demented development when it takes the form of ultra views upon such subjects as woman's suffrage and a feverish desire to hold political office, physical culture clubs, dress reform movements, and the like." The home is woman's proper sphere, not politics.

191   WATTERSON, HELEN. "Women's Excitement over 'Woman.'" Forum
       16 (September):75-85.
       Observes that women used to be content to do their work quietly and unostentatiously; now they want the limelight. Believes the typewriter has done more for women than the ballot ever would. Implies that women have gone too far, that they are infatuated with the idea of "woman." All this talk just keeps alive "that intangible something called the 'Woman Question,' of which men are already tired and of which women ought to be." Women need to be emancipated from themselves.

1894

192   "Woman Suffrage." Outlook 49 (14 April):657-58.
       Worries that suffrage will add a burden to already over-worked women and that they will lay aside other duties to take up this new duty. Opposes women working outside the home because it lowers men's wages. Supports the division of labor, which "has its reason in the eternal laws of God."

193   RAMEE, MARIE LOUISE de la [Ouida]. "The New Woman." North
       American 158 (May):610-19.
       Objects to women asking for rights and also insisting on retaining privileges. Alleges that women have plenty of fields for action already in private life but instead want to be admitted to public life. Objects to higher education for women because "the perpetual contact of women with other women is very far from good" and "the publicity of a college must be odious to a young girl of refined and delicate feeling." Objects to putting any power in woman's hands. Opposes coeducation or anything that would "obliterate the contrast of the sexes."

194   BARR, AMELIA E. "Have Women Found New Weapons?" <u>Ladies'</u> <u>Home</u> <u>Journal</u> 11 (June):4.

      Believes "women are as unnecessary to politics as politics are to women." Women have their own work to do. If they desert their homes and children to move into the public arenas of life, their poor children will suffer. Intelligent, manly men find the strong-minded woman objectionable and unwomanly.

195   COPE, EDWARD D. "The Oppression of Women." <u>Open</u> <u>Court</u> 8 (7 June):4103-5.

      Says government and all human acts are expressions of force. Therefore, women will never be able to stand equal to men in this regard. But women now occupy a position at least as good as men's, excluded from the struggle men must undergo. Asserts that what is at the bottom of the woman's movement is ignorance of the facts--"it is on the sex instinct of men that they have ultimately to depend, and not on any preponderance of force."

196   ELIOT, ELTON. "Women and Women." <u>Southern</u> <u>Magazine</u> 5 (September):199-203.

      Invidiously compares southern and northern women, finding the former true women, gentle, pure, womanly, the latter restless, craving the ballot, shrieking for freedom. The northern woman is by nature a reformer and wants to depose man and reign in his stead. "She would perform duties for which nature and education has not fitted her." Alleges that few southern women are interested in the suffrage.

197   "The New Woman under Fire." <u>Review</u> <u>of</u> <u>Reviews</u> 10 (December):656-57.

      Warns the New Woman that she should be aware that "her condition is morbid, or, at least, hysterical." What man "would bind himself to spend his days with the anarchist, the athlete, the blue stocking, the aggressively philanthropic, the political, the surgical woman?" Reprinted from <u>Quarterly</u> <u>Review</u> (London) 179 (October):289-318.

<u>1895</u>

198   DOANE, Rt. Rev. WILLIAM CROSWELL. <u>Extracts</u> <u>from</u> <u>Addresses</u> <u>to</u> <u>the</u> Classes Graduated from <u>St.</u> <u>Agnes'</u> <u>School,</u> <u>Albany,</u> <u>June</u> <u>6th,</u> <u>1894,</u> and <u>June</u> <u>6th,</u> <u>1895</u>. Albany: Albany Anti-Suffrage Association, 6 pp.

      Insists upon separate duties for the two sexes. No wild and unwomanly fanaticism wanted. No mannishness or neglected home or political discord. Reprinted in 556.

199   GOESSMANN, HELENA T. <u>The</u> <u>Christian</u> <u>Woman</u> <u>in</u> <u>Philanthropy</u> <u>(A</u> <u>Study</u> <u>of</u> <u>the</u> <u>Past</u> <u>and</u> <u>Present)</u>. Amherst, Mass.: Carpenter & Morehouse, 62 pp.

:s that the only true life for woman is "that of un-
)or." Condemns as unattractive and un-Catholic the
ghts agitators. Urges the Catholic woman of today to
her womanly manner and modest bearing." Says woman can
do anything but enter professions of politics, law, and arms—can
be a physician to her own sex.

200   MALLON, ISABEL ALLDERDICE [Ruth Ashmore]. Side Talks with
      Girls. New York: C. Scribner's Sons, 252 pp.
         Warns her "girls" that if they follow "the so-called ad-
vanced women of to-day," they will become nervous, irritable,
fretful, feared by society and in their own homes. Objects
emphatically to women speaking in public. Asserts that the best
work a woman can do is to set a good example in her own home.
Does not want her girls to be advanced women. Says that "she who
spends her time seeking votes, making speeches and arranging blue
books will find it impossible to think out the proper way to
perform household duties, to make life pleasant for others, or to
build a nest as it should be built if it is to bear in golden
letters the name of 'Home.'" Also objects to club women.

201   NOTT, CHARLES C. The New Woman and the Late President of
      Williams. N.p., 5 pp.
         Opposes women doing "men's work" for men's pay. Says it
will not benefit children, men, or women. Men and women are
component parts, not distinct classes and rivals. Asserts that
"the chief and lasting evil of this New Woman movement is, that it
is, directly and indirectly, consciously and unconsciously, inim-
ical to marriage, stigmatizing it as the last resort of the
incapable and the unfortunate, robbing it of its dignity and of
its old contentment." It keeps our brightest and ablest young
women from marrying and becoming mothers, thus "hastening the
degeneration of our American race." Reprinted in 556.

202   WILKIN, Rev. GEORGE FRANCIS. The Prophesying of Women.
      Chicago: Fleming H. Revell, 348 pp.
         Insists that all human government and authority rest on
physical force. "The hand that holds the helm of state must be
ever ready to back its mandates with the thunderbolts of war, or
it will fall paralyzed and impotent." Since women lack physical
force, they should not vote. If women rebel, men will cease to
love and respect them. Calls equal rights treason against womanhood. "God has made subjection to be of the essence of womanhood." Thinks if women start speaking in church, all barriers
will fall disastrously. Women's rights lead to violence, murder,
and divorce.

203   MOODY, HELEN WATTERSON. "The Woman Question Once More."
      Century 27 (March):796.
         Denies that there is a woman question. Says women should
stop talking about their advancement and do their work. Sees the

real improvement for women coming from "quiet workers who have no convictions of duty to their sex."

204   SMITH, Mrs. BURTON.   "The Mother as a Power for Woman's Advancement."   Popular Science Monthly 46 (March):622-26.
       Suggests that the mother can offer sympathy yet counsel moderation "to those restless sisters whose demands so often grow out of bitter personal experience and too often rise to a discordant clamor." Sees danger in the extravagances of some of the women's rights enthusiasts and regrets their encouraging antagonism between men and women, which is contrary to God's laws and "death to the best development of mankind." Counsels that "if there is to be a 'new woman,' let us have her by evolution, not revolution."

205   PATRICK, G.T.W.   "The Psychology of Woman."   Popular Science Monthly 47 (June):209-25.
       Describes women as physically and mentally approaching the child type. Says that in dress women have been arrested or retarded at a primitive stage. Woman is representative of the past and future of humanity. Her qualities are concentration, passivity, calmness, and reserve of force. Since the burdens and responsibilities of future generations rest on her shoulders, she should be protected from being roughly jostled in the struggle for existence. She also deserves to be exempted from man's duties. Reprinted in 206.

206   PATRICK, G.T.W.   "The Psychology of Women."   Review of Reviews 12 (July):82-83.
       Reprinted from 205.

                                    1896

207   HANSSON, LAURA MARHOLM.   Six Modern Women, Psychological Sketches.   Translated by Hermione Ramsden.   Boston: Roberts Brothers, 213 pp.
       Sketches of six contemporary representative women, all of whom had achieved some success: Marie Bashkirtseff, Sonia Kovalevsky, George Edgerton, Eleanora Duse, A.C. Edgren-Leffler, Amalie Skram. Her main point is that they all suffered disillusion, were unhappy women—their achievements brought them no happiness. Believes women cannot stand alone; each needs a man: "A woman's life begins and ends in man." He is the only meaning in her life. Has little sympathy with the women's rights movement and indeed shows how feminists died early because their ideas were in conflict with their womanly nature.

208   MITCHELL, S. WEIR, M.D.   Address to the Students of Radcliffe College, Delivered 17 January 1895.   Cambridge, Mass., 23 pp.
       Would allow women freedom to choose so long as it is within "the noble limitations of sex." Objects to women becoming

preachers, lawyers, or platform orators. Warns against knowledge becoming an overwhelming passion in women. "It can destroy happiness, obliterate the moral sense and substitute for love of family the extreme of selfishness and even contempt for the decencies of existence." Urges the students to pay attention to dress. "If you want to see ill-dressed people, the worst are women-doctors, platform-ladies, college professors. . . . I never saw a professional woman who had not lost some charm." Drawing on his medical practice, describes women wrecked in health by ambition and competition with men. Condensed and reprinted in 1049.

209   BARR, AMELIA E. "Discontented Women." North American 162
       (February): 201-9.
       Asserts that there has never been a time in the world's history when women were so discontent with their home duties, which are their first natural duty; with their marriages; and with their husbands. Working women are also discontented and talk a great deal about their grievances. The most foolish complainers are women who object to their political position. Points out that all discontented women are dull, are always egotists, and breed dislike and distrust. Marriage is the cure for discontent.

210   MALLON, Mrs. ISABEL ALLDERDICE [Ruth Ashmore]. "The Conserva-
       tive Woman." Ladies' Home Journal 13 (February):16.
       Believes that the best position a woman can occupy is as a companion to a man. What we want is the conservative woman, not "the loud scream of those sisters of hers who, in their desire to repudiate their womanhood, become sexless." Woman has no right to the vote for physical reasons--she cannot go as a soldier to protect her country.

211   ABBOTT, LYMAN. "Marriage and Divorce." Outlook 53
       (14 March):477-79.
       Upholds the separation of the spheres. Man is the defender and burden-bearer. Regrets "the new era in which women are rushing into every kind of employment and lowering the wages of men by doing men's work." Opposes woman suffrage.

212   WINSTON, ELLA W. "Foibles of the New Woman." Forum 21
       (April):186-92.
       Asserts that woman has asked for much in the past forty years and been given it but is still not satisfied. The New Woman calls herself a slave because she cannot vote, ignoring her great privileges and opportunities. Denies that women can do nothing without the ballot. Let women influence their children and protect their homes. Women have never lacked power but have not always used it well--gives examples from history. Warns that the children of women who neglect them to campaign for temperance may become drunkards. Duty, like charity, begins at home.

213   TALBOT, GEORGE F.   "The Political Rights and Duties of Women."
       Popular Science Monthly 49 (May):80-97.
          Warns that giving women suffrage will affect their char-
       acter and welfare; women have neither time nor facility for
       public duties. Says "a few restless women, mostly those whose
       domestic relations are out of gear or who have failed in a con-
       genial social career," will be the ones who run for office, not
       the best women. Women are a privileged group now, exempted from
       the burdens of war, dangerous work, even earning their liveli-
       hood. It is only "shrill insurgent womanhood," not universal
       womanhood, which demands its rights. Woman suffragists wish to
       enter into competition with men for jobs, thereby aggravating
       industrial strife. Then men will no longer feel obliged to
       support and protect the weaker sex. Leave woman in her high
       estate.

214   BLOUET, PAUL [Max O'Rell].   "Petticoat Government." North
       American 163 (July):101-9.
          Loathes the domination of woman. Wants her to persuade.
       Calls the New Woman "the most ridiculous production of modern
       times and destined to be the most ghastly failure of the cen-
       tury." Pictures the rosy, contended mother in contrast with the
       thin, sulky, haughty joiner of causes, teetotaller, faddist.
       Mocks the cause of temperance. Says women should stay at home.

215   MAC CORRIE, JOHN PAUL.   "'The War of the Sexes.'" Catholic
       World 63 (August):605-18.
          Says the New Woman becomes "unpardonably ridiculous" when
       she demands every right and liberty enjoyed by man. Women's true
       rights are to mould young minds and be a loving wife and mother.

216   OAKLEY, CHARLES SELBY.   "Of Women in Assemblies." Living Age
       211 (28 November):572-77.
          Says that it is impossible for men to have a real discus-
       sion of important matters in any assembly where women are present
       either as voters or fellow debaters. Although physically weaker,
       women have enormous influence over men through fascination.
       Asserts that men's chivalry will prevent them from contradicting
       or attacking women, so issues will not get properly aired. "The
       vital point is that the mere presence of her sex must necessarily
       disturb the freedom of style and the possibility of rudeness
       where necessary, which is indispensable to the real treatment of
       public questions." It would be the end of the men's club. Wants
       to limit the public functions of women to "the collecting of
       evidence, which men must afterwards debate." Reprinted from
       Nineteenth Century (London) 40 (October):559-66.

                              1897

217   BELL, LILLIAN.   From a Girl's Point of View. New York:
       Harper & Brothers, 192 pp.

Likes the term "equal suffrage" rather than "woman's rights," which she thinks has "a masculine, assertive, belligerent sound." Wants women to please men, not try to be their equals. Mocks independent women--"I shrink from the idea of independence and cold, proud isolation with my emancipated sister-women, who struggle into their own coats unassisted and get red in the face putting on their own skates, and hang on to a strap in the street-car." She would much rather have a man on his knees before her than have him consider her an equal. Does not like women shrieking on platforms, wearing bloomers and bending over their handlebars, wanting to hold office and smoke and talk like men. But then we have always had unconventional, rowdy women.

218 PARKHURST, CHARLES H. Talks to Young Women. New York: Century Co., 136 pp.
Says that only a "false civilization" would try to transform women into men. If women want to retain their present supremacy, they must become more womanly, not mannish. Asserts that there is an element in society suffering from "andromania"--"a passionate aping of everything that is mannish." Nature has decreed that woman's sphere is the home. Women who try to resist nature's intentions for them are motivated by a desire for celebrity. If women want a better world, they should do their work in the home better. Opposes woman suffrage.

219 STUTFIELD, HUGH E.M. "The Psychology of Feminism." Living Age 212 (13 March):707-18.
Insists that women's preoccupation with their own psyches is just self-torture, neurotic and decadent, affected, hysterical, unhealthy. Blames "the literature of vituperation and of sex-mania, with its perpetual harping on the miseries of married life, and its public washing of domestic dirty linen" for widening "the breach between men and women" and making them "more mutually distrustful than ever." Reprinted from Blackwood's Edinburgh Magazine 161 (January):104-17.

220 JOHNSON, HELEN KENDRICK. "Woman Suffrage and Education." Popular Science Monthly 51 (June):222-31.
Counters suffragists' claims with arguments that the barriers of sex are not broken down in education, nor should they be. There is sex in mind. "The education that did not, through cultivation, emphasize that fact, would be a lower and not a higher product." Women need education, not suffrage. Womanliness is the desired end. Excerpt from Woman and the Republic (see 700).

221 TYRRELL, GEORGE, S.J. "The Old Faith and the New Woman." American Catholic Quarterly 22 (July):630-45.
Describes the New Woman "in her extreme type" as "an abomination to Catholic instincts." Blames J.S. Mill for many false

principles of the woman's movement. Finds it imbued with principles of rationalism, individualism, and equalitarianism. Insists
that there are distinctions between women and men and that women
must subordinate themselves to and obey men because they are
morally and intellectually inferior to men. Sees in the New
Woman the downfall of the family and the profanation of marriage.
The Christian lady is the ideal.

222   DESART, ELLEN. "Women." Eclectic Magazine 129
      (September):377-82.
         So far the women's movement has made real gains, but we
have reached the outer limit of what women will try to do. The
present-day "Advanced Woman" has lost her way and wants to become
a man. Believes woman should not vote because she cannot fight.
Holds up Queen Victoria as a model--influence, not doctrines and
demands. Women should admit their limitations and glory in their
inability to make direct laws and wars. Reprinted from National
Review (London) 29:711ff.

223   "The Fin-de-Siècle Woman." Living Age 215 (11 December):
      743-48.
         In reviewing books by two feminists, comes round to naming
"the gravest characteristic defect of the Fin-de-Siècle woman
[and] the most damaging flaw in the theories of certain advocates
of Woman's Rights," namely, that they are destroying the founda-
tions of conduct and morality. Deplores the fact that many of
the best and sanest leaders of the movement join the "herd of
hysterical and irrational she-revolutionaries, like the authors
of the 'Woman's Bible'--contemptible these in their own persons,
but formidable and almost appalling if considered as signs of the
times." Reprinted from London Quarterly 89 (October):99-108.

                              1898

224   BARR, AMELIA E. Maids, Wives, and Bachelors. New York:
      Dodd, Mead & Co., 323 pp.
         Grants that working women have some cause to be discontent
but rails against women wanting political privileges: "Of all
the shrill complainers that vex the ears of mortals, there are
none so foolish as the women who have discovered that the found-
ers of our republic left their work half finished, and that the
better half remains for them to do." Sensible women are trying
to put their homes in order while these restless, discontented
women dabble in questions of the utmost gravity. Warns that once
women enter into politics, priests and preachers "would gain
enormously in influence and power." Much of this is reworked and
repeated from her article on discontented women (see 209).

225   BINGHAM, HARRY, LL.D. The New Education of Woman, an Address
      Delivered before the Grafton and Coos Bar Association,

Plymouth, New Hampshire, 29 January 1897. Concord, N.H.:
Rumford Press, 20 pp.
    Says the movement for improved education and employment of
women "is not promoted but rather retarded and exposed to ridicule by reason of the farcical performances of those women who
unsex themselves, put on masculine attire, scream about the
tyrant man, and put themselves forward as candidates for office."
Says they are "mere fireflies" who will pass away and be forgotten. Severely criticizes feminists, calling them "stormy vira-
goes," "a vociferous band of female iconoclasts," and more.
Wants higher education for women to maintain them as women.

226   DONNELLY, ELEANOR CECILIA, ed. Girlhood's Hand-book of Woman:
      A Compendium on Woman's Work, Woman's Sphere, Woman's Influ-
      ence and Responsibilities. St. Louis: B. Herder, 203 pp.
    Donnelly writes in "Wife and Mother" against women who
dress and talk like men and force themselves into manly occupations to the criminal neglect of their normal duties. Warns that
in this "wild, unnatural struggle," women will lose men's devotion and worshipful reverence. "All that is gentle, attractive,
womanly withers under the hot sun of publicity and notoriety."
Katherine E. Conway in "The Normal Christian Woman" insists that
woman has no vocation to public life and says Catholic women
oppose suffrage and women's organizations because "the Catholic
woman is the normal woman." Last essay in book favors woman
suffrage.

227   MOODY, HELEN WATTERSON. The Unquiet Sex. New York:
      C. Scribner's Sons, 159 pp.
    Largely a reworking of magazine articles. See 191, 228,
901, 903, 1042.

228   MOODY, HELEN WATTERSON. "The Unquiet Sex: Women and
      Reforms." Scribner's Magazine 23 (January):116-20.
    Finds women by temperament "more inclined to extremes in
all things than men are." Agrees that reforms may be necessary
but says it is crucial that the reformer remain sane and
pleasing--"particularly pleasing." Warns that reformers run the
risk of becoming "egoistic, downright, declaratory, and dead-in-
earnest," while most of us prefer our women mild and serene.
Counsels that reform will come when the time is ready; cites
dress reform, shocking forty years ago but now accepted, to prove
her point.

229   BISLAND, ELIZABETH. "The Abdication of Man." North American
      167 (August):191-99.
    Before the stern realities of war, the woman question is
deferred. "War legitimates man's claim to superiority." Women
are revolting because men have ceased to be heroic, to dress
well, to behave dramatically. It is man who is "forcing a democracy of sex upon woman." Blames man for abdicating his responsibilities, causing woman to move out into industry, forcing

equality upon her, depriving her of her protection. Yearns for
the day when man was hero and master, woman dependent.

1899

230   DOUMIC, RENÉ. "Feminism During the Renaissance." Living Age
      220 (21 January):139-47.
         Holds up Renaissance feminists as a warning for modern
      feminists. Says the principle on which they rested their claims
      was fundamentally false. "The women of that era wrought only for
      themselves, and their end and aim was the gratification of their
      own vanity." Present-day feminists are trying to be independent
      and are causing social life to decline. Calls women back to
      being the guardians of honor and purity, of religion and moral-
      ity. Reprinted from Revue des deux mondes.

231   GOSSE, EDMUND. "The Reverses of Britomart." North American
      168 (June):720-29.
         Explains the reduced clamor for woman's rights as resulting
      from fighting the world over. Peace encourages the individual;
      war causes the family unit to gather closely together. Confesses
      that "the exaggerated thesis of feminism exasperates me beyond
      words." Asserts that he is too gallant to oppose extreme femi-
      nism, but then refers to the arguments of Mrs. Lynn Linton, Miss
      Arabella Kenealy, and Mme Anna Lemperiere as evidence that women
      also oppose feminism.

232   PECK, HARRY THURSTON. "The Woman of To-day and of To-morrow."
      Cosmopolitan 27 (June):148-62.
         Is woman's discontent justified? Actually men have been
      courteous and considerate of women in public as well as private,
      resulting in intolerable selfishness, lack of consideration, and
      thanklessness on woman's part; "it has encouraged her to rant and
      brawl and make herself offensive in pretty nearly every way that
      ingenuity can discover." Some "meek and spineless men" even join
      women on the public platform. Strongly opposes Gilman's call for
      economic independence for women, which is causing women to shun
      marriage and regard maternity with loathing. Soon "the terrible
      significance of these strange theories will come home with force
      to all men" and with brutal male roughness they will force women
      to become serene and charming again.

233   VIVARIA, KASSANDRA. "On the International Congress of Women."
      North American 169 (August):154-64.
         Expresses disappointment in the Congress. Describes her-
      self as slowly realizing, as she listened to the sessions, that
      "there was something young and amateurish and beside the mark in
      many of the papers read." Opposes bringing to the front so many
      women of mediocre talent and isolating the work of women from
      that of men. Calls feminism "a modern form of morbid vanity."
      Opposes pay for housework. The nature of woman's perfectibility

is to absorb good on all sides and radiate it toward others, not
to clamor for more rights for which she is unprepared, especially
when many of her duties need to be better performed.

234   LOW, FRANCES H.   "A Woman's Criticism of the Women's Congress
      (London 1899)." Eclectic Magazine 133 (November):641-49.
          Says the majority of the discussions were of the futile
      sort, "characterized by wild notions"--no central or fundamental
      principles. Women's Congresses are "a lamentable waste of energy
      and a painful exhibition of ignorance and folly." Finds in them
      the tendency to foster enmity between the two sexes which have
      their own characteristics and duties and yet are interdependent
      upon one another. Believes that "any attempt to achieve the
      welfare of one without regard to the race at large is mischie-
      vous." Reprinted from Nineteenth Century (London) 46
      (August):192-202. Reprinted in Living Age 222 (23 September):
      793-801.

                                  1900

235   ALLEN, GRANT. Plain Words on the Woman Question. Chicago:
      M. Harman, 44 pp.
          Alleges that he sympathizes with woman's desire for emanci-
      pation, but her emancipation must not interfere with her produc-
      ing four children to continue the population at its present
      level. Argues that women's rights women are "drawing the atten-
      tion of thinking women from the true problem of their sex to fix
      it on side issues of comparative unimportance." Women ought to
      glory in their femininity, not seek to be unsexed. Calls women's
      education a mistake; they should be educated "to suckle strong
      and intelligent children and to order well a wholesome, beauti-
      ful, reasonable household." Worries that the sexuality of both
      English and American women is becoming enfeebled and destroyed.

236   CORBIN, CAROLINE F. The Woman Movement in America. Chicago:
      Illinois Association Opposed to the Extension of Suffrage to
      Women, 8 pp.
          Gives the history of antifeminism in America, focusing
      mainly on antisuffrage. Argues that only a very small minority
      of women desires the suffrage and that woman suffrage has accom-
      plished little in western states. Opposes coeducation because it
      "feminizes" the university. Vehemently opposes women's political
      rights: "It is only for purposes of selfish ambition, political
      intrigue, and noisy notoriety, that the ballot avails anything to
      woman." Reprinted as Woman's Rights in America (see 267).

237   THOMPSON, FLORA MC DONALD. "One Woman's Point of View."
      Harper's Bazar 33 (10 February):110.
          One page of short essays, many antifeminist. Thinks it a
      disgrace that a school in Philadelphia is teaching boys to cook:

"To put an apron on a boy and set him to cooking is to make him
ashamed of himself, and so to corrupt his best capital in life--
his self-esteem." Opposes equal wages for equal work, saying
that women are paid less than men because men support them. Any
law that provides equal pay should also give control of woman's
labor to the man who supports her. Finally, opposes woman suffrage: "clearly extension of woman's rights is not in the interests of society." Blames men for letting their higher faculties
atrophy and causing women to extend their prerogatives to fill
the vacuum men left.

238   IRELAND, WILLIAM W. "Degeneration: A Study in Anthropology."
       International Monthly 1 (March):235-79.
           Alleges that "we are going through a critical time, and
       some dangers look ominous for the future of the race." Finds the
       most far-reaching danger to be that women are withdrawing from
       their natural duties, refusing to bear or nurse children, ne-
       glecting their children. Calls women's rights and independence
       just "a shadowy myth."

239   THOMPSON, FLORA MC DONALD. "Retrogression of the American
       Woman." North American 171 (November):748-53.
           Describes the American woman of today as "the fatal symptom
       of a mortally sick nation." Compares unfavorably the American
       woman as described by de Tocqueville with the present-day degen-
       erate. "The aggressive spirit of the 'new' woman" has overthrown
       the economically ideal organization of the American family, so
       that now women advance into men's industries and men into domes-
       tic labor and personal service. Says that when the American
       woman competes with the man, it is not only to his disadvantage
       but also to his degradation.

240   AN AMERICAN MOTHER. "Why Are We Women Not Happy?" Ladies'
       Home Journal 18 (December):22.
           Warns against taking the noisy minority who are constantly
       in the public eye and ear as typical American women and over-
       looking "the silent millions in the background who are as busy,
       and helpful, and noiseless as God's angels." This silent influ-
       ence keeps America moral and sane. Asserts that it is this
       silent multitude opposing the ballot that has saved women from
       suffrage for so many years. Charges some American women with
       being restless, nervous, and unhappy because of misplaced values;
       they worry about appearance, money, and social standing.

                            1901

241   BLOUET, PAUL [Max O'Rell]. Her Royal Highness Woman and His
       Majesty--Cupid. New York: Abbey Press, 311 pp.
           Mocks "petticoat government." Says New Women are the "ugly
       women, old maids, and disappointed and neglected wives." Calls
       her "the most ridiculous production of modern times . . . a woman

with a grievance . . . the greatest nuisance of modern society."
Describes her as thin, sallow, wrinkled, sulky, haughty, dis-
gusted with life. WCTUers are no better: "fussy, interfering,
faddists, fanatics, of all sorts, old women of both sexes,
shrieking cockatoos, that will by-the-by make life intolerable to
any man of self-respect." Has an extremely long list of women he
hates, including those who make after-dinner speeches, scientific
women, lady physicians, lawyers, school board members, preachers,
presidents, secretaries, and more.

242   CORBIN, CAROLINE F. The Position of Women in the Socialist
       Utopia. Chicago, 16 pp.
       Alleges that Stanton and the other feminists got their
ideas from socialists and communists. Upholds the traditional
woman, roles, etc.

243   GORDON, NANCY MC KAY. Woman Revealed: A Message to One Who
       Understands. 2d ed. Chicago, 152 pp.
       Thinks it an error when women "have tried to enter man's
sphere or attempted to regulate man's work." Woman already has
privileges. Warns her against putting herself "in greater bond-
age, by flinging away those divine and inner qualities, to assume
command of something intangible and unreal."

244   FINCK, HENRY T. "Are Womanly Women Doomed?" Independent 53
       (31 January):267-71.
       Blames coeducation for woman's loss of womanly qualities
but says woman suffrage poses the worst threat--"some extremists
even wear trousers, and others want to go to war, not as nurses,
but as soldiers." But says that this "invasion of man's domain
by women" is merely "a temporary anomaly against which a strong
reaction has already set in." Says that it is mostly mannish
women who want the vote. Worries that if women get the vote,
they will outvote men and put only women in office.

245   HART, LAVINIA. "The Ideal Wife and Helpmeet." Cosmopolitan
       30 (April):638-42.
       The ideal wife and helpmeet is a complement to her hus-
band's nature. These ideal women are the ones who, "slowly and
steadily, are accomplishing what the high-voiced advocates of
'Woman's Rights' never will: the social equality of the sexes."

246   "Why Men Don't Like Her." Independent 53 (11 April):852-54.
       Editorializes on the New Woman. Says men do not like her
because she takes herself seriously, her learning has made her
"just a little bit 'fresh,'" and she runs on too much about
woman's rights. Implies that she is unlikeable.

247   SLOSSON, EDWIN E. "Man and the Woman's Club." Current
       Literature 30 (May):600-601.

Jocular: piqued that he, a professor at the University of Wyoming, could not join a woman's club. "Was it possible that emancipated woman is bent on the same policy of exclusion which has for so many centuries been the reproach of dominant man?" Reprinted from Independent 53 (14 February):387-89.

248   MÜNSTERBERG, HUGO. "The American Woman." International
      Monthly 3 (June):607-33.
         Worries that the home and family are being undermined. Charges higher education with making marriage less attractive to women and coeducation with making the two sexes indifferent or disillusioned about each other. Finds educated American girls under great mental strain and excitement, nervous, pathologically tense, all of which damages them as mothers. Worries that the American woman's movement is feminizing the whole higher culture as well as universities, and pushing men out. Asserts that "American intellectual work is being kept down by women." Women will eventually take over medicine, law, and religion, because they work for less; but equality is unnatural.

249   WILCOX, ELLA WHEELER. "The Restlessness of the Modern Woman."
      Cosmopolitan 31 (July):314-17.
         Declares that women are restless because they do not have enough to do. Believes that "this restlessness of woman is a giant evil, and one of serious growth." American women do not know when they are well off. At the bottom of this feminine restlessness is "a lack of good, every-day common sense."

1902

250   LATHERS, RICHARD. This Discursive Biographical Sketch of
      Colonel Richard Lathers Was Compiled as Required for Honorary
      Membership in Post 509, Grand Army of the Republic.
      Philadelphia: J.B. Lippincott, 207 pp.
         Includes an address delivered at New Rochelle--"Woman and Her Relations to Society." Says when woman yields to masculine impulses, it invariably produces evil. "Nature seems to revolt at any attempt to overcap or set aside the law of sex, or to tolerate competition between them." Alleges that when women attempt to be men, "forgetting the native modesty of their sex, they simply induce a species of disgust in those who value their sex."

251   GIBBONS, Cardinal JAMES. "The Restless Woman." Ladies' Home
      Journal 19 (January):6.
         Regrets that women have laid aside modesty and gentleness and taken up "masculinity and aggressiveness" in their stead. Asserts that women who participate in the public life ultimately neglect or even abandon their homes. Regards women's rightists as "the worst enemies of the female sex," robbing women "of all

that is amiable and gentle, tender and attractive" and giving in
return "masculine boldness and brazen effrontery." Warns that
anyone who enters the political sphere "is sure to be soiled by
its mud." Says the model woman is Mary, the Christian wife and
mother, not "she who takes up all the 'ologies' and scientific
studies" or the public woman or the bold worker in men's spheres.

252   SUTHERLAND, Lady MILLICENT. "Woman and Her Sphere." North
      American 174 (May):632-39.
          Provides an unflattering description of feminists scram-
      bling up the ladder of political and intellectual success,
      dressed in "shapeless shirt-waists, indifferent to clearness of
      complexion and pearly teeth." Wants to see progress for women
      but doubts it will come from "the shrieking band of ignoramuses,
      exorbitant in demands and unfit in capacity."

                                1903

253   MALLARD, ROBERT Q., D.D. Martha's Fault and Mary's Choice.
      Richmond, Va.: Whittet & Shepperson, 43 pp.
          Opposes the sort of women's rights that would have us "sent
      to school to infidels and to unsexed women, who have endeavored
      to throw off the trammels of marriage, and even decency, to learn
      them." Likens the modern woman's rights woman to Jezebel.
      "Martha's fault" is becoming too preoccupied with household
      duties. Mary chose to sit at Jesus' feet.

254   "Woman's Privileges." Harper's Weekly 47 (3 January):21.
          Reports that Miss Josephine Dodge Durham told members of
      the New York Legislative League that she would advise a young
      girl who asked her advice "to hang on to her privileges and let
      her rights go."

255   WATSON, H.B. MARRIOTT. "The Deleterious Effect of American-
      ization upon Woman." Living Age 239 (5 December):609-18.
          Asserts that American women are living their lives not
      wholly in harmony with nature, refusing to bear children, working
      only to bedeck themselves. Reprinted from Nineteenth Century
      (London) 54 (November):782-92.

                                1904

256   ABBOTT, LYMAN. "The Advance of Women." World's Work 8
      (July):5033-42.
          Applauds the improvement in woman's education, the enlarge-
      ment of employment opportunities, but insists that "there are
      distinctive feminine and masculine spheres of activity, and that
      each sex renders the best service to society within its appro-
      priate sphere." Since most women do not wish to vote, it should

                                 62

not be imposed upon them. The education of women should be
different than men's and be a preparation for motherhood. Urges
the public not to listen to a few hysterical or aggressive women.

1905

257 HAGAR, FRANK N. The American Family, a Sociological Problem.
     New York: University Publishing Society, 196 pp.
     Insists that women cannot and should not share the burdens
of men in government. The idea of sex equality weakens the
family. Says it has blasted "the rising bloom of romantic love,"
fostered "strife, conflict and sex warfare" rather than "amity
and love." It has made women ambitious and hostile to "a con-
tented and successful wifehood" and has destroyed men's chivalry,
benevolence, and kindness toward women. It has pushed women into
industrial employments. Argues that sex equality will cause
degeneracy.

258 KEENE, FLORENCE ROSINA. "The Nobler Part." Overland, n.s. 46
     (July):26-28.
     Regrets the "insane ranting" about woman's sphere in the
last decade. Woman is like a child crying for the moon. She
should realize that hers has always been the nobler part. A woman
today can do anything she wants to. If men are bad to women, it
is the fault of women. Opposes women "shrieking on the platform."

259 THE COUNTRY CONTRIBUTOR. "The Ideas of a Plain Country
     Woman." Ladies' Home Journal 22 (November):26, 63.
     Calls the woman's movement "a delusion." Asserts that
"most of the aspirations that women are struggling with are fool
notions promulgated by somebody who hasn't anything better to
do." Says she is "dreadfully tired" of the suffragists. Woman
already has too many rights and duties; suffrage "would be the
last straw."

1906

260 HYDE, WILLIAM DE WITT. The College Man and the College Woman.
     Boston: Houghton Mifflin, 333 pp.
     Devotes two chapters to college women. This president of
Bowdoin College champions the womanly ideal over women's rights
and equality. Would prefer to emphasize the differences between
man and woman. Woman is happiest not in competing with man but in
consuming goods. Women should not engage in masculine occupations and avoid squandering their vitality "to gain some paltry
academic honor or ephemeral social success." Alleges that nature
exacts terrible penalties: "muscular flabbiness, nervous exhaus-
tion, sharp-featured irritability, flat-chested sterility." Opposes woman's activity in politics and believes that "all sane men
and wise women" will agree.

261   HALL, G. STANLEY. "The Feminist in Science." Independent 60
       (22 March):661-62.
            Disagrees with Lester Ward that equality is the goal of
       civilization: "with civilization the dimensions of the woman's
       body, her life and her psychic traits become more different from
       those of men rather than less so."

262   BOK, EDWARD. "Behold, the Emancipated Woman!" Ladies' Home
       Journal 23 (April):20.
            Responding to a recent suffrage speech, mocks "emancipa-
       tion": "isn't it a big, fine, soul-inspiring picture: the
       picture of a ballot that will 'emancipate' women from tyranny:
       from being 'suppressed': from 'cowering': from being 'puppets':
       from being mothers rather than women: from motherhood itself:
       from babies: from everything--everything except 'emancipation'!"

263   THE COUNTRY CONTRIBUTOR. "The Ideas of a Plain Country
       Woman." Ladies' Home Journal 23 (April):30.
            Insists that the franchise would "complicate the 'woman
       question'" just as the Civil War did the "negro problem." Argues
       that "woman is not built to be man's rival in the business or
       professional world. Deplores wrong thinking about and hesitation
       over marriage. Says this too is caused by the "woman question."

264   "An Ontological Indictment of the Human Female." Current
       Literature 40 (April):433-35.
            A summary of Weininger's Sex and Character, recently pub-
       lished in the United States. Weininger believes that "it is only
       the male element in emancipated women that craves for emancipa-
       tion." He asserts that "there is not one woman in the whole
       history of thought, not even the most manlike, who can be com-
       pared with men of fifth- or sixth-rate genius."

265   HARRIS, Mrs. L.H. "The Monstrous Altruism." Independent 61
       (4 October):792-98.
            Argues against Gilman's call for breaking down the nuclear
       family. Asserts that "no self-respecting man ought to want a
       'citizen' for his mother, and no wise woman will wish to follow
       her sons to the polls and henpeck them while they are looking
       after that part of the world's business, which is as essentially
       man's as rolling logs and building dams." The great women of our
       time and all times are not those who demand citizenship but
       mothers.

                                  1907

266   CORELLI, MARIE. "Man's War against Woman." Harper's Bazar 41
       (May):425-28; (June):550-53.
            Describes herself as listening "somewhat amusedly" to the
       screaming, screeching, and yelling for votes for women. Finds
       "the very desire for a vote on the part of woman is an open

                                    64

confession of weakness--a proof that she has lost ground and is
not sure of herself." A real woman tries to persuade, enthral,
and subjugate man, not come down from her pedestal and mingle in
his political frays. If man treats woman badly, it is her fault.
Warns her "suffragette sisters" that men will no longer admire
them if they try to be and look like men. "A masculine woman is
nothing more than a libellous caricature of an effeminate man."
Really clever women know how to hold men in subservience; only
stupid women are clamoring for their rights.

1908

267   CORBIN, CAROLINE F. Woman's Rights in America, A Retrospect
      of Sixty Years. New York: New York Association Opposed to
      Woman Suffrage, 8 pp. Date is estimated.
      Reprint of The Woman Movement in America (see 236).

1909

268   BROWN, CHARLES REYNOLD. The Modern Young Woman. Sermon
      Preached at the First Congregational Church, Oakland,
      California, to the Students of Mills College, 21 March 1909.
      Oakland, 16 pp.
      Feels no sympathy with reformers who would wipe out dis-
      tinctions between the sexes. "They would have women so strong-
      minded, so completely self-sufficient for the rough give and take
      of the outer world, so intent upon the rights and privileges
      sometimes reserved for men, that except for her clothes--and then
      not always--a stranger would hardly know whether he was talking
      to a woman or a man." Believes that sex runs all the way through
      a person. Abjures Mills College women not to sacrifice their
      womanliness for a career. Neither Mills nor any of the better
      institutions for the higher education of women wants to obscure
      the feminine by "certain mannish accomplishments."

269   LOMBARD, LOUIS. Observations of a Bachelor. Boston:
      D. Estes, 181 pp.
      Women are mentally inferior to men. Those women, "angular
      and mannish," who urge other women not to marry are really using
      the sour-grapes argument. Hates "the mannish girl," whom he
      describes as "narrow-hipped, straight-jacketed, short-haired, and
      flat-chested, . . . who, with both hands in coat pocket, walks
      with pugilist-like tread." Alleges that her heart is "shrunk
      like a dried nut." This "hybrid" challenges Nature, is ashamed
      of her sex. "We should perhaps pity rather than condemn her. . . .
      To ridicule her may be as unjust as to laugh at an epileptic.
      She cannot help having been born a weak, pitiable tomboy. She is
      an accident." The higher education of women unfits them for
      marriage, makes them unattractive and sterile.

65

270   PARKHURST, Rev. CHARLES H. Woman: An Address Given in
       Mendelssohn Hall, 17 December 1909. New York: Irving Press,
       14 pp. Date is estimated.
           Address was given under the auspices of the National League
       for the Civic Education of Women. Says that woman suffrage is
       only part of a larger whole, and in making it so conspicuous,
       women have shown "the logical infirmity of mind which constitutes
       one of the weaknesses, and I might say, one of the charms of the
       feminine constitution." Alleges that the woman's movement is an
       "eruption" and casts slurs on those involved as being women who
       change husbands. Mocks "hysterical extravagances of speech."
       Believes that the "animus of feminine antagonism to the male sex
       is latent in the movement." Biological law insists that the
       higher the species, the wider the gap between male and female.

271   ABBOTT, LYMAN. "The Assault on Womanhood." Outlook 91
       (3 April):784-88.
           Says he believes in woman's rights but finds that "the
       movement for the emancipation of woman has been accompanied by
       extravagances which constitute nothing less than an assault on
       womanhood." Among these are the abolition of marriage, easy
       divorce, trial marriage, the crowding out of men in the labor
       market, and the rearing of children by experts, not parents.
       Opposes woman suffrage, as do most women: women have a more
       important function to perform.

272   BISSELL, EMILY PERKINS [Priscilla Leonard]. "The Ideal of
       Equality for Men and Women." Harper's Bazar 43 (May):525-26.
           Denies equality between women and men. Cites biology to
       prove that the higher the organism, the greater the differences
       between the sexes. Woman's sphere "has all biology and all
       civilization behind it." Believes government to be man's work
       and the vote his symbol of service. Women have better functions
       in the community than politics. They should not duplicate man's
       work. Brings up the specter of congested cities, the black belt
       in the South, and socialism to refute woman suffrage.

273   RAMEE, MARIE LOUISE De La [Ouida]. "Love versus Avarice; A
       Frank Analysis of the Causes Which Make for Social Evil."
       Lippincott's 83 (June):712-17.
           Characterizes woman's rights crusaders as "hard, exag-
       gerated, vanity-inflated." Says feminists and adventuresses are
       alike in rebelling "against the imprisonment of a domestic and
       monotonous career." Asserts that "the same desires in womanhood
       which abhor privacy and domesticity lead on the one hand to the
       suffragist, and on the other to Faustina and all her infamous
       sisterhood." The cure is to ennoble women and turn them away
       from a lust for riches (see note at 609).

274   ATHERTON, GERTRUDE. "The Present Unrest among Women."
       Delineator 74 (August):118, 156.

Reminds us that women must be passive in regard to romantic attachments, waiting for men to take the lead: "romantic love still interferes with independence." Detess suffragettes—— "personally I hate the sight and sound of a suffragette," calling them ridiculous extremists.

275   "The Present Net Results of Woman's 'Emancipation.'" Review
       of Reviews 40 (December):731-32.
            A survey of articles from France and Great Britain that
       condemn feminism and find it in a state of decline. Several
       Frenchmen criticize feminists as anti-Christian; feminists are
       against marriage and a separation of the sexes——and this leads to
       libertinage.

276   BABCOCK, EDWINA STANTON. "Melancholia and the Silent Woman."
       Outlook 93 (18 December):868-74.
            Likens the exponent of the women's movement to Durer's
       "Melancholia" in her "greed for power, intensity of aggression,
       and display of the symbols of knowledge." In contrast is the
       Silent Woman who sits by the fireside, supports her husband,
       tends her children. States, with emphasis, that "if the influ-
       ence of the home is failing, it is because energies that should
       have been conserved to its development and support have been
       dissipated elsewhere." Asserts that the women's movement is
       making women discontent and individualistic; it is doing away
       with the home and damaging women's natural instincts. It is also
       hurting men by lowering their wages, deflating their ambitions,
       disillusioning them, and causing them to forsake their
       responsibilities.

1910

277   CORBIN, CAROLINE F. Equality. Bulletin no. 4. Chicago:
       Illinois Association Opposed to Woman Suffrage, 4 pp.
            Insists that nature and God dictate inequality of the
       sexes. "The inequalities which spring from sex are the dynamic
       force of evolution."

278   CORBIN, CAROLINE F. Socialism and Sex. Bulletin no. 6.
       Chicago: Illinois Association Opposed to Woman Suffrage,
       4 pp.
            Says socialism "seeks to elevate the maternal half of the
       race by obliterating all its normal conditions and aspirations."
       It robs the mother of the child and demands of her equal work.
       But political rights are impossible because men and women are
       different.

279   MAC PHAIL, ANDREW. Essays in Fallacy. New York: Longmans,
       Green & Co., 359 pp.

Argues that men and women are complementary to each other. "In so far as the woman acquires the qualities and characteristics of the man she becomes to that extent futile." Women are becoming lawless, which leads to the increase in the divorce rate.

280   BOK, EDWARD. "My Quarrel with Women's Clubs." Ladies' Home Journal 27 (January):5-6.
      Believes it is all right for woman to join one, and only one, club so long as it does not interfere with her home duties. But most clubs are very shallow and superficial in their studies and have accomplished little in their civic-betterment projects. Does not want woman out of the home at all.

281   HARRISON, ETHEL B. "Then and Now." Living Age 264 (15 January):137-42.
      Surveys gains for women in education and in employment up to 1905. Congratulates feminists up to that point but deplores the militants and believes they have set back the cause. Takes up the militants' grievances: "we consider it grossly unjust to suggest that men have sought of deliberate purpose to exploit women." Says the law is indulgent, not unfair and unjust, to women. Says that the vote is not a right but a public trust. Denies that votes for women would overthrow immorality and intemperance; foresees easy divorce, too much discussion of sexual questions, etc. Alleges that "women desire all the privileges without the duties and responsibilities of men." Women are actually retrogressing. Reprinted from Nineteenth Century (London) 66 (December 1909):1051-57.

282   BOK, EDWARD. "Dutchman's Breeches or Ladies' Slippers." Ladies' Home Journal 27 (March):6.
      Declares that women will have to make the choice in the title, to be men or ladies. "Hide it as the shrieking suffragists may--that is the question."

283   "An Italian View of Woman in Modern Society." Review of Reviews 41 (March):370.
      Summary of and quotations from an article by Signor Mazzei in the Italian Rassegna Nazionale, where the author deplores attempts to make the mission of women and men equal. Children suffer in the woman's quest for equal rights. Women should work in female employments if they must; better to do good in society.

1911

284   The Book of Woman's Power, with an Introduction by Ida M. Tarbell. New York: Macmillan, 285 pp.
      A collection of 115 essays, not all of them by anti-feminists, showing that women have had power in the past and

arguing that woman suffrage is not the best route to power in the present. Tarbell argues in her introduction that women are different from men and should not do the same work. Others argue that the ballot will solve no problems for women but will rather create them.

285   BURGESS, GELETT. The Maxims of Noah, Delivered from His
      Experience with Women Both Before and After the Flood as Given
      in Counsel to His Son Japhet. New York: Frederick A. Stokes
      Co., 119 pp.
          General nasty, but humorous misogyny, with swipes at suf-
      fragettes and women in public. Noah warns his son to avoid
      suffragettes and any woman who prefers her rights to her priv-
      ileges. Pseudobiblical sayings: "It is ever the homely woman
      who maketh a show of herself in public."

286   HECKER, EUGENE A. A Short History of Women's Rights. New
      York: G.P. Putnam's Sons, 292 pp.
          Prowoman, but has very useful analysis of and quotations
      from antiwoman sources. See especially pp. 150-56, 236-87.
      Breaks down opposition to woman suffrage as based on five
      grounds—theological, physiological, social or political,
      intellectual, and moral—and shows weaknesses of each.

287   Men for the State; Women for the Home. Bulletin no. 8.
      Chicago: Illinois Association Opposed to Woman Suffrage,
      4 pp.
          The old order established the duality of the race. Social-
      ism would do away with this, making the individual the unit of
      society, leaving marriage and the home out of account. Thus
      "woman is to be free and irresponsible in her sexual choice as
      the men of Socialism are, and the voice of passion is to override
      the voice both natural and divine which makes in sexual, as in
      all other relations of life, self-sacrifice, self-discipline and
      spiritual aspirations the price of all true and lasting success."
      Woman suffrage is opposed to natural law. If woman becomes a
      worker and voter, man degenerates and loses his manliness, cour-
      age, and ambition.

1912

288   Modern Thought. Bulletin no. 15. Chicago: Illinois
      Association Opposed to Woman Suffrage, 4 pp.
          Links woman suffrage, progressivism, socialism, and the
      propaganda of the Industrial Workers of the World. All encourage
      divorce, labor of women outside the home, luring young women into
      restaurants, cafés, hotels, places that encourage them to adopt
      "masculine habits, even in such personal matters as smoking,
      drinking and the like."

289   ROOSEVELT, THEODORE. "Women's Rights; and the Duties of Both
       Men and Women." Outlook 100 (3 February):262-66.
          Believes in woman's rights but says that normally men and
       women should perform completely dissimilar functions. "I believe
       in woman suffrage wherever the women want it." But does not like
       the actions of the woman suffrage leaders, "who seem desirous of
       associating it with disorderly conduct in public and with thor-
       oughly degrading and vicious assaults upon the morality and the
       duty of women within and without marriage."

290   S., M.E. "Feminine versus Feminist." Living Age 272
       (9 March):587-92.
          Says that the antisuffragists wish "to cultivate and pre-
       serve woman's independent identity and personality" whereas the
       suffragists would "extinguish and subjugate the same by merging
       it in the man's." Finds the position of the suffragists humili-
       ating to women, an "execration of the world-old idea of woman's
       sphere." The sex has been lowered by feminists, taught to des-
       pise housekeeping and revolt against child care. Warns that
       "this hideous feminism is sapping our vitality as a nation . . .
       it is at the root of half the unhealth and disease of which to-
       day's unrest is symptomatic." Reprinted from National Review
       (London) 58 (February):938-45.

291   ALMA TADEMA, Miss LAURENCE. "The Suffrage Danger." Living
       Age 274 (10 August):330-35.
          Warns that it is not just suffrage that women want. "Be-
       hind the present passionate unrest stands the ideal of unsexed
       womanhood, pining to show her strength, no longer satisfied to
       feel it, asking to seem rather than to be, burning to exchange
       veiled powers, of which somehow she has lost the secret, for
       common, obvious, tangible rights." Women are now competing with
       men and the home is breaking up. Calls the feminist movement
       "actually an outrage upon womanhood." But women will come back
       to true womanhood if enough women exert their influence. Re-
       printed from National Review (London) 59 (July):876-83.

                                    1913

292   HEAPE, WALTER, M.A., F.R.S. Sex Antagonism. New York: G.P.
       Putnam's Sons, 217 pp.
          Says unrest among women is leading to sex war. Denies that
       sexual equality is possible because nature has made the two sexes
       different, in both mind and body. Asserts that the accurate
       adjustment of society requires that the male and female be under-
       stood as complementary. Invokes pseudoscience to allege that the
       bulk of those women who take part in the women's movement are
       spinsters who are sexually unsatisfied and mentally deranged
       because of degeneration of the generative organs.

293   MARTIN, EDWARD S. The Unrest of Women. New York:
       D. Appleton & Co., 146 pp.
       Much of this material appeared earlier in periodicals.
Argues that woman's great vocation is motherhood, not out-of-the-
home work, which is just temporary, an avocation. But today
women are restless, particularly for the vote, and they force
disturbance on other women who are happy in the home. Most women
prefer that men govern. Says the vision of the feminists that
husbands and wives can both work and rear children "is nine-
tenths delusion." Accuses suffragist writers of not appreciating
what a competent mother does for her family. Many of them give
evidence in their personal lives of failure as women, yet "women
who seem to have made a mess of all life's relations are not
abashed to offer themselves as pilots to their sex."

294   TAYLER, J. LIONEL. The Nature of Woman. New York: E.P.
       Dutton, 186 pp.
       Opposes women participating in business life because they
acquire "an irritable, bickering spirit" which they then carry
into the home, ruining married life and diverting women from the
care of their children. Quotes Laura Marholm Hansson (see 206)
at length and with general agreement. Opposes coeducation
("quite unbiological") and economic independence for women,
arguing that they "dewomanize the woman and destroy her real
inborn individuality of body and mind." Argues that increased
physical activity by women probably has retarded womanly development, increased nerviness in women, and made childbirth more
difficult. Wants woman's education, professions, and expecta-
tions to be womanly.

295   FITE, WARNER. "The Feminist Mind." Nation 96
       (6 February):123-26.
       Mentions several books on women; praises Ida Tarbell and
Ellen Key, mentions Harold Owen, finds that "the literature of
feminism neither enlarges the mind of the reader nor increases
his self-respect," and then launches into a consideration of
woman's intellectual fitness for suffrage. Asserts that whereas
the masculine mind reaches maturity, "the feminine mind seems
hardly to get beyond the stage of adolescence." Women are illogical, lack a sense of justice. Feminism is adolescent romanti-
cism, "the mark of an undeveloped self-consciousness." Faults
women for their unscientific attitude toward housekeeping. Wants
women to do the work at their doors, not seek a career of
suffrage.

296   "The Future of Free Womanhood." Living Age 277
       (12 April):119-21.
       Faults feminists' logic of equality, saying that men and
women can never be totally equal in education, employment, par-
enthood, and the home. Calls this a "mechanical logic of equality which, ignoring or deprecating the natural obligations and

the social significance of sex, lays out the whole career of woman on the basis of that human nature which she possesses in common with men." Calls Gilman an "extremist." Says this militant feminism is against Nature's plan. It is men like Earl Barnes, W.L. George, and Dr. Saleeby who warn against this extravagance. Reprinted from Nation (London) 12 (8 March):919-20.

297   "Woman's Unrest through Conservative Eyes." Current Opinion
       55 (September):192.
           Summarizes Edward S. Martin's The Unrest of Women (see
       293).

298   COLQUHOUN, ETHEL. "Modern Feminism and Sex Antagonism."
       Living Age 278 (6 September):579-94.
           Finds no remedy for woman's present condition in the feminist position, which only leads to sex antagonism. What women need is to be strengthened in their normal, natural sphere and to develop along the lines suggested by their sex needs and characteristics. Reprinted from Quarterly Review (London) 219 (July):143-66.

299   BOK, EDWARD. "Restless American Women." Ladies' Home Journal
       30 (October):5.
           Alleges that it is only a small percentage of American women who are restless and discontent--a negligible quantity. Asserts that "for every noisy woman clamoring for some 'right' or other there are tens of thousands of quiet women, who have all the rights they want, and a few privileges to the good."

300   CROMER, E.B. "Feminism in France." Living Age 279
       (6 December):589-93.
           Links feminism and anarchy, also feminism and socialism. Feminism will lead to the destruction of the family and menaces morality. Says feminism in France is receiving little support. Reprinted from National Review (London) 62 (November):403-8.

                                    1914

301   BARUCH, Mrs. SIMON. Feminism Is a Bar to Social Betterment;
       and The Affiliation of Suffrage and Feminism. N.p., 4 pp.
       After spring 1914.
           Writes in response to an article by a feminist on feminism and suffrage. Insists that feminists intend to have no home and to practice free love. But women are incapable of rule, as has been proved in history. Divorce is higher in suffrage than in nonsuffrage states. Her unidentified male coauthor contributes three quarters of this essay.

302   MAC ADAM, GEORGE. Feminist Revolutionary Principle Biologically Unsound. New York: Man-Suffrage Association Opposed
       to Extension of Political Suffrage to Women, 14 pp.

Reports views of William T. Sedgwick, professor of biology and public health at M.I.T. It is masculine women, "mistakes of nature . . . who are largely responsible for the feminist movement." Warns that "if the feminists are allowed free sway, there will be a total destruction of wifehood and the home, a total destruction of all the tender relations and associations that home involves." But insists that women will never rule man because men can always fall back on brute strength. Actually women enjoy being mastered—we are all still rather primitive. Predicts that "feminism will soon be looked back on as the most absurd and dangerous vagary of a restless age." Reprinted from New York Times, 18 January 1914.

303   The Right and Wrong of Feminism: Sermon, Central Congrega-
       tional Church, Providence, Rhode Island. N.p., 16 pp.
       Will support woman suffrage if it comes gradually but not
the dissolution of home and marriage which, he alleges, the more
extreme feminists advocate. Wants women to be feminine and to
accept their condition as women. Opposes individualism. Christianity is the answer.

304   MARTIN, EDWARD S. "Much Ado about Women." Atlantic 113
       (January):9-12.
       Likens feminists to "little boys who run beside the band in
a procession. It is all right that they should run, and even
holler (for the band is loud) and be happy. But they are not the
procession." Let them make noise; it is better that they should
clamor about their debatable and even preposterous hopes "than
that their mental disturbance should not be advertised."

305   CROWELL, CHESTER T. "The Worm Turns: An Indictment of Women
       and a Defense of Men." Independent 77 (12 January):68-69.
       Says he is in favor of woman suffrage and higher education
for women but deplores their abuse, attack, and misrepresentation
of his sex. Feels that "the feminist movement is running amuck."
Wants women to acknowledge how much men have done for them.
Asserts that "a man is a more valuable unit of society than a
woman" and "contributes more to the world." Women are still
barbaric so the excesses of the British suffragettes do not
surprise him. Women are also less than truthful; they are dis-
loyal, unmerciful to one another, neither punctual nor indus-
trious, and scornful of rules. Much misogyny. Alleges that his
goal in writing the article was to get feminists to change their
attitude toward men. See responses that follow in 307.

306   HARRISON, ETHEL B. "Abdication." Living Age 280
       (24 January):195-200.
       Taking stock of the woman's movement again (see 281) finds
that "there never was a time when fewer solid contributions were
made by women to society than the present." Blames "a destructive campaign" for engrossing "time, energy, and money which

might have been employed in constructive work." Asserts that as
soon as women begin to traffic in votes, they lose their true
influence, and at great loss to the country. Opposes mothers
working outside the home. Feminism destroys the ideal of the
family and denigrates the home, leading to unpleasant, uncomfort-
able homes. Sex antagonism is "the worst and most unscientific
feature of the [feminist] campaign." Women are morbid and abnormal. Reprinted from Nineteenth Century and After (London) 74
(December 1913):1328-35.

307   "The Worm that Turned Is Trodden On." Independent 77
       (16 February):239-40.
       Fifteen excerpts from responses to Chester Crowell's arti-
cle (305), more than half disagreeing with him. But he is supported by a few men and women, including a trained nurse.
Editors report that they have rarely received more mail on an
article in their publication. More replies published 9 March
1914 but almost all emphatically disputed Crowell's points.

308   COLQUHOUN, ETHEL. "Woman and Morality." Living Age 280
       (28 February):515-24.
       Asserts that feminists are teaching a "false doctrine that
man has usurped a place in society which belongs by right to
woman." Says that as a result of the militants, women are no
longer being treated courteously in public. Women lack political
principal. The result is moral retrogression. Reprinted from
Nineteenth Century and After (London) 75 (January):128-40.

309   "The 'Brute in Man' as an Argument against Feminism." Current
       Opinion 56 (May):370-71.
       Presents the views of Professor William T. Sedgwick, from
the New York Times, where he calls feminism the "most absurd and
dangerous vagary of a restless age" and says feminists are the
"mistakes of nature" who want the "privilege of seeking sex
adventure." If women do not watch out, the brute in man will put
them in their place. Replies quoted from Dr. Frederick Peterson
and C.P. Gilman.

310   SCHEFFAUER, HERMAN. "The Passing of the Gentlewoman." North
       American 200 (July):71-84.
       Describes feminists as "heated and dishevelled Amazons who
carry on the siege against intrenched masculinity." Although
much that was false is passing away, still deplores the modern
trend against the gentlewoman and toward the vigorous, sport-
loving feminist. Women are becoming too much like men and there
is evolving "a colorless hybrid of both sexes." Complains that
"the movement for political 'rights,' aiming at masculine prerogatives and standards, has produced strange types, shorn of all
the glory of sex, ascetic, grim, mannish spirits in female
frames."

311   ELLIS, L.B.   "Same Old Thing."   Harper's Weekly 59
      (29 August):208.
           Says that what is now called feminism is merely a new name
      for what men used to call "feminine unreason" or "the peskiness
      of the sex." Men must fight back. Cites a long list of histor-
      ical examples of female militancy. Article supposedly humorous.

312   POWERS, F[RED] P[ERRY].   "The Curse of Adam and the Curse of
      Eve." Unpopular Review 2 (October-December):266-79.
           Denies that women and men are essentially the same and
      equal. On the contrary, "the differentiation of men and women is
      the most valuable product of ages of gradually developing civili-
      zation." Blames the rise of feminism for the increase in mate-
      rialism and paganism. "Manners have coarsened, modesty is
      disappearing," and the fiction and drama of the day are vicious.
      Some allege that women are taking to alcohol and tobacco, which
      merely proves that when the distinctions between the sexes break
      down, women are lowered and men not raised. Further asserts that
      "the period of aggressive Feminism coincides with decrees of
      fashion that are designed to expose as much of the female figure
      as the police will permit."

313   DRAKE, DURANT.   "Ethics of the Woman's Cause."   North American
      200 (November):771-80.
           Warns that militant women are after much more than the
      vote--they also want free divorce and free love. Counsels women
      to be content with their home duties and to leave to men the
      tasks of production. They should not be lured into business or
      professional life. Stresses: "It is not a question, ultimately,
      of what women want, but of what they ought to want, not a ques-
      tion of rights, but of duties." Also warns against letting women
      succeed by militant methods as they will set examples for other
      classes and parties. Hopes that the mass of "sound-hearted"
      Englishwomen will rise to rebuke "their mad sisters who put the
      winning of an end before scrupulousness about means, class advan-
      tage before the general welfare, victory before ideals."

314   WALKER, HENRY.   "Feminism and Polygamy."   Forum 52
      (December):831-45.
           Believes that the true goal of the feminist movement is
      polygamy--"legalized, regulated by the state; respectable, and
      'moral.'" Polygamy would satisfy every normal woman's desire for
      motherhood and "a complete, wholesome sexual life" as well as
      men's ongoing normal need for sexual intercourse. Argues that
      polygamy is the only way to meet the legitimate demands of women.
      It would almost eliminate prostitution. It would also take women
      out of the work force, thus opening wider and more remunerative
      fields of employment for men.

1915

315   HUBBARD, BENJAMIN VESTAL. <u>Socialism, Feminism, and
       Suffragism, the Terrible Triplets: Connected by the Same
       Umbilical Cord, and Fed from the Same Nursing Bottle</u>.
       Chicago: American Publishing Co., 300 pp.
          The subtitle accurately expresses the author's approach!

316   WHEELER, EVERETT P. <u>What Women Have Done without the Ballot</u>.
       New York: Man Suffrage Association, 8 pp. Date is estimated.
          Alleges that much reform legislation has been passed with
       the aid of intelligent women who saw evils and brought them to
       the attention of the public. Women are active in charity and
       philanthropic work, in settlements. Women should be content with
       educating public sentiment and not inflict suffrage upon women
       who already have enough to do. Likens the feminist movement to
       Napoleon and says it "will have the same career." Approves of
       their trying to secure equal civil rights and opportunities, but
       now its leaders want political power and aim at domination.
       "They are fighting against natural law. They also will find
       their Moscow."

317   TAGORE, RABINDRANATH. "Beehive: Feminism Contrasted with the
       Zenana." <u>Craftsman</u> 27 (January):364-68.
          Feminism is "uneasiness and buzzing." Women are at work
       rather than engaged in homemaking. Urges women to return to the
       home: "Love, not struggle, must animate Woman, the Comforter."
       Much poetic language.

318   POWERS, FRED PERRY. "Feminism and Socialism." <u>Unpopular
       Review</u> 3 (January-March):118-33.
          Argues that women do not need the vote to remove legal
       disabilities as men have already removed them. Mocks the femi-
       nists' desire to "mother" the community, which he says "rises
       with their aversion to mothering anything else," and says they
       are interested in municipal housekeeping because "they are in
       revolt against domestic housekeeping." Quotes feminists only to
       mock them; quotes antifeminists approvingly. Argues that equal-
       izing the pay of women and men would be enormously unjust, unless
       men were at the same time relieved of the legal and customary
       requirement of supporting their wives. Shows how feminism and
       socialism are allied and "both are antagonistic to the private
       family."

319   REPPLIER, AGNES. "Women and War." <u>Atlantic</u> 115 (May):577-85.
          Deplores the fact that feminists oppose the war. Men
       fight, she says, to protect and defend women. Women should not
       sever their interests from men's, as the feminists are doing.

320   "Confessions of an Anti." <u>Unpopular Review</u> 4 (October-
       December):255-73.

Entered manhood an advocate of woman suffrage but gradually became disillusioned, first by the failure of a woman suffragist in her household duties and family work because she was too busy doing "man's work" on a platform. Says "the very qualities that make women great as women, generally make them ridiculous as politicians and economists." They are also tragically inadequate as physicians and surgeons. Wants women in the homes, making them "our centres of social sweetness and light," not running around wasting energy on questionable causes. Any woman who wanted to vote "couldn't be a darling if she tried." Objects to books written by feminists that attack chastity and the family. Says feminism stinks in sensitive nostrils.

321   HENLE, JAMES. "The New Woman." Harper's Weekly 61
      (20 November):502-3.
      Thinks the feminist movement is "the product of hysteria, sincere but cockleshell enthusiasm, a badly deranged sense of proportion, and general mental indigestion." Denies that women are capable of equal education. "Woman is readily receptive to facts and singularly unresponsive to ideas." She cannot produce new ideas and never will be able to; nor can she understand or form abstract ideas. She is interested in the ballot because it is tangible. But because she cannot grasp an abstract idea, woman is incapable of ideals. Points out that "no woman has ever remained true to a cause; no woman has ever sacrificed herself for an idea." Finds on all sides "infinite twaddle," "infinite mush," "meaningless phrases," and "frothy nothingness."

1916

322   HALE, ANNIE RILEY. The Eden Sphinx. New York, 238 pp.
      Calls feminists "peeved disciples of sex-grouch." Says woman suffrage is futile and superfluous because women have achieved all their rights (legal, educational) without it. Mocks male supporters of woman suffrage as hen-pecked, impractical, or idealistic. Reveals that woman suffrage is just the means to the end--feminism, which would emancipate woman from womanly occupations and conventions. But feminism is "unsound and untenable" and "positively harmful to women and to the race." Argues that it was "sex-dissatisfaction--and not political or economic, dissatisfaction--[that] was the root of the 'woman movement.'" The remedy is for women to demand self-control and chastity from men, to enforce a higher standard of sex-morality.

323   [LUBY, RICHARD]. Diplomacy; or, Separate Self-Government for
      Each Sex. Monrovia, Calif., 64 pp.
      Opposes coeducation and cosuffrage. Alleges that co-suffrage is "the most subservient to the sex-passion and the most inimical to rationality in human government." Finds "enforced promiscuity of the sexes" in school to be "exceedingly repugnant to natural law." Reprints many short news articles to show what

escapades coeducated students engage in. Wants each sex to
manage its own affairs, for there to be male and female legislatures, governors, as well as schools. Calls this "diplomacy"--"a
double or two-fold form of human government in which the two
sexes, as aggregates, are co-ordinate and co-equal, being segre-
gated politically, educationally and, as far as practicable,
industrially." Calls this the only civilized form of government.

324   MARTIN, JOHN, and MARTIN, PRESTONIA MANN. Feminism: Its
       Fallacies and Fancies. New York: Dodd, Mead & Co., 359 pp.
           John, writing first, opposes feminism with humanism. Femi-
       nism is individualistic, anarchic, family-destroying; humanism
       the opposite. His humanism would stress sex differences and
       "exempt women from competitive industry in order to produce
       greater human beings." Opposes higher education for women as
       leading to fewer and more sterile marriages because feminism
       starves women's instincts. Would set up schools of household
       craft and mothercraft. Prestonia says feminism destroys the
       family, places child-rearing in the hands of "experts," and con-
       vinces superior women not to marry. Alleges that professional
       women are selling the race by denying their own motherhood poten-
       tial. Finds woman suffrage innocuous (author appears confused
       over meaning of "innocuous").

325   ROBINSON, MARGARET C. "The Feminist Program." Unpopular
       Review 5 (April-June):318-31.
           Says feminists oppose monogamous marriage, favor one title
       for all women, and are "trying to remove every safeguard, social,
       moral, or legal against illegitimate relations." Blames feminism
       for poisoning our literature. Quotes feminists at length.

326   "Some of the Fallacies and Follies of Feminism as Seen by a
       Man." Current Opinion 60 (June):425.
           Recounts the arguments of John Martin in Survey (1243),
       where he states that working women regard economic independence
       as a curse and would prefer adequate remuneration of their hus-
       bands to work for themselves. Feminism has led to the exploita-
       tion rather than the protection of women. Feminists cavalierly
       treat motherhood as incidental.

327   RAVENEL, Mrs. S.P. "The Eternal Feminine." Unpopular Review
       6 (October-December):348-66.
           Calls feminism inconsistent. It looks back to a golden
       past where men and women were co-workers, whereas this was a time
       of unremitting toil, a dreary prospect. Feminists always main-
       tain that "the man's gain is and always has been the woman's
       loss," and so "the campaign of sex antagonism is begun." Says
       feminists want to undo the work of centuries to become man's
       equal. But woman cannot because she is mentally and physically
       handicapped. Nature has cut woman off from the highest imagina-
       tive and intellectual pursuits in order to allow her to be the
       mother of the race.

328   RICHARDSON, ANNA STEESE.   "'Parasites Lost' and 'Parasites
      Regained.'"   McClure's 48 (December):25-26, 62-63.
          Asserts that woman's twenty years of economic independence
      are causing her to react with an abnormal yearning for protected
      wifehood and motherhood, a desire to escape all responsibility
      and become a parasite on man.   These women are marrying without
      love.   Examples are chorus girls, movie actresses, saleswomen,
      teachers--all products of enforced economic independence.
      Alleges that she is not attacking feminism (although she actually
      is).

1917

329   WALSH, CORREA MOYLAN.   Feminism.   New York: Sturgis & Walton,
      393 pp.
          Argues that feminism violates nature by stirring up sex-
      antagonism.   Feminism destroys the family and makes all members
      individuals.   Feminism is allied with socialism.   "Women simply
      are not equal to men in capacity for self-support or indepen-
      dence, not being able to stand the same stress and strain."
      Their bodies and brains are smaller and weaker--all the tradi-
      tional distinctions are cited, with copious references.   Women
      should not go into business but rather should bear and rear
      children.   Examines arguments for and against woman suffrage, and
      comes out opposed.   The solution is to bring women back into the
      home and occupy them there, so they do not interfere elsewhere
      and endanger the race.

330   "The Real Feminist Ideal: Editorial."   Unpopular Review 7
      (April-June):440-41.
          The mocking story of Mrs. Burke-Jones, "a philanthropist,
      and socialist and a suffragist," who neglects her husband to
      attend meetings day and night, go to conventions.   The husband
      gets indigestion eating at his club.   When she is finally elected
      president of the State Federation of Women's Clubs, she ironi-
      cally gives an address on "Woman's Sphere, the Home."

1918

331   KIRKLAND, WINIFRED MARGARETTA.   The Joys of Being a Woman, and
      Other Papers.   Boston: Houghton Mifflin, 281 pp.
          In title essay takes a derogatory attitude toward femi-
      nists, which she defines as women wishing to become men.   "To
      become a genuine feminist, a woman would have to forego her most
      enviable possession--her sense of humor."   What women really want
      is to satisfy men, not to terrify or to emulate them.   The rest
      of the book consists of desultory essays, neither anti- nor
      prowoman.

1919

332   DAVIS, EMERSON. <u>An</u> <u>Address</u> <u>Delivered</u> <u>at</u> <u>the</u> <u>Sixteenth</u> <u>Anni-</u>
      <u>versary</u> <u>of</u> <u>the</u> <u>Mt.</u> <u>Holyoke</u> <u>Female</u> <u>Seminary,</u> 4 <u>August</u> <u>1853</u>.
      N.p., 12 pp. Date is estimated.
          Takes on modern reformers who insist that there is no
      difference in the mental constitution of the sexes, that women
      should not be excluded from any employments, and that women
      should vote. Says women should be separately educated and remain
      in their sphere.

1920

333   KENEALY, ARABELLA, L.R.C.P. <u>Feminism</u> <u>and</u> <u>Sex-Extinction</u>.
      London: T. Fisher Unwin; New York: E.P. Dutton, 313 pp.
          Objects to feminism because it seeks to eliminate sex
      differences and sex distinctions. Progress for the race requires
      two distinct sexes, not rivalry, antagonism, and competition.
      Rather shaky biology: right side of body and brain is male,
      dominant; left side is female, dormant. This holds for the face,
      eyes, hands, ears, etc. Left arm and hand of woman hold and
      caress her infant. If a woman develops along masculine lines, is
      tall or strong or mentally virile, her sons will be emasculated,
      for she has squandered their inheritance. In masculinizing
      women, feminism is "burdening the Race and deteriorating type by
      producing an ever-increasing number of neurotic, emasculate men
      and boys." Feminism leads to hermaphroditism.

334   MC EVILLY, MARY. <u>To</u> <u>Woman,</u> <u>from</u> <u>Meslom</u>—<u>A</u> <u>Message</u> <u>from</u> <u>Meslom</u>
      <u>in</u> <u>the</u> <u>Life</u> <u>Beyond,</u> <u>Received</u> <u>Automatically</u> <u>by</u> <u>Mary</u> <u>McEvilly</u>.
      New York: Brentano's, 108 pp.
          In the form of communications from the life Beyond. Lofty
      teachings on the subject of woman's duty and destiny. Woman
      "must learn that nothing can or should ever make her man's equal.
      There can be no equality between the sexes—there is the marvel-
      ous completion of one another when each be true to nature."

335   FLYNN, THOMAS E. "Revolutionary Legislation; Proposal to Rob
      Husbands of Their Rights in the Making of Wills." <u>Overland</u>,
      n.s. 76 (November):14-16, 88.
          Alleges that women having been given the right to vote,
      "one of the important propositions put forth in the name of the
      sex, is that they shall be empowered to steal the property of
      their husbands." Objects to changes in community property laws
      and blames a committee of women. This is what happens when women
      can vote.

1921

336   CURRIE, BARTON W.   "The Humbug of Sexlessness."   <u>Ladies' Home</u>
       <u>Journal</u> 38 (May):24.
            Points out that even though the feminists have achieved
       political equality, they are still pushing for economic equality--
       "aggressively, militantly, noisily." Finds the "extreme feminist"
       to be "about the worst snob the world has yet produced." She
       thinks of herself as superwoman and wants to become sexless, a
       biological impossibility. "Let's have done with all this humbug
       about sexlessness. It's just meaningless twaddle."

337   WILSON, MARGARET WOODROW.   "Where Women in Politics Fail."
       <u>Ladies' Home Journal</u> 38 (September):10, 70.
            Opposes separate organizations for women like the Woman's
       Party and the League of Women Voters. Thinks it "dishonest for
       women to act as if they were not citizens along with men, after
       all, but a class apart." Faults them for thinking that, with
       their superior consciences, "they must work alone for the benefit
       of humanity."

Woman Suffrage

Some opposition to woman suffrage was expressed in the 1830s, but it was not until woman suffrage became a shaky plank in the early women's rights movement in the 1850s that antisuffrage writings began to appear in significant number. Many writers accepted improved female education and even wider employment but balked at the franchise.

As with women's rights in general, suffrage activity slowed during the Civil War, to pick up again late in the 1860s, when women hoped to win the vote. Correspondingly, antisuffrage writings increase in number in the late 1860s and 1870s, slow dramatically late in the 1870s and early 1880s, and then periodically peak as new campaigns and tactics are tried: in 1885, for example, when suffragists tried to have woman suffrage passed in Massachusetts; in 1894, as they sought to have woman suffrage adopted at the New York State Constitution Convention. Activity slowed late in the 1890s and remained moderate, rising gradually after the turn of the century, jumping in 1909, and remaining high until 1916, when America entered the war and woman suffrage appeared certain. By then even some staunchly antisuffrage periodicals like the Outlook had accepted the inevitability of women's voting.

Reasons for opposing woman suffrage did not change much over time. Women are too good to vote, should remain nonpartisan, should influence men, should not be coarsely jostled at the polls, should not descend to men's level. Negatively, suffragists are monsters, women are more likely to be bribed and corrupted by politicians, women lack force to uphold any laws they might make. As immigration swelled in the 1880s and 1890s, the specter of the ignorant foreign vote, now more than Biddy at the washtub, was raised. For the twenty years after the turn of the century, being an antisuffragist must have been a full-time activity.

<u>1837</u>

338   WILKES, GEORGE. <u>A</u> <u>Review</u> <u>of</u> <u>Miss</u> <u>Martineau's</u> <u>Work</u> <u>on</u> <u>Society</u>
      <u>in</u> <u>America</u>. Boston: Capen & Lyon, 54 pp.
      Faults Martineau for criticizing America for not giving
woman political equality. Argues ingeniously that people are
entitled to the protection of the community when they fulfill all
their duties and occupy their natural station. Since the only
natural situations of women are as wife and mother, unless a woman
is a mother she is neutral, "simply an accidental visitor, whom
the laws of the hospitality demand we should respect and defend,
and in this capacity she can have no political character." In
her natural situation as mother woman needs man's protection.
She is certainly not qualified to take a political or active role
in society. Says that "we shall evade giving [women] the right
of suffrage for ever."

<u>1839</u>

339   [BY A LADY OF CHILLICOTHE]. "The Proper Sphere of Woman."
      <u>Hesperian</u> 2 (January):181-86.
      Believes it would be injurious to woman's true interests to
extend political rights to her. It would be "a waste and mis-
direction of her mental energies" and call her out of her proper
sphere.

340   "American Women." <u>Democratic</u> <u>Review</u> 6 (August):127-42.
      Begins by reviewing Sedgwick's <u>Means</u> <u>and</u> <u>Ends</u> (see 26) and
then considers aspects of woman's condition. Favors improved
education but opposes woman suffrage, accusing those who are
championing the right of women to "an equal participation in
public affairs" of "sailing on a wrong tack." Objects to women
departing from "the more appropriate sphere of woman's action and
influence," the home.

<u>1841</u>

341   BURNAP, Rev. GEORGE WASHINGTON. <u>Lectures</u> <u>on</u> <u>the</u> <u>Sphere</u> <u>and</u>
      <u>Duties</u> <u>of</u> <u>Woman</u> <u>and</u> <u>Other</u> <u>Subjects</u>. Baltimore: J. Murphy,
      272 pp.
      Generally standard fare but notable for opposing woman
suffrage at this early date: "The political rights of women have
been often discussed, but generally without either wisdom or
moderation on either side." Finds it impossible to maintain that
they ought "to aspire to the right of suffrage," but will allow
that they should have property rights.

1849

342   WALKER, T. "The Legal Condition of Women." Western Law
      Journal 6 (January):145-59.
          Points out that precisely the same situation that preceded
      the American Revolution exists in the case of women--taxation
      without representation. Yet most women do not want the vote and
      would exclude themselves from "the noise, the glare, the turmoil,
      the corruption attendant upon elections." Says these "form no
      congenial element for female sensitiveness, diffidence, and deli-
      cacy." Argues that those very characteristics that make woman "a
      ministering angel" at home utterly unfit her for public life;
      predicts that such "could have no other effect than to transform
      them into a race of Amazons." Concludes that any "woman who best
      understands her true interest and glory, will probably be most
      thankful for her political disfranchisement."

343   F., K. "Women and their Occupations." Monthly Religious
      Magazine 6 (June):269-72.
          Wants the condition of working women to be improved--"why
      should a girl of good habits and cultivated mind, even though an
      obscure needle woman, not receive as much courtesy and kindly
      consideration in her avocation, as her fairer and more favored
      sisters?" Hopes more occupations--"various, pleasant and elevat-
      ing"--can be opened to them. Does not women to have to marry for
      a living. Yet is "far from advocating 'women's rights,' in the
      sense of admission to the political arena, or to the unfeminine
      privilege of the polls." Considers all such relations "entirely
      unsuited to the peace and purity of woman's sphere."

1851

344   L., M.U. "The Sphere of Woman." Monthly Religious Magazine 8
      (February):63-66.
          Says woman has a noble sphere, "to watch at the very foun-
      tain of life." No one who knows this sacred trust would wish it
      to be jostled at the ballot-box. It is best for her to infuse a
      purer spirit into those who vote for her.

345   HALE, SARAH JOSEPHA. "Editors' Table." Godey's Lady's Book
      43 (July):57-58.
          In a letter of congratulations to Mr. Godey on his Lady's
      Book reaching twenty-one years of age, thanks him for supporting
      the journal and says that if women could vote, they would elect
      him president. But does not advocate any change in woman's
      sending the male members of her household to vote while she stays
      home quietly to read. Vigorously protests the "notion of female
      voting" and fears that next women will have to serve in the
      military and as firemen. "A pretty sight it would be to see our
      lovely ladies parading at beat of drum, or running after the
      fire-engines!"

346   BERRY, KATE. "How Can an American Woman Serve Her Country?"
       Godey's Lady's Book 43 (December):362-65.
           Opposes women's associations because they make "the sex
       quite needlessly conspicuous." Woman's sphere is private, not
       public, individual, not collective. Finds female politicians
       "unlovely and unfeminine," and political discussions unbecoming.
       Women are not supposed to understand politics and need not move
       into the political arena to prove themselves patriots. Women
       impair their usefulness and true character in trying to move into
       the male sphere.

                                  1852

347   HALE, SARAH JOSEPHA. "Editors' Table: How American Women
       Should Vote." Godey's Lady's Book 44 (April):293.
           The American woman should vote by rightly influencing the
       votes of men, not by seeking suffrage for herself.

348   M., L.S. "Enfranchisement of Woman." Southern Quarterly
       Review 21 (April):322-41.
           Asserts that God has established woman's position. She
       must stay in it or fail and be degraded. Such mental aberrations
       of woman as seeking suffrage excite both pity and disgust.
       Woman's duty and nature is to govern, sway, teach, civilize,
       by love. Says that the women at the Worcester Woman's Rights
       Convention are of the third sex. Finds woman's rights entirely a
       Yankee notion of "petticoated despisers of their sex,--these
       would-be men,--these things that puzzle us to name. . . . Moral
       monsters; they are things which Nature disclaims." Reminds read-
       ers that woman suffrage and abolition are closely allied--"Mounted
       on Cuffee's shoulders, in rides the lady." The freest woman is
       the truest woman.

                                  1855

349   WILLIS, NATHANIEL PARKER. The Rag-Bag, a Collection of
       Ephemera. New York: C. Scribner, 356 pp.
           Argues that women are already superior to men in America--
       physically, intellectually, morally, in religion, taste, senti-
       ment, consistency of opinion. They already have power and re-
       forms are needed, but doubts that female freedom to vote would
       bring about the needed reforms. "We agree with Mr. Greeley that
       the worst women would probably drive the best from the ballot-
       box. An easier first step is wanted--something that does not
       conflict directly and rudely with the inbred habits of the sex."
       Proposes that women ostracize offending members of legislative
       bodies. Women should use their influence.

1858

350   MONTEZ, LOLA. Lectures of Lola Montez, Including Her Auto-
      biography. New York: Rudd & Carleton, 292 pp.
          Mocks women who call and attend women's rights conventions
      and wish to vote. Asserts that "the will of every intellectual
      and adroit woman does go to the ballot-box" with her husband,
      which is far preferable to having her rush into the coarse crowd
      and carry it there herself. Insists that "in such a contact the
      mass of women would only lose the delicacy and refinement which
      now constitute their only charm, without getting any benefit for
      the terrible sacrifice."

1867

351   An Appeal against Anarchy of Sex, to the Constitutional Con-
      vention and the People of the State of New-York, by a Member
      of the Press. New York: John A. Gray & Green Printers,
      21 pp.
          Foresees that barbarism will follow if women get the vote
      because men will no longer treat them with tenderness and cour-
      tesy. Says the few strong-minded women who started the agitation
      "are unequivocally and almost universally repudiated by the sex."
      Calls them "somewhat monstrous," a sort of third sex. Warns that
      "Biddy is to be there as well as her mistress. . . . What
      ignorant and vulgar women, inflamed by drink and unamenable to
      order and discipline in a degree that no men are, will do upon
      exciting election days, is beyond picturing."

352   Universal Suffrage. Female Suffrage. By a Republican (Not a
      "Radical"). Philadelphia: J.B. Lippincott, 116 pp.
          First opposes universal suffrage (freed slaves are not
      ready to vote); then takes up female suffrage. Says only a few
      women want to vote. Women have not enough time and energy to
      vote and do the duties assigned to them by Providence. Worries
      that female servants "and the large class of ignorance which they
      represent" shall have a vote. Women without the vote can serve
      as peacemakers, can turn talk away from politics. Alleges that
      woman suffragists admire men, denigrate women. Asserts that if
      women do man's work, they will lose their femininity and do
      indifferent work. Warns that if women harp on their rights, they
      may get more than they bargained for—courtesy will go out the
      window.

353   HALE, SARAH JOSEPHA. "Editors' Table: Ought American Women
      to Have the Right of Suffrage?" Godey's Lady's Book 75
      (October):354-55.
          Supports the Bible's distinctions between the sexes and
      government based on man as authority and woman as influence.
      American women are the best protected and cared-for in the world.

Opposes placing women in competition with men in industrial
pursuits because it would harm feminine nature and make society
too materialistic. Urges that women be educated in domestic
science. Laws require force to be upheld; women should content
themselves with moral influence and persuasion.

1868

354   CLEMENT, CORA. A Woman's Reasons Why Women Should Not Vote.
       Boston: J.E. Farwell & Co., 16 pp.
          Believes that "no person having a just appreciation of the
       cares devolving upon the mother of a family, would ask her to
       take an additional, permanent responsibility." If women try to
       move into men's sphere, they abandon their influence over men.
       Woman suffrage would bring out the ignorant and licentious vote
       and would lead to domestic discord.

355   PEABODY, A.P. "Man and Woman." Monthly Religious Magazine 39
       (June):436-43.
          Wants men and women assimilated on a spiritual plane, but
       objects to "external (so-called) reforms" which would only retard
       or frustrate [this] religious elevation." Warns that woman suf-
       frage would degrade and pollute society. Pictures ignorant and
       vicious women being bribed, drugged, brought to the polls intoxi-
       cated. The presence of women at political parades, "orgies,
       riots, and debauches" sickens him.

356   HALE, SARAH JOSEPHA. "Editors' Table: Independence--The Old
       and the New." Godey's Lady's Book 77 (July):82-83.
          As part of her ongoing opposition to woman suffrage, pre-
       sents a paean to the home and then an excerpt from Gail Hamilton's
       Woman's Wrongs, which is actually not antisuffrage.

1869

357   BEECHER, CATHARINE E. Something for Women Better Than the
       Ballot. New York: D. Appleton, 12 pp.
          Wants institutions established that will train women to
       their appropriate professions. Then we will not need the ballot
       for women, with all its "risks and responsibilities."

358   BUSHNELL, HORACE. Women's Suffrage: The Reform against
       Nature. New York: Charles Scribner & Co., 184 pp.
          Grants that women have economic, social, educational, and
       legal disadvantages, and supports coeducational colleges, women
       in medicine, in law (with limited scope), as deaconesses (but not
       ministers), and many other kinds of work, but draws the line at
       suffrage. Asserts that women and men are so unlike as to be more
       like two species than two varieties. Like their skin, women's

brains are finer, more delicate than men's. Masculinity carries
the governing function, femininity submission and subordination.
"Women are out of place in the governing of men." Can "only look
with supreme pity" on the women who campaign to be men. Predicts
that suffrage will change women both morally and physically.
Refutes Mill and Henry Ward Beecher.

359   DEWEY, CHARLES C. Woman Suffrage: Speech Delivered in the
      Council of Censors, Montpelier, Vermont, 4 August 1869.
      Montpelier: Journal Press, 29 pp. Date is estimated.
         Apparently Vermont was asked to amend its constitution;
this body sat to consider change. Opposes woman suffrage as
contrary to divine revelation and against the natural law of the
sex. Predicts "the most lamentable consequences to the race."
Attacks Lucy Stone: like Eve, she has been tempted out of her
sphere, denied her husband power over her, and been disobedient.
Pictures "multitudes of harpies" roaming through the country bent
on leading women into "an Amazonian" battle against marriage and
for the ballot. Says these "ravenous wolves" will "debauch the
hearts and minds of our wives and daughters." Insists "the
ballot and the bayonet go together." Much antifeminist
criticism.

360   FULTON, JUSTIN DEWEY, D.D. The True Woman: To Which Is Added
      Woman vs. Ballot. Boston: Lee & Shepard, 264 pp.
         Says woman suffrage is founded in infidelity to the word of
God and infidelity to woman. Objects to making men and women
rivals. Says women who ask for the ballot are infidels. "Give
to woman the ballot, and this country is hopelessly given up to
Romanism." Those who claim the ballot "lose social respect,
because they step out of the path marked out for them by Provi-
dence and by Nature." In sum, "three facts stand in the way of
Woman's being helped by the Ballot,--God, Nature, and Common
Sense."

361   FULTON, JUSTIN DEWEY, D.D. Woman as God Made Her: The True
      Woman. Boston: Lee & Shepard, 262 pp.
         A reworking of material in 360, with the same approach.

362   LOGAN, OLIVE SIKES. Apropros of Women and Theatres with a
      Paper or Two on Parisian Topics. New York: Carleton, 240 pp.
         Adopts a humorous tone: "If you want me to tell you the
candid, the true truth, I'll confess at once to you that the
blessing of not being allowed to vote is one of the best-
disguised blessings I ever met." Says she is easily deceived
and does not like fights. When her writing fingers "have wrought
their last battle, then it will be a sweet thought, that amid all
the strife and turmoil of political life, I was content to remain
a woman, and never troubled my intellect about any question
graver than that of the newest thing in bonnets."

363   "Female Suffrage." <u>Monthly</u> <u>Religious</u> <u>Magazine</u> 41 (January):93.
        Argues that ignorant and bad women will vote, good women
will not. Women of the highest culture and refinement tell him
they would be grieved to have suffrage forced upon them.

364   BY A LADY. "Editors' Table: What Can Woman Do?" <u>Godey's</u>
        <u>Lady's</u> <u>Book</u> 78 (February):187-88.
        Thinks the majority of women do not know enough to vote
intelligently. Most women take pride in their incapacity for
impartial judgment and their narrow and prejudiced views of
public men and affairs. Most women are also too busy with home
duties and home life to vote. Characterizes one who demands
woman suffrage as "the frivolous woman of fashion, ignorant of
all useful knowledge, and wise only in the trivialities of dress
and etiquette." Commends the German women's reform movement for
focusing on children's health, domestic affairs, and dress
reform.

365   HALE, SARAH JOSEPHA. "Editors' Table: Woman Suffrage."
        <u>Godey's</u> <u>Lady's</u> <u>Book</u> 79 (October):359.
        Recounts an amendment to the state constitution of New
Hampshire proposed on July of 1869 entitling women to vote. A
remonstrance opposing this amendment was signed by 267 ladies of
Warner; they argued that woman's moral influence would be dimin-
ished and "the best interests of home and society endangered" if
woman obtained the vote.

                              <u>1870</u>

366   FAIRCHILD, JAMES HARRIS. <u>Woman's</u> <u>Right</u> <u>to</u> <u>the</u> <u>Ballot</u>.
        Oberlin: G.H. Fairchild, 67 pp.
        This president of Oberlin College opposes woman suffrage
because it will break down the family and make the individual the
unit in society. Faults the present woman movement for intensi-
fying the individual tendency. Says there is a danger in pushing
women out of the home and into public occupations and employments: "There is such eagerness to open all these doors to women
that the higher proprieties and sentiments will be trampled on to
accomplish it, a proof that the leading thought is rude force,
rather than high character."

367   BEECHER, CATHARINE E. "Is Woman Suffrage Contrary to Common-
        Sense?" <u>Christian</u> <u>Union</u> 1 (12 February):98-99;
        (19 February):114-15.
        The Creator instituted two great classes, the strong and
the weak. Men, the strong, have one class of duties and rights,
women, the weak, another. Women have merely to unite in asking
for reforms and they will get them. The ballot is not the answer
but rather the opening of new employments to women, those connected with the family. "Opening the honors and excitements of

political life would operate as a most disastrous drain on forces
now so much needed to sustain the honor and duties of the family
state." Commends the suffragists for raising the question of
woman's condition but wants the discussion rightly directed.

368   MC KIM, J.M. "The Vexed Question." Nation 10 (24 March):189-
       90; (31 March):205-6; (14 April):237-38.
       Says giving the vote to women, after extending it to freed-
men, would "more than double as much ignorance and unfitness as
that which is now putting to the test the ship of state's capacity." Woman should not vote because she cannot fight. Calls it
"simply preposterous" to think of women "performing military
duty, either as noncombatants or as fighters."

369   MYROVER, J.H. "Woman Suffrage: Or, the New Era." New
       Eclectic 6 (April):459-66.
       Mockery in the form of a drama that includes characters
Elizabeth Stady Canton and Miss Fanny, who wants to vote and
loses her suitor; a riotous scene at the polls and one in the
family dining-room, with Brown at home cooking in his wife's
apron, caring for a squalling child, his wife coming in with her
cohorts from a political convention. In the last scene Mrs.
Brown unexpectedly decides to "stay at home and attend to my
proper affairs," tired of seeing her house and furniture be
ruined, having bad food, etc. Her friends concur.

370   BENSON, CARL. "The Woman Question." Galaxy 9 (June):841-44.
       Declares that at best the ballot would make no difference
to woman's condition, while at worst very positive evils would
result. Women are unfit for the suffrage on moral and emotional
rather than intellectual grounds--they are too impulsive.

371   HALE, SARAH JOSEPHA. "Editors' Table: Definitions." Godey's
       Lady's Book 81 (August):181.
       Declares that woman is delicate, man strong. He has the
hard work to do, she the persuasive work. Voting not only will
not help woman to rise; it must degrade her. She would then have
to share in man's hard work and leave her own work undone.

1871

372   BEECHER, CATHARINE E. Woman Suffrage and Woman's Profession.
       Hartford, Conn.: Brown & Gross, 211 pp.
       A series of addresses. Argues that the woman movement
unites many others: spiritualism, free-love, free divorce, in-
dulgences, avoidance of large families, etc. On woman suffrage,
says it will not arrive soon because it is contrary to the cus-
toms of Christian people, who accept the division of labor. A
large majority of women do not want to be forced to assume another responsibility. Believes woman suffrage would greatly
increase the number of incompetent and dangerous voters. Blames

the present woman's rights agitation for a lack of appreciation
for woman's work in the home. The remedy is not woman suffrage
but rather preparation of women for their appropriate duties.

373   DAHLGREN, Mrs. MADELINE VINTON. Thoughts on Female Suffrage,
       and in Vindication of Woman's True Rights. Washington, D.C.:
       Blanchard & Mohun, 22 pp.
           Describes a moral battle to keep women from "the oppression
       of having suffrage forced upon them." Gives history of present
       protest and then reprints several articles previously published
       under the pseudonym Cornelia: "An Appeal for Women," in which
       she foresees the advent of communism from woman suffrage and asks
       to be saved "from this promiscuous mingling of the sexes, now
       advocated under this new phase of irreligion"; reprints excerpt
       from R.H. Davis's "Pro Aris et Focis" (see 119); another on
       children's rights that expresses worry over effect on children if
       women get their rights; repeats that woman's rights equals commu-
       nism; a section entitled "Change--not Progress" criticizes the
       life and career of E.C. Stanton.

374   LATONA. "Woman: Her Mission and Influence." Southern
       Magazine 8 (February):206-8.
           Objects to "those man-hating, bellicose females of the
       present day" who are an embarrassment to gentle, home-loving
       creatures. Objects to the language of the suffragists. Sees no
       good in sundering "the magical links in the chain of exclusive-
       ness that should be girded about one's own home." Woman's sphere
       is in the home.

375   COOPER, Mrs. SARAH B. "Ideal Womanhood." Overland 6
       (May):453-60; 7 (July):69-76; (August):167-75; (October):359.
           Believes that woman is approaching the ideal state, "but
       not in the Ballot do we expect to find a universal panacea for
       feminine grievances." Says woman, "self-consecrated and up-
       reaching," must regenerate herself. Supports coeducation and
       self-dependence but not woman suffrage.

376   "Woman Suffrage in England." Every Saturday 10 (10 June):530.
           Contrasts the suffrage movement in England and the United
       States. Predicts that property-holding Englishwomen will get the
       vote before American women because the suffrage leaders in
       England have made their cause one of "morals and justice,"
       whereas in the States the leaders have allowed themselves asso-
       ciation with "unclean and half-brained creatures of either sex
       and no sex." Englishmen respect the English woman suffragists,
       whereas in the States, woman suffrage "has become associated in
       many minds with free love and free divorce and half a dozen other
       forms of freedom dangerous to social order and the general wel-
       fare." Warns American women to emulate their more decorous
       British sisters.

377   "The Voice of Apollo Hall." Every Saturday 10 (17 June):
      554-55.
           Warns that the convention at Apollo Hall did not advance
      the cause of woman suffrage. Resolutions, platform speakers, and
      personalities, specifically Woodhull's, were "an abomination
      repugnant to the moral sense and hateful in the eyes of purity."
      Pleads with woman suffragists to modify their stance and take
      into account "prejudice and inborn conservatism and the force of
      numbers." They must convince men that woman suffrage will im-
      prove society, which the proceedings of Apollo Hall deny.

378   "Three Pieces of the Woman Question. Editorial." Scribner's
      Monthly 2 (July):316-17.
           Opposes woman suffrage as a revolution that will not
      improve things.

379   "Free-love and Free-divorce." Every Saturday 11 (22 July):75.
           Warns that the free-love cause is hurting woman suffrage.
      Calls it "a fester abhorrent to truth and purity, a scandal to
      the hope of elevation and advancement, a defilement of noble
      longing and progressive civilization." Warns that men will not
      give women the ballot until they are satisfied that it will not
      be used to advance "these shameful theories." Calls upon the
      good women of the country to repudiate those who advocate free-
      love and free-divorce.

380   HYDE, ALEXANDER. "The Coeducation of the Sexes." Scribner's
      Monthly 2 (September):519-24.
           Favors coeducation for prowoman reasons, but opposes woman
      suffrage: it will "make woman less of a woman." Insists that it
      is only "a few of the strong-minded [who] are clamorous on this
      point," not the majority of women.

381   CONANT, WILLIAM C. "The Right Not To Vote." Scribner's
      Monthly 3 (November):73-85; (December):209-17.
           Says the temptation to vote is "the crisis of a Second
      Temptation" for woman. Is it in woman's best interests to assume
      an identical position with man? Says some who propose to speak
      for women are "individuals whose sex is suspected to be rather a
      disguise." Says the right to vote is not the real question;
      rather, it stands "for all the various masculine functions which
      women are invited [by feminists] to assume." Feels the "zeal or
      ambition of a minority" should not plunge women into the fray.
      In the social sphere woman is nearly omnipotent. She may lose
      this omnipotence if she assumes man's position.

                              1872

382   BEECHER, CATHARINE E. Woman's Profession as Mother and
      Educator with Views in Opposition to Woman Suffrage.
      Philadelphia: George Maclean, 223 pp.

Objects to women speaking across the land "advocating principles and measures destructive to both the purity and the perpe-
tuity of the family state." Collection includes "An Address on
Female Suffrage" delivered December 1870 and published earlier
(see 372) as well as "An Address to Christian Women of America,"
in which she objects to the teachings of Mill and his followers
as "in direct opposition to the teachings both of common sense
and Christianity." Says there is a safer and speedier way to
improve woman's condition than granting suffrage—through influence and through establishing a woman's university to train women
to be housekeepers and schoolteachers and so stay in the home.

383   SAMSON, GEORGE W., D.D. Modifications of the Established
       Curriculum Requisite and Legitimate in Colleges for Young
       Women. Albany, 12 pp.
           In this address at an 1872 convocation, privately published
       by order of the Regents, the president of Rutgers Female College
       in New York City alleges that female advocates of woman suffrage
       are unsexed and misrepresent their sex from personal ambition.
       "Woman's sphere in the family manifestly unfits her for all these
       three offices: the legislative, judicial and executive functions
       of government."

384   HALE, SARAH JOSEPHA. "Editors' Table: Invention and Intui-
       tion." Godey's Lady's Book 84 (January):93.
           Calls on women who oppose woman suffrage to speak out to
       state legislatures and Congress to make them realize that "these
       complainers represent a very small fraction of American women."
       Woman has intuition to balance man's invention. Man works on
       brute matter, woman on human nature. Hers is the loftier sphere.

385   [SMALLEY, Mrs.]. "Thoughts for the Women of the Times: By
       One of Themselves." Catholic World 14 (January):467-72.
           Argues that whereas Protestantism has been adverse to the
       interests of women, the Catholic Church has elevated women.
       Describes woman suffrage as an idle dream. Woman would have to
       cease to be a woman, wife, and mother before she could vote.
       Women have everything to lose and nothing to gain in the woman
       suffrage movement. It would "only betray their feet into a
       political slough, and bespatter them with political defilements
       from which none but an omnipotent power can rescue and cleanse
       them."

386   COOPER, Mrs. SARAH B. "Woman Suffrage—Cui Bono?" Overland 8
       (February):156-65.
           Does not believe that suffrage will elevate woman. "The
       natural, pre-ordained sphere of man and woman is radically dif-
       ferent." The fact that most women are indifferent to suffrage
       proves that most are not dissatisfied with their lives. If woman
       affects masculine accomplishments and becomes a quasi-man, love
       and reverence toward her will diminish. Woman can best improve

society by her moral influence. Good women would not vote; bad
ones would. Education will emancipate women. As civilization
progresses, the two sexes become more unlike. Motherhood, not
suffrage.

387   JONES, ALCIBIADES. "Suffrage." Southern Magazine 10
      (April):456-59.
         Says that either woman suffrage would be useless--women
      would vote with their husbands--or it would destroy the family
      relation by causing antagonistic wives. Opposes it.

1873

388   DUBBS, Rev. J[OSEPH] H[ENRY]. Woman's Culture: An Address
      before Allentown Female College, 27 June 1872. Philadelphia:
      J.B. Rogers, 16 pp.
         Believes that woman should be excused from the performance
      of tasks like voting that "appear to conflict with that modest
      shrinking from publicity which is the chief charm of her nature."

389   DUBBS, Rev. J[OSEPH] H[ENRY]. "Woman's Culture." Mercersburg
      Review 20 (January):78-91.
         Reprint of 388.

1874

390   STRAKER, D. AUGUSTUS, Esq. Citizenship, Its Rights and
      Duties--Woman Suffrage. Washington, D.C.: New National Era
      Print, 20 pp.
         An interesting pamphlet by a black man urging suffrage for
      black men but not for women. Says suffrage is a privilege to be
      granted depending upon the fitness and qualification of the
      applicant and then goes on to say that "sex is a good objection
      against woman suffrage." Only a few women want suffrage. Laws
      should not be changed to suit the minority.

391   WHITE, ELIZA A. [Alex]. As It Should Be. Philadelphia: J.B.
      Lippincott & Co., 274 pp.
         In an earlier book had supported woman suffrage but now has
      changed her mind--says she favors woman's rights but not woman
      suffrage. Does not believe the ballot will obtain rights for
      women. "We cannot help but feel that the time spent in clamoring
      for suffrage is worse than time wasted, while women only lower
      themselves in the estimation of men by such a demand." Women
      should do their own work in an exemplary fashion rather than
      descend from their true womanly position to demand a privilege
      that is of so little consequence, and that cannot make them
      better women. Woman now has the power of controlling the world
      in "the moulding of the infant mind."

392   GODKIN, E.L. "Woman Suffrage in Michigan." Nation 18
        (14 May):311-13.
            A cautionary tale for the people of Michigan, who are
        considering woman suffrage. Argues that the influence of sex is
        "so subtle, so penetrating, that even the most powerful charac-
        ters [are] affected by it." Foresees that if men and women are
        thrown together in the political arena, we will see "corruption
        the like of which has never been seen in a free country." Then
        describes the fall of a minister (undoubtedly Henry Ward Beecher)
        at the hands of unchaste women in the suffrage movement. If
        women go into politics, they will either tempt men or entrap them
        with false charges which nevertheless ruin them and their families.

393   "The Moral Power of Women: Editorial." Scribner's Monthly 8
        (June):238-39.
            Argues that women have moral power because they do not have
        the ballot and are not political. If woman had the ballot, a
        moral crusade like that for temperance would be impossible.
        Those in this crusade have never asked for the ballot. They
        would consider the conferment of suffrage upon them a calamity,
        as it would be. It would rob women of their peculiar power--"a
        power which all experience proves cannot be preserved too care-
        fully." The ballot would tie woman's hands, "weaken her influ-
        ence, destroy her disinterestedness in the treatment of all
        public questions, and open into the beautiful realms of her moral
        power ten thousand streams of weakness and corruption."

394   "Shall Women Be Charged with the Duty of Participating in the
        Government of the State?" Republic 3 (July):36-44.
            Criticizes Stanton, whom he calls "the representative agi-
        tator of the question," for alleging that men are hostile to
        women. Says every man cares about his wife, mother, and daugh-
        ter. Denies that suffrage is an inherent natural right. Men
        vote because they can defend the country. Men are stronger,
        heavier, more powerful. Women have the duties of maternity and
        the internal government of the family. Alleges that men already
        neglect their political duties and will do so even more when "the
        interminable and unreasoning gabble of brassy tongued women is
        added." Calls them women "of the lawless stamp of Mrs. Woodhull
        and Miss Susan B. Anthony." Wants to see the moral energies of
        women expended in the appropriate sphere.

395   SMITH, GOLDWIN. "Female Suffrage." Eclectic Magazine 83
        (August):171-81.
            Says he previously had favored female household suffrage
        until he saw the public life of women in the States. Insists
        that "the want of domestic authority lies at the root of all that
        is worst in the politics of the United States." Predicts that if
        women had political power, free government would fall. "Chances
        are, that, being more excitable, and having, with more warmth and
        generosity of temperament, less power of self control, women
        would, when once engaged in party struggles, be not less but more

violent than men. All our experience, in fact, points this way."
Women would vote emotionally, not rationally; marital disharmony
would increase. Reprinted from Macmillan's Magazine (London) 30
(June):139-50. Reprinted in 396.

396   SMITH, GOLDWIN. "Female Suffrage." Popular Science Monthly 5
       (August):427-43.
          Reprint of 395.

397   PORTER, D.G. "Republican Government and the Suffrage of
       Women." Christian Quarterly 6 (October):471-96.
          After tracing the origin of republicanism and the nature of
       suffrage, opposes woman suffrage. Suffrage belongs only in the
       hands of those who represent the natural independent forces of
       society. Woman is naturally weak and dependent; giving her the
       suffrage would not make her stronger. Further, woman suffrage
       would weaken government and the social order. It is also against
       biblical teachings. Any evils in woman's condition can be reme-
       died with present suffrage. Men can be moved by both justice and
       chivalry to protect women. Suffrage would degrade women.

                              1875

398   "Woman Suffrage: Editorial." Scribner's Monthly 9
       (March):628-29.
          States that the movement is waning. It has made a good
       many blunders, among them attracting "those entertaining loose
       social theories." Says those good and pure men and women asso-
       ciated with it "have been obliged, again and again, to wash their
       hands, and protest." Asserts that it has always had a "social
       bad odor."

399   CROFTON, F.B. "A Bachelor on Woman's Rights." National
       Quarterly Review 32 (December):60-75.
          Opposes Mill's desire to encourage women to abandon their
       domestic duties for the political arena. Believes that woman
       suffrage would lower "the standard of legislation, and of offi-
       cial morality and talent." Only bold and "manly" women would
       vote, and they are "of doubtful purity." Women in general are
       more prejudiced and impressionable. Woman suffrage would in-
       crease the influence of the clergy in politics. It would lead
       women to court rather than shun notoriety and "to mingle in the
       toils and dissipations of men." Does not want to see women
       become cynical, hard-hearted, skeptical, and shameless. Believes
       woman suffrage would also harm the character of men, making them
       less concerned for women, less tender and magnanimous.

                              1876

400   BULLOCK, Hon. ALEXANDER HAMILTON. The Centennial Situation of
       Woman. Address at the Commencement Anniversary of Mt. Holyoke

Seminary, Massachusetts, 22 June 1876. Worcester:
C. Hamilton, 45 pp.
    Favors and celebrates all sorts of improvements in women's
condition but stops short of suffrage because he believes women
cannot form political judgments. "Women have ranged with free
volition over the whole domain of speculative thought, and the
fact that they have either avoided the severities of political
economy or have added nothing of value to it, is their own volun-
tary tribute to the wisdom of the division of duties under which
society has so long existed." To have both men and women involved
in politics would bring about "confusion, awkwardness and impos-
sibility of progress in domestic life," so that women instinctively reject it. Cites France to show what happens when women
meddle in politics.

1879

401   B. "An Open Question—Women's Suffrage on School Committees
       in Massachusetts." Nation 29 (23 October):272-73.
           Insists that women have a permanent natural disqualifica-
       tion for that amount of public life which voting implies. Points
       out that women are the real enemy to the cause of woman suf-
       frage—they do not want the vote.

402   GODKIN, E.L. "The Last Report of the Woman Suffragists."
       Nation 29 (30 October):286-88.
           Declares that the woman suffrage issue has lost ground in
       the past ten years. Is still waiting for the suffragists to show
       that they have made some progress in enlisting the support of
       women themselves. Finds no increased discussion of political
       issues by women. Alleges that the agitators do not speak for the
       great body of women, most of whom are either indifferent or
       hostile to woman suffrage.

403   S., E.L. "Suffrage and the Higher Education for Women."
       Nation 29 (27 November):364-65.
           Letter from a former suffragist who has been alienated by
       their "intense radicalism and fervid enthusiasm." Agrees with
       antisuffragists that women lack breadth of mind and steadfastness
       of character and urges that daughters be given mental discipline
       and breadth of outlook to combat their "want of reasoning capa-
       bility, impetuousity in forming judgments, and 'irresolute
       pertinacity.'"

1880

404   DOLE, E[DMUND] P. "Legal Rights of Married Women in New
       Hampshire." Granite State Monthly 3 (April):264-68.

Supports personal and property rights for women but concludes with a demurrer against political duties and responsibilities, which he characterizes as not a question of justice, like
property rights, but one of "mere expediency, and of very doubt-
ful expediency, indeed, until such objections as those urged by
Mr. Parkman [see 163] . . . can be fairly and reasonably answered."

1881

405   "The Prejudice against Woman Suffrage." American 1
        (29 January):243-44.
        Editorializes that woman's sphere consists of the care of
persons. To men belongs the care of principles, including politics. "The great mass of mankind feel instinctively that there
is something incongruous in the association of the sex with the
exercise of political duties, and therefore they have never been
able to take the matter seriously. They have regarded it as a
bad joke, and have soon ceased to feel even a languid interest in
it."

1882

406   [WATSON, ELLEN H.]. Pros and Cons of Woman Suffrage: Review
        of a Legislative Report: By One of the Sex. Boston: Clarke
        & Carruth, 32 pp.
        Objects to the suggestion in the report (which seems to be
from Rhode Island, 1874) that voting women would be subject to
the draft. Doubts whether allowing only women with property to
vote would have much effect on elections. Thinks married women,
especially mothers, would be much too busy to vote. Prefers
keeping the sexes and their duties separate.

1883

407   [WATSON, ELLEN H.]. Rights of Men and Women, Natural, Civil,
        Political, with Replies to Popular Speakers and Writers.
        Boston: Cupples, Upham, 62 pp.
        Asserts that women have a natural instinct against public
speaking. Prefers "the calm earnestness of sober thought and
reflection" to "the excitement and impulsiveness of a public
gathering." "Natural" rights indicate that interior work belongs
to women, exterior work to men. Women do not need the ballot to
get what they need. If women desire the ballot, it is because
they become "perverted." "We maintain that the native, genuine
growth of the feminine sex is not for the ballot; that any
appearance of this kind has been induced upon it by outward
influences, and is only of partial development." That is why
most women are indifferent on the subject.

408   GODKIN, E.L. "Female Suffrage." Nation 36 (8 March):204-5.
            Reports that woman suffrage has just been defeated in the
       Massachusetts legislature. Says the most serious obstacle that
       suffragists have to face is "the indifference or hostility of the
       great body of the women, including, too, the most earnest, thought-
       ful, and conscientious."

409   CORT, Rev. CYRUS. "Woman Suffrage." Reformed Quarterly 30
            (July):343-64.
            Raises the specter of foreign born, factory hands, and
       southern Negroes voting--better to limit suffrage than extend it.
       Says woman is disqualified for public or political life by phys-
       ical unfitness. Men should vote because they defend the common-
       wealth. Alleges that suffragists are hostile to Christian ideals
       of marriage and look upon maternity as a calamity rather than a
       blessing. Cites S.B. Anthony as supporting easy divorce. The
       woman's movement demoralizes women, causing them "to shirk the
       obligations of wifehood and the duties of maternity." Agrees
       with and quotes Bushnell, Goldwin Smith, and Mrs. Admiral
       Dahlgren. Points to the Beecher-Tilton scandal as an example of
       suffrage supporters; also refers to "the Woodhull." All are
       "foul birds."

                                   1884

410   LEONARD, Mrs. CLARA T. Woman Suffrage, a Letter. Boston:
            Massachusetts Association Opposed to the Further Extension of
            Suffrage to Women, 4 pp.
            Invokes the standard arguments to oppose woman suffrage:
       it is not an inherent right; women cannot enforce their ballot
       with physical force; women are represented by men; ignorant and
       irresponsible foreign women will vote; the lives of men and women
       are essentially different. Women have more power without the
       ballot. If women enter the political arena, it would be "repul-
       sive to a large portion of the sex, and would tend to make women
       unfeminine and combative, which would be a detriment to society."
       This letter was read by a man before the Legislative Committee on
       Woman Suffrage. Reprinted in 556.

411   P., J.W. A Remonstrant View of Woman Suffrage. Cambridge,
            Mass.: J. Wilson, 43 pp.
            Although the subject is overworked, one must speak out when
       the true cause of woman is endangered. Believes that women will
       lose power with the vote and that "the collective vote of the sex
       must be a great injury to the country in general, and the sex in
       particular." Alleges that woman suffrage would impair the effi-
       ciency of the government. Maintains that "the great argument
       against suffrage is the comparative unfitness of women for gen-
       eral politics, arising from the character of their minds, their
       natural tastes, and their present if not future occupations and
       training." Can justify unequal pay for equal work because men

have greater muscular strength, larger brains, and better training and health, and so are worth more.

412   GOODWIN, H.M. "Women's Suffrage." New Englander 43
         (March):193-212.
              Warns that woman suffrage signifies "a radical and revolu-
       tionary change in our whole social system." Alleges it would
       hurt the family by creating discord and rivalries between
       spouses. Finds it "a rebellion against the divinely ordained
       position and duties of woman." Calls the leaders of the movement
       "strong-minded and masculine women" and says "the very names of
       some of these leaders give on an inward shudder when thought of
       in the relation of wife." Denies Mill's claim that woman is in
       subjection. Says woman suffrage is advocated only by those "few
       whose instincts have been repressed and conquered by their will."
       Warns that it would make women repulsive by giving them masculine
       traits and abilities.

413   CAMPO-GRANDE, Viscount de. "Woman: Her Moral and Political
         Influence." Education 4 (July):633-49.
              Says politics is not a suitable field for women. Women's
       best action is influence. Translated from the Spanish.

414   BLOODGOOD, E.A. "A Word from a Woman Against Female
         Suffrage." Lippincott's 34 (August):169-73.
              Calls woman suffrage "one of the maddest pieces of polit-
       ical mischief ever attempted in this long-suffering country." It
       would be adding to the votes of ignorant and dishonest men the
       votes of even more ignorant and dishonest women. Good women do
       not want to vote. Raises the specter of "Biddy at the wash-tub."
       Asserts that women cannot comprehend rules, are illogical and
       unjust. Women would not defend their vote or their country.
       Predicts that if women ever rule, we will see "a country ruled by
       impulse" with justice "decided by a headache or a fit of hyster-
       ics." Women in power would be those enjoying publicity, notori-
       ety, voting for the handsomest men, meeting opposition with
       childish stubbornness. Not an appealing picture.

                                  1885

415   [DEXTER, HENRY MARTYN, D.D.]. Common Sense as to Women
         Suffrage. Boston: W.L. Green, 33 pp.
              Argues that we already have too many incompetent voters
       imperiling the country. Woman's "intellectual peculiarities" do
       not fit her to exercise the calmness of research, completeness of
       investigation, or unprejudiced coolness of judgment that are
       necessary for "wise political action." Rather, she jumps to
       conclusions, is illogical, and is easily distracted. "Woman's
       nature is adjunctive and complemental, not self-complete, irrela-
       tive and independent. She was not divinely planned to do alone,

or to be alone, but to be a help-meet for man." Woman suffrage
is "an unnatural, and therefore unwholesome and really monstrous
thing." Gives many more standard objections. Says the movement
has already "broken up thousands of happy homes" through divorce.

416   LOWELL, JOHN. Address Delivered before the Committee on Woman
        Suffrage, in Boston, 9 March 1885. N.p.: Printed by the
        Remonstrants, 4 pp.
            Traditional arguments. Denies that paying taxes should
        entitle women to vote. Reprinted in 556.

417   TAPPAN, WILLIAM H. Minority Report of the Committee on Woman
        Suffrage, in Opposition to the Bill Reported to the Massa-
        chusetts Legislature of 1885. Boston, 4 pp.
            Says the vast majority of women in Massachusetts have
        enough to do without having the vote thrust upon them. Woman
        suffrage would mar family happiness and not improve women's
        influence. Reprinted in 556.

1886

418   DODGE, MARY ABIGAIL [Gail Hamilton]. Letter from Gail
        Hamilton. N.p., 2 pp.
            Supports better education for women but claims exemption
        from political duty and responsibility for them. "I regret to
        see women engaged in the movement, because it indicates a failure
        to discern the natural place of woman in the order of creation--
        the place of eternal superiority and supremacy." Reprinted in
        533.

419   RAMEE, MARIE LOUISE De La [Ouida]. "Female Suffrage." North
        American 143 (September):290-306.
            Believes that were women to vote, it would bring into
        politics "inferior intelligence and hysterical action." Women
        are also mentally and morally inferior to men--they are neither
        tolerant nor calm in judgment; they are also subjective, "uncon-
        sciously unscrupulous," and able to be bribed. Women would
        intensify the present despotisms and weaknesses of political
        life" and lose their own charm. "The woman is the enemy of
        freedom. Give her power and she is at once despotic. . . ."
        Alleges that even in the best women there is "a sleeping poten-
        tiality for crime, a curious possibility of fiendish evil." She
        could be "a worse curse to the world than any man has ever been."

1887

420   CROCKER, GEORGE G. Letter to the Committee on Woman Suffrage.
        Boston: Rand Avery, 7 pp.

Believes that woman suffrage cannot do much good but may do immense harm by promoting discord in the family and taking women away from their home and child-rearing duties. Warns that "the excitement and nervous strain of an active participation in public affairs may prove injurious to women's physical and mental condition." Reprinted in 556.

421   FAY, CLEMENT K. Municipal Woman Suffrage: An Argument for Remonstrants. Brookline, Mass.: Chronicle Press, 22 pp.
      Says municipal woman suffrage "would usher in a train of evils." The ignorant, the bad, and the abandoned would vote as well as the wise, the good, and the pure. Public sentiment is opposed to municipal woman suffrage. Says woman suffrage clings parasitically to the temperance movement, but whereas the latter protects our homes, the former invades them.

422   FOXCROFT, FRANK. Municipal Suffrage for Women--Why? Boston: Massachusetts Association Opposed to the Further Extension of Suffrage to Women, 2 pp. Date is estimated.
      Asserts that aside from declamations, tedious reiterations, and vague generalizations, no statement has been made as to what great benefit women would derive from municipal suffrage. Nor has anyone shown that the community would benefit or that women will vote more wisely and steadily than men. Reprinted in 556.

423   FOXCROFT, FRANK. Some Objections to Municipal Suffrage for Taxpaying Women. Boston: Massachusetts Association Opposed to the Further Extension of Suffrage to Women, 2 pp. Date is estimated.
      Asserts that those who seek the ballot for taxpaying women ask legislators "to ignore the fundamental distinctions of function, training, education, and aptitude which are inherent in sex, and to set up the purely arbitrary distinction of property." Objects to giving a double vote to men who have given their wives property. Says, finally, that voting on the basis of property ownership is not an American ideal. Reprinted in 556.

424   CLARK, E.P. "Woman Suffrage in Operation." Nation 44 (14 April):310.
      Using the results of the first voting of women in Kansas, examines the effects and finds no perceptible difference in the results in small villages but noticeable effects in large towns, where organized women sometimes decide an election. Finds "the spectacle of negro women who cannot read their ballots voting at the dictation of a woman politician" to be "certainly not full of promise." Considers "the most striking and serious feature of the experiment" to be "the precipitation of sexual controversies into municipal elections."

425   INGALLS, JOHN JAMES. "The Sixteenth Amendment." Forum 4 (September):1-13.

Argues that suffrage is a privilege bestowed upon those who can enforce its decrees. "Politics is the metaphysics of force." Raises the specter of immigrant hordes, anarchists, etc. Believes that women's virtues would do more harm in politics than their vices. Also argues that women do not want the ballot. Points out that "there is no legislation that can annul the ordinances of nature, or abrogate the statutes of the Almighty."

1888

426 COPE, EDWARD DRINKER. The Relation of the Sexes to Government. New York: DeVinne Press, 17 pp.
        Reprint of 428. Reprinted in 495 and 533.

427 INGALLS, ETHEL. "A Congress of Famous Women." Cosmopolitan 5 (May):217-24.
        Believes that the great obstacle to woman suffrage is the indifference of women. Women are not voting in Kansas. Insists that "the great mass of American women are content with their own condition, and prefer to remain queen of their own domain than to usurp the scepter of a foreign realm. History teaches us that no class of society asks for a change unless dissatisfied. As the majority of our mothers, wives, and daughters are content they are not asking for this change." Rest of article is a description of the dress and appearance of women delegates.

428 COPE, EDWARD D. "The Relation of the Sexes to Government." Popular Science Monthly 33 (October):721-30.
        Repeats the traditional notions about the sex: man is more rational, better at mechanical skills; woman breaks down more easily under strain, etc. Argues that since the functions of the sexes are different in nature, they should be different in society. The progress of society is marked by protecting woman from the struggle for existence. Says woman suffrage would change all this. Argues that woman is physically incapable of carrying into execution any law she may enact. "Immunity from service in executing the law would make most women irresponsible voters." Women would enter public life and use extreme and irresponsible language, as Mrs. Stanton and Mrs. Lathrop do now. Urges the sexes be kept in separate spheres. Reprinted in 426 and 533.

1890

429 BISSELL, EMILY PERKINS [Priscilla Leonard]. A Help or a Hindrance. New York: New York State Association Opposed to the Extension of Suffrage to Women, 8 pp. Date is estimated.
        Says ballot will not help working women. In fact, once women get the vote, men may stop passing special legislation for them. "A vote is a very poor and mechanical substitute for true

womanly influence." Calls political activity "a barren gain" and
says it "cheapens womanhood in a vain struggle for the wrong kind
of influence." Only foolish women ask for the ballot that they
may destroy with their own hands the protection and sanctity of
their womanhood and their homes. Reprinted in 556.

430   LORD, ARTHUR. Argument before the Legislative Committee on
      Woman Suffrage, in Behalf of the Remonstrants against Munici-
      pal Suffrage for Women. Boston: George H. Ellis, 26 pp.
         Disputes the three arguments in favor of woman suffrage:
      (1) argument of necessity--laws already protect and favor women;
      (2) suffrage is a right--it is not; (3) the argument of expedi-
      ency--actually woman suffrage would weaken women's moral influence.

431   WHITNEY, ADELINE D.T. The Law of Woman Life, from the
      Remonstrants Against Woman Suffrage in Massachusetts. Boston,
      20 pp.
         Woman suffrage is useless unless woman has done her work in
      the home. Thinks women cannot do both. "Woman always deserts
      herself when she puts her life and motive and influence in mere
      outsides." Women cannot be spared from the household to go to
      the polls. "The law of woman life is central, interior, and from
      the heart of things."

432   SMITH, GOLDWIN. "Woman's Place in the State." Forum 8
      (January):515-30.
         Wants to restrict suffrage to men because laws must be
      backed by force: "muscle is the coarse foundation on which the
      most intellectual and august fabric of legislation rests." Warns
      that women would produce "arbitrary and sentimental legislation"
      and no doubt pass prohibition. Then legislation against the use
      of tobacco would follow. Women thrown into the political fray
      would no longer be angels and would be tempted to take bribes and
      worse.

433   CLARK, CHARLES WORCESTER. "Woman Suffrage, Pro and Con."
      Atlantic 65 (March):310-20.
         Denies that the right to vote is a natural right or that
      the individual is the unit of society. Woman does her work for
      the state in rearing future citizens. Behind the ballot is
      coercion. Believes that the very female qualities which do good
      in molding character would do ill in public action. Women are
      ruled by the heart, a trait that would be mischievous in public
      activities. Woman suffrage would overburden women.

434   COOKE, ROSE TERRY. "Should Women Vote?" Home-maker 3
      (March):471-74.
         Believes women should not vote because of physical inabil-
      ity and "because they are too sympathetic by nature, too little
      discriminating to keep their politics and their social relations

apart." Predicts that if women become active politicians, "society will degenerate into a squabble, and good-breeding be a
lost art." Women are more easily influenced and less resistant
and independent, and would be prey to all sorts of political
dishonesty and chicanery. Argues that it is only a few women of
strong character and masculine mind who wish to vote. Quotes
Cardinal Gibbons.

435   SANGSTER, MARGARET E. "Should Women Vote?" Home-maker 4
      (May):120-22.
          Finds women's status changing gradually. Better to trust
      in the chivalry and loyalty of men than to make women and men
      opponents. Women are already overburdened. Women are not
      trained to vote or suited to hold public office. Political
      activity by women would cause men to cease to be deferent, would
      introduce hostility into the home. The weak, wicked, ill-
      educated, and uneducated women of the cities would outvote bet-
      ter women. Is willing to trust men to take care of women, for
      mothers rule the world.

436   FROTHINGHAM, O.B. "The Real Case of the 'Remonstrants'
      against Woman Suffrage." Arena 2 (July):175-81.
          "It is because womanhood stands so high, not because it
      lies so low, that its mingling with political enginery is de-
      plored." Feeling is strong in women, and emotion--"virtuous
      women cannot be aware of the dangers they will have to encounter
      if they enter the political arena." Women should remain "moral
      inspirers."

                                   1891

437   WOMEN REMONSTRANTS OF THE STATE OF ILLINOIS. To the Honorable
      the Senate and House of Representatives of the State of
      Illinois, Greeting. Chicago, 4 pp.
          Say they have no grievances which their husbands, fathers,
      etc., do not address. Criticize the tactics of women's rights
      supporters, who "have formed themselves into a sect, and have
      zealously propagated their ideas, which we believe to be false
      and unnatural." Deny that the feminists speak for them and
      resent their belittling women's home interests and trying to woo
      young women out of the home. "They behave in such a manner as to
      bring reproach upon the ancient good repute of womanhood." Feel
      they must now come forward to protest these misrepresentations.
      Urge the lawmakers to continue their good work and not to lay
      further burdens on women.

438   COOKE, ROSE TERRY. "A Symposium: Woman's Suffrage."
      Chautauquan 13 (April):74-76.
          Woman is physically unfit to vote; she is subject to ner-
      vous fluctuations that affect her reason and judgment. "Under

some conditions of a woman's physical nature she is incapable of seeing correctly or judging impartially the character or conduct of others." She acts hysterically, unreasonably, and impulsively, and then later repents. "But neither regret nor repentance could recall a vote once cast." Second, women are mentally incapable of grappling with contemporary issues. Holds up the specter of ignorant masses being told how to vote by their priests. Finally, woman suffrage would usurp the rights of men. "The sexes are reciprochal, not identical, a truth the eager shriekers for woman's rights persistently ignore."

439   HENDERSON, JOSEPHINE. "A Symposium: Woman's Suffrage."
        Chautauquan 13 (April):76-77.
        Says the conscientious, thoughtful women hesitate to ask for the vote because it would be another responsibility, and they already have enough burdens. "Woman has only so much strength, nerve, and brain; just so much of these as she gives to public affairs, just so much she takes from her own life and the lives of those dependent upon her. Why give up a positive good for an uncertain one?" Included in this symposium are prosuffrage articles by Lucy Stone and Frances Willard.

440   LINTON, E. LYNN. "The Wild Women: As Politicians." Eclectic
        Magazine 117 (September):297-303.
        Describes wild women as unnatural, distasteful, unfeminine, never lovely. Calls the demand for political activity by women a "pernicious craze." But the ultimate end of women is maternity: "the cradle lies across the door of the polling-booth and bars the way to the Senate." Foresees woman suffrage opening a floodgate of the uneducated, unrestrained, irrational, and emotional. The higher the society, the more distinct the two spheres. Calls the demand for political rights "woman's confession of sexual enmity" and the most anti-Christian thing imaginable. The one unanswerable objection to women's political activity is her inability to serve in the military. Reminds readers of political women in history--they started wars. Reprinted from Nineteenth Century (London) 30 (July):79-88.

1892

441   ADAMS, OSCAR FAY. The Presumption of Sex, and Other Papers.
        Boston: Lee & Shepard, 149 pp.
        Says that women who want the ballot presume that they will be able to set everything to rights with the vote; disagrees. Objects to "sex piety"--the assumption that anything done by a woman is good. Alleges that women are "the mannerless sex" in a chapter by that title, and in another that women are "the ruthless sex."

1893

442   PARKMAN, FRANCIS. <u>An</u> <u>Open</u> <u>Letter</u> <u>to</u> <u>a</u> <u>Temperance</u> Friend.
       N.p., 1 p. Date is estimated.
          Opposes license suffrage for women. Says it is just an
       entering wedge to get universal woman suffrage. All women are
       not reformers. More are part of the "rude masses" who "will
       reinforce that ignorant male vote which already puts our institu-
       tions to so perilous a strain." Reprinted in 556.

443   SMITH, GOLDWIN. <u>Essays</u> <u>on</u> <u>Questions</u> <u>of</u> <u>the</u> <u>Day,</u> <u>Political</u> <u>and</u>
       <u>Social</u>. New York: Macmillan & Co., 360 pp.
          In a chapter on suffrage, insists that men retain the right
       of suffrage because man alone can uphold government and enforce
       the law. If women passed laws, they would have no force behind
       them. Sees looming behind woman suffrage prohibition, outlawing
       of tobacco, and extension of capital punishment to sex offenses.
       Women would get men into wars but not share responsibility.
       Woman suffrage equals "national emasculation." Laws are already
       more favorable to women than to men. Women can enter trades and
       professions. Connects woman suffrage and easy divorce. Women
       have more political power without the vote. If thrown into
       political strife, women, being weak, will lose self-control, not
       elevate politics. Opposes coeducation.

444   MAYNARD, CORA. "The Woman's Part." <u>Arena</u> 7 (March):476-86.
          Woman's special power and mission is love. Fears that "the
       woman who is bending every energy to obtain the suffrage of her
       sex" may, in the fray, be robbed of "her womanhood's gentleness
       and sweetness, grace and charm." Her mission is to uplift man to
       the level of her purer nature--"to love, to redeem, to save!"

445   WILLIAMS, Rev. JOHN MILTON. "'Woman Suffrage.'" <u>Bibliotheca</u>
       <u>Sacra</u> 50 (April):331-43.
          Believes woman suffrage will damage both the family and the
       state but not remedy woman's ills. Finds the woman suffrage
       movement not "creditable to woman's good sense." It is more like
       a revenge than a reform, creating unrest and dissatisfaction
       among women and causing divorce to increase alarmingly by intro-
       ducing strife into the home. "Woman is not improved by any
       effort to make herself a man." Worst of all, it will increase
       the political strength of the Roman Catholic Church. Thinks it
       unwise "to triple the political strength of a politico-religious
       hierarchy which is so successfully intriguing for power and
       place, waiting and working for the hour when the will of a for-
       eign potentate shall be supreme in the New World."

446   WILLIAMS, Rev. JOHN MILTON. "'Woman Suffrage.'" <u>Literary</u>
       <u>Digest</u> 6 (29 April):2-3.
          Condensation and reprint of 445.

447   LIEB, General HERMANN. "Mothers, Not Politicians, Wanted."
      Open Court 7 (28 September):3816-18.
            Says Susan B. Anthony and the other woman's rights sup-
      porters are "bright and earnest, . . . undoubtedly, sincere,
      conscientious women; but they are all unbalanced, the effect of
      mental indigestion, more or less." Wants suffrage restricted to
      men because women have "natural disabilities" and other duties
      imposed upon them. Predicts that woman suffrage will damage
      offspring of unnaturally excited women. Most women "instinc-
      tively shrink from the very thought of politics; the finer sensi-
      bilities of her nature revolt at such promiscuous associates."
      Thinks "it would be cruel to tear womanhood from her aesthetic
      pedestal" and allow her to be jostled about at polling places.

                                  1894

448   ABBOTT, Mrs. LYMAN. Mrs. Lyman Abbott on Woman Suffrage:
      Address before the Anti-Woman Suffrage Society of Albany, New
      York. Albany, 6 pp. Date is estimated.
            Holds up the specter of the South after the Civil War to
      show the disastrous consequences of unrestricted male suffrage.
      Predicts that "if suffrage is imposed upon women, the vicious in
      our great cities, the ignorant, of whom the number in the black
      race and among the so-called poor whites in the South cannot be
      here reckoned, would be used by unscrupulous partisans for their
      selfish ends." Then moral and intelligent women would have to
      lay aside pressing tasks and enter into the political fray.
      Women can do their duty better without the ballot. The great
      mistake of thrusting women into male employments has already been
      made; suffrage would be worse. Urges opponents of suffrage to
      remain calm, vigorous, dignified, assured.

449   CAIA [pseud.]; W., M.L.; and ROBBINS, MARY C. Woman Suffrage,
      by Three Massachusetts Women. N.p., 58 pp. Date is
      estimated.
            According to Caia, woman suffrage would do more harm than
      good. Men and women are not meant to be antagonists. "The best
      interests of society are bound up in their unity, and this unity
      is best promoted by a difference of position which excludes
      direct competition." According to M.L.W., women are neither
      intellectually, morally, nor physically fitted to vote. "The
      effect on the home and home life can only be disastrous if women
      are to enter into political life." Mary C. Robbins says women
      are more valuable and influential to the state without the vote.
      Reprinted in 495; M.L.W. only reprinted in 533.

450   COMMITTEE ON PROTEST. The Right to Vote or Hold Office Is Not
      a Test of Citizenship. Brooklyn, N.Y.: Brooklyn Auxiliary of
      the New York State Association Opposed to the Extension of
      Suffrage to Women, 2 pp.

This two-page pamphlet was arranged by a committee of
Brooklyn lawyers at the request of the Protest Committee. It
lists certain rights and privileges that women have but that are
denied to men under New York State law, and also immunities
enjoyed by women but not shared with men, all in an attempt to
persuade women to sign a protest against eliminating the word
"male" from the New York State constitution. Women are better
off without the ballot.

451   Committee on Protest against Woman Suffrage. Brooklyn, N.Y.:
       Committee on Protest against Woman Suffrage, 6 pp.
           A protest arising out of the Constitutional Convention to
be held in Albany in May 1894. Believes that "woman suffrage
would be against the best interests of the state, its women and
the home." Characterizes suffrage as a burdensome duty. The
household, not the individual, is the unit of the state. "The
duties and life of men and women are divinely ordered to be
different in the State, as in the home." Signed by twenty
Brooklyn women supposedly active in public affairs.

452   CUYLER, Rev. THEODORE L. Shall Women Be Burdened with the
       Ballot? Brooklyn, N.Y.: Brooklyn Auxiliary of the New York
       State Association Opposed to the Extension of Suffrage to
       Women, 4 pp. Date is estimated.
           Says women already have enough to do without voting.
Points out that when they were entrusted with civil power in
the past, they did not do very well. Cites as examples queens
Margaret, Mary, and Elizabeth—men did everything good under
Queen Elizabeth. Bad women would vote; good women would not.
Women are physically disabled from voting.

453   FROTHINGHAM, O.B., et al. Woman Suffrage, Unnatural and Inex-
       pedient. Boston, 28 pp.
           Most of these essays were originally collected at the time
of hearings on woman suffrage in Massachusetts early in 1886.
Frothingham advances the government-equals-force argument. Says
the movement would be cruel to women in lifting their exemptions
and privileges. Prentiss Cummings believes only "some grave
exigency, or a demand from women as a whole of the right to vote,
would warrant the risk attendant upon such an extension of the
franchise." John Boyle O'Reilly writes that "it would be no more
deplorable to see an angel harnessed to a machine than to see a
woman voting politically, giving up her divine intuition for a
vulgar material compromise." Richard H. Dana says evil and
corruption result from woman's rule.

454   GILDER, JEANNETTE L. Why I Am Opposed to Woman Suffrage.
       Boston: Massachusetts Association Opposed to the Further
       Extension of Suffrage to Women, 4 pp.
            Reprinted from 477. Reprinted in 556.

455   HALE, MATTHEW. <u>Why Women Should Not Vote</u>. Albany: Anti-
       Woman Suffrage Association of Albany, 4 pp. Date is
       estimated.
            Address at a mass meeting called by the Anti-Woman Suffrage
       Asssociation of Albany, 11 May 1894. Says women have never been
       discriminated against in New York; all disabilities have been
       removed. Women have not needed the ballot to accomplish great
       results, so why should they want to expose themselves to "the
       foul language, disgraceful contests and bloody noses" of poli-
       tics? Women are represented by father, husband, son, etc. We
       should not introduce disreputable women, whose votes will be for
       sale, into politics. Charges proponents of woman suffrage with
       showing "great lack of self-restraint, and an unfortunate ten-
       dency to exaggeration" in their speeches. They often show them-
       selves ignorant of the law.

456   HEWITT, Honorable ABRAM STEVENS. <u>Statement in Regard to the
       Suffrage</u>. New York: New York State Association Opposed to
       the Extension of Suffrage to Women, 3 pp.
            States that men and women are different. She enjoys cer-
       tain privileges and immunities because of her maternal function.
       Woman would lose her capacity to elevate the moral tone of indi-
       viduals if she got the vote. Woman suffrage would add discord
       and injustice to the family. Women have no grievances that
       cannot be addressed through already existing agencies. Woman
       suffrage would unsex men and women by eliminating male courtesy
       toward women. Woman suffrage entails too much risk and offers
       too little improvement. Advises women to remain independent of
       the suffrage. Reprinted in 533.

457   JAMISON, HELOISE. <u>The Wrong of Suffrage</u>. N.p., 4 pp. Date
       is estimated.
            Argues that the ballot must have behind it force: "to be a
       citizen is to be a possible soldier." But would women fight?
       Serve on juries? Do police duty? Women now have advantages.
       "Let us remember and prize the fact that we have the right not to
       vote." Reprinted from <u>American Woman's Journal</u> of May 1894,
       which I have not seen.

458   JOHNSON, ROSSITER. <u>The Blank-Cartridge Ballot</u>. New York:
       New York State Association Opposed to Woman Suffrage, 8 pp.
            Argues that "woman suffrage would be a serious mistake. A
       ballot put into the box by a woman would be simply a blank
       cartridge." Men and women both pay property tax but only men pay
       what he calls "service tax"--jury service, police service, mili-
       tary service. "Representation goes with this kind of taxation,
       and not with the other." Women should get what they want through
       influence and persuasion. Reprinted in 495 and 533.

459   MILLER, JAMES. <u>Is God Supreme? Or Are Man, Woman, and the
       Devil Supreme? A Letter Addressed to Rev. W.H.H. Murray on</u>

the Subject of His Lecture on Woman Suffrage. N.p., 4 pp.
Date is estimated.
    Insists that man should not try to make laws to help God;
that is caused by promptings of the devil. Pleads, "Oh, save
your wife from casting a ballot, for that is a declaration that
she is higher than God himself."

460   New York State Association Opposed to Woman Suffrage.
       Brooklyn, N.Y.: Brooklyn Auxiliary of the New York State
       Association Opposed to the Extension of Suffrage to Women,
       5 pp.
           Urges women who do not want to vote to bestir themselves,
       because woman suffragists are pushing vigorously to get support.
       Argues that women already have enough duties and would have to
       put some aside to vote. The division of labor between the sexes
       "has its reason in the eternal laws of God."

461   PRUYN, Mrs. J.V.L. Resolution to Constitutional Convention of
       State of New York. Albany: Anti-Suffrage Association, 4 pp.
       Date is estimated.
           Remonstrates against the imposition of political duties
       upon women. Woman has already been emancipated by male voters.
       She does not need the ballot, which would take her away from her
       home duties.

462   ROOT, Hon. ELIHU. Address Delivered before the New York State
       Constitutional Convention, 15 August 1894. New York: New
       York State Association Opposed to Woman Suffrage, 4 pp.
           Argues that woman suffrage would be a loss to all women and
       an injury to the state. Politics is modified war, and were women
       to enter into the political arena, they would become "hard,
       harsh, unlovable, repulsive." Women must be protected from such
       strife.

463   SCHURZ, CARL. Woman Suffrage. Boston: Massachusetts Asso-
       ciation Opposed to Extension of Woman Suffrage, 4 pp. Date is
       estimated.
           Reprinted from 483. Reprinted in 556.

464   SCOTT, FRANCIS M. Address to Committee on Suffrage, New York
       Constitutional Convention, 14 June 1894. N.p., 28 pp.
           Says he is speaking for a large body of women who wish to
       protest such a radical and revolutionary amendment as woman
       suffrage. Charges support for woman suffrage to "the unrestful
       spirit of Socialism abroad throughout the land." The government
       would have no strength if weak, noncombative women voted. Laws
       would have no force and could thus be disregarded. Reprinted in
       556.

465   SCOTT, Mrs. FRANCIS M., et al. To the Constitutional Conven-
       tion. New York, 9 pp.

Committee reports that until about three weeks before the Constitutional Convention opened, they had thought that "the opposition of silence would be sufficiently effective," but began to fear that silence be misinterpreted as acquiescence, so have determined to speak against woman suffrage. Woman suffrage "would undo much of the good which earnest effort and untiring philanthropy have achieved for their sex within the last twenty years." Fear that women will lose certain privileges and exemptions if the duty of suffrage is imposed upon them. Signed by eight members of the executive committee, Mrs. Scott, chairman.

466   Taxation without Representation. Boston: Massachusetts Association Opposed to the Extension of Suffrage to Women, 2 pp. Date is estimated.
        Denies that tax paying by women is the issue. Rather, sees "a body of women who are constantly seeking some change in the existing condition of things, and who use this 'voiceless' cry . . . as an incentive to other women." Alleges that tax-paying women do not care to vote; they let men vote for them. Also published by Albany Auxiliary Association of New York State Association Opposed to Woman Suffrage.

467   VAN RENSSELAER, Mrs. SCHUYLER. Should We Ask for the Suffrage? New York: J.J. O'Brien & Son, 57 pp.
        Says the country is passing through a time of disturbance and uncertainty and has enough risks to deal with without woman suffrage. Reminds readers of the "tens of thousands of illiterate and vicious women in New York City" and "the scores of thousands of ignorant negresses at the South." Denies that suffrage is a right. Does not want women and men to separate their interests from one another, women to care for women's interests, sex antagonism--all of which would result from woman suffrage. Women have special duties to perform for the state. Women are smaller and weaker than men and cannot engage in the same work as men. Reprinted in 495 and 533.

468   WALSH, Father. Protest Against Woman Suffrage. Albany, 4 pp.
        Opposes woman suffrage because it degrades women. Describes polling places as "pestilential spots, seething with perjury, bribery, unclean language and rowdyism." Does not want women mingling there. Alleges that when women become active in public affairs, "there is an insolent cruelty, and a moral debasement, that shames the worst male profligacy." Women must remain in the home, aloof from politics, a refuge and a restraint, with unbiased influence. Woman's delicate nervous system, tending to hysteria, gives her charm except in emergencies, when "it is liable to explode in violent paroxysms, when all the mental and physical faculties are perverted, and thrown into a condition of startling turbulence." That is why she must not vote. Reprinted in 556.

469   WELLS, Mrs. KATE GANNETT. An Argument Against Woman Suffrage
       Delivered before a Special Legislative Committee. Boston:
       Massachusetts Association Opposed to the Extension of Suffrage
       to Women, 4 pp. Date is estimated.
           Says antisuffrage women would prefer to stay at home doing
       their part through the home, but it is time to speak out against
       woman suffrage. Country already has enough to do to educate the
       ignorant foreign vote without also having to educate women.
       Reprinted in 556.

470   Woman Suffrage and Wages. Boston: Massachusetts Association
       Opposed to the Extension of Suffrage to Women, 3 pp. Date is
       estimated.
           Asserts that if suffrage helped wages, there would be no
       underpaid or unemployed men, and no more strikes. Working women
       cause men's wages to fall--by the law of supply and demand.
       Urges that we stay with the present system. "Let us oppose the
       effort to grasp an unknown and untried system that may prove to
       be an illusive phantom, or worse."

471   "An Anti-Suffrage Movement." Outlook 49 (28 April):738-39,
       760.
           Believes that the extension of suffrage to women would be a
       distinct disadvantage to both women and the community. Refers
       readers to the antisuffrage statement and movement (p. 760).

472   "A Woman's Protest Against Woman Suffrage." Outlook 49
       (28 April):760.
           Describes meetings and a protest written by the Brooklyn
       Association Opposed to the Extension of Suffrage to Women, lists
       signatures, and asks interested women to join.

473   "As Seen by Women." Outlook 49 (5 May):798-99.
           Letters for and against woman suffrage. Those opposed call
       for an organized antisuffrage movement; predict that the Roman
       Catholic church will gain control; say they are too busy to vote
       or have other means of improving society; etc.

474   "For and Against Woman Suffrage." Literary Digest 9
       (5 May):5-6.
           Describes the countermovement against amending the New York
       State constitution. Names signers and gives their reasons. Re-
       prints paragraphs from leading newspapers on the subject, some of
       them antisuffrage. Also excerpts an article by M. Ostrogorski in
       which he insists that expediency, not natural right, must be the
       ground on which suffragists base their claim.

475   GOODWIN, MAUD WILDER. "The Woman Suffrage Question: Part
       II--A Plea for Postponement." Outlook 49 (12 May):821-22.
           Opposes woman suffrage in New York because of "its enormous
       foreign population and the choking masses, unenlightened and un-

Americanized, in its great cities." Says woman suffrage is an
experiment but is irrevocable. The antisuffragists "deprecate
revolutionary legislation at a period when the State is struggling with so many difficulties and dangers." Positive side
offered by Mary Putnam Jacobi (pp. 820-21).

476   "The Woman-Suffrage Agitation: The Constitutional Conven-
       tion." Literary Digest 9 (12 May):5.
       Quotes newspapers in the East on the question before the
New York Constitutional Convention, namely, striking "male" from
the suffrage article. Some of them antisuffragist.

477   GILDER, JEANNETTE L. "Why I am Opposed to Woman's Suffrage."
       Harper's Bazar 27 (19 May):399.
       Believes in the mental but not the physical equality of the
sexes. Women can enter any trades or professions (does not like
the idea of a woman preacher and would not retain a woman lawyer). Thinks women have no place in politics—it is too public,
too wearing. Woman suffrage would "let loose the wheels of
purgatory." What will become of home life? Who will look after
the children? Women cannot cultivate home life and enter the
political arena. Woman suffrage is like a bomb that may go off
in woman's hands and produce great mischief. Reprinted in 454
and 556.

478   "Is the Suffrage a Duty?" Outlook 49 (19 May):860-61.
       Insists that the majority of women do not wish the suf-
frage. Argues that the role of government is "the exercise of
force for protection," which has never been woman's duty. The
whole idea of woman suffrage is founded on a false conception of
equality. Women and men have different work to do. "Man is the
natural protector; to him belongs the exercise of force; to him,
therefore, the making of law." To woman belongs the nurturing of
life. The fundamental and radical objection to woman suffrage is
that it will force woman to become a protector of the state,
something from which she naturally and instinctively shrinks.

479   "Is Suffrage Her Right?" Outlook 49 (26 May):908-9.
       Argues that the right to vote is an acquired right, con-
ferred by the community, not a natural right. Woman suffrage
will introduce dissension in the home, burden women, unburden
men, etc.

480   CROUNSE, LORENZO. "Woman Suffrage in Practice." North
       American 158 (June):741-44.
       Nebraska defeated an amendment for woman suffrage in 1882
(only men voted). Crounse, governor of the state, argues that
the votes of the men represented the sentiments of their women-
folk, who trust their men to represent them or who do not wish to
have the vote thrust upon them. Says educated and refined women
will be compelled to lay aside their modesty and oppose the
suffragists when these "bold," "bad," and "ambitious" women move

in the direction of "bad legislation and loose government."
States that women have plenty of rights in Nebraska.

481   HALE, MATTHEW. "The Useless Risk of the Ballot for Women."
       Forum 17 (June):406-12.
       Argues that women do not need the suffrage, for men have
taken care of their needs. Sees many dangers in woman suffrage:
false registration and repeating would be greatly increased by
adding women to suffrage; the prostitute vote could be bought,
and this element would be enough to turn the scale in a close
election; and there are physical and mental weaknesses in women
that make it inexpedient that the vote be imposed upon women.
Woman suffrage will "drag angels down."

482   "Woman Suffrage: Her Redemption Must Come from the People's
       Party." Literary Digest 9 (9 June):153-55.
       Summarizes pro- and antisuffrage articles in various peri-
odicals. Discussion on antisuffragist side is reprinted from
480 and 481.

483   [SCHURZ, CARL]. "Woman Suffrage." Harper's Weekly 38
       (16 June):554.
       Says supporters of woman suffrage have an advantage, being
accustomed to speaking in public. Opponents are accustomed to
home circle and do not like to be drawn into public. Reminds
supporters that unfit as well as fit women would be enfranchised.
Believes that there are more ignorant women than men so proportion of ignorant voters would increase. Says the country already
has enough problems without adding another. Reprinted in 463 and
556.

484   [GILDER, RICHARD WATSON]. "The New Woman-Suffrage Movement:
       Editorial." Century 26 (July):469-70.
       Says the real question is not the right to vote but rather
the right not to vote. "Shall men, at the request of some women,
load upon all women, equally with men and in addition to their
present burdens, the duties and obligations of civil government?"
Believes women should continue in their customary channels and
with their customary influence, not impelled into the political
sphere. Warns that "the compulsion of all womanhood into the
political arena . . . would be a revolution of greater magnitude
and effect than any the world has yet witnessed."

485   BUCKLEY, J.M. "The Wrongs and Perils of Woman Suffrage, with
       Postscript." Century 26 (August):613-23, 625-26.
       Argues that "the coherence and permanence of the family
depend upon the difference in the mental and emotional constitution of men and women." Woman suffrage "would unfit woman for
her position in the family" by imbuing her with "the governing
spirit." Cites and quotes notable reversals of opinion on woman
suffrage: Bushnell, Bright, Goldwin Smith, Spencer, Gladstone,
Bishop Vincent. Women are better than men only because they are

shielded and protected in the home. Raises the menace of the
foreign and black vote. Predicts "religious feuds" if women
vote. Reminds readers of feuds in two suffrage associations,
within WCTU, at World'a Fair. Woman suffrage will harm the moral
tone of most women and bring corruption to politics.

486   G[ILDER], H[ELENA] DE K. "A Letter on Woman Suffrage, from
       One Woman to Another." Critic 25 (4 August):63-65.
          Insists that women are not the equals of men so far as
       government is concerned. Accuses woman suffragists of being
       "dazzled by a word" and attaching too much value to the vote.
       Woman has a wide enough domain without the vote. Woman suffrage
       would strain family relations. Men have kept women free of all
       that is politically coarse and vulgar. Alleges as an artist that
       "to make little men of women is so ugly; to unsex them, so
       intensely inartistic." Women are now protected and secluded and
       can reward men with their praise, rather than descend from their
       elevated position to struggle with them. Warns that woman suf-
       frage is closely allied to socialism. Reprinted in 495, 533, and
       596.

487   BUCKLEY, JAMES M. "For and Against Woman Suffrage." Review
       of Reviews 10 (September):307-8.
          Reprint of 485.

488   KINNICUTT, ELEANORA. "The American Woman in Politics."
       Century 27 (December):302-4.
          Worries that "opening the sluice-gates to all women" in
       woman suffrage would double the "ignorant" vote. Urges a combi-
       nation of educated men and women in voting through women becoming
       aware of public affairs and then influencing men. "Disinterest-
       edness of motive is a mighty weapon and a strong shield." Argues
       against women serving on juries because it "would clog many a
       wheel in domestic machinery." Reprinted in 489.

489   KINNICUTT, ELEANORA. "Is the Vote Necessary for Woman's
       Influence?" Review of Reviews 10 (December):657.
          Reprint of 488.

                              1895

490   CRANNELL, Mrs. W. WINSLOW. Wyoming. Albany: Albany Anti-
       Suffrage Association, 4 pp.
          Alleges that woman suffrage in Wyoming is not a success and
       that Wyoming cannot be a precedent for New York State because of
       vastly different populations.

491   MC INTIRE, MARY A.J. Of No Benefit to Woman: She is a Far
       Greater Power without Suffrage. Boston, 8 pp. Date is
       estimated.

Denies that suffrage is a natural right or that women are taxed without representation. Woman suffrage will not help the community or women or working girls. It will introduce discord and disunion into the family. Women will lose the special privileges they now possess. Women have more influence without suffrage. Reprinted from Boston Sunday Herald. Reprinted in 556.

492   P., A.P. As to Suffrage in New York State. Albany, 3 pp. Date is estimated.
       Reprint of a letter to the editor of the Sun. Says women do not want to vote. Suffragists are using objectionable methods.

493   SCOTT, Mrs. FRANCIS. Extension of the Suffrage to Women: Address Delivered before the Judiciary Committee of the New York Senate, 10 April 1895. Boston: Massachusetts Man Suffrage Association, 3 pp.
       Insists that civilization rests on force of law, nor moral suasion. Speaks of the petition signed by 7,000 against woman suffrage. "These women do not want publicity, they do not want to be mixed up in politics, they just want to be women and do a woman's work, and they are the great majority of our sex, and they should be respected." The disinclination for motherhood seen in the younger generation is the result of "this unrestful desire for a life outside the home." Reprinted in 556.

494   SCOTT, FRANCIS M. Woman and the Law. New York, 7 pp.
       Asserts that, contra suffragists, the law of New York does not discriminate against women in any respect except that of voting. Further, women have many special privileges and immunities not enjoyed by men.

495   Why Women Do Not Want the Ballot. Vol. 1. New York: J.J. O'Brien & Son, 182 pp. Date is estimated.
       A collection of five previously printed pamphlets: 426, 449, 458, 467, 486.

496   The Woman-Suffrage Movement in the United States, a Study by a Lawyer. Boston: Arena Publishing Co., 153 pp.
       Alleges that the agitation against and discussion of woman's rights goes back to "that female outlaw, Mary Wollstonecraft, whose book on that subject was written not for the betterment of her sex, but to destroy a belief in God and His revealed Word." Says that woman suffrage is "simply a denial of the right of God to reign, and of the infallibility of his Word as his revealed will." Says woman suffrage would destroy civilization, degrade woman, unsex men, and lead to bickering, lawsuits, divorce suits, street fights, bloodshed, and murder. "It is impossible to grasp or to describe in all their horrible details the effects to be wrought in and upon society and its various relations . . . by this principle."

497   LEONARD, CLARA TEMPLE. "What Women Can Do Best." Century 27
       (January):475-76.
          The most vital objection to woman suffrage is "the awful
       danger of doubling the suffrage." Says women already have the
       power to do good by influence in public matters, but most do not
       and know nothing about politics. Women who do public service do
       not wish public notice, but "the women who see the danger of an
       enormous extension of the suffrage have been forced into a public-
       ity which they do not desire, because their own protest seems
       necessary to avert the threatened evil."

498   WATSON, ANNAH ROBINSON. "The Attitude of Southern Women on
       the Suffrage Question." Arena 11 (February):363-69.
          Offers racist reasons for opposition to woman suffrage.
       "There can in no sense be a just balance in this matter between
       the immigrant or illiterate classes of the North and the illit-
       erate negro class of the South. The ballot should be withheld
       from both but with greater reason from the latter." Is sure that
       the "better women" of the South, even that small minority in
       favor of woman suffrage, would forego the right if it must be
       used also by Negroes, whereas "the colored element, elated by the
       power put into their hands, would, beyond a question, make use of
       it."

499   PARKHURST, CHARLES H., D.D. "Women Without the Ballot."
       Ladies' Home Journal 12 (June):15.
          Compares suffragists to jealous children. Women now have
       many more rights and opportunities for improving society than
       they are using. No need for the ballot.

500   WINSTON, ELLA W. "Woman's Part in Political Sins." American
       Magazine of Civics 6 (June):575-83.
          Argues that the average woman has enough work to do without
       voting, if she would only do it. If there is wrong and wicked-
       ness in the world, it is the fault of mothers; they have the
       power of the home and so are the controlling factor in human
       affairs. Refutes Frances Willard.

501   WINSTON, ELLA W. "Women in Politics." Review of Reviews 12
       (July):84-85.
          Reprint of 500.

502   DOANE, Bishop WILLIAM CROSWELL. "Why Women Do Not Want the
       Ballot." North American 161 (September):257-67.
          Repeats all the clichés: suffrage is not a right; it will
       not help the working woman; equality does not mean identity of
       duties, rights, or privileges; etc. Quotes from Mrs. Schuyler
       Van Rensselaer's articles in the New York World (see 467).
       Insists that "the most serious, intelligent, cultivated women,
       with the largest money interest in the government, and the most
       quiet, thoughtful, earnest women, are conscientiously, and on
       clear conviction, opposed to woman suffrage." These women would

not vote but fallen women would. Warns that religion (Roman
Catholic) would be dragged into politics. Woman suffrage would
be a retrogression, not progression. Women should use their
powers of persuasion and stay out of politics.

503   WEIR, JAMES, Jr. "The Effect of Female Suffrage on Poster-
       ity." American Naturalist 29 (September):815-25.
          Believes that female suffrage will bring about a return to
matriarchy, which "would be distinctly, and emphatically, and
essentially retrograde in every particular." It is an atavistic
desire, "a reversion to the mental habitudes of our savage ances-
tors." Calls the pronounced advocates and chief promoters of
woman suffrage "viragints [from virago]--individuals who plainly
show that they are psychically abnormal." Blames the woman's
rights movement for increase in suicide and insanity among women.
Having lost all restraint, women are heading for serious psychic
and physical degeneration. "Equal rights" will lead to an "abyss
of immoral horrors."

504   "Extraordinary Protest against Woman-Suffrage." Literary
       Digest 11 (26 October):5.
          Reports on the formation of a Man-Suffrage Association in
Massachusetts to combat the woman suffrage movement. Lists sign-
ers and quotes from their manifesto. Also quotes press comments,
most of them critical of the Man-Suffrage Association.

505   MATHESON, Mrs. FLORENCE PERCY. "Woman's Natural Debarments
       from Political Service." American Magazine of Civics 7
       (December):591-98.
          Argues that the majority of women do not want to vote but
will not speak out of a sense of delicacy and modesty and also
because they fear ridicule by suffragists. Admits that among
suffragists are many noble women but also disappointed and
thwarted ones who crave excitement and notoriety. Expects that
women will not stop with the vote but will also want to hold
public office, which she opposes even more than suffrage. Raises
anatomical objections to woman suffrage, insisting that woman is
not fit to undertake serious mental or physical work during
menstruation, gestation, or child-rearing. But if she forgoes
marriage, she becomes a cranky, crochety, thorny old maid. Suffrage allowable only to women over fifty.

                                 1896

506   [CORBIN, CAROLINE F.]. The Home Versus Woman Suffrage.
       Boston, 12 pp.
          Says woman suffrage would destroy marriage and the home,
and bring in a reign of socialism and anarchy. Quotes from her
essays on Aveling, articles in Chicago papers, etc. Extracted
from appendix to A Woman's Philosophy of Love (see 188). Reprinted often in various forms--see Socialism vs. Legal Marriage
(625).

507   CRANNELL, Mrs. W. WINSLOW. Address before the Committee on
      Resolutions of the Republican National Convention at St.
      Louis, 16 June 1896. Albany: Anti-Suffrage Association of
      the Third Judicial District of the State of New York, 4 pp.
          Says she appears before them "with reluctance and trepida-
      tion," representing women who had to choose either to remain
      silent and seem implicated or to speak out against woman suf-
      frage. Women are already protected by laws. Woman suffrage
      would "increase the evils that already threaten to overcome the
      principles for which our fathers fought." These are hard times,
      with "an undercurrent of anarchy that roils the waters of our
      social and political life." Begs the legislators to keep their
      wives and daughters out of "the mire of political life." Re-
      printed in 556.

508   MASSACHUSETTS ASSOCIATION OPPOSED TO THE EXTENSION OF SUFFRAGE
      TO WOMEN. First Annual Report. Boston: Massachusetts Asso-
      ciation Opposed to the Extension of Suffrage to Women, 8 pp.
          Mary Guild, secretary, reports on activities, which have
      consisted mainly of parlor meetings to hear papers. The antisuf-
      fragists decline to take part in public discussion. They also
      distribute papers, including those from other associations op-
      posed to woman suffrage. Included is a treasurer's report and an
      address by the chairman of the Executive Committee, Margaret F.G.
      Whitney.

509   PARKMAN, FRANCIS. Some of the Reasons Against Woman Suffrage.
      Boston: Massachusetts Man Suffrage Association, 16 pp. Date
      is estimated.
          God and nature have made women weaker both mentally and
      physically. Woman suffrage would be a cruelty to women. It
      would also enormously increase evil because the female vote "is
      often more numerous, always more impulsive and less subject to
      reason, and almost devoid of responsibility." Female politicians
      would exhibit "artfulness, effrontery, insensibility, a pushing
      self-assertion, and a glib tongue." The best women let their
      husbands, fathers, etc., represent them. Most women are averse
      to woman suffrage. Women cannot fight, therefore should not
      vote. Finally, woman suffrage is a "most unnatural and pestilent
      revolution." Published from an earlier address by Parkman at the
      request of an association of women. Reprinted in 556.

510   SCOTT, Mrs. FRANCIS M. Annual Report, New York State Associa-
      tion Opposed to the Extension of Suffrage to Women. New York,
      11 pp.
          Lists the Standing Committee, Executive Committee, and
      others. Describes the forming of the association in April 1895
      and its recent activities. Insists that never again will such a
      small proportion of women in New York State (suffragists) assume
      to speak for all. Believes that "this Association is the voice
      of the majority of the intelligent and thinking women of this
      State, and as such is prepared to stand between the unwise,

socialistic and illogical demands of the Woman Suffragists, and
the unwise, hasty and inexpedient action of the Legislature."
Announces the availability of pamphlets.

511   WILEY, C.W., Esq. "Woman Suffrage--by a Bachelor." American
       Magazine of Civics 8 (April):376-84.
          Accuses suffragists of being intemperate and prejudiced, of
       denouncing and vilifying man. Says women enjoy equal rights and
       privileges with men except voting. Denies any legal oppression
       remains. Woman suffrage will result in little or no benefit to
       the country or to women. Counsels waiting to see how woman
       suffrage proves in Colorado, Utah, and Wyoming.

512   SCAIFE, WALTER B., Ph.D. "Civic Education and Woman's Rela-
       tion Thereto." Public Opinion 20 (2 April):429-30.
          It is partly women's fault that men are not better citi-
       zens. Instead of asking for suffrage, which would give bad as
       well as good women the vote, women should ostracize every man
       found lacking in the performance of his civic duties, thereby
       purifying public life.

513   MARSH, HARRIET A.; DENISON, DEMIES T.S.; and WHEELOCK, LUCY.
       "The Benefit to Women of Suffrage Rights: Various Opinions."
       American Magazine of Civics 8 (June):605-15.
          By the only antisuffragist contributors to a ten-page arti-
       cle. Harriet Marsh, principal of Hancock School in Detroit,
       claims that woman's finer nature would become blunted by poli-
       tics. Demies Denison, a member of the Patria Club in New York,
       finds women are discontent to be women. Says woman suffrage
       would reverse the order of nature and cause degeneracy in the
       home and society. Supports the scriptural prescription of
       woman's position. Lucy Wheelock feels strongly that "the tender,
       womanly qualities are not conserved when one must of necessity
       assume sometimes an aggressive attitude in the world." Women
       should become absorbed in work for children.

514   DOANE, Bishop WILLIAM CROSWELL. "Some Later Aspects of Woman
       Suffrage." North American 163 (November):537-48.
          Mocks Victoria Woodhull Martin and her support of woman
       suffrage: she proves the unfitness of women for political life.
       Contrasts the actions of Mrs. W. Winslow Crannell of Albany, who
       shows what kind of political power a true woman can exercise
       without voting. Quotes Mrs. Crannell at length and from an
       article on feminism by Pierre-Leroy Beaulieu in Revue des Deux
       Mondes. Insists that experience shows that woman is not better
       than man and that woman suffrage would not improve the moral
       atmosphere in the country.

1897

515   SCOTT, Mrs. FRANCIS M. Address Delivered before the Judi-
       ciary Committee of the State of New York, 24 March 1897. New
       York: J.J. O'Brien & Son, 7 pp.
            Insists that women cannot enforce laws; therefore, they
       have no part in making them. "Motherhood must interfere with the
       performance of public duty." Women already have enough to do--we
       should not hamper their lives and give them added obligations.
       Speaks for the New York State Association Opposed to the Exten-
       sion of Suffrage to Women.

516   DILKE, EMILIA F.S. "Woman Suffrage in England." North
       American 164 (February):151-59.
            Calls feminists foolish and pathetic, says they "are wont
       to embarrass those who value self-control, reticence, right judg-
       ment, and weighty speech." Describes herself as an early suffra-
       gist who came to feel that it were better to appeal reasonably to
       public opinion than to vote.

517   BISSELL, EMILY PERKINS [Pricilla Leonard]. "Woman Suffrage in
       Colorado." Outlook 55 (20 March):789-92.
            Finds patterns unchanged, life unimproved after three years
       of woman suffrage in Colorado.

518   ELLIOTT, ELLEN COIT. "Let Us Therewith Be Content." Popular
       Science Monthly 51 (July):341-48.
            Insists that home is woman's sphere, motherhood her highest
       calling. American women have the freedom to do anything they
       want. American men are neither tyrannical nor condescending to
       women. The majority of American women is content and instinc-
       tively draws back from the prospect of voting.

1898

519   FOXCROFT, FRANK. Objections to License Suffrage from a No-
       license Point of View: Address before Massachusetts Legisla-
       tive Committee. Boston: Massachusetts Association Opposed to
       Further Extension of Suffrage to Women, 2 pp.
            Says women would harm the no-license (temperance) cause
       because they could not enforce their vote. Opposes allowing
       women the vote on this issue. Reprinted in 556.

520   LEONARD, CLARA TEMPLE. "Women's Work for Women and Children."
       Century 33 (March):793-94.
            Describes the work of Massachusetts women without political
       power who established a woman's prison: "Legislation necessary
       to the improvement of public charitable methods can be influenced

by women without the ballot better than with it, as comes through
the efforts of non-partizans who have no personal ends to gain."

1899

521   Address to the Judiciary Committees of the Senate and Assembly
      of the State of New York, 22 February 1899. New York: New
      York State Association Opposed to the Extension of Suffrage to
      Women, 8 pp. Date is estimated.
            Prepared by a subcommittee consisting of Mrs. Rossiter
      Johnson and Mrs. Winfield Moody and read by Mrs. Arthur M. Dodge.
      Women do not need the property vote. "Nature, not man, has
      exempted woman from the fighting line where rests the ballot-
      box." Woman suffrage and women's progress are distinct and
      antagonistic. Reprinted, with slight adaptation, by Massa-
      chusetts Association Opposed to Extension of Suffrage to Women.
      Reprinted in 556.

522   DANA, STEPHEN WINCHESTER, D.D. Woman's Possibilities and
      Limitations: A Message to the Young Women of To-day. New
      York: Fleming H. Revell Co., 110 pp.
            Describes the distinctive characteristics of woman: emo-
      tional nature; intuitive faculty; love of admiration; convention-
      ality and conformity. Favors wider employments for women and
      good education but thinks suffrage unnecessary. Says its strong-
      est opponents are "women of intelligence and character, who do
      not wish to have this added responsibility thrust upon them."
      They feel they can work for their country in other ways, espe-
      cially by making good citizens. Believes that woman suffrage
      would weaken the family.

523   JOHNSON, HELEN KENDRICK. Woman's Progress versus Woman
      Suffrage. New York: New York State Association Opposed to
      Woman Suffrage, 4 pp.
            Argues that women have made progress without suffrage.
      Asserts that "the suffrage movement is to-day allied with co-
      education as against woman's higher education in colleges of her
      own; with 'isms' as against tried principles; with prohibition as
      against temperance; with Mormonism as against separation of
      church and state; with socialism as against representative gov-
      ernment; with radical labor movements as against the best organ-
      ized and unorganized efforts of wage-earning men and women; with
      'economic independence' and the co-operative household as against
      family life and the home." Woman suffrage is based on sex antag-
      onism, whereas sex harmony is the best route to woman's progress
      according to both science and Christianity. Reprinted in 533.

524   KNAPP, ADELINE. An Open Letter to Mrs. Carrie Chapman Catt.
      New York: New York State Association Opposed to the Extension
      of Suffrage to Women, 8 pp.

In a letter dated 10 November 1899, from Berkeley, California, the writer asserts that women are too busy to vote. There is "as true patriotism in the quiet conservation of the inner things of the home and of society which are permanently in women's hands, as the insistence upon rights so-called which are not yet successfully demonstrated to be human rights in the sense which is claimed for them."

525   BELL, ALDEN. "Shall the Ballot Be Given to Women?" Gunton's Magazine 17 (December):474-84.
Believes that it is not in the best interests of womanhood or of the state to impose the responsibility of voting upon women. It would unfit woman for her natural position in the family. Quotes male recanters like John Bright, Herbert Spencer, Horace Bushnell, Gladstone, Goldwin Smith, and Bishop John H. Vincent. Believes that "there are pathological and physiological reasons" for women to abstain from political work and voting. Warns that "women as voters would increase the bitterness of political life." Women would become demoralized and sullied, and chivalry would pass away.

1900

526   BISSELL, EMILY PERKINS. A Talk to Every Woman. Richmond: Virginia Association Opposed to Woman's Suffrage, 24 pp. Date is estimated.
Asserts that not one tenth of American women want to vote. Like her, they already have enough to do. The ballot would be a useless burden. It would not help the working girl or the woman property owner or the social service worker or the college graduate. Says that behind suffrage agitation is sex antagonism and sex disloyalty. "The suffrage ideal of womanhood is that of woman putting on masculinity, assuming men's tasks, and laying aside as cumbering femininity."

527   BISSELL, EMILY PERKINS [Priscilla Leonard]. Woman as a Municipal Factor. N.p., 12 pp.
Alleges that suffragists have the advantages of being on the positive side of the question and of premising that their argument is an axiom, not to be debated. But righteous and public-spirited women are already doing valuable work without the vote. Even without the vote, a righteous and public-spirited woman can combine her efforts with those of similarly minded men to combat the vote of a bad or indifferent man, but not both his and his wife's vote. A voteless woman represents purity and progress. "The positive, the progressive work of to-day in our large cities is done by women who are not asking for the ballot," she claims, while in the same breath mentioning Jane Addams in Chicago! Reprinted in 556.

528   Do We Want It in Massachusetts? Boston: Massachusetts Man
      Suffrage Association, 1 p. Date is estimated.
         Quotes a long paragraph by James T. Gardiner about elec-
      tions in Kansas in which women are described as just as fully
      involved in bribery, intimidation, and cajolery as men to show
      that Massachusetts men should vote against woman suffrage.

529   LEWIS, Mrs. HELEN ARION. Woman Suffrage a Menace to the
      Nation. Omaha: Nebraska Association Opposed to Woman Suf-
      frage, 6 pp. Date is estimated.
         Says she was prosuffrage for fifteen years until she had an
      actual experience with the vote in Utah and Colorado. Now is
      active in antisuffrage in Nebraska. Reports being filled with
      horror at the "degradation of womanhood . . . when she becomes
      embroiled in political intrigue." Says she "witnessed revolting
      and disgusting sights of debauchery of women at the polls, such
      as are impossible of adequate description." Good women do not
      vote or vote as their husbands direct. Has been shocked and
      ashamed by some of the tactics of the suffragists in gaining
      recruits. Argues that women should remain dependent, for depend-
      ency "nourish[es] the love and respect of man for woman."

530   MC KEEN, Mrs. M.E.L. Will the Ballot Help the Working Girl?
      N.p., 4 pp. Date is estimated.
         Repeats the traditional arguments on this topic.

531   MC VICKAR, Mrs. ESTELLE R. What Is an Anti-Suffragist? Mount
      Vernon, N.Y., 11 pp. Date is estimated.
         Read before the Mt. Vernon Auxiliary of Society Opposed to
      the Extension of Suffrage to Women. Says women have already made
      progress, although questions the wisdom of women taking men's
      jobs. Defines an antisuffragist as one who believes in mascu-
      line and feminine as created by God, who believes in different
      work for men and women, and who thinks woman's place is in the
      home. "We also believe that it would be equally as injudicious
      for her to quit her proper sphere of influence, and go down into
      the strife and turmoil of the world's political life, as it would
      be for the generals of a vast army to quit their posts of vantage
      in a great battle and plunge into the thick of the fight." If
      men are bad, it is women's fault.

532   Of What Benefit to Woman? Boston: Massachusetts Association
      Opposed to the Further Extension of Suffrage to Women, 7 pp.
      Date is estimated.
         Men vote because they have the force to back up laws and
      compel respect and observance. Denies that voting is a natural
      right, that if taxed women should vote, or that women would
      reform politics. Ballot would not help the working woman. Most
      women do not wish to vote. Women have enough to do, would lose
      privileges, would endanger home and children if they vote. Women
      have more influence without the ballot.

533   Why Women Do Not Want the Ballot. Vol. 1. Rev. ed. New
      York: J.J. O'Brien & Son, 169 pp. Date is estimated.
           A collection of fourteen pamphlets, fliers, letters, and
      newspaper articles. Many have been listed in this bibliography:
      418, 426, 449, 456, 458, 467, 486, 523, 700.

534   WILBUR, ALICE HEUSTIS. Woman Suffrage Not Wanted in Oregon.
      Portland: Irwin-Hodson Co., 7 pp.
           Outline of a talk given at a parlor meeting of the Oregon
      State Association Opposed to the Extension of Suffrage to Women
      on 10 March 1900. Opposes woman suffrage because "we fail to
      find sufficient force in the arguments for making this extension"
      and because "we believe that such a change would be inexpedient
      and to the disadvantage of the state and of woman herself." It
      is "the duty of every patriotic, home-loving, God-fearing woman
      of the State of Oregon" to oppose woman suffrage.

535   BAILEY, JOSEPH W., M.C. "Where Women Fail as Parliamen-
      tarians." Harper's Bazar 33 (24 February):154.
           Cites a multitude of reasons why women fail as parliamen-
      tarians: they have no legislative business important enough to
      force them to master parliamentary process; they lack the mental
      ability to comprehend parliamentary law; the feminine mind lacks
      the "perfect mental poise absolutely indispensable to success in
      governing a deliberative body"; and because parliamentary process
      is totally outside woman's sphere. Believes that woman suffrage
      would be a disaster, degrading womanhood and lowering the moral
      tone of the nation.

536   "Conditions of Suffrage." Outlook 64 (24 February):434-36.
           Believes that it is only "a small number of persistent and
      vigorous women" who demand suffrage. Most women know that they
      have more important services to perform for the community than
      voting. Further, most do not want to have to help enforce the
      laws. Liberty demands not that women have suffrage imposed upon
      them but rather that they be exempted from it.

537   "Concerning Woman's Suffrage." Outlook 64 (10 March):573-74,
      599.
           Believes that suffrage is a duty and a burden. Women
      should allow themselves to be protected by men, to enjoy men's
      gallantry. Woman suffrage is a reform against nature, quoting
      Bushnell. "It is not strange that, after many years of agita-
      tion, it makes no true progress." Hastens to add that woman is
      not inferior to man, just weaker, needing protection. Insists
      that woman suffrage "will not make headway in the best and most
      highly cultivated communities . . . because it is against the
      nature of both man and woman, it contravenes their native and
      righteous instincts and whatever so-called reform contravenes the
      divine order never permanently endures."

538   GREEN, ALICE STOPFORD. "Growing Bureaucracy and Parliamentary
      Decline." Living Age 225 (23 June):774-80.
          Argues against suffrage for women; too many people already
      vote. Reprinted from Nineteenth Century (London) 47 (May):
      839-46.

539   "Woman Suffrage in the West." Outlook 65 (23 June):430-31.
          Points out that woman suffrage has been defeated after a
      two-year trial in Washington because the people decided it was
      not in the best interest of the community. Oregon has also
      rejected woman suffrage, learning from the experience of its
      neighbor state.

                                1901

540   HERSEY, HELOISE EDWINA. To Girls: A Budget of Letters.
      Boston: Small, Maynard, 247 pp.
          Opposes woman suffrage for elitist reasons. Says it will
      allow women from the lowest ranks to vote, and they are too
      ignorant to vote wisely. Describes women as divisible into two
      classes, "the women who are too ignorant for the suffrage and the
      women who are too good to spend themselves on it." Women do not
      need suffrage to improve civic life.

541   SEDGWICK, Mrs. MARY K. "Some Scientific Aspects of the Woman
      Suffrage Question." Gunton's Magazine 20 (April):333-44.
          Believes that woman suffrage would retard human progress
      and confer new burdens on women. Education should emphasize the
      differences between the sexes, not obliterate them. Each sex has
      its work to do. The more advanced the race, the more pronounced
      are sex differences. The family, not the individual, is the
      social unit. Women are too emotional to vote.

542   FINCK, HENRY T. "Woman's Glorious Opportunities."
      Independent 53 (30 May):1238-42.
          Compares the suffragists' demands to "an infant's bawling
      for the moon." It is unwise to let women vote because none of
      them need it, most of them do not want it, and if they got it,
      more harm than good would result to themselves and others.
      Argues that it is in the domestic sphere that woman's most
      glorious opportunities lie. It is mothers who rule the world.
      Alleges that woman can practically rule the world without woman
      suffrage "by making proper use of her beauty, sympathy, winsome-
      ness, and of soft, refined blandishments--that is, by being what
      men want her to be, an enchantress and not a rival."

543   ABBOTT, LYMAN. "The Rights of Man: A Study in Twentieth
      Century Problems." Outlook 68 (8 June):349-55.
          Says there is no natural right of suffrage, so the real
      question is, is it necessary for the protection of her rights

that woman should vote? Should the suffrage be multiplied by
two? Asserts that "history shows us that the personal and property rights of women can safely be intrusted to the rest of the
community." The majority of women do not wish to vote--it would
be a burden thrust upon them. It is not part of woman's duty to
serve as protector of the state; the ballot is, after all, "nothing but a mutually protective society."

544   [ABBOTT, LYMAN]. "The Right of Suffrage." Outlook 68
       (27 July):711-12.
       Opposes universal suffrage--that is, extending suffrage not
only to women but also to Negroes, Indians, Filipinos--because
the men of the dominant race can alone determine the best conditions of suffrage to produce and conserve the best government.
The best conditions would be those which "men of intellectual and
moral character can comply with."

1902

545   SMALL, ALBION W. "Social Mission of College Women."
       Independent 54 (30 January):261-66.
       Opposes the extension of suffrage to women because it would
"further complicate our political machinery." Calls for college
women who need not work to be "the stewards of the mysteries of
appropriate human life." Reminds women that they are responsible
for the quality of life.

546   SCRUGGS, WILLIAM L. "Citizenship and Suffrage." Independent
       54 (24 July):1774-77.
       Declares that women can be and are citizens but that does
not imply suffrage. Wants suffrage restricted to "an impartial
standard of intelligence, virtue, and personal responsibility."
Implies that this excludes women.

1903

547   ABBOTT, LYMAN. Why Women Do Not Wish the Suffrage. Boston:
       Massachusetts Association Opposed to the Further Extension of
       Suffrage to Women, 8 pp. Date is estimated.
       Reprint of 552. Reprinted in 556.

548   SAUNDERS, CHARLES R. Taxpaying Suffrage. Boston:
       Massachusetts Association Opposed to the Further Extension of
       Suffrage to Women, 2 pp.
       Insists that the payment of taxes and the right to suffrage
are not connected. Woman suffrage is "inexpedient in the highest
degree." Reprinted in 556.

549   DRAPER, A.S. "Co-education in United States." Educational
       Review 25 (February):109-29.
              An address before the Century Club in Boston. Favors
       coeducation and equal education but opposes woman suffrage. Says
       that as the "natural protector," man is the natural voter. Just
       because men do not always vote wisely, it does not follow that
       women would do better--probably worse. But predicts that when
       the majority of women wish the vote, men will give it to them.
       "It is a matter of expediency."

550   "Twenty-Five Years of Woman's Suffrage." Catholic World 76
       (February):706-7.
              Editorial that argues that suffrage agitation is losing
       momentum. Women do not want the right to vote and indeed are
       protesting against it. Better to solidify the family. Warns
       that "the right of voting in the hand of woman is a wedge to pry
       asunder what God has joined together."

551   [ABBOTT, LYMAN]. "Woman Suffrage in New Hampshire." Outlook
       73 (21 February):418.
              Advises readers in New Hampshire to vote against woman
       suffrage on 10 March because (1) women in neighboring Massa-
       chusetts rejected suffrage, (2) women have other more important
       functions to fulfill, and (3) suffrage in this country is already
       too far extended.

552   ABBOTT, LYMAN. "Why Women Do Not Wish the Suffrage."
       Atlantic 92 (September):289-96.
              Speaks for the silent women who know that woman suffrage
       would be an undesirable revolution. The sexes are different not
       only physically and incidentally but also psychically and essen-
       tially, temperamentally, in every way. Their functions are dif-
       ferent, and so talk of equality is meaningless. Masculine women
       and feminine men are "the monstrosities of Nature." The basis of
       the family is the difference between the sexes. Government is
       involved in protection, which is man's function. Only he can
       compel obedience. Therefore, only he should vote. Woman may
       counsel but she shrinks from commanding if she is womanly. This
       is the negative reason why woman does not want to vote. The
       positive reason is that she has more important things to do.
       True women will not be forced or enticed from their allotted
       sphere "by their restless, well-meaning, but mistaken sisters."
       Reprinted in 547 and 556.

553   MC CRACKEN, ELIZABETH. "Woman's Suffrage in Colorado."
       Outlook 75 (28 November):737-44.
              Says that women active in Colorado politics have hurt
       themselves cruelly. Public life there is hysterical; women are
       intoxicated by political power. Women in the East use influence,
       which is less crude and less rasping than power. The ballot has
       made Colorado women less womanly, blunted their sense of taste,
       and weakened their personal dignity. It has also caused women to

perform acts of charity for selfish, political reasons. These
women, "by perverting the most tender of human feelings to a hard
and practicable political use, . . . have become less fitted to
guide the children growing to manhood and womanhood in their
State." Woman's ideals have been lowered, her delicacy of perception blunted, by this blow to her womanhood. Reprinted in
556.

554   SCRUGGS, W.L. "Citizenship and Suffrage." North American 177
       (December):837-46.
          Asserts that a person may be a citizen and not have the
       right to vote. Opposes universal suffrage, which is "but another
       name for licensed mobocracy."

                              1904

555   GUILD, Mrs. CHARLES E. Municipal Suffrage for Women. Boston,
       3 pp.
          Wants women left free to do their natural work, which has
       been "confirmed and sanctioned by Christian civilization."

556   Why Women Do Not Want the Ballot. Vol. 2. New York: J.J.
       O'Brien & Son, 224 pp. Date is estimated.
          A collection of sixty pamphlets, fliers, letters, and news-
       paper articles, many already noted in bibliography.

557   BISSELL, EMILY PERKINS [Priscilla Leonard]. "The Ladies'
       Battle." Current Literature 36 (April):386-88.
          It is woman rather than man who is keeping woman from the
       ballot-box. "It is a 'ladies' battle' that the suffragists are
       fighting. Suffrage does not appeal to the average woman, and so
       it hangs fire."

                              1905

558   CORBIN, CAROLINE F. Socialism and Christianity with Reference
       to the Woman Question. Chicago, 31 pp.
          Christianity is contrasted with socialism. Argues that
       woman suffrage is the cornerstone of socialism and would lead to
       the abolition of marriage and of protection of women; women would
       have to work and thereby be degraded. Accuses feminists of
       "pulling down the roof-tree to boil the kitchen pot."

559   FOXCROFT, FRANK. The Check to Woman Suffrage in the United
       States. Boston: Massachusetts Association Opposed to the
       Further Extension of Suffrage to Women, 8 pp. Date is
       estimated.
          Reports that the suffrage movement has come to a standstill
       because people have discovered that only a small minority of

American women want the suffrage. Women are organizing to oppose
woman suffrage. Gives great credit to the antisuffragists. Reprinted from Nineteenth Century and After (London) 56 (November
1904):833–41.

560   MC CRACKEN, ELIZABETH. The Women of America. New York:
       Macmillan, 397 pp.
         Argues that women suffragists in Colorado have hurt them-
selves in voting--have weakened their personal dignity, blunted
their sense of taste, and become less womanly. They have also
"pervert[ed] the most tender of human feelings to a hard and
practicable political use" and so "have become less fitted to guide
the children growing to manhood and womanhood in their State."

561   PETERS, MADISON C., D.D. Will the Coming Man Marry? and Other
       Studies on the Problems of Home and Marriage. Philadelphia:
       J.C. Winston, 192 pp.
         States that woman would lose dignity and refinement if she
voted. Woman suffrage "would not only violate the sacred laws of
her being, but add nothing to the high and holy mission which her
own nature unmistakably defines." Warns that "woman must fail
the moment she passes the boundary that God has indicated in her
being."

562   Why Women Do Not Want to Vote. Albany: Anti-Suffrage Asso-
       ciation of the Third Judicial District, 6 pp.
         Reprinted from New York Post, 8 March 1905. Author praises
Mrs. W. Winslow Crannell's demeanor and tone, contrasting it
favorably with that of the "new woman." Her speech is quoted at
length "because it is unusual, and an expression from the side of
a question which is seldom heard outside the homes of the land."

563   CLEVELAND, GROVER. "Would Woman Suffrage Be Unwise?" Ladies'
       Home Journal 22 (October):7–8.
         Declares that God has assigned the places of men and women,
a natural equilibrium which must not be jolted out of balance by
feminism. Deplores the false doctrines being taught by and to
women to subvert women from their true mission into the "stern,
rugged, and unwomanly duties and responsibilities allotted to
man." Regrets that extremists have forged to the front; calls
them "clamorous," radical, noisy, notoriety-seeking, and bad-
tempered. Woman suffrage would be "an inexpedient and venture-
some experiment" and women's clubs are its ally. Warns that the
votes of the thoughtful and conscientious would be "outweighed by
those of the disreputable, the ignorant, the thoughtless, the
purchased and the coerced."

564   MC CRACKEN, ELIZABETH. "Woman Suffrage in the Tenements."
       Atlantic 96 (December):750–59.
         A series of anecdotes about school suffrage in Boston by a
social settlement worker proves that tenement women are not

interested in the ballot. They have more pressing concerns, or
they manifest only an ephemeral interest in voting. More anec-
dotes about woman suffrage in Colorado—it confuses women, while
poor women vote for money. Colorado women were not ready for the
gift.

1906

565   An Appeal to Voters and Arguments Against Equal Suffrage
      Constitutional Amendment. Portland: Oregon State Association
      Opposed to the Extension of Suffrage to Women, 23 pp. Date is
      estimated.
           Asks men to oppose woman suffrage. Reprints "Woman's Pro-
      test Against Woman Suffrage," statement by Abram S. Hewitt,
      address by the Reverend Father Walsh of Troy, New York, and
      outline of talk by Mrs. R. W. Wilbur. See 556. Repeats all the
      old arguments and phrases.

566   [CORBIN, CAROLINE E.]. A Protest against the Granting of
      Municipal Suffrage to Women in the City of Chicago. Chicago:
      Illinois Association Opposed to Woman Suffrage, 15 pp.
           Reports that women have not voted in any great numbers for
      school elections and opposes extension of suffrage to women.
      Good women do not vote or engage in politics; bad women do.
      Urges the committee not to take women out of their God-appointed
      sphere.

567   LEWIS, LAWRENCE. How Woman's Suffrage Works in Colorado.
      Oregon State Association Opposed to the Extension of Suffrage
      to Women, 12 pp.
           Reprinted from Outlook, 27 January 1906.

568   A Remonstrance against Granting of Municipal Suffrage to Women
      in the City of Chicago. Chicago: Illinois Association
      Opposed to the Extension of Suffrage to Women, 3 pp.
           Believes that "the propaganda of woman suffrage is an
      attack upon the whole order of civil government as it exists
      under Christian civilization." Men and women are forever dif-
      ferent, although equal. "To confound and 'equalize' these func-
      tions would be to undermine and subvert the whole order of
      society and introduce anarchy." Signed by eleven women, Caroline
      Corbin at the top.

1907

569   HAZARD, Mrs. BARCLAY. How Women Can Best Serve the State: An
      Address before the State Federation of Women's Clubs, Troy,
      New York, 30 October 1907. Chicago: Illinois Association
      Opposed to the Extension of Suffrage to Women, 8 pp. Date is
      estimated.

Argues that women now have the advantage of complete political independence, so their pleas will be considered on merit
alone. Urges young women not to forget their true position,
"beguiled by any specious arguments about the so-called equality
of women." Warns them against "change, masquerading as progress." Beseeches them not to surrender their powerful and absolutely unique position for hope of personal gain or restless
ambition or desire to play a part in public life.

570   STEPHEN, CAROLINE E. "Women and Politics." Living Age 253
       (9 March):579-86.
       Proposes to speak "on behalf of a great though silent
multitude of women" who shrink from the prospect of woman suffrage, which would "inflict" upon women, "against their will and
without a hearing, a grave injustice." Says many women are
silent "because the very cause itself which they would advocate--
the cause of reserve, of modesty, of personal dignity and refine-
ment--appears to forbid public discussion of a position which till
lately has seemed to be its own security." Nature has laid
burdens on women that allow them to be exempted from political
duties. For women to neglect those duties would ruin the state.
Reprinted from Nineteenth Century and After (London) 61
(February):227-36.

571   [ABBOTT, LYMAN]. "Women and Politics." Outlook 85
       (6 April):786-88.
       Commends, summarizes, and quotes from an article by
Caroline Stephen (see 570) opposing women in politics and doing
so "in a spirit of calmness and womanly reserve which is in
refreshing contrast to some of the unwomanly utterances which
have been given forth by advocates upon the other side." Asserts
that the majority of women do not wish the vote and do not want
additional burdens.

572   CHAPMAN, THEODORE. "Women and Politics." Living Age 253
       (4 May):271-76.
       Agrees with Caroline Stephen (see 570) that woman suffrage
ignores the facts of nature and proposes human disaster. Similar
functions cannot be allotted to men and women. Alleges that
suffrage agitators in Great Britain are ill-tempered, indecorous,
loud, rude, and careless. Reprinted from Nineteenth Century and
After (London) 61 (April):595-601.

573   STEPHEN, CAROLINE E. "Women and Politics: A Rejoinder."
       Living Age 253 (4 May):270-71.
       Responding to Miss Gore-Booth's prosuffrage article, con-
tinues to assert that woman suffrage would mean a total redistri-
bution of labor between the sexes. Urges women to be true to
their natural duties. Reprinted from Nineteenth Century and
After (London) 61 (April):593-94.

574   DELAND, MARGARET. "The New Woman Who Would Do Things."
       Ladies' Home Journal 24 (September):17.
            Warns that the New Woman is reaching out for dangerous
       power in suffrage, "willing to multiply by two the present ig-
       norant and unconscientious vote." Asserts that women approach
       social questions in a shallow way, without thoroughness, thinking
       they can reform complex wrongs. Deplores the arrogance of the
       New Woman.

                                   1908

575   CORBIN, CAROLINE F. The Antisuffrage Movement. Chicago:
       Illinois Association Opposed to the Extension of Suffrage to
       Women, 3 pp. Date is estimated.
            Useful for a short history and lists of those active in the
       antisuffrage movement. Reprinted from Chicago Daily News, 24
       November 1908.

576   KNAPP, ADELINE. Do Working Women Need the Ballot? Address to
       the Senate and Assembly Judiciary Committees of the New York
       State Legislature, 19 February 1908. New York: New York
       State Association Opposed to Woman Suffrage, 8 pp.
            Insists that the ballot will not help women get equal pay
       for equal work. Repeats same old arguments.

577   [ABBOTT, LYMAN]. "An Imposition on Women." Outlook 88
       (8 February):296.
            Points out that women have hitherto been exempted from
       political duties as from police, militia, and jury duty. If they
       do not want to vote, "it is both a hazardous experiment and an
       act of doubtful justice to impose these duties upon them."

578   MASSIE, EDITH M. "A Woman's Plea Against Woman Suffrage."
       Living Age 257 (11 April):84-88.
            Believes that woman's condition has been vastly improved
       without the vote. Thinks women can gain little with the vote but
       lose much. Women should stick to indoor work and not assume
       extraneous and unnecessary burdens. Votes for women would harm
       both women and the commonwealth. Reprinted from Nineteenth
       Century and After (London) 63 (March):381-85.

579   HARRIS, Mrs. L.H. "The Women and the Future." Independent 64
       (14 May):1090-92.
            Asserts that every thinking woman dreads the day when the
       ballot is thrust on her; it will be a burden. Says she prefers
       being "the victim of man's love and injustice rather than compete
       with him politically, face his temptations and risk the chance of
       being elected to some indelicate office, like that of sheriff."

580   [ABBOTT, LYMAN]. "Woman's Suffrage in Oregon." Outlook 89
       (27 June):402.
            Applauds the defeat of woman suffrage in Oregon and com-
       mends the courageous silent antisuffrage leaders who have been
       subjected to unscrupulous abuse from suffragists.

581   [ABBOTT, LYMAN]. "'As Others See.'" Outlook 89
       (25 July):633.
            Recounts a letter by Mrs. Humphrey Ward recently published
       in the Times (London) in which Mrs. Ward alleged that the woman
       suffrage movement in the United States is being defeated by women
       and called for silent women in England who oppose woman suffrage
       to be more active in their opposition.

582   THE COUNTRY CONTRIBUTOR. "The Ideas of a Plain Country
       Woman." Ladies' Home Journal 25 (September):38.
            Opposes woman suffrage because there are many times when
       home is the only proper place for a woman. Would have women mix
       with men at the polls only after they are fifty years of age.
       Does not say this flippantly; believes it. Thinks that "sex is
       the real barrier to women's rights." Finds women unnatural in
       the male business world.

583   LE ROY, VIRGINIA B. "A Woman's Argument Against Woman Suf-
       frage." World To-Day 15 (October):1061-66.
            Denies that there are any a priori and absolute rights. The
       ballot is simply an instrument, a question of social expediency.
       Her main objection to woman suffrage is that it would "direct
       woman from her real social purpose." Wants woman to preserve her
       social spirit and maintain public and patriotic motives rather
       than competing for political prizes with men and becoming per-
       sonal and selfish. We "cannot afford to lose her as a generator
       of pure social spirit unpolluted by lust of political gain."
       Reminds women that men are what women make them.

584   WARD, MARY A. (Mrs. HUMPHREY). "The Women's Anti-Suffrage
       Movement." Living Age 259 (3 October):3-11.
            Recounts the activities of the antisuffragists since 1889,
       when the "Appeal against Female Suffrage" was issued. Says women
       have many opportunities for participation in local government
       without suffrage. Describes a need for more active antisuffrage
       work and reprints the manifesto of the National Women's Anti-
       Suffrage League, begun in 1908, and a speech given on that occa-
       sion. Asks for time, money, and work from those who oppose woman
       suffrage. Reprinted from Nineteenth Century and After (London)
       64 (August):343-52.

585   WARD, MARY A. (Mrs. HUMPHREY). "Some Suffragist Arguments."
       Educational Review 36 (November):398-404.
            Insists that the educated female without voting already
       exerts more influence than the uneducated male voter. Says
       suffragists "are endangering their true power and their true

sphere." Progress depends upon specialization. Quotes Frank
Foxcroft at length on suffrage agitation in the United States
(see 559). Reprinted from the Times (London).

586   WARD, Mrs. HUMPHREY. "Why I Do Not Believe in Woman Suf-
       frage." Ladies' Home Journal 25 (November):15, 72.
          Believes there is and always will be a natural division
between the spheres of men and women. The modern state depends
ultimately on force. Says "women have no right to claim full
political power in a state where they can never themselves take
the full responsibility of their actions, because they can never
be called upon finally to enforce them." For the educated woman,
the vote would reduce her power; for the poor woman it would
increase hers, ignorantly. Let us in the name of common sense
leave the franchise to men.

587   "The British Amazons." Independent 65 (5 November):1078-79.
          Editorial that expresses belief in woman suffrage but finds
the militant British suffragettes "little less than an abortion,
an abomination, a gross parody on womanhood and disgusting to
manhood." Recalls that in the 1870s we had "a little bevy of
extreme women, Pantarchian rebels against marriage law," but they
were rejected by both women's rights camps and they never smashed
windows. These British women are not ladies, they are termagants.

588   "Theodore Roosevelt and Elihu Root on Woman's Suffrage."
       Outlook 90 (19 December):848-49.
          Describes the formation of a League for the Civic Education
of Women and appends letters from President Roosevelt and Secretary of State Elihu Root. Roosevelt is a lukewarm woman suffrage
supporter, thinks it not very important, and does not see that it
has made any difference in the West. Woman's place is in the
home. Root opposes woman suffrage.

1909

589   ADAMS, Miss MARY DEAN. Wages and the Ballot. 2d ed. New
       York: New York State Association Opposed to Woman Suffrage,
       7 pp.
          Alleges that "the suffrage craze is quite unscrupulous as
to the means employed to attain its ends." Asserts that voting
will not make jobs or raise wages. On the contrary, "the surest
and quickest way to bring about the moral and physical destruction of the working woman would be to thrust her into American
politics," for then she will be prey to the political boss.

590   BISSELL, EMILY PERKINS. A Talk to Women on the Suffrage
       Question. New York: New York State Association Opposed to
       Woman Suffrage, 8 pp.
          Opposes woman suffrage because it is man's, not woman's,
duty; because "it would set modern society on the road back to

savagery" by making woman do man's work and taking her out of the
home, which should not be agitated by turmoil from outside. "The
vote, which means public life, does not fit into the ideal of
family life." The vote fosters individualism, which is a threat
to family life. Raises the specter of the vote by blacks and
immigrants.

591   BOK, EDWARD W. Real Opponents to the Suffrage Movement Are
      the Women Themselves Whose Peculiar Field of Work Lies Outside
      of Politics. New York: New York State Association Opposed to
      Woman Suffrage, 12 pp.
         Gives his standard reasons for opposing woman suffrage.
      Characterizes the woman's movement as not a movement but rather
      "an excitement, an outbreak, an expression, and, to my mind, an
      unnatural expression of an unnatural condition that goes much
      deeper than mere woman suffrage." Woman is a creature of nervous
      energy and excitement which is supposed to be channeled into
      motherhood. Lately women have been avoiding motherhood, leaving
      them unsatisfied, with their nervous energy unspent. That is
      when they look to the outside, to clubs, bridge, vivisection,
      woman suffrage. Sees a hopeful sign in the child-study movement.
      Reprinted from New York Times, 18 April 1909.

592   BUCKLEY, JAMES M., LL.D. The Wrong and Peril of Woman Suf-
      frage. New York: Fleming H. Revell, 128 pp.
         Argues that "to impose upon women direct responsibility for
      civil government is incompatible with the nature of womanhood,
      and with the highest conception of the state." If the family is
      to be preserved, women must stay independent and submissive;
      voting would entirely alter that. Refutes arguments for woman
      suffrage and alleges that in places where woman suffrage is
      legal, women vote for pay just as men do. "Woman suffrage cannot
      achieve what its advocates expect." It would lead to religious
      feuds because women are much more partisan than men. Men would
      no longer be chivalrous to women. Family relations would be
      strained. Political life would become more bitter because women
      cannot be impartial.

593   The Campaign of Noise. Bulletin no. 2. Chicago: Illinois
      Association Opposed to Woman Suffrage, 4 pp.
         Asserts that woman suffrage is a campaign of noise and
      demonstration, "a general disturbance of the social and political
      elements."

594   CLEWS, HENRY. Shall the Suffrage Be Given to Women? An
      Address Delivered 19 November 1909 under the Auspices of the
      National League for the Civic Improvement of Women. New York,
      15 pp.
         Says if women should get the vote and become the equal of
      men, they would lose that superiority over men that is manifested
      in men's deference and gallantry. Home life and children would

be neglected. Women would risk physical dangers at public meetings and polls--imagines a lady being verbally insulted and then
physically attacked by a coarse, ignorant woman. Women would
become masculine and men effeminate. Woman should stick to her
natural sphere, which is the home.

595   GEORGE, Mrs. ANDREW J. Address before the Brooklyn Auxiliary.
      New York: New York State Association Opposed to Woman Suf-
      frage, 8 pp.
         Denies that woman suffrage is making progress worldwide.
      Says woman suffrage would not benefit the state but would "crip-
      ple the energies, the activities, and the influence of public-
      spirited women."

596   GILDER, HELENA [DE K.]. A Letter on Woman Suffrage, from One
      Woman to Another. New York, 15 pp.
         Reprinted from 486. Reprinted in 495 and 533.

597   Opinions of Eminent Persons Against Woman Suffrage. Boston:
      Massachusetts Association Opposed to the Further Extension of
      Suffrage to Women, 7 pp.
         Daniel Webster, Horace Bushnell, Francis Parkman, Edward
      Everett Hale, Jacob Riis, Abram S. Hewitt, and many others--forty
      in all, twelve of whom are women; also some from England.

598   SCOTT, Mrs. WILLIAM FORSE, and ADAMS, Miss MARY DEAN. In
      Opposition to Woman Suffrage: Two Papers Read at Albany, 24
      February 1909, before the Joint Senate and Assembly Judiciary
      Committee. New York: New York State Association Opposed to
      Woman Suffrage, 8 pp.
         According to Mrs. Scott, "The characteristics which most
      ensure woman's fitness for her vocation, most positively bar her
      from any promise of fitness to deal with broad and high questions
      of Statesmanship." Miss Adams, investigator for the New York
      State Commission of Immigration, worries about extending the vote
      to immigrant women: "The immigrant woman is a fickle, impulsive
      creature, irresponsible, very superstitious, ruled absolutely by
      emotion and intensely personal in her point of view. In many
      things much resembling a sheep." Asserts that she would be quick
      to see the commercial value of her vote.

599   To the Voters of the Middle West. Bulletin no. 1. Chicago:
      Illinois Association Opposed to the Extension of Suffrage to
      Women, 10 pp.
         Insists that the majority of women do not want to vote.
      Woman suffrage is part of a world wide movement to overthrow the
      present order of society and replace it with a revolutionary one.
      Woman suffrage would be a monstrous burden and oppression.

600   Why the Home Makers Do Not Want to Vote. Chicago: Illinois
      Association Opposed to the Extension of the Suffrage to Women,
      4 pp. Date is estimated.

Argues that woman in the home is independent and nonpartisan. What is needed is not woman suffrage but education of women
for the home and home duties.

601   BOK, EDWARD. "What Forty-six Women Decided." Ladies' Home
       Journal 26 (February):6.
           Canvassed women about suffrage. Reports that the wife of a
       recent president was indifferent, her friends opposed or indif-
       ferent, a woman's club overwhelmingly opposed, and women's club
       leaders admitted that their membership opposes woman suffrage.
       Concludes that "the field of politics as a new excitement for a
       few restless American women is barred to them by their own sex."

602   SIMKINS, M.E. "Suffrage and Anti-Suffrage." Living Age 260
       (6 February):323-29.
           Calls the woman suffrage movement a sign of national deca-
       dence. Says "no single factor at this date threatens us with
       such rapidly accelerated degeneration." Says average women are
       not equipped to exercise the vote. Better to "instruct women how
       better to discharge the duties, the grand and awful duties, they
       are already invested with [than] to impose on them new ones."
       Blames women that men drink too much, that the poor work in
       factories, that pay is so bad. Alleges that it is only priv-
       ileged women who want to vote; it would impose a triple burden on
       working women, who prefer the home. Describes herself as a woman
       worker who has tried "to combine first teaching and then histor-
       ical research with housekeeping." Reprinted from National Review
       (London) 52 (January):784-93.

603   WATTERSON, HENRY. "The Wisdom of Watterson." Harper's Weekly
       53 (27 March):25, 31.
           Opposes woman suffrage because it would introduce "an equal
       quantum of similar ignorance, intemperance, and corruption" as
       the male vote now contains but also add new evils. Has great
       scorn for woman suffragists: "I look upon the professional
       'suffragette' with horror and disgust. When she is not a crank,
       pure and simple, or a poor, plain fool, she is a creature with a
       grievance--a thing abominable whether male or female--a soured
       nature, a jaundiced mind--the victim either of misusage or the
       barren state, redolent of mental whimsies." Alleges that if a
       woman takes more interest in public than in private life, she
       either has a bad husband or no husband. "The poor suffragette--
       He-woman--the bow-legged, bandy-shanked."

604   "The Anti-Suffrage Movement." Harper's Bazar 43 (April):424.
           Insists that the antisuffrage position is entitled to as
       much respect and attention as the suffrage movement. Describes
       the history of the movement and names participants, briefly
       giving some of their achievements.

605   SHAW, Mrs. G. HOWLAND, et al. "Woman Suffrage in the United
       States: A Correction of Misstatements." Educational Review
       37 (April):405-8.
       A reply to Julia Ward Howe, who in turn had replied to Mrs.
Humphrey Ward. These officers of the Massachusetts Association
Opposed to Woman Suffrage insist that interest in woman suffrage
is on the decline in the United States, as Mrs. Ward had stated.
Believe that organizations opposing woman suffrage in the United
States "are composed of as high-minded and intelligent women as
the country possesses." Reprinted from the Times (London).

606   ABBOTT, LYMAN. "The Profession of Motherhood." Outlook 91
       (10 April):836-40.
       Objects to woman suffrage because of what it will do to
mothers: cause them to get caught up in party emotions, argue
with their husband, neglect their children. Denies that working
women need the ballot, that it would improve woman's legal situation, that woman suffrage would add a new moral tone to politics.

607   DICEY, A.V. "Woman Suffrage." Living Age 261 (10 April):
       67-84.
       Presents a "calm" examination of the pros and cons of woman
suffrage in England, the conclusion of which is that "a revolution of such boundless significance cannot be attempted without
the greatest peril to England." Reprinted from Quarterly Review
(London) 210 (January):276-304.

608   REYNOLDS, STEPHEN. "'Seems So'--the Suffragettes." Living
       Age 261 (24 April):240-43.
       Alleges to be knowledgeable about working-class attitudes
toward woman suffrage. Says working-class women have enough to
do and distrust those women who tell them they need the vote.
Says suffragettes provide amusement ("sport") for working-class
men. Does not want to give up the ideal of the lady and domesticity for the mud-splasher type of woman). Reprinted from the
Spectator (London) 102 (20 February):296-97.

609   RAMEE, MARIE LOUISE De La [Ouida]. "Shall Women Vote? A
       Study of Feminine Unrest--Its Causes and Its Remedies."
       Lippincott's 83 (May):586-92.
       Editor says in a footnote that Ouida sold the magazine this
and another article more than twenty-five years ago with the
stipulation that they not be published until after her death.
She had recently died. See also 273. Ouida faults women clamoring for their rights, particularly for suffrage, who will not
waive their demands for deference, homage, chivalry. They demand
everything but will concede nothing. Wants to see women better
educated and more capable of self-support. For that reason
regrets to see the cause of woman's education mixed up with vague
and preposterous cries for "female rights." Let women achieve
intellectually before they ask for suffrage. Reprinted from
Review of Reviews 39 (May 1909):624-25.

610   HAZARD, Mrs. BARCLAY. "The New York Anti-Suffrage Associa-
       tion." Harper's Bazar 43 (July):730.
           Alleges that the majority of women oppose or are indif-
       ferent to suffrage.

611   WARFIELD, ETHELBERT DUDLEY. "The Moral Influence of Women in
       American Society." Annals of the American Academy of Polit-
       ical Science 34 (July):106-14.
           After praising women's earlier activities, including in
       education, abolition, and the WCTU, states that "The Woman Suf-
       frage movement . . . is rooted in an idea that is antagonistic to
       the family, and if worked out to its logical conclusion would
       destroy its solidarity." Says there are always abnormal women--
       anarchists, free lovers, ones who drink moonshine and smoke cob
       pipes, drink champagne and smoke cigarettes--but the normal
       prevails.

612   CHITTENDEN, ALICE HILL. "The Counter Influence to Woman Suf-
       frage." Independent 67 (29 July):246-49.
           Alleges that woman suffrage is on the decline in the United
       States. Oregon voted it down, and it has not been effective in
       Colorado, Idaho, Utah, or Wyoming. Enumerates the many failures
       in the attempt to achieve suffrage for women. Argues that women
       have failed in this reform, although they have succeeded in
       others, because it is against the natural laws of specialization
       and different sex activity. Credits the activities of the anti-
       suffragists for the fact that woman suffrage has made no progress
       since the early 1890s.

613   JONES, Mrs. GILBERT E. "Some Impediments to Woman Suffrage."
       North American 190 (August):158-69.
           This founder of the National League for the Civic Education
       of Women asserts that the antisuffragists want differentiation
       rather than equality between the sexes. Men are the natural
       protectors of women and must be "the basic power and the leaders
       to guarantee safety to our country." Suffrage will not help the
       working woman. Deplores that the suffragists "have created a
       spirit of unrest among all classes of women." Alleges that many
       suffrage organizations are affiliated with and endorsed by social-
       ists. Does not want women to be equal to men because men would
       no longer support their wives, marriage would become less common,
       and divorce granted at will. Says men and women instinctively
       oppose woman suffrage.

614   CHESTERTON, G.K. "The Modern Surrender of Women." Living Age
       262 (21 August):462-67.
           Argues that voting is based on coercion and collectivity,
       and woman's role has always been to oppose both actions. Asserts
       that the woman suffrage movement "is simply the breakdown of the
       pride of woman." She used to be able to laugh at men's political
       activities; now she wants to participate in them, to everyone's
       loss. Reprinted from Dublin Review 144 (January):1-32.

615   BOK, EDWARD. "Woman or Mother? Woman's Real Progress."
       Ladies' Home Journal 27 (October):6.
           Faults the equal suffrage movement as "fundamentally
       wrong." It fails because it arrays itself against effective
       motherhood. Moral force is more effective than the power of the
       ballot. Asserts that "to oppose woman suffrage is distinctly to
       advance woman's real progress." Woman cannot compete with the
       stronger, more aggressive force of man. God has established the
       respective spheres, and neither sex can usurp the functions of
       the other.

616   BISSELL, EMILY PERKINS [Priscilla Leonard]. "The Working-
       Woman and Anti-Suffrage." Harper's Bazar 43 (November):
       1169-70.
           Insists that politics do not control economics. Argues
       that the ballot will not help the working girl.

                                   1910

617   BARRY, RICHARD H. The Truth Concerning Four Woman-Suffrage
       States. New York: National League for the Civic Education of
       Women, 16 pp.
           Reprint of 648. Also reprinted by New York State Associa-
       tion Opposed to Woman Suffrage.

618   BIRDSALL, Mrs. WILLIAM W. Woman Suffrage and the Working
       Woman. N.p., 3 pp. Date is estimated.
           Says votes for women will not improve the condition of
       women workers either in homes or factories. Asserts that working
       women are not interested in the ballot; they see it as a burden.

619   BRONSON, MINNIE. The Wage-Earning Woman and the State: A
       Comparison of the Laws for Her Protection in Various States of
       the Union. Boston: Massachusetts Association Opposed to the
       Extension of Suffrage to Women, 10 pp.
           Says lawmakers have enacted laws to protect women workers
       because so many women are taking industrial jobs. The best laws
       were not passed in woman suffrage states. Denies that woman
       suffrage would help female teachers because variations in pay are
       due to the operation of the law of supply and demand. Worries
       that "the constantly reiterated demand that woman shall be
       allowed to stand on exactly the same footing as man may render
       ineffective much of the law which now gives her an advantage."

620   BROWN, HENRY. Woman Suffrage: A Paper Read by Ex-Justice
       Brown before the Ladies' Congressional Club of Washington,
       D.C., April 1910. Boston: Massachusetts Association Opposed
       to the Further Extension of Suffrage to Women, 16 pp. Date is
       estimated.
           Says the fact that traditionally only men vote is strong
       evidence of the wisdom of such policy. Most laws are more

                                   143

favorable to women than to men. Women and men are equal but different. Most women, particularly of the upper classes, are
indifferent or opposed to suffrage. Woman suffrage would be
dangerous, as indeed Negro suffrage has been. Fears that letting
women compete with men would "brush away that bloom of delicacy
and refinement" which evokes men's admiration and chivalry toward
women. Women "will lose something of the instincts of motherhood," become less private, more vulgar and mannish.

621   CHITTENDEN, ALICE HILL. The Inexpediency of Granting the
       Suffrage to American Women: Address at the Tenth Biennial of
       the General Federation of Women's Clubs, 4 May 1910. New
       York: State Association Opposed to Woman Suffrage, 12 pp.
           Repeats the same arguments she presented at her Cazenovia
address (see 662).

622   [CORBIN, CAROLINE F.]. Letter to the Honorable Henry W.
       Blair, United States Senator from New Hampshire. Albany: New
       York Anti-Suffrage Association, 4 pp. Date is estimated.
           Woman Suffrage will form a class of women like those in
ancient Greece, brilliant and intellectual but without faith and
virtue.

623   CROSBY, JOHN F. The Advisability of Inserting the Word Sex
       before the Word Race in the Fifteenth Amendment to the Consti-
       tution of the United States. Washington, D.C.: Georgetown
       University, 16 pp.
           Argues that the right to vote is a political privilege, not
a natural one. "It is a registry of will" and as such must be
backed up by force. Men will give women anything they need.
Most women do not want to vote. Woman suffrage has as its corner-
stone sex antagonism. The emancipation of women in Rome brought
about degeneracy, decadence, and a decrease in the birthrate.
Our birthrate too is falling. What we need is a reevaluation of
the ideal of motherhood. Woman suffrage would divert women from
their life work. "Woman's place is in the home and if she does
not fill that place it will be empty." Winner of the Mallory
Prize for an essay on the constitution at Georgetown University.

624   MARSHALL, EDWARD. A Woman Tells Why Woman Suffrage Would Be
       Bad. New York: New York State Association Opposed to Woman
       Suffrage, 14 pp. Date is estimated.
           Quotes Mrs. Francis M. Scott at great length. According to
Mrs. Scott, "the danger in the ballot for our womankind lies
mostly in the conditions which exist at present and which it must
destroy between women and their most necessary work." She believes that no woman can be an ideal mother and engage in an
active outside life. Woman must choose between the ballot and
the baby--she cannot have both. Believes that work for suffrage
has undermined man's regard for women. Deplores women's attempts
at economic independence. Says woman suffrage and socialism are

closely allied. Predicts that poor women would be less scrupu-
lous in politics than men. Blames women for lowering men's
wages.

625   Men and Women. Bulletin no. 3. Chicago: Illinois Associa-
       tion Opposed to Woman Suffrage, 4 pp.
           Women must do their work as mothers better, training their
       children in purity and self-knowledge. Keep American men virile
       and strong and powerful. Don't set back progress by giving women
       the vote.

626   SCOTT, Mrs. FRANCIS M. The Legal Status of Women: A Reply to
       Mrs. Johnston-Wood. New York: New York State Association
       Opposed to Woman Suffrage, 7 pp.
           Insists that women's legal status is actually quite favor-
       able. They do not need the ballot. Reprinted from the New York
       Times, 31 March 1910, p. 10.

627   Significance of the Woman Suffrage Movement; Session of the
       American Academy of Political and Social Science, 9 February
       1910. Philadelphia: American Academy of Political and Social
       Science, 37 pp.
           Reprints Mrs. Gilbert Jones's "The Position of the Anti-
       Suffragists (643)," in which she refutes the assertion that
       taxation without representation is tyranny. Asserts that suf-
       frage has not helped women in suffrage states. "The real truth
       is that woman suffrage is absolutely futile." Also reprints
       Lyman Abbott's "Answer to the Arguments in Support of Woman Suf-
       frage" (from "The Profession of Motherhood," 606), and Charles H.
       Parkhurst's "The Inadvisability of Woman Suffrage" (from an
       address delivered in New York on 17 December 1909).

628   Socialism versus Legal Marriage. Bulletin no. 5. Chicago:
       Illinois Association Opposed to Woman Suffrage, 4 pp.
           Woman suffrage is the cornerstone of socialism. Socialism
       destroys legal marriage. If women discard legal marriage, they
       will lose rights and safeguards. Woman suffrage would be a
       radical departure from the civilized, Christian ideal of the home
       as the unit of the state.

629   STIMSON, HENRY A. Is Woman's Suffrage an Enlightened and
       Justifiable Policy for the State? New York: Brooklyn
       Auxiliary of New York State Association Opposed to Woman
       Suffrage, 12 pp.
           Reprint of 640.

630   The Truth about Wage-Earning Women. New York: National Asso-
       ciation Opposed to Woman Suffrage, 1 p. Date is estimated.
           Insists that the best laws for working women are to be
       found in male-suffrage states. The ballot will not help the
       working woman.

631   Views on Woman Suffrage. Albany: Anti-Suffrage Association,
      3 pp. Date is estimated.
         Antisuffrage views of Herbert Spencer; Bishop John H.
      Vincent, the founder of Chautauqua; and John Bright, English
      patriot. Reprinted from 556.

632   Why Should Suffrage Be Imposed on Women? Boston:
      Massachusetts Man Suffrage Association, 4 pp.
         Women do not want the vote. It would not promote the
      general welfare or benefit the cities. Town meetings would be
      impossible--who would watch the children? Woman suffrage would
      impose great hardship on many women. Women's interests are safe
      in the hands of men.

633   ABBOTT, LYMAN. "Why the Vote Would Be Injurious to Women."
      Ladies' Home Journal 27 (February):21-22.
         Alleges that he originally favored woman suffrage but that
      his wife persuaded him otherwise, showing him that voting is a
      duty rather than a right and that it is good that women have been
      exempted from this burden. The great majority of women do not
      wish to vote. Advocates woman's rights: "her right to be exempt
      from the duty of protecting persons and property." Asserts that
      "few sober-minded women" desire the vote, "whatever a few hyster-
      ical suffragettes may claim." Warns that woman suffrage would
      cause great marital friction "in the so-called homes of the slums
      of our great cities and our mining and manufacturing towns."

634   BUCKLEY, JAMES M. "Moral Objections to Woman Suffrage."
      Current Literature 48 (February):177-79.
         Woman suffrage was wrong from the start. Women in public
      almost always appear at their worst. Women's participation in
      government would lower its tone. Summary of his The Wrong and
      Peril of Woman Suffrage (see 592).

635   [ABBOTT, LYMAN]. "Do Women Wish to Vote?" Outlook 94
      (19 February):375-77.
         Encourages the move in New York State to have a special
      election in which women alone would vote and indicate whether
      they want to vote. Is confident it will fail: "The Outlook is
      opposed to woman suffrage primarily because it is an advocate of
      woman's rights, and believes in her right to be exempt from the
      responsibility of participating in the duties and burdens of
      government." Woman has more important work to do for the com-
      munity. Grants that if women vote to have suffrage, they should
      have it.

636   DELAND, MARGARET. "The Change in the Feminine Ideal."
      Atlantic 105 (March):289-302.
         Is concerned that women are becoming less unselfish than
      their mothers. Finds real danger in individualism that the
      family will become secondary and divorce rampant. Sees in the

call for social responsibility a shallowness. Particularly opposes woman suffrage, for women have already secured through
"intelligent influence, and plain unsensational common sense, a
large number of rights and privileges without the ballot." Calls
the ballot a "plaything" and a "toy." Raises the specter of the
ignorant Irish vote. Also condemns woman's public-spiritedness
as shallow, sentimental, and lawless.

637   BISSELL, EMILY PERKINS [Priscilla Leonard]. "Temperance and
        Woman Suffrage." Harper's Bazar 44 (April):289.
        Denies that woman suffrage is necessary to the temperance
campaign. Believes that temperance workers to best in the
schools and churches, not in politics. Women must use their
influence. Woman suffrage would be a mistake.

638   MC GRIFF, JESSIE ATKINSON. "Before the American Woman Votes."
        Ladies' Home Journal 27 (April):56.
        Believes that there is much work for women to do without
suffrage, which is "a meaningless bauble." Thinks immediate and
universal suffrage is "the most demoralizing obstacle placed in
the way of the American woman's natural and vigorous development." Woman must be awakened to her real duty and influence as
a wife and mother.

639   SCOTT, Mrs. WILLIAM FORSE. "Woman's Relation to Government."
        North American 191 (April):549-58.
        States that in higher species there is ever-greater spe-
cialization. Women cannot do men's work because they have
evolved along different lines. Woman's public work should be
education and the molding of public opinion. It would be wrong
to go against evolution, "wrong to encourage woman to engage in
political activities which would interfere with her natural development and with the performance of strictly womanly duties."

640   STIMSON, HENRY A. "Is Woman's Suffrage an Enlightened and
        Justifiable Policy for the State?" Bibliotheca Sacra 67
        (April):335-46.
        Characterizes advocates of woman suffrage as "an eruption"
and deplores "obstreperousness, the vulgarity of self-assertion,
the ineffectiveness of argument based on self-interest, and the
ill-manners of ridicule or personalities." Sums up the arguments
against woman suffrage: "it will not do what is claimed for it;
and it will occasion unanticipated evil." Is particularly concerned that it will "bring new temptations to weak women, and
crowd them upon them with new force," exposing them to public
life. "It will add a new excitement to lives already greatly
overexcited, especially in the cities." Finally, "it introduces
a terrible risk into the life of the state because, once given,
it is unalterable." Reprinted in 629.

641   ABBOTT, LYMAN. "Answer to the Arguments in Support of Woman
       Suffrage." Annals of the American Academy of Political
       Science 35 (May):supp. 28-32.
            Answers arguments in favor of woman suffrage: (1) Woman
       suffrage is not a natural right. (2) Woman suffrage would cause
       sex antagonism, whereas what is needed is an appeal by women to
       remove any remaining legal disabilities. (3) Woman suffrage
       would not benefit women wage earners. (4) Wage-earning women do
       not want the ballot. (5) Woman suffrage will not bring moral
       reforms; women are worse in suffrage states.

642   JONES, Mrs. GILBERT E. "Facts about Suffrage and Anti-
       Suffrage." Forum 43 (May):495-504.
            Believes that woman suffrage would prove "unwise, inex-
       pedient, and generally speaking, futile. Women are too protected
       to know about government and politics, and should remain so.
       Laws are already more favorable to women than men. Voting power
       is based on force, which women do not have. "Man forms the ONLY
       basis on which any government can rest." It hardly speaks well
       for woman suffrage that polygamy prevails in Utah. Deplores
       women entering unsuitable professions, causing the birth rate to
       decline and infant mortality to increase. Men must work to keep
       women out of competitive industries. It is insulting to men that
       women say they need the ballot to protect themselves, for the
       American male instinctively protects women.

643   JONES, Mrs. GILBERT E. "The Position of the Anti-Suffragists."
       Annals of the American Academy of Political Science 35
       (May):supp. 16-22.
            Record of a session of the American Academy of Political
       and Social Science in February 1910 on the significance of the
       woman suffrage movement. Speakers were evenly balanced, three
       pro and three con. Refutes the notion that women should vote
       because they pay taxes. Denies that ballot will help wage-
       earning woman. Wants women not to work in unsuitable occupa-
       tions. Examines record in suffrage states and finds it wanting.
       Woman suffrage is "absolutely futile." Reprinted in 627.

644   MEYER, ANNIE NATHAN. "Miss Johnston and Woman Suffrage."
       Bookman 31 (May):312-14.
            A critique of a prowoman suffrage article by Mary Johnston
       in Atlantic, April 1910. Says that the women who have really
       brought reforms in the country were "either outspoken anti-
       suffragists or at best lukewarm suffragists who were too busy
       doing their work to bother about imaginary wrongs."

645   PARKHURST, CHARLES H., D.D. "The Inadvisability of Woman
       Suffrage." Annals of the American Academy of Political
       Science 35 (May):supp. 36-37.
            Women should remain on their pedestal, not sacrifice their
       distinctive influence. Women should not make themselves men to

get what they want. Opposes woman suffrage. Extracts from an
address delivered in New York in December 1909.

646   HAZARD, Mrs. BARCLAY. "New York State Association Opposed to
      Woman Suffrage." Chautauquan 59 (June):84-89.
         Gives the history, policy, methods, and activities of the
      Association. Lists pamphlets it has sent out. "The policy is to
      present an unwavering opposition to the suffrage for women; to
      hold no public conventions; to avoid needless discussions; to
      advocate the duty of women towards the state through appointive
      office; to impress upon the public the belief that women without
      a vote exert upon the government the best influence in their
      power, and that such influence would be limited by the affilia-
      tion with parties made necessary by the use of the ballot."

647   SEAWELL, MOLLY ELLIOT. "The Ladies' Battle." Atlantic 106
      (September):289-303.
         Opposes woman suffrage for two basic reasons: "First, no
      electorate has ever existed, or ever can exist, which cannot
      execute its own laws. Second, no voter has ever claimed, or ever
      can claim, maintenance from another voter." Women would be kept
      away from the polling place by ruffians. Then they would make
      laws that they could not enforce. Alleges that suffrage states
      lead in the numbers of divorces. Suffrage leads to divorce.
      Says there has never been a time when the ballot would not have
      been a hindrance and burden to her. Pleads for women: "defend
      them from suffrage, and protect their property privileges, their
      right to maintenance from their husbands, and their personal
      dignity." Reprinted in 653.

648   BARRY, RICHARD. "What Women Have Actually Done Where They
      Vote." Ladies' Home Journal 27 (1 November):15-16, 68-69.
         Asserts that there have been more improvements in laws
      pertaining to women and children in states where only men vote
      than in those with woman suffrage. Alleges that prostitution,
      illegitimacy, free love, and divorce are greater in woman suf-
      frage states. Woman suffrage has not improved women's wages.
      Alleges he "saw scores of women accept money for the election
      held in Denver on May 17, 1910." Quotes a Denver politician:
      "It is inevitable . . . that women should lose not only their
      fineness but also their characters when they mix in poli-
      tics. . . . Woman suffrage in this state is a joke, when it is
      not a shame. High-minded men ignore the woman voter; to low-
      minded men she is—well, the less said about that the better."
      Reprinted in 617.

                                 1911

649   Facts and Fallacies about Woman Suffrage. Bulletin no. 7.
      Chicago: Illinois Association Opposed to Woman Suffrage,
      8 pp.

Argues that there has been a steady decline in the morals
of suffrage states and that "illiteracy is much greater and the
care of children much less." Suffrage will not help working
women. Woman's true work is bearing and rearing the next generation. Women can do better civic work without the vote. Urges
men not to listen to "the shallow and oftentimes misleading
arguments of agitators, and renounce the distinctive manhood with
which nature and civilization have crowned them." Asks them not
to degrade women or "reverse all that wonderful machinery which
nature has devised to ensure the ever-increasing progress of the
world in gentleness, peacefulness, and spiritual aspiration."

650   Fifteenth Annual Report. Bulletin no. 10. Chicago: Illinois
       Association Opposed to Woman Suffrage, 8 pp.
           Denies that the woman suffrage movement should be called
       the woman movement. Rather, that name should be reserved for the
       antisuffrage movement because it "upholds woman as the origin and
       moral savior of the race."

651   LYON, ERVIN F. The Successful Young Woman. Boston: R.G.
       Badger, 130 pp.
           Allows that women may have a public role but opposes "the
       boisterous woman suffragist" and deplores her methods. "The
       first and most important place of woman is in the home." Oppo-
       site the title page is a picture of "The Young Woman as a
       Bride"--that is the success he is talking about.

652   SANFORD, J.B. Extracts from a Speech Against Woman Suffrage in
       the California State Senate. N.p., 4 pp.
           On the cover: "Go to the Polls on October 10th and Vote
       Against . . . the Equal Suffrage Amendment. . . . Read and pass
       on to your neighbor." Intones that "the bedside prayer of one
       pure, noble, Christian woman far outweighs all the work of all
       the mannish female politicians on earth" (Applause). Insists
       that "the real mothers and home builders are opposed to this
       measure." Insists that woman suffrage has been a failure where
       it has been instituted. Keep the homes pure and independent. A
       mocking description of the new man and new woman brings prolonged
       applause and laughter. Defines suffragette: "a mannish woman
       who kisses lap dogs instead of babies and who wants to raise h---
       but no children." Much laughter and applause.

653   SEAWELL, MOLLY ELLIOTT. The Ladies' Battle. New York:
       Macmillan, 119 pp.
           Reprint and expansion of 647.

654   Woman Suffrage and the Constitution of the United States:
       A Catechism Which He Who Runs May Read. Bulletin no. 9.
       Chicago: Illinois Association Opposed to Woman Suffrage,
       4 pp.
           Socialism and woman suffrage degrade both men and women.
       Traditional arguments, this time in the form of catechism.

655   Woman Suffrage and the Equal Guardianship Law. New York: New
      York State Association Opposed to Woman Suffrage, 2 pp.
           Says it was antisuffragists, not suffragists, who got the
      equal guardianship bill passed in New York. Asserts that "woman
      can accomplish more along all lines of human betterment without
      the ballot, than with it. It all depends on the woman!" The
      woman who takes credit for getting the bill passed says that
      woman suffragists' support would have killed it.

656   "Do You, as a Woman, Want To Vote? Some Prominent Women of
      America Answer the Question." Ladies' Home Journal 28
      (1 January):17.
           A refutation of the supposition that thinking women support
      woman suffrage. One-sentence responses from authors like Margaret
      Deland, Kate Douglas Wiggin, Mary Wilkins, Octave Thanet, Ida
      Tarbell; prominent women like Caroline Hazard, former president
      of Wellesley; Agnes Irwin, former dean of Radcliffe; paragraph-
      length responses from the National League for the Civic Education
      of Women and the New York State Association Opposed to Woman
      Suffrage; from Mrs. Francis W. Goddard, president of Colonial
      Dames of Colorado; and more. A useful resource. See also 659.

657   "Women Voters' Views on Woman's Suffrage." Outlook 97
      (28 January):143-44.
           Says the greatest obstacle to woman suffrage is women
      themselves--they do not wish to vote. Says that in England, a
      majority even of those who vote opposes woman suffrage.

658   RICHARDSON, ANNA STEESE. "The Work of the 'Antis.'" Woman's
      Home Companion 38 (March):15, 70-71.
           Richardson is a suffragist, but this is a useful article in
      summarizing the history, goals, and concerns of the antisuffra-
      gists. Illustrated with pictures of their headquarters and also
      of prominent antisuffragists, including Mrs. Andrew Carnegie.
      Says they worry about "the unsexing of women, the dethroning of
      motherhood, the destruction of family ties, family life and
      family responsibility." Asserts that in twenty years as a re-
      porter, "I have never met a more elusive yet effective body of
      women than these few courageous souls, the 'antis,' who are
      calmly placing their slender shoulders against the apparently
      popular movement in favor of the ballot for women. And I have
      never met a body of women so sublimely confident of the outcome."

659   "Is Mrs. Goddard Alone in Her Position That Woman Suffrage in
      Colorado Is a Failure?" Ladies' Home Journal 28 (1 April):6.
           Response to the statement in the Ladies' Home Journal by
      Mrs. Francis W. Goddard that woman suffrage has been a failure in
      Colorado (see 656). The Journal canvassed more Colorado women
      "of undisputed social and civic prominence" and prints their
      opinions. All eighteen oppose woman suffrage. The comment of
      Mary Mackenzie Gambrill is typical: "I think women are too

hysterical, too personal in feeling, and not well enough balanced
to exercise the right of suffrage."

660   HERRICK, CHRISTINE TERHUNE. "Do Women Want to Vote?" Woman's
       Home Companion 38 (July):10.
            Alleges that most women she knows do not want to vote
       because they are too busy. Interviews several, and all agree.
       One complains that an English suffragette ridiculed antisuf-
       fragists by name and that turned her against woman suffrage.
       Herrick concludes that women must be educated for suffrage and
       political responsibilities and says it may take a decade.

661   [ABBOTT, LYMAN]. "Result of Woman's Suffrage." Outlook 98
       (5 August):757.
            Argues that woman's suffrage has not been a success in
       Colorado. Women do not want to vote. "It seems to us quite
       clear that suffrage ought not to be forced upon a reluctant
       constituency."

                                 1912

662   CHITTENDEN, ALICE HILL, and FAIRCHILD, CHARLES S. Addresses
       at a Public Meeting in Opposition to the Extension of Woman
       Suffrage. Cazenovia, New York, 14 August 1912. [Cazenovia,
       N.Y.], 18 pp.
            According to Chittenden, opposition to woman suffrage is so
       strong that it must be based on some fundamental principles.
       Antisuffragists have the welfare of the state and race at heart.
       Suffrage would add burdens to women without giving them any
       compensating advantages. It would also weaken the state by
       "attempting to equalize and identify the practical activities of
       the sexes" and by allowing women who cannot enforce their princi-
       ples to vote. Nature has created woman to be the biological
       conserver, not the dispenser, of energy. To do the latter would
       be a step backward. Fairchild presided and opened the meeting.
       Alleges that women he knows do not really care to vote.

663   CORBIN, CAROLINE F. Woman's Best Work: The Making of Voters.
       Bulletin no. 13. Chicago: Illinois Association Opposed to
       Woman Suffrage, 6 pp.
            Shaping the moral trend of the child is woman's highest and
       most important work. "It is therefore the making of the adult
       citizen, which is woman's most important and inalienable polit-
       ical work."

664   Dignity of Womanhood. Bulletin no. 11. Chicago: Illinois
       Association Opposed to Woman Suffrage, 8 pp.
            Asserts that woman should do her work better rather than
       doing man's. In that way she makes a better woman of herself and
       a nobler and more useful man of him. Reprints "One Woman's
       Experience of Emancipation" for the third time on the occasion of

visit of Maxim Gorky and a female companion ("paramour") to
expound doctrines of socialism in the United States. Woman
should do her job better. "If the legitimate voters had been
properly brought up, they would not need the help of their sisters." Blames woman suffragists for loose morals and neglected
homes.

665   HINMAN, HAROLD JAY. Why I Am Opposed to Woman Suffrage. New
      York: New York State Association Opposed to Woman Suffrage,
      8 pp.
         Says women and men are equal but have dissimilar functions.
      Most women do not want the vote. Included is an editorial from
      the New York Sun of 21 March 1912: "Woman suffrage should not be
      foisted upon New York by a minority or by the cowardice or mental
      inertia of the men folks."

666   JEPSON, NELS P. The Woman's Suffrage from a Religious and
      Judicial Point of View; Address Delivered at Eau Claire,
      Wisconsin. N.p., 23 pp.
         Says woman suffrage has religious implications—it will
      destroy Divine Law; it has social implications—it will harm the
      family. Uses Scriptures to show God originally made woman equal
      to man but when woman violated God's commandment, she was pun-
      ished by being made subordinate and dependent upon man. Much
      legal language in discussion of Divine Law. Insists that Divine
      Law must not be set aside for woman suffrage—it would be blas-
      phemous, treasonous, rebellious, permissive, and unconstitu-
      tional. Wants woman to be superior in the home, church, school,
      and society, and man in business, government, and war. Urges
      Wisconsin voters to adhere to God's law and vote against woman
      suffrage.

667   LOCKWOOD, GEORGE ROBINSON. Why I Oppose Woman Suffrage. A
      Pamphlet, Not an Essay. St. Louis: Privately printed, 20 pp.
         Says this is a pamphlet because it is colloquial, familiar,
      a friendly talk with his readers. Expresses his love and respect
      for women. Opposes woman suffrage because (1) where there is
      universal manhood suffrage, women and children are represented by
      men; (2) universal womanhood suffrage would add nothing to the
      voting wisdom of the present electorate; "woman is hysterical,"
      characterized by "an unbalanced and weak emotionalism," and
      therefore unsuited to such things as voting; (3) there are few
      legal discriminations against women in this country; the enfran-
      chisement of women is not necessary to correct them; and (4)
      woman suffrage would have an injurious effect on the relation of
      the sexes and be detrimental to women.

668   OWEN, HAROLD. Woman Adrift: A Statement of the Case Against
      Suffragism. New York: E.P. Dutton & Co., 333 pp.
         Says woman suffrage is "at best a dangerous experiment and
      at worst a positive retrogression." If women become independent,
      they will no longer become mothers, and the white races will

decrease. Woman is "horribly handicapped by the fact that Nature
assigned to her the function of giving birth to children." Men
are workers; women are mothers. Power is essential to the vote.
"The underlying idea of the Woman Suffrage movement is a disrespect for man, amounting in the worst cases to a real androphobia."

669   TIBBLES, C[HARLES] E. Books of Letters: How to Make the Best
       of Life vs. Woman Suffrage. 2 vols. N.p., 194 pp.
           Contains excerpts of letters written over fifty years of
       "active, strenuous and successful business life" to employees and
       friends on subjects like falsehood, strong drink, gambling, and
       woman suffrage. Alleges that no happily married women are for
       woman suffrage. "The whole agitation for woman suffrage has been
       brought about by adventuresses, those who expect to be benefited
       by holding government offices and by having political sway over
       the mothers of this country." Women cannot both vote and rear
       children, so the state will have to take over child care. Al-
       leges that free-love and common-law marriages will follow woman
       suffrage. Crime increases among women in public life because
       they meet more temptations.

670   TIBBLES, C[HARLES] E. Nonpartisan Political Lecture on Uni-
       versal Suffrage at the Republican National Convention, Held in
       Chicago, June 1912, and Colonel Roosevelt's Reversal of Doc-
       trine on Woman Suffrage. Chicago: C.E. Tibbles, 16 pp.
           Criticizes Roosevelt for changing his stand on woman suf-
       frage, calling him disloyal to the American people. Presents the
       standard arguments against woman suffrage with some bizarre addi-
       tions: alleges that agitation for suffrage has increased the
       number of husbands murdered by their wives. In Chicago this has
       reached two a month. "These murderesses have been driven par-
       tially insane by the agitation and teaching of the Woman Suffrage
       Doctrines." Woman suffrage causes "innumerable incurable dis-
       eases," including leprosy, which cannot be cured or controlled
       and which "are carried down through many generations indefinitely."

671   WHEELER, EVERETT. The Right and Wrong of Woman Suffrage. New
       York: New York State Association Opposed to Woman Suffrage,
       12 pp.
           Denies that woman suffrage would effect reforms. Opposes
       subjecting mothers to the turmoil and heat of political strife.
       Impugns the motives of some of the suffragists, saying they just
       want excitement and notoriety.

672   Where Woman's Work Is Most Needed. Bulletin no. 14. Chicago:
       Illinois Association Opposed to Woman Suffrage, 4 pp.
           Men and women occupy "duplex spheres." Quotes from
       Outlook, "The Enemy at the Gates," 6 April 1912 (1330), and from
       Ladies' Home Journal of October 1912 (692). Woman suffrage is "a
       vital and dangerous folly."

673   Woman Suffrage. Is It Sure to Come? Bulletin no. 12.
       Chicago: Illinois Association Opposed to Woman Suffrage,
       4 pp.
          Traditional arguments.

674   ABBOTT, LYMAN. "Women's Rights." Outlook 100 (10 February):
       302-4.
          Opposes woman suffrage because he does not believe men
       should "impose on women a share in the responsibilities of gov-
       ernment from which they have hitherto been exempt."

675   TARBELL, IDA M. "The Business of Being a Woman." American
       Monthly Magazine 73 (March):563-68.
          Excerpt from the book by the same name (see 969). Woman's
       task is to rear citizens. She does not need the vote to do this.

676   [ABBOTT, LYMAN]. "The Militant and Riotous Suffragettes."
       Outlook 100 (16 March):566-67.
          Applauds the firmness of the British government in dealing
       with the militant suffragettes. Says they show an utter lack of
       patriotism in pushing their claims when their country is in the
       midst of an industrial and social crisis.

677   "Broken Glass and Votes for Women." Literary Digest 44
       (23 March):584-85.
          Quotes several editorials from England deploring the de-
       struction of plate-glass windows by militant suffragettes. Says
       it is "the work of a few unbalanced women."

678   [ABBOTT, LYMAN]. "Anti-Suffrage in England." Outlook 100
       (13 April):797.
          Says the English suffragettes are as active as ever but are
       not getting their way. Reports on a great antisuffrage meeting
       held recently in Albert Hall.

679   HENDERSON, MANFORD E. "The Anti-Suffrage Argument."
       Collier's 49 (20 April):27.
          Is against woman suffrage because "man is the rightful law
       giver," appointed by God. Man would lose his respect for a woman
       who had equal political rights. Bad women, women of the lower
       class, will outvote the better class of women. Woman's place in
       government is to be the mother of man and train him to be a good
       citizen. "God forbid that man, because of the clamoring of a few
       women who have been disappointed in life, and of some who are
       seeking popularity and notoriety, should bring down upon woman--
       his mother, his wife, and daughters--the curse of woman suffrage;
       but instead give us back the days of chivalry, when woman looked
       upon man as her protector, and man did his best because of this
       faith in him."

680   TARBELL, IDA M. "The Irresponsible Woman and the Friendless
       Child." American Monthly Magazine 74 (May):49-53.
            Women should concern themselves with the plight of children
       in their neighborhood. Woman should mind her business--she does
       not need to vote for that.

681   WATKINS, ANN. "For the Twenty-two Million: Why Most Women Do
       Not Want To Vote." Outlook 101 (4 May):26-30.
            Says that with the exception of the ballot, everything the
       early suffragists fought for has been given to them, and more.
       Better to use influence than the ballot. Loathes politics and
       does not want to have to wallow in mire. Woman's strength is in
       her inability to use men's weapons.

682   [ABBOTT, LYMAN]. "The Right of the Silent Women." Outlook
       101 (18 May):105-6.
            Observes that ten thousand women marched in a suffrage
       procession, but that leaves 990,000 silent. Says we need to ask
       them whether they want to vote. Reminds readers that woman
       suffrage means women will enter the public arena with men, go to
       public meetings, etc. Politics is a conflict of wills. Women
       should be asked if they want to participate in this conflict.

683   BOK, EDWARD. "The Signal Failure of Woman Suffrage." Ladies'
       Home Journal 29 (June):6.
            Asserts that in states where there is woman suffrage, women
       have failed to create legislation that will protect life or to
       retard or prevent the growth of saloons, the social evil, vene-
       real diseases, easy marriage and easier divorce. Therefore,
       woman suffrage is a failure.

684   "A Famed Biologist's Warning of the Peril in Votes for Women."
       Current Literature 53 (July):59-62.
            Summary of Sir Almroth Wright's view on woman suffrage as
       they appear in the Times (London). He finds much mental disorder
       in suffragists as well as fatuousness, dishonesty, immorality.
       Two prosuffrage replies are also summarized and quoted.

685   GOODWIN, GRACE DUFFIELD. "The Non-Militant Defenders of the
       Home." Good Housekeeping 55 (July):75-80.
            Believes the suffrage movement presents "elements of grave
       danger to our home life in this country." Blames foreign ideas
       rather than American ones for this heresy. Women must keep homes
       safe--that is their political function. Also deplores the antag-
       onism toward men which she finds in the woman suffrage movement.
       If men are not trustworthy, it is the fault of mothers; the way
       to remedy this is for women to improve their homes and keep
       "hands clean of all political pitch."

686   MARTIN, I.T. "Concerning Some of the Anti-Suffrage Leaders."
       Good Housekeeping 55 (July):80-82.

Provides photographs and capsule biographies of several antisuffrage leaders to prove that "the women opposing suffrage are not the drones and parasites the suffragists love to call them, but earnest, thoughtful women."

687   [ABBOTT, LYMAN]. "Shall Women Vote?" Outlook 101 (3 August): 754-55.
Restates the Outlook's position on woman suffrage: (1) "Suffrage is not a natural right. . . . (2) It is not the duty of women to take part in government. . . . (3) "This burden cannot be put upon part of the women without putting it upon all the women. . . . (4) Voting is only a part, and a small part, of government. . . . (5) At the present time the majority of women are either opposed to assuming or reluctant to assume this additional responsibility." (6) If a majority of women wish to vote, let them--better than having them discontented. (7) Women can do more without suffrage than with it. (8) Women should be able to express their desires on this issue.

688   "Shall Women Vote? A Discussion by Readers of the Outlook." Outlook 101 (3 August):767-78.
Seventeen letters, twelve pro, four anti, one neutral. Of the antisuffragists, Mrs. Jacob H. Greene, Hartford, Connecticut, says men should "protect women from the excitement and temptation of politics and the burden of active participation in the government." H.A. Bereman, Florence, Nebraska, says woman suffrage is "a fad, put forward by women whose household cares (?) [sic] sit lightly upon them and who seek for stimulus among women's clubs, politics, and other extraneous activities." Clara M. Hobbs, Utica, New York, speaks for the average woman who already has enough to do. Julia T. Waterman, secretary, District Association Opposed to Woman Suffrage, Washington, D.C., finds significance in the small number of NAWSA dues-payers.

689   ROFF, O.M. "Woman and the Suffrage." Harper's Weekly 56 (17 August):6.
Asserts that woman is so constructed psychologically that she cannot come to any purely logical conclusion. Instead, she obeys her instincts. Education cannot make her any less capricious and unstable than she has always been. Therefore, women are unfit to use rationally the power of the ballot.

690   "England's Reign of Terror." Literary Digest 45 (24 August): 293-94.
Describes militant suffragettes as initiating a new terrorism in England by breaking windows, setting fire to buildings, attempting murder, and so forth. But some are finally being convicted and sentenced to prison. Such extremists have hurt the cause of woman suffrage in England, which has never been very popular.

691   "Failure of Finnish Feminism." Literary Digest 45
       (7 September):365-66.
            Summary of an article by Edith Sellers in Nineteenth Cen-
       tury and After (London) 72 (July):167-81 asserting that woman
       suffrage in Finland is a failure. Says "the section of the Diet
       which comprises women is of a heterogeneous character, and in-
       cludes those who have lived in domestic service." Some servants
       are becoming arrogant, and "politically minded wives and mothers
       neglect their households and their babies." Asserts that most
       women are the worse for having the vote.

692   "His Letters to His Mother: What Is the Truth about Woman
       Suffrage?" Ladies' Home Journal 29 (October):24.
            Points out that improvements in women's education have come
       without the ballot. Barriers against women's employments are
       down. Conditions for women are not better in suffrage states.
       Women do not want the ballot. They can be more effective in
       quiet civic work.

693   JOHNSTON, CHARLES. "An Equal Suffrage Dialogue: The Boy-Girl
       Threshes out a Burning Question with the Idealist." Harper's
       Weekly 56 (19 October):11.
            The Idealist argues that women should leave the issue of
       woman suffrage to men and men's chivalry. In this cute dialogue,
       the idealist male clearly bests the young "boy-girl" woman
       suffragist.

694   [ABBOTT, LYMAN]. "Votes for Women." Outlook 102
       (2 November):476.
            Says the chief opposition to woman suffrage comes not from
       liquor interests or politicians or men but "from women who find
       themselves already bearing all the responsibilities they feel
       themselves able to bear."

                                    1913

695   BOCK, ANNIE. Woman Suffrage: Address to the Committee on
       Woman Suffrage, United States Senate. Senate document no.
       160. Washington, D.C., 10 pp.
            Formerly a suffrage worker in California, says she appears
       "with a feeling of great temerity" but must work to get woman
       suffrage removed from California. Considers it "disastrous"--
       women in politics are no better than men and do not want to vote.
       "Suffrage robs women of all that is gentle, tender, attractive."
       Men are rude to women. Only socialists are pleased with it.
       Supporters are dupes of the socialists, who scorn our laws,
       denounce the Bible, trample the flag under foot, and want to tear
       down the Constitution. Woman suffrage is not in God's plan for
       women. Women should be protected by men from voting. Gives a
       stirring conclusion; pictures blood running in the streets.

696   CASWELL, Mrs. GEORGE A. <u>Address in Opposition to Woman</u>
        <u>Suffrage</u>. Boston: Massachusetts Association Opposed to the
        Further Extension of Suffrage to Women, 12 pp.
            Gives eleven reasons, none of them new, why she opposes
        woman suffrage. Estimates that "the thoughtful, reasoning woman
        is to the sum of the uneducated plus the semi-educated plus the
        indifferent plus those outside the pale plus the immigrants as,
        say--1 to 35 or 1 to 50." Reports that the Massachusetts Asso-
        ciation Opposed to the Further Extension of Suffrage to Women
        numbers 20,000 women. Its creed: "The ballot will not--cannot--
        remedy wrongs. In the name of the women whom we represent, in
        the name of the freedom of all women, we ask you not to place
        this state among the suffrage states; not to mistake a minority
        for the majority; not to thrust the ballot upon the women of
        Massachusetts."

697   GEORGE, Mrs. A[NDREW] J. <u>Woman Suffrage</u>: <u>Address before the</u>
        <u>Committee on Woman Suffrage, United States Senate, 19 April</u>
        <u>1913</u>. Washington, D.C.: Government Printing Office, 20 pp.
            Argues that a majority of women in the United States do not
        desire the suffrage. This is proved by the fact that women in
        Massachusetts defeated woman suffrage in 1895 and the suffragists
        have opposed putting it to women ever since. Women's civil and
        legal rights have been recognized without the ballot. She has
        educational and employment opportunities. If men are doing
        poorly in government (and this she denies), it is the fault of
        their mothers and wives. Suffrage is allied with socialism. It
        takes women out of the home and away from children. It is allied
        with militancy and feminism, which mean violence. Women should
        remain nonpartisan.

698   GOODWIN, GRACE DUFFIELD. <u>Anti-Suffrage</u>: <u>Ten Good Reasons</u>.
        New York: Duffield & Co., 141 pp.
            Denies that women as a whole suffer without suffrage or
        that the ballot would improve women's condition. Asserts that "a
        large part of the suffrage movement at present, in its fervor and
        fury, represents the acme of hysterical feminine thoughtlessness
        and unrest." Most of her ten reasons are a restatement of those
        already advanced, except that she includes the charge that woman
        suffrage agitation is coming from abroad and that we should not
        base our actions and policies on foreign conditions (an argument
        not original with her). Concludes that universal adult suffrage
        "will be a menace to American government and to American woman-
        hood, and that it is lacking in the fundamental principle of
        patriotism."

699   HARTWELL, EDWARD M. <u>Small Interest Taken by Women</u>. Boston:
        Massachusetts Association Opposed to the Further Extension of
        Suffrage to Women, 4 pp. Date is estimated.
            This statistician for the city of Boston analyzes statis-
        tics on school suffrage to show that women take small interest in
        voting. Reprinted from the <u>Boston Globe</u>, 19 January 1913.

700   JOHNSON, HELEN KENDRICK. Woman and the Republic: A Survey of
       the Woman-Suffrage Movement in the United States and a Discus-
       sion of the Claims and Arguments of its Foremost Advocates.
       New and enlarged ed. New York: Guidon Club Opposed to Woman
       Suffrage, 368 pp.
          Originally published in 1897, with postscripts added in
       1909 and 1913. Insists that the demand for woman suffrage is not
       evidence of progress. It arrays sex against sex. Woman can
       advance only as the race advances. Argues that woman suffrage is
       incompatible with true republicanism and will destroy the indi-
       vidual home. Asserts that the woman suffrage movement has not
       changed laws, opened professions or trades to women, or improved
       women's education. In her 1909 postscript asserts that "woman
       suffrage is the child of Rationalistic Communism." Excerpt
       printed in 533.

701   MACLAY, ARTHUR C. Is Christianity Hostile to the Cause of
       Woman Suffrage? Plainfield, N.J., 31 pp.
          God established the relative position of the sexes and
       mankind cannot change it. The woman suffragists reflect the
       spirit of hell rather than the spirit of heaven and insult the
       dignity of their sex. Alleges that the ballot-box "is merely a
       provisional substitute for war." Since women cannot go to war,
       they may not vote. It is only disloyal, unpatriotic, and effemi-
       nate men who support woman suffrage.

702   PYLE, JOSEPH GILPIN. Should Women Vote? Remarks Made at a
       Meeting of the Informal Club, St. Paul, 28 March 1913. N.p.:
       Privately printed by special request and unanimous consent,
       19 pp.
          Asserts that women should not vote because they are supe-
       rior to men. "The very qualities that give charm to womanhood
       impair the efficiency of the voting machine." There is plenty of
       good work for women to do without voting. Differentiation of the
       sexes is the higher state; woman suffrage would be regression.
       Agitation for the ballot has led to sex hostility. Woman suf-
       frage "is really a movement for the degradation of women."

703   SAMS, CONWAY WHITTLE, Esq. Shall Women Vote? A Book for Men.
       New York: Neale Publishing Co., 345 pp.
          This member of the Virginia bar regards woman suffrage as
       "one of the greatest afflictions which could happen to any
       State." It would "undermine the family, the home, and society
       itself." Brings forth many legal examples to show that man's
       authority is being broken down, men are becoming subordinated to
       women, women no longer obey their husbands, fathers' rights over
       children are eroded. Points out that Negroes have been disfran-
       chised, thus preventing a "menace to the peace and good order of
       the State." So women also should be prevented from voting.
       Control is the desideratum.

704   Some Facts about California's Experiment with Woman Suffrage.
       New York: National Association Opposed to Woman Suffrage, 7
       pp. Date is estimated.
           Argues that "the better moral element among women does not
       vote." Further, bad women "do vote for undesirable and vicious
       measures." Woman suffrage is also increasing the divorce rate.

705   TIBBLES, C[HARLES] E. The Doctrines of Woman Suffrage and
       Monogamous Marriage Antagonistic. N.p., 31 pp.
           Alleges that the woman suffrage movement preaches trial
       marriage, marriage contracts, easy dissolubility of marriage, no
       punishment for infidelity, and miscegenation, with the result
       that young men are afraid of marriage and disinclined to marry.

706   TYLER, Rev. ROBERT E. The Human Trinity: Is the Home
       Passing. New York: Shakespeare Press, 146 pp.
           Opposes woman suffrage. Believes that "it will not be a
       healthy day for the home when wives and mothers resort to the
       club, and talk of the right of suffrage, while immoral nurses
       pace about the streets with their children." Women should real-
       ize that their sons', brothers', friends' votes are their own.
       "Any extra discord in the home will likely be more harmful than
       good." Opposes "the woman who wants to hold office--shriek on
       political platforms, neglect her family, smoke and talk like
       men." Blames the women's movement for weakening home ties and
       contributing to the falling birth rate.

707   Votes for Men. New York: Duffield, 80 pp.
           A particularly hostile piece. Says only disappointed women
       would vote more than the first time (for novelty). Suffrage is
       just the latest fad. Alleges that "the true suffragette is a
       man-hater. Her chief end and aim, to stir up sex-antagonism."
       Most suffragists are in that dangerous time of life, middle age,
       when women are subject to "forms of mental aberration." Warns
       that such women "ought not to be making fools of themselves on
       platforms or in politics, but retired to the quiet of private
       life until they are in touch with normal feelings and sympathies
       again." Women are mentally disqualified from voting--"They are
       constitutionally incapable of fair play, of justice." Wants
       female malcontents to be put and kept in their place.

708   WHEELER, EVERETT P. For the Preservation of the Home:
       Address at Berkeley Lyceum, 6 March 1913. New York: New York
       State Association Opposed to Woman Suffrage, 7 pp.
           Believes that thirty years from now people will look back
       on woman suffrage as an hysterical outbreak. Neither man nor
       woman can change the laws of human nature. God has established
       the essential differences between the sexes, and "this will
       continue to be the source of the beauty and happiness of human
       life when all these rebels against it are forgotten."

709   WHEELER, EVERETT P. Home Rule: An Argument before Committee
        on Rules, House of Representatives, December 1913, against
        Proposition to Establish a Special Committee on Woman Suf-
        frage. New York: Man Suffrage Association, 7 pp.
             Says the Man Suffrage Association stands for "the sacred-
        ness of the home, the security of the home, the protection of the
        mother and the family." Calls the "suffrage doctrine of the
        independence of woman . . . odious."

710   Woman Suffrage: A Socialistic Movement. Bulletin no. 17.
        Chicago: Illinois Association Opposed to the Extension of
        Suffrage to Women, 8 pp.
             Insists that more progress for women has been made in
        nonsuffrage than in suffrage states. Asserts that "woman suf-
        frage is not and never has been a woman's movement. It was in
        its beginning fathered by men who had the destruction of our free
        constitution at heart, and the building up of a government upon a
        new economic system, which required as one of its most important
        foundation stones the equality of the sexes, instead of that
        equality of marriage which both science and revelation plainly
        recognize." What has resulted is "the neglect of the home duties
        which nature exacts of women and the pushing of them forward into
        the ranks of paid workers." Men become idle and unemployed.

711   Woman Suffrage and the Feminist Movement. Omaha: Nebraska
        Association Opposed to Woman Suffrage, 10 pp. Date is
        estimated.
             Quotes various sources to prove that leading suffragists
        support feminism--free love, voluntary motherhood, women keeping
        their own names, no wedding rings for women, shared housework,
        experts to care for children. Asks, "What is more destructive of
        home than feminism? What is more productive of licentiousness
        than feminism?" Quotes many feminists and antifeminists to show
        dangers.

712   WRIGHT, Sir ALMROTH E., M.D., F.R.S. The Unexpurgated Case
        against Woman Suffrage. New York: Paul B. Hoeber, 188 pp.
             Argues that the woman suffrage movement "has no real intel-
        lectual or moral sanction." Suffrage should be denied to women
        because if women vote, the vote will no longer represent physical
        force. Women also have "intellectual defects" which should pre-
        vent them from voting. Finally, the woman voter "would be perni-
        cious to the State also by virtue of her defective moral
        equipment."

713   DELAND, MARGARET. "The Third Way in Woman Suffrage." Ladies'
        Home Journal 30 (January):11-12.
             Describes herself as a moderate. Wants women to have to
        take a test for intelligence in matters of government before they
        can vote. Her description of both suffragists and antisuffra-
        gists is uncomplimentary; suffragists are "a loud and clamorous

body of women of sometimes illogical and occasionally lawless minds."

714   MARTIN, EDWARD S. "Editorial from Life on Feminine Unrest."
       Ladies' Home Journal 30 (January):23.
            Says woman suffragists are restless, and they force their
       restlessness on other women. Describes woman suffrage as an
       experiment. Not strongly anti but believes flatly that to marry
       and have and rear children is and always will be woman's natural
       destiny.

715   "Suffragette Intolerance." Forum 49 (February):254-56.
            Deplores the lengths to which the woman suffrage movement
       in England has gone. Believes that the militant movement has
       "passed beyond the proper bounds of reason and decency, in its
       public conduct," and that in private discussion the militants
       have passed the bounds of common courtesy.

716   [ABBOTT, LYMAN]. "Suffragette War Again in England." Outlook
       103 (8 February):281-82.
            Faults the militant suffragettes and their lawless, de-
       structive campaigns. The "suffragettes are not like other folks.
       They are possessed of an idée fixe."

717   "The Prospects of Woman Suffrage." Living Age 276
       (22 February):502-4.
            A discussion of the strategies of the woman suffragists in
       Parliament and a forecast that woman suffrage will take many
       years. The country must undergo "a long period of 'education.'"
       Seems to be neutral but then asserts that "if [woman suffrage]
       ever happens it will be a bad thing for the country and a very
       bad thing for women." Reprinted from the Spectator (London) 110
       (1 February):182-83.

718   SMITH, FREDERICK EDWIN. "The Future of Female Suffrage in
       England." Living Age 277 (5 April):10-14.
            Welcomes the fact that woman suffrage in England has been
       dealt a moral blow because not it will become clear that it is an
       agitation which is conducted "entirely from a handful of vocifer-
       ous women," making "no appeal to the great body of women," and
       "repudiated with indignation by the great majority of men."
       Reprinted from Pall Mall Magazine (London).

719   [ABBOTT, LYMAN]. "Ask Her." Outlook 103 (19 April):839-40.
            Says men need to know whether the vote is something most
       women want. All indications are that a majority of women either
       oppose or are indifferent to woman suffrage. Statistics are
       cited in support.

720   WHITE, Mrs. HELEN MAGILL. "An Open Letter on Woman Suffrage."
       Outlook 103 (26 April):893-94.

Says she is a suffragist but deplores the lawlessness of
British suffragettes and will give no money to the National
American Woman Suffrage Association until its leaders forcefully
denounce their British sisters' actions. Letter contains some
misogyny in attacks on women's foolishness, absurd dress, card-
playing, mannerless children, immoral dancing. High prices are
blamed on women. Women are inferior to men or they would not act
as the Englishwomen are doing.

721   BURROWS, FREDERICK B. "A Call to Sanity." New England
       Magazine, n.s. 49 (May):109-10.
       Calls it "foolish for the suffragettes to grow excited over
their supposed wrongs." Objects to dire predictions by antisuffragists. Women will never participate actively in politics
because it is against their nature. Counsels the suffragists to
behave sanely--"Militancy is folly. Women have lost an opportunity to show the world that they were capable of conducting a
campaign with restraint and reason."

722   [ABBOTT, LYMAN]. "Don't Ask Her." Outlook 104 (10 May):
       54-55.
       Abbott had proposed that there be a special election to
determine whether women want the vote. Reports that he has
received five responses from suffragists saying, in effect, do
not ask her. Says that proves that "only a small minority of
women favor this political revolution."

723   "The Victory of Militancy." Living Age 277 (13 May):569-71.
       Cheers the defeat of woman suffrage as the defeat of the
militant suffragettes, for "the triumph of woman suffrage in
England would have been the classical example of the efficacy of
force and violence." Warns that then every minority would have
been encouraged to follow the same path, even to arson and murder. Conjectures as to the source of militancy. Blames Fleet
Street for its growth. Reprinted from the Economist (London) 76
(10 May):1083-84.

724   [ABBOTT, LYMAN]. "Woman Suffrage Defeated by Suffragettes."
       Outlook 104 (17 May):83-84.
       Declares that the lawlessness of the militant faction in
England has contributed to the defeat of a bill allowing limited
suffrage to women. Deplores the activities of the Pankhurst
faction.

725   "England's Defeat of Woman-Suffrage." Literary Digest 46
       (31 May):1217-18.
       Blames the militants for the defeat of woman suffrage in
England because they have acted violently and irresponsibly; a
compilation of quotations from British sources.

726   "The Argument against Woman Suffrage." Independent 75
       (7 August):301-2.

Editorial that mocks the "choice sentiments" of Albert
Taylor Bledsoe, LL.D., against woman suffrage, calling his logic
confused. Bledsoe is quoted as blaming "the strong-minded women
of the North" for coming south to unsex the souls of southern
womanhood. The Senate repudiated the speech.

1914

727   BRONSON, MINNIE. Woman Suffrage and Child Labor Legislation.
New York: National Association Opposed to Woman Suffrage,
8 pp.
Says women have done more to protect children through creating public opinion than they could with suffrage. The best child
labor laws are in states where only men vote.

728   DODGE, Mrs. ARTHUR M. "Woman Suffrage Opposed to Women's
Rights." In Women in Public Life. Edited by James P.
Lichtenberger. Philadelphia: American Academy of Political
and Social Science, pp. 99-104.
Calls woman suffrage "a retrogressive movement toward conditions where the work of man and woman was the same because
neither sex had evolved enough to see the wisdom of being a
specialist in its own line." Women's civil and legal rights have
been established without woman suffrage. Women's higher education and access to professions have been improved without woman
suffrage. Women can render the best service to the state by
remaining exempt from political responsibility.

729   GIGLIOTTI, CAIROLI. Woman Suffrage: Its Causes and Possible
Consequences. Chicago: Barnard & Miller, 92 pp.
Pays homage to womanhood. Maligns militant English suffragettes, who have no respect for the law. Claims they are all
"old maids, or sore-heads, or ugly looking women, or hysterical
females." Impugns their motives. "Only the abnormal woman is
looking for equal suffrage." Insists that laws discriminate in
favor of women. Real mothers have enough to do; they should
concentrate on doing their duty at home. Deplores having women
involved in politics. Says woman suffrage places control in
hands of immigrants; Americans face race suicide. Quotes scientists who assert that women who engage in activities outside the
home are no longer women. Would allow only unmarried women and
widows to own property or do business. Arguments are old by now.

730   HALE, Mrs. CLARENCE. Against Woman Suffrage, An Argument.
Maine Association Opposed to Suffrage for Women, 8 pp. Date
is estimated.
Argues that only a small minority of women want suffrage.
They must go to extreme methods to recruit followers. The great
majority is silent. Denies that suffragists will support temperance. Objects to the tone of sex antagonism in suffrage arguments. Woman suffrage will not help working women or children.

731   Manifesto. Omaha: Nebraska Men's Association Opposed to
       Woman Suffrage, 11 pp.
            Insists that the Association reveres and respects women and
       will grant them everything necessary for their true womanhood,
       but does not believe women are adapted to political work. If
       women vote, we would be liable to insurrections, seditions, and
       revolutions, so emotional and excitable are women. Signed by
       thirty Omaha men.

732   Nebraska Clergymen Condemn Suffrage. Omaha: Nebraska Men's
       Association Opposed to Woman Suffrage, 12 pp.
            Five Nebraska clergymen condemn woman suffrage and feminism
       in the usual terms. Notable is the Reverend Adolf Hult, pastor
       of Immanuel Lutheran Church in Omaha, who equates suffragism with
       feminism and says it is led by dangerous minds like Gilman, Inez
       Milholland, and Mrs. Belmont, who have taken over good women like
       Jane Addams and great magazines. Alleges that "a feministic
       American womanhood will give us a destroyed American home life.
       A wrecked American home means a doomed America. The hosts of the
       Orient will flock like vultures upon the emasculated citizenship
       of our beautiful land." Others call it immoral, un-Christian,
       against God's teaching, etc.

733   TEN EYCK, JOHN C. Suffrage and Government. New York: Guidon
       Club Opposed to Woman Suffrage, 8 pp.
            Insists that manhood suffrage is "the expression of the
       will of those whose power in the aggregate supports the state."
       It cannot be shared with women because it comes from men's phys-
       ical organization. . . . The power of men in the aggregate is
       the coercive force that energizes government."

734   WHEELER, EVERETT P. Home Rule: An Argument before Judiciary
       Committee, House of Representatives, March 1914. New York:
       Man Suffrage Association, 6 pp.
            Repeats some material from December 1913 address. Believes
       each state should regulate the suffrage according to the judgment
       of its own citizens. Opposes adoption of a constitutional amend-
       ment. Repeats what the Home Rule party stands for.

735   WHEELER, EVERETT P. The Woman and the Vote: Discussion under
       the Auspices of the Civic Forum, Carnegie Hall, New York, 26
       January 1914. New York: Man-Suffrage Association Opposed to
       Extension of Political Suffrage to Women, 10 pp.
            Does not want political activity forced upon women. Says
       women already have equal opportunities. Political suffrage for
       women has produced bad results--"All history shows that when
       women are engrossed with public contests and ambitions they
       become vindictive and implacable." Good women can do more for
       social betterment without suffrage. Fears that "what the most
       zealous advocates of woman suffrage really want is independence
       and domination."

736   Woman Suffrage in Practice. Boston: Massachusetts Associa-
      tion Opposed to the Further Extension of Suffrage to Women,
      15 pp.
          A critique of an article by George Creel, "What Have Women
      done with the Vote?" in Century for March 1914. Cites errors of
      fact, of interpretation, of emphasis. Says antisuffragists are
      the good folks who "oppose woman suffrage because they believe it
      to be a menace both to women and to the state, and because they
      believe that the interests of women and children can be better
      served by disinterested and non-partisan influence than by thrust-
      ing women into the strife of politics and loading them with men's
      responsibilities."

737   BEYER, THOMAS PERCIVAL. "Creative Evolution and the Woman
      Question." Educational Review 47 (January):22-27.
          Uses Bergson's Creative Evolution to show why the woman
      suffrage movement is fundamentally unwise. Women are instinct,
      men intelligence. Describes three types of women who want suf-
      frage: frenzied women who must compete with men for jobs; prod-
      ucts of coeducation who "wish to beat men at their own game"; and
      "mannish women" who "are in reality women only by accident" and
      push toward "masculine restlessness rather than towards feminine
      security." Woman suffrage would be a retrograde step and "give
      vast encouragement to women in the anomalous attempt to become
      the same as men." Warns that woman suffrage is just the entering
      wedge of feminism.

738   SEAWELL, MOLLY ELLIOT. "Two Suffrage Mistakes." North
      American Review 199 (March):366-82.
          Insists that woman suffrage would create a helpless and
      irresponsible class of voters who would enact laws they could not
      enforce and legislate upon affairs they do not understand. Calls
      the proposed suffrage amendment a "shrieking and screaming ab-
      surdity" and holds up the spectacle of "alien races" taking over
      in the South and West. Deplores the suffragist opposition to the
      income tax.

739   BROUGHAM, H.B. "How Woman Suffrage Has Worked." Unpopular
      Review 1 (April-June):307-32.
          A survey of the workings of woman suffrage. Articles by
      both suffragists and antisuffragists, with little evaluation save
      this: "In the length and breadth of this Union there are no
      distinctive results of woman suffrage where it has been granted
      in part or in whole." Compliments the feminists on not following
      the English model.

740   ROBBINS, ELLEN R. "Why Woman Suffrage?" National Magazine 44
      (May):266-71.
          Insists that woman suffrage has not performed as expected
      in those states which have granted women suffrage. Women do not
      want the ballot and would not use it. They can do more without

it. All law rests on force; women could not back up laws with
force.

741   BEEBE, C. WILLIAM. "The Jelly-fish and Equal Suffrage."
       Atlantic 114 (July):36-47.
          Does not want to deny the gulf between man and woman, which
       woman suffrage would do. Advances not equality but rather "spe-
       cialization and a thoughtful, respectful cooperation between the
       sexes--this is the true sex equality." Uses biology, especially
       jellyfish, to prove his points.

742   DODGE, Mrs. ARTHUR M. "Woman Suffrage Opposed to Woman's
       Rights." Annals of the American Academy of Political Science
       56 (November):99-104.
          Opposes woman suffrage because "stability of government
       demands that the control of government should remain in the hands
       of those who can be responsible for results. . . . Woman suf-
       frage in its last analysis is a retrogressive movement toward
       conditions where the work of man and woman was the same because
       neither sex had evolved enough to see the wisdom of being a
       specialist in its own line." Laws unfavorable and unjust to
       women have been removed. Women can be educated in the trades and
       professions. Women have the right to be exempted from political
       duties to do the work for which they are suited. It is right
       that the state surround them with protective legislation. Part
       of an issue devoted to women in public life--this is the only
       anti.

1915

743   Brief on Woman Suffrage: Political Suffrage for Women Subver-
       sive of American Ideals. New York: Man Suffrage Association,
       18 pp.
          Says that woman suffrage would lower the quality of the
       electorate by adding indifferent voters. Woman suffragists are
       described as vain and lusting for power. "Man's government by
       woman is a political absurdity." Men govern by physical power;
       woman could not. Asserts that woman suffrage has been tried and
       failed. Woman suffrage is allied with feminism and socialism and
       would lead to social revolution.

744   The Case Against Woman Suffrage: The Most Important Question
       on the Ballot at the State Election, 2 November 1915. Boston:
       Massachusetts Anti-Suffrage Committee, 48 pp.
          Insists that woman suffrage would hurt both women and the
       state. Various suffrage states are examined to show that woman
       suffrage has been damaging there. Divorce is increasing in woman
       suffrage states.

745   Eminent Catholic Prelates Oppose Woman Suffrage. Boston:
       Massachusetts Anti-Suffrage Committee, 4 pp.
          Reprint of 755.

746   LEATHERBEE, Mrs. ALBERT T. Anti-Suffrage Campaign Manual.
      Boston: A.T. Bliss & Co., 31 pp.
          Explains the antisuffrage position. Alleges that only "a
      small body of intensive and fanatical women" want to vote. The
      real danger is the indifferent vote. Explains why the vote could
      not help married women, single women, wage-earning women. Many
      statistics. Gives reasons why men should oppose woman suffrage,
      quoting Frank Foxcroft. Complains that feminism is unpleasant
      but must be discussed because it is affiliated with woman suf-
      frage. Describes all the problems with feminism. Denies any
      connection with woman suffrage and prohibition. Denies that
      women with the ballot will stop war.

747   LEWIS, W.D. "Woman's Rights." Fort Worth: Panther City
      Printing Co., 11 pp.
          Reports and prints the resolution adopted in 1914 by the
      State Convention of the Farmers' Educational and Co-Operative
      Union of Texas. Woman's "noble achievements should not be marred
      or her hallowed influence blighted by the coarser duties of
      citizenship." Calls for southern chivalry to preserve woman
      unsullied. Alleges that "directing the affairs of government is
      not within woman's sphere, and political gossip would cause her
      to neglect the home, forget to mend our clothes and burn the
      biscuits." Warns women: "Touch not the ballot box. In it are
      the charm of the serpent, the lure of the spider and the sting of
      the adder." Asks God to save the country from "becoming a hen-
      pecked nation; help us keep sissies out of Congress."

748   [M., G.]. The Red Behind the Yellow: Socialism in the Wake
      of Suffrage. New York: National Association Opposed to Woman
      Suffrage, 4 pp. Date is estimated.
          Asserts that "socialists are behind woman suffrage." De-
      tails what socialism means: no more private property, no more
      marriage, no more homes but state nurseries instead. "If you
      hold your family relations, your home, your religion, as sacred
      and inviolate, if you desire to preserve them for yourself and
      for your children for all time, then work with all your might
      against the companion, the handmaid, the forerunner of socialism--
      Woman Suffrage."

749   MARTINE, JOHN E. Article on Woman Suffrage from District
      of Columbia Association Opposed to Woman Suffrage, Introduced
      by Senator Martine (New Jersey) in U.S. Senate on 25 February
      1915. Washington, D.C., 14 pp.
          States that woman suffrage has had a pernicious effect in
      states where it now exists. Says it is "unjust to place the
      burden on a majority of women in order that the few aggressive,
      forward, notoriety-seeking women can break into politics, some of
      whom resent the fact that they were created women and not men."
      Alleges that woman suffrage would increase the power of the Negro
      in politics. Opposes women in the work force, saying they lose
      their delicate charm and sympathy. Quotes Senator Vest of

Missouri, who asks what man would want to go home after a hard
day of work and "fall into the arms of a constitutional lawyer or
a politician for rest, consolation, and comfort?"

750   OLIN, STEPHEN H. An Argument Against the Woman's Suffrage
      Amendment to the Constitution of New York. Rhinebeck, N.Y.,
      8 pp.
         Reprinted from Rhinebeck Gazette of 16 October 1915.
      Insists that small groups rule better than large ones. Urges
      that the vote not be doubled. Women should continue to trust men
      to do well by them.

751   OSBORNE, DUFFIELD. Xanthippe on Woman Suffrage. New York:
      National Association Opposed to Woman Suffrage, 14 pp.
         Reprint of 761.

752   PARKER, WILLIAM. The Fundamental Error of Woman Suffrage.
      New York: Fleming H. Revell, 125 pp.
         Extremely reactionary considering the date. Argues that
      woman suffrage is morally wrong, against the God-given nature of
      women, and detrimental to their highest interests. Men and women
      cannot and must not perform the same work; "any confusion of
      their workings means disorder, disease, and sometimes death."
      Opposes women wearing men's clothing as "contrary to both moral
      and civil law." According to an unnamed authority, women cannot
      engage in physical exercise without developing a masculine mind.
      Alleges women in business or on the stage become degraded; they
      are also causing the church to degenerate. "In its final analy-
      sis, woman suffrage is opposed to all law, precedent, or estab-
      lished order of things." Upholds "true womanhood."

753   ROBINSON, MARGARET C. Woman Suffrage a Menace to Social
      Reform. Boston: Women's Anti-Suffrage Association of Massa-
      chusetts, 12 pp. Date is estimated.
         Insists that woman suffrage would destroy women's nonparti-
      san power and moral influence. The great body of home-making
      women would not vote, only the wrong-minded women. Women must
      work to keep their opportunities for civic reform rather than
      accepting political rights.

754   SHURTER, EDWIN DU BOIS, ed. Woman Suffrage: Bibliography and
      Selected Arguments. Austin: University of Texas, 86 pp.
         A handbook used for interscholastic debates. Contains
      articles pro and con, most of which appeared originally else-
      where. Articles by former Supreme Court Justice Brown, Henry L.
      Stimson, James Buckley, Mary Sedgwick, Priscilla Leonard, William
      Croswell Doane, Rose Terry Cooke, O.B. Frothingham, and others.

755   Some Catholic Views on Woman Suffrage. N.p., 4 pp.
         Quotes the Catholic Encyclopedia: "The indirect influence
      of women which in a well ordered state makes for the moral order,
      would suffer severe injury by political equality. The opposition

expressed by many women to the introduction of woman suffrage as
for instance, the New York Association Opposed to Woman Suffrage,
should be regarded by Catholics, as, at least, the voice of
common sense" (15:694). Quotes James, Cardinal Gibbons, and many
more. Archbishop Moeller requests women to sign the antisuffragist list and says, "Pastors might urge the women from the pulpit
to declare themselves in this regard to this matter when the
opportunity presents itself." Reprinted in 745.

756   STIMSON, HENRY L. Suffrage Not a Natural Right. New York:
      New York State Association Opposed to Woman Suffrage, 4 pp.
           In this letter from the former secretary of war, he opposes
      woman suffrage because he believes "it would throw an additional
      strain upon the efficiency of popular government which would tend
      to make it less competent to grapple with the increasing problems
      of to-day." Women today are more privileged than men. They have
      no idea of government, though, and no understanding of methods of
      force. Thus they would imperil the country if permitted to vote.
      City women would vote more readily than country women, which
      would destroy proportionate representation between city and
      country.

757   TAYLOR, ROBERT S. Woman Suffrage: An Argument against It.
      N.p., 18 pp. Date is estimated.
           Says woman suffrage is not only unnecessary, "it would be
      injurious to the highest interests of society." Men build homes
      and women must take care of them. Woman suffrage would destroy
      the home.

758   Woman Suffrage and the Liquor Question: Facts Show that
      Women's Votes Have Not Aided Prohibition. New York: Women's
      Anti-Suffrage Association, 4 pp.
           Alleges that actually, suffragists seek the support of
      brewers, brewery workers, and their affiliated interests. Cites
      Susan B. Anthony and many others. Women's votes will not solve
      the liquor problem. Vote no on woman suffrage on 2 November
      1915.

759   ROBINSON, MARGARET C. "The Other Side of Suffrage." New
      Republic 1 (16 January):24.
           Cites facts to prove that "human values" have not been
      operative in suffrage states; uses Colorado as an example. Ob-
      jects to the New Republic's stand in favor of woman suffrage and
      alleges that "facts are abhorrent to the suffrage mind."

760   "Chivalry in Congress." New Republic 1 (23 January):8-9.
           Mocks the chivalrous gentlemen in the Congress who oppose
      woman suffrage—useful for quotations, especially of Mr. Bowdle
      of Ohio, who is pilloried by the author for his leering, lewd
      contempt of women, his "cave man idea." Congress chastized for
      greeting him with applause and laughter.

761   OSBORNE, DUFFIELD. "Xanthippe on Woman Suffrage." Yale
       Review, n.s. 4 (April):590-607.
            In cute form of a dialogue among Xanthippe, Socrates, and
       Aspasia. Socrates is rational, Xanthippe prosuffrage but frivo-
       lous. Socrates has all the customary antisuffrage arguments.
       Aspasia has doubts about suffrage and about women entering into
       business because men are no longer courteous or deferential to
       women. Aspasia says Socrates has convinced her. "I never really
       felt as if I wanted to vote. Now I see that woman suffrage would
       be an innovation dangerous for the state and even more dangerous
       to our own well-being." Xanthippe remains unconvinced but
       Socrates has the last word. Reprinted in 750.

762   ROBINSON, MARGARET C. "The Suffrage Prophets." Unpopular
       Review 4 (July-September):127-39.
            Says woman suffragists have made many prophecies regarding
       women and the vote, none of which have come true. Things have
       improved without it and have not been improved with it. Finds
       the latest prophecy, that woman suffrage will do away with war,
       equally unfounded. Much use of evidence from the militant suf-
       fragettes' actions in England.

763   MC KEE, JOSEPH V., A.M. "Shall Women Vote?" Catholic World
       102 (October):45-54.
            Finds untenable the claims that suffrage is a natural right
       or that taxation without representation is tyranny. Nature has
       preserved the physical and psychological differences between the
       sexes. Woman suffrage would blur them. Women have progressed
       without the vote. They should not sacrifice their disinterest-
       edness. Woman suffrage would destroy the family by emphasizing
       the individual. Woman suffrage leaders are aligned with
       socialists.

764   PUTNAM, Mrs. G.H. "Wayland the Feminist." Unpopular Review 4
       (October-December):237-54.
            A fictional account of one Wayland, who starts out his
       venture confused about woman suffrage, although ostensibly a
       feminist. Through various experiences Wayland comes to see the
       futility of woman suffrage, the unwisdom of doubling the number
       of ballots; his common sense opposes woman suffrage.

765   GEORGE, ALICE N. "Woman Suffrage Must Fail." Independent 84
       (11 October):59.
            Insists that woman suffrage must fail because it is based
       on the fallacious notion that "there is in our social order a
       definite sex division of interests, and that the security of
       woman's interests depends upon her possession of the elective
       franchise." Believes that real equality between the sexes would
       be brutal and retrogressive for women. Calls the woman suffrage
       movement "an imitation-of-man movement, and as such merits the
       condemnation of every normal man and woman." Calls woman suf-
       frage the political phase of feminism, which would totally revise

the relations of the sexes. Antisuffragists know that such a false, uneconomical, unnecessary, and unnatural movement cannot achieve a permanent success.

766   "No Votes for New Jersey Women." Literary Digest 51
       (30 October):946-47.
            Useful for quotations from New Jersey antisuffragists.
       Mrs. Breese doubts that woman suffrage will ever come to or be
       desired by women in the East. James R. Nugent says: "New Jersey
       leads off in the fight for sane government and rational politics,
       the purity of the home, and the protection of her womanhood."
       Asserts that the strongest argument against woman suffrage "has
       been a procession of long-haired men and short-haired women
       streaming across the Hudson River into New Jersey" but that their
       appeal does not reach "the intelligent, responsible, and sober-
       minded citizenship of New Jersey," which stands for women in the
       home, woman as moral force, protector, and guide of children.

767   RAND, Professor E.K. "Professor Perry and the Condescending
       Man." Harper's Weekly 61 (30 October):428.
            Responding to a prosuffrage article by Professor Ralph
       Barton Perry, he states flatly: "Woman as a class is not fitted
       for these strenuous acts of state, and unless she can as a class
       enter freely into them she should not have the right to vote
       about them." Furthermore, the majority of women do not want the
       burden of the vote imposed upon them.

768   "Both Sides Encouraged by the Suffrage Defeat." Literary
       Digest 51 (13 November):1065-67.
            In a generally balanced, even prosuffrage article about the
       defeat of woman suffrage in New York State, one statement stands
       out. James Brett Stokes in the New York Tribune says that the
       defeat proves "that the great, thinking Eastern States are not
       ready to join in a movement started by the Mormon Church to
       increase its power, and backed by Socialists and IWWs, plus the
       strong indorsement of Harry Thaw."

769   EBY, TH. "The Admirable Anti." New Republic 5 (13 November):
       36-37.
            Analyzes the woman antisuffragist and her fears. Believes
       they stem from her awareness that participation in politics will
       require the whole art of being a leisure-class lady to be re-
       worked. The admirable antisuffragist is bound to fight to pro-
       tect her vested interests in the existing order of womanhood.

                                  1916

770   Anti-Suffrage Essays by Massachusetts Women. Introduction by
       Ernest Bernbaum, Ph.D., Harvard University. Boston: Forum
       Publications, 154 pp.

Materials from the 1915 Massachusetts campaigners and speak-
ers. In his introduction Bernbaum says that Massachusetts men
voted against woman suffrage because most women did not want the
vote, because the creation of a large body of voters who did not
vote would be bad for government, and because "they grew dis-
gusted with the temperament, the notions, and the methods typical
of the few women who clamored for the vote." A short biography
precedes each of the seventeen essays as well as an introductory
statement by Mrs. John Balch. Essays cover traditional ground.

771   The Case Against Woman Suffrage. Boston: National Anti-
       Suffrage Association, 31 pp.
          Advances the standard arguments. "Woman Suffrage is wrong
in theory and bad in practice."

772   VERTREES, JOHN J. An Address to the Men of Tennessee on
       Female Suffrage. Nashville, Tenn., 20 pp.
          Does not believe that the men of Tennessee really approve
of woman suffrage or that "the strident and conspicuous few now
clamoring for their 'rights,' truly represent the womanhood of
Tennessee." Besides, it is not a question of what women want but
what they ought to have, which men must determine. Repeats old
arguments. Warns that "if civilization is to be preserved, much
less advanced, woman's rights and woman's duties must be as
motherhood requires. . . . Anything which takes her abroad,
whether it be business or politics, injures the race, the family,
and her." Raises the specter of race, pointing out that Negroes
support woman suffrage and the rights of individuals. Many
quotations linking feminism and suffrage.

773   "Votes for Women: Editorial." Unpopular Review 5 (January-
       March):209-13.
          Quotes a letter from a militant objecting to "Confessions
of an Anti" (see 320) and then, in agreement with Rossiter
Johnson, opposes woman suffrage because there would be no force
behind a woman's vote. Says the woman's movement has done much
damage to woman's character, as witness the letter from "Militant" and "the make-up of every feminist gathering."

774   "Labor's Position on Woman Suffrage." New Republic 6
       (11 March):150-52.
          Describes recent action of the Minnesota Federation of
Labor in refusing to adopt a resolution approving woman suffrage.
The Minneapolis Labor Review upheld this action "because of the
fear that the women, if given the ballot, will hasten the cause
of prohibition," which would increase unemployment. Sees significant involvement of liquor interests in persuading the labor
movement to oppose woman suffrage. A prosuffrage article useful
for sources and analysis of opposition.

775   BRAY, WILLIAM M. "Do Women Want the Vote?" Atlantic 117
       (April):433-41.
           Describes the activities of a (fictitious?) state senator
       in polling the women of his district as to whether they want to
       vote. Two thirds did not. The young legislator even defies his
       suffragist mother, who wants the vote to outlaw the saloon,
       because, he reasons, if men want the saloon, should woman suf-
       frage put women in the position of voting against most men?
       Besides, equal suffrage is for all time and therefore dangerous.
       Clever narrative.

776   "Suffrage Sabotage: Editorial." Unpopular Review 6 (July-
       September):219-20.
           Comments on a vote at a recent state convention of the
       suffrage party in New York City where the members resolved not to
       contribute to any charities until women secure the vote. Calls
       the move absurd: "it is plain to certainty that women passing
       this [resolution] have not yet reached a point of sufficient
       poise and judgment to qualify them for the suffrage."

777   MEYER, ANNIE NATHAN. "As Another Anti Sees Hughes." New
       Republic 8 (2 September):115-16.
           Tries to explain her antisuffragist position. Says women
       oppose suffrage because they "feel safer in the hands of men."
       Prefers "freedom from party strife" because it makes "the non-
       partisan voice of women the strongest kind of a moral spur" and
       then women's activities can be directed to the home, philan-
       thropy, and the arts. Prefers not to have our already crowded
       and overbalanced electorate further extended by votes for women.

778   R., M. "Amendment Anti-Democratic." New Republic 8
       (21 October):298.
           Opposes the federal suffrage amendment as undemocratic. It
       would let the legislatures of states decide to give suffrage to
       women when the majority opposes woman suffrage. Thus the suffra-
       gists would have to convince only Congress and thirty-six legis-
       latures, not the average man, who "votes against woman suffrage
       because he finds the average woman has no use for it."

                              1917

779   An Appeal to the Electors of the State of New York to Vote
       Against Woman Suffrage on 6 November 1917. [New York], 6 pp.
           Gives standard reasons against woman suffrage plus two new
       concerns: it would introduce feminism into government, which
       would "overthrow long-established governmental policies and in-
       troduce instability, sentimentalism and caprice." Second, the
       war is a solemn demonstration and warning against woman suffrage
       because it "emphasizes the importance of not dragging [woman]
       into politics and feminizing our government." Quotes Bishop
       Vincent, founder of the Chautauqua, Cardinal Gibbons, Cardinal

Farley, and Rabbi Joseph Silverman, who says that woman suffrage
equals socialism and that it "will destroy all that God and man
have in the past years built up."

780   DOS PASSOS, JOHN R. Equality of Suffrage Means the Debasement
       Not Only of Women but of Men. New York: National Association
       Opposed to Woman Suffrage, 8 pp. Date is estimated.
           Finds woman suffrage spreading with "an enthusiasm approach-
       ing a religious or fanatic frenzy." Says women have all the
       rights they need and should be thankful for what they have, not
       claim more. Fundamentally objects to woman suffrage because of
       the "physical, moral and natural differences of the two sexes"
       and their separate missions. Opposes any step which would impair
       the efficiency of women to bear children. Predicts that "all of
       the nice and refining barriers which now separate the two sexes
       will disappear and a common, vulgar and even savage basis of life
       and intercourse will be established between them." Already we
       see women becoming masculinized in dress, habits, and speech.

781   FOXCROFT, LILY RICE. Why Are Women Opposing Woman Suffrage?
       Boston: Women's Anti-Suffrage Association of Massachusetts,
       11 pp. Date is estimated.
           Wants women to continue to work disinterestedly and nonpar-
       tisanly. Worries about "apathetic, ignorant, sordid women" vot-
       ing. Argues that women know little about business, which is
       necessary to cast a thoughtful vote, and that women do not vote.
       Where they do, it is not assured that they will support temper-
       ance. Says that suffragists routinely reassure liquor interests
       and drinking men that suffrage does not equal temperance. Be-
       lieves that the movement is diverting women away from home duties
       and mothering, slurring domesticity, and providing bad examples.
       Cites easy divorce, trial marriages, state rearing of children,
       and voluntary motherhood. Reprinted from Wellesley Alumnae
       Quarterly, April 1917.

782   HALE, Mrs. ANNIE RILEY. Woman Suffrage: An Article on the
       Biological and Social Aspects of the Woman Question.
       Washington, D.C.: Government Printing Office, 8 pp.
           Says that the feminists' contention that women need mascu-
       line activities for their development is "as scientifically un-
       sound as it is socially pernicious." Quotes S. Weir Mitchell,
       Ida Tarbell, Sir Almroth Wright, Herbert Spencer, and many oth-
       ers. Insists on structural, physiological, and psychical sex
       differences and that these increase as we ascend the evolutionary
       scale. Feminist goals lead to racial degeneracy. Raises the
       specter of transvestism. Faults Olive Schreiner. Blames woman's
       lack of creativity on sex differentiation. Says feminists and
       suffragists are bad logicians and bad psychologists. Finds sex
       distrust and sex hostility lurking behind woman suffrage. No new
       antisuffrage arguments.

783   HARTLEY, CATHERINE GASQUOINE. <u>Motherhood</u> <u>and</u> <u>the</u> <u>Relationship</u>
      <u>of</u> <u>the</u> <u>Sexes</u>. New York: Dodd, Mead & Co., 402 pp.
      Argues that the war restored women to their place and
taught them the possible results of their "sex rebellion."
Faults the suffrage movement for its "wild pranks" and its desire
to crush and level sex characteristics. "Mixed up with all that
was fine in their movement was an infinity of glitter and tinsel,
vanity and restlessness. There was present always an intense and
theatrical egotism, a yearning to make an impression and force
applause at any cost." Argues that women got caught in militant
suffragism because something was missing in their lives--a cause,
a focus of passion. Now that cause can be reasserted--motherhood
and sex differentiation.

784   JOHNSON, ROSSITER. <u>Helen</u> <u>Kendrick</u> <u>Johnson:</u> <u>The</u> <u>Story</u> <u>of</u> <u>Her</u>
      <u>Varied</u> <u>Activities</u>. New York: Publishers Printing Co., 64 pp.
      Recounts how Mrs. Johnson became convinced that the suf-
frage movement was unsound through reading the illogical and
unworthy arguments of the suffragists. Useful for a discussion
of her antisuffrage activities as well as a bibliography of her
writings.

785   ROBINSON, MARGARET C. <u>Woman</u> <u>Suffrage</u> <u>in</u> <u>Relation</u> <u>to</u> <u>Patriotic</u>
      <u>Service</u>. N.p.: Public Interests' League of Massachusetts,
      12 pp.
      States that women in the past have always done their part
in national emergencies. Wonders whether "the hiking, parading
woman whose ideal is publicity and the limelight [has] destroyed
men's trust in woman's willingness to serve?" Insists that
suffragists generally have not supported the war and are therefore unpatriotic, whereas patriotic antisuffragists immediately
began working for humanity. Much invidious contrasting of suffragist and antisuffragist war work. Alleges that suffragists
put suffrage above war work.

786   TERRY, EDMUND T. <u>Votes</u> <u>for</u> <u>Women:</u> <u>Why</u>? New York: Hamilton
      Press, 63 pp.
      Alleges that women want to vote because they are restless
and want to be like men. "This foolish demand for 'Votes for
Women' is not so much a logical demand for the rectification of
an unjust condition, but rather a sort of unthinking, hysterical
protest against the fact that the God of Nations has made them
women." Says the logical extension of suffrage is that father is
no longer important, rape no longer a crime, chastity "a dis-
graceful folly," illegitimacy no problem. "Easy divorce is another rotten and obtrusive plank in the suffragette platform."
Characterizes women who demand the vote as noisy, reckless,
obstreperous, illogical, untruthful--a motley crowd of little
value to themselves, their sex, or their country.

787   MURDOCK, J.B.   "Woman Suffrage: A Protest."   Outlook 117
       (21 November):457-58.
           Protests what he sees as a change in policy as announced in
       a prowoman suffrage editorial on 14 November 1917. Editors add
       this note: "The duty of good citizens with regard to woman
       suffrage is now to cease theoretical discussion of the question
       and put all their energies into helping the women to make the
       best of the new civic opportunities which have been given them."
       Woman suffrage had just passed in New York State.

788   MEYER, ANNIE NATHAN.   "The Anti-Suffragist Replies."   New
       Republic 13 (1 December):124-25.
           Asserts that the leaders of the woman suffrage cause have
       been poor patriots. They have nagged the president, been disre-
       spectful to him, given more money to suffrage causes than the war
       effort, tried to keep the country out of the war, and diverted
       women's attention from needed war work. Concludes her letter by
       recounting the intolerance she has suffered because of her anti-
       suffrage position.

                                 1918

789   CARVER, THOMAS NIXON.   Woman Suffrage from a Neutral Point of
       View: Address Delivered at the Annual Meeting of the Cambridge
       Branch of the Women's Anti-Suffrage Association of Massachu-
       setts, 13 May 1918.   Boston: A.T. Bliss & Co., 16 pp.
           Says we should put aside discussions of woman suffrage
       during the great war but suffragists "persist in pestering the
       public and trying to divert attention of law makers and adminis-
       trators from the problems of the war to the pet hobby of the
       suffragists, hoping by the stridency of their appeals to force
       weak and vacilating men to give them what they ask for in order
       to get rid of them." Objects to the methods of the more aggres-
       sive suffragists. Points out that woman suffrage is simply part
       of the drift toward individualistic as opposed to familial units
       which is also fostering divorce and lowering the birth rate.

790   HAZELTON, JOHN H.   Just a Few Thoughts Upon the Woman Suffrage
       Question.   New York: Erle W. Whitfield, 69 pp.
           Insists that suffrage is not a right. Takes up legal cases
       (Minor v. Happersett) and the proposed constitutional amendment.
       Opposes the latter because it would make states that do not
       support the amendment rightly discontented. Reprints letters to
       newspaper editors from 1915. Quotes many antisuffragists. Says
       women should not vote because they are foolish, feminine, in-
       stinctual, and illogical.

791   PEEBLES, ISAAC LOCKHART.   Is Woman Suffrage Right? The Ques-
       tion Answered.   Meridian, Miss.:   Tell Farmer, 25 pp.
           Insists that "God's word is the only authority" for settle-
       ment of the issue of woman suffrage. Uses Scriptures to show

that Christ is the head of every man and man the head of every woman, and this must be a relationship of inequality. Voting would make it possible for women to become governor or president, becoming a head over man and therefore changing God's order. Asserts that woman suffrage robs women of ladylike modesty and delicacy, drives them to desperate acts, deprives woman of man's protection, destroys homes, disregards God's order, and ignores nature.

792   "Three Cheers for the Poor." New Republic 13 (26 January): 364-65.
       Useful for its quotations and analysis of the opponents of woman suffrage in the House of Representatives. One senator predicts that political debates within the family will become so bitter that "a veritable conflagration of domestic infelicity would be kindled, consuming the marital tie, destroying the home, and sending the children, to all intents and purposes, orphans out on the cold charity of the world to become charges of the state."

1919

793   CONAWAN, WAITMAN HARRISON. The Subjugation of Man Through Woman Suffrage. N.p., 31 pp.
       A handful of misguided women are heckling the president and intimidating Congress to get the Anthony Amendment passed, so those conscientiously opposed must speak out. Presents two choices: either stick to the "strong and tried fundamental principles of our government" or "adopt extreme and dangerous views of a capricious nature tending to disintegration and weakness." Argues that woman suffrage is fundamentally wrong from a military and political standpoint. Particularly objects to the League of Women Voters, formed in March 1919. Foresees that it will attempt to control American politics and align women against men, causing sex antagonism and the eventual subjugation of man. Appeals to patriotism, masculinity, and tradition.

1920

794   LITTELL, P. "Books and Things." New Republic 21 (11 February):319.
       A humorous, satiric, prowoman look at two antisuffrage documents, one from the Men's Patriotic Association of Pittsburgh, the other an unsigned and undated circular. Points out that these documents present man as threatened, egotistic, vain. "What a piece of work is man, so exposed, so irresolute, so addicted to whistling in order to keep up his feeling of superiority, so easily disheartened, such a quick dispairer!" Useful for the sources.

795   LAPE, ESTHER EVERETT.   "What Do Women Want with the Vote?"
       Ladies' Home Journal 37 (March):39, 91-92, 94.
           Believes that most women are working to secure laws to
       protect women in industry, to put rural health nurses in every
       county, and to train the foreign-born. They focus on human needs
       rather than sex equalization. Believes it would be a great
       danger for the new woman voter to "carry sex into politics,"
       persisting in the "sex campaigning attitude which she necessarily
       had as a suffrage worker." Alleges that in some states and
       communities, women with the vote still seem to be fighting for
       it. When that is true, then instead of women's participation in
       politics, what we really have is feminism in politics--"the last
       thing in the world that most of us want to see."

796   TAFT, HELEN HERRON.   "Women in Politics." Woman's Home
       Companion 47 (April):4, 127.
           Opposes the idea of a Woman's party. Women need to learn
       from and work with men. Does not want women and men to separate
       along sex lines on issues. Warns that "nothing would do more to
       develop sex antagonism--an anti-suffrage bogy which hardly has
       shown its head in this country--than a Woman's Party, an organ-
       ized militancy based on sex."

797   "Woman Suffrage." Weekly Review 3 (1 September):181-82.
           Defends antisuffragists. Says they had the greatest re-
       spect for women and sympathy with their aspirations and believed
       that woman suffrage would "impair to a disastrous extent those
       distinctive attributes of women which are so unspeakably precious
       an element of human life." Warns that "there is danger of a loss
       profound and penetrating affecting the very finest and most
       precious elements of life."

798   "Awful Dangers of Woman Suffrage." Literary Digest 67
       (23 October):24.
           Excerpts from and summary of an article in the Saturday
       Review (London) which hopes woman suffrage will be defeated in
       Great Britain and America. Man must take his last stand against
       "the subversion of his rights of virility by a tyranny" that is
       "humiliating because it is the submission of the superior to the
       inferior sex [and] dangerous, because, if it be pushed beyond a
       certain point, it will be overthrown by an appeal to physical
       force." Blames women for prohibition in the United States,
       saying that since women cannot digest alcohol, they support
       prohibition. Fears that men will resort to "the argument of the
       black eye" as "the only means of recovering the lost Rights of
       Man."

ANTISUFFRAGE PERIODICALS

799   The True Woman. Edited by Mrs. Charlotte E. McKay. 4 vols.
      Baltimore, 1871-73.
           This was the first of the antisuffrage periodicals. It
      printed petitions and published excerpts, poems, stories, let-
      ters, articles, addresses by ministers, and notices of books by
      antifeminists. In addition to woman suffrage, objected to women
      receiving medical training in mixed (coeducational) classes and
      opposed training single young women for medicine. Regular con-
      tributors included Madeline V. Dahlgren, Harriet Beecher Stowe,
      and Almira Lincoln Phelps.

800   The Remonstrance. 30 vols. Boston: Massachusetts Associa-
      tion Opposed to the Extension of Suffrage to Women, 1890-1920.
           Published at first yearly, in 1907 it became a quarterly. It
      also moved in size from four pages to eight to ten to twelve in
      1914, then back down to eight in 1916. Ceased publication in
      1920. Every issue quoted active antisuffragists; there was no
      new material. An issue in 1901 was addressed to the voters of
      South Dakota. A running tally was kept of defeats of woman
      suffrage. Useful to students of the Massachusetts Association
      Opposed to the Further Extension of Suffrage to Women. Provided
      lists of state organizations opposed to woman suffrage, as well
      as lists of officers.

801   The Anti-Suffragist. Edited by Mrs. W. Winslow Crannell. 4
      vols. Albany, 1908-12.
           This journal was "devoted to placing before the public the
      reasons why it is inexpedient to extend the ballot to women."
      Published for four years, it merged with the Woman's Protest in
      1912.

802   The Woman's Protest. 6 vols. New York: National Association
      Opposed to Woman Suffrage, 1912-18.
           The organ of the National Association Opposed to Woman
      Suffrage, which was founded in November 1911. It reprinted
      articles, newspaper stories, printed poems, cartoons, lists of
      officers of state organizations, and lists of pamphlets avail-
      able. Ceased publication in February 1918.

803   The Reply. Edited by Helen S. Harman. 2 vols. New Canaan,
      Conn., 1913-15.
           This antisuffrage magazine was published monthly for two
      years. In it appeared all the familiar names: Grace Duffield
      Goodwin, Mrs. William Forse Scott, Helen Kendrick Johnson,
      Caroline F. Corbin, Everett P. Wheeler, Rossiter Johnson, and
      others. There were some original articles. Included advertise-
      ments and fashions, with patterns offered for sale.

804   The Woman Patriot. Edited by Minnie Bronson. 33 vols.
      Washington, D.C., 1918-31.

This weekly national newspaper was "for home and defense
against woman suffrage, feminism, and socialism." It had an
active and well-known list of contributing editors, including
Henry Watterson, Octave Thanet, Annie Nathan Meyer, and Margaret
C. Robinson. Headlines were often inflammatory: "Suffrage Burn-
ings Create Riots," "Rights of Women to Choose Husbands No Longer
Exists under Feminism in Russia," "'All Women Are Liars' Says
Anna Howard Shaw," "Bureaus of Free Love Established by Feminists
and Socialists in Russia." Alleged that woman suffrage was pro-
German and that German brewers supported suffrage. During the
war, one headline declared, "Policeman Ready to Testify that
Suffragist Cursed Flag and Assaulted Police Matron."

Domesticity, Femininity, and Motherhood

The materials in this section have a limited and repetitive
message: woman must stay in her proper sphere, the home; woman must
be gentle, pure, modest, selfless, "a rainbow of hope." Women and
men are complementary, and women must remain subject to their husbands. There would be no social problems if mothers did their jobs
properly, and if women stayed in their proper sphere. "All the
wickedness of the human race can be traced to incompetent motherhood"
(929).

In the second half of the nineteenth century, particularly in the
last third, concern began to be expressed over the falling birthrate.
Now women were urged not only to remain in the home but to have many
children. Feminism is blamed for women's declining to marry, shunning maternity, and neglecting their homes. No doubt this emphasis
on domesticity and motherhood was also an indirect reaction to wom-
en's demanding political rights, better education, and wider employment, but women were definitely beginning to limit pregnancies.
Physicians provided dire warnings of the consequences of birth control. Dr. R.C. Brannon warned in 1915 that preventing large families
had caused "an increase in insanity, tuberculosis, Bright's disease,
diabetes, and cancer" (989).

Divorce also becomes an issue toward the end of the nineteenth
century and is blamed on feminism and women's individualism. Antifeminists insist that the family should be the unit of society, not
the individual. Marital problems are the fault of women. A final
target was women's clubs. Early in the twentieth century articles
began to appear, some by former presidents of the United States,
blaming the organized club movement for making women discontent with
home life. In the Ladies' Home Journal, Edward Bok campaigned cease-
lessly against women's clubs.

1833

805   Sketches of the Lives of Distinguished Females, Written for
Girls, with a View to Their Mental and Moral Improvement. By
an American Lady. New York: J. & J. Harper, 227 pp.

The mother has harsh words for female sovereigns, praise for women in private life. In relating the history of Queen Christina, the mother admonishes her daughters that "'woman shines but in her proper sphere,' and whatever may be her talents or education, qualities or situation, if she step beyond the boundaries of her sex, she becomes ridiculous and disgusting to every well-regulated mind."

1834

806   FAIRFIELD, SUMNER LINCOLN. "The Privileges and Influences of the Sexes." North American 4 (October):382-87.
    Reacts with horror at the statement by some women that they would be men. Insists that "no woman can mingle with the rude sports and revels of man without contamination." Home is her empire, the "heart is her altar, and her children the cherubim." Woman will only be humiliated and scorned if she tries to assume men's manners or privileges. "She is, or should be, a being of purity and holy light, shrined in the sanctuary of a blest and blessing home; not the amazon that drives the scythed chariot of carnage, nor the drudge that delves in the noonday fields."

1836

807   CUSHING, C. "Social Condition of Women." North American 42 (April):489-513.
    For women to fill our councils and man our armies would be for them to sacrifice all the charms of womanhood. Her domain is the moral affections, not "the rude commerce of camps and the soul-hardening struggles of political power." Man wants to look up to her as something brighter and purer, "an emanation of some better world, irradiating like a rainbow of hope, the stormy elements of life."

1837

808   A Manual of Politeness, Comprising the Principles of Etiquette, and Rules of Behaviour in Genteel Society, for Persons of Both Sexes. Philadelphia: W. Marshall, 287 pp.
    In a chapter on "Advantages of Female Conversation," advises young men to "talk to women, talk to women as much as you can. This is the best school. This is the way to gain fluency, because you need not care what you say, and had better not be sensible. They, too, will rally you on many points, and, as they are women, you will not be offended."

809   "Condition of Woman in Ancient Greece." Southern Quarterly
       Review 16 (January):324-42.
            Presents a long discussion of women in the past for the
       purpose of examining contemporary women. Finds the sexes un-
       equal, with man superior in both mental and physical power.
       Believes the differences probably are less than supposed but has
       no desire to call woman away from her position. Woman's "greater
       delicacy of organization, both mental and physical, keener sus-
       ceptibilities and intensity of affection and sympathy" render her
       less fit for public stations than man and, at the same time,
       point to "the domestic circle and social life as [her] proper and
       peculiar sphere."

1851

810   BEECHER, CATHARINE E. The True Remedy for the Wrongs of
       Woman. Boston: Phillips, Sampson, 263 pp.
            Written as a series of letters to her sister, Harriet
       Beecher Stowe. Says the real wrong of woman is that her profes-
       sion is disgraced, that she is not educated for her true voca-
       tion, and that she cannot find remunerative employment. Says it
       is folly to entice woman into man's employments. She should be
       better prepared for her own. Counsels: "Instead of rushing into
       the political arena to join in the scramble for office, or at-
       tempting to wedge into the overcrowded learned professions of
       man, let woman raise and dignify her own profession, and endow
       posts of honor and emolument in it, that are suited to the char-
       acter and duties of her sex."

1852

811   WEST, CHARLES E. An Address Delivered before the Patrons and
       Pupils of the Buffalo Female Academy at the Dedication of
       Goodell Hall, 6 July 1852. Buffalo: G. Reese, 42 pp.
            Faults reformers who "would rob woman of that modesty of
       demeanor which is the ornament of her character and the source of
       her power." Says they would make her dissatisfied with the
       sphere Providence has assigned to her. They would make women of
       men and men of women. "Their teaching is not only revolutionary
       but destructive of all that is pure in morals and holy in reli-
       gion." Opposes the throwing down of all barriers to women's
       education and employment.

1853

812   HALL, L.J. "Eliot's Lectures to Young Women." Christian
       Examiner 55 (September):187-201.

Review of <u>Lectures</u> <u>to</u> <u>Young</u> <u>Women</u>, delivered in the Church
of the Messiah, by William G. Eliot, Jr. Recommends this book
because it is lively. "In order to arrest the attention of the
airy, gay creatures, whose besetting sin is that they hate
thought, we require no ordinary means."

813   SAINTE-FOI, CHARLES. "The Mission of Woman." <u>Metropolitan</u> 1
       (September–December):388-90, 435-37, 536-38, 589-91; 2
       (April):139-42; (August):395-98.
           Standard stereotypes: woman's mind is intuitive, not logi-
       cal; she "does not reason, she contemplates; she is not con-
       vinced, but carried away." The family is her sphere. Woman
       should please, not preach. She should not take an active part in
       any discussion, never make a display of her knowledge and erudi-
       tion, "but rather let her strive to conceal it from others, and,
       if possible, even from herself." Woman may work out her salva-
       tion through either virginity or maternity. Man was made to act,
       woman to love. She needs someone to direct her, to be her head.
       The world is full of more dangers to woman than man--curiosity,
       frivolity, vanity, coquetry.

                                1854

814   OSGOOD, SAMUEL. <u>The</u> <u>Hearth-Stone:</u> <u>Thoughts</u> <u>upon</u> <u>Home-Life</u> <u>in</u>
       <u>our</u> <u>Cities</u>. 3d ed. New York: D. Appleton, 290 pp.
           Insists that it would be a great mistake to "take woman
       from her sphere of dignity and power, and make her the rival of
       man in pursuits which require his ruder nature and sterner will."
       Girls should never be trained to be men in cast of mind or way of
       life. "We can never slight the hint of nature without bringing
       down her retribution, and temporary success but delays the evil
       day." Cites Margaret Fuller as an example, alleging that the
       stern discipline of her father's training "repressed the springs
       of feminine power."

815   WEISS, J. "The Woman Question." <u>Christian</u> <u>Examiner</u> 56
       (January):1-34.
           Any woman who urges her right to be a politician "has
       little but her sex and her attire to vouch for her feminality
       [<u>sic</u>]." Urges that "the delicate influence of a true woman is
       better than her judgment, however sound, upon affairs of state,
       or her administration, however effective, of a public office."
       Promotes domestic, not political, influence.

                                1855

816   PIERSON, LYDIA JANE. "'She Merely Does Her Housework.'" <u>Lily</u>
       7 (1 August):119-20.

Tells of two women, one too weak to do more than her own housework, the other who sets up a shoemaking establishment in her home. The former has a happy marriage and her husband is respected and grows rich, whereas the husband of the more self-sufficient woman neglects her and his work, takes to drink, loses his custom and shop, ceases to provide for his family, and becomes abusive. Urges women not to do custom work when they marry but to expect husbands to provide for them. God fixed the punishment of Eve and all women to be the bearing and rearing of children and dependence on and subjection to a husband. Men are supposed to earn the bread. Women should not infringe upon God's will by assuming part of their husband's burden.

1857

817   HALE, SARAH JOSEPHA. "Editors' Table: Grammatical Errors." Godey's Lady's Book 55 (August):177-78.
        Objects to the use of the word "female" because it pertains to the animal designation of the sex and is vulgar when applied to women. Favors feminine endings—"poetesses" rather than "female poets." Believes that "this error regarding the name of woman is of grave importance" because "it lowers the idea of the sex to consider them only as females, and therefore tends to foster that tendency to masculine pursuits and appellations which we are sorry to see prevail among our young and gifted countrywomen."

1858

818   "Woman and Womankind." Eclectic Magazine 43 (March):392-401.
        Insists that a woman's sphere of action is her home. Anything that would take her out of that home is wrong, including politics. Who would care for the children and her other domestic duties while she is out voting? Reprinted from Tait's Magazine.

1859

819   "Female Influence in the Affairs of State—Politics Not Woman's Sphere." Democratic Review 43 (April):175-84.
        Notes that although Providence has assigned the spheres, manly women and womanish men occasionally suggest reforms. Fanny Wright was the first to do so in this country. Says great evils are produced when women step out of their proper sphere. Many examples are provided from history of women's intrigue, treachery, and immorality. American women should stay in the "domestic vineyard."

1860

820   STORRS, Rev. HENRY M. Position and Necessities of the Edu-
      cated Woman: An Address, Delivered at the First Anniversary
      of the Lake Erie Female Seminary, Painesville, Ohio, 19 July
      1860. Boston: T.R. Marvin, 24 pp.
          Discusses ways that woman can employ her education--through
      reading, conversation, and composition. Praises woman's ability
      to converse but opposes her speaking in public. Wants her to
      speak not "with unveiled exposure before some promiscuous assembly
      as a strolling lecturer, dropping the graceful skirts of her
      modest womanhood, to don the unbecoming breeches of manhood."
      Rather, he would have her bring forth her mental treasures "with
      the bewitching eloquence of the fireside. . . . I am then her
      slave."

821   HALE, SARAH JOSEPHA. "Editors' Table." Godey's Lady's Book
      60 (January):79-80.
          Warns that when women step out of their own sphere, when
      they encroach on man's sphere, they lose their great womanly
      advantages but cannot perform the duties of men. Thus they
      become "unhappy, undignified beings."

1862

822   "Husbands and Wives." Monthly Religious Magazine 27
      (May):273-78.
          Asserts that "a thousand woman's conventions" will not
      alter the true nature of men and women. Nature makes them com-
      plementary, not equal.

1863

823   HAYDEN, WILLIAM BENJAMIN. Ten Chapters on Marriage: Its
      Nature, Uses, Duties, and Final Issues. 2d ed. Boston: W.
      Carter & Bro., 160 pp.
          Upholds the doctrine of separate spheres. Warns that if
      woman "cultivates the masculine faculties of study, acquiring
      knowledge, and of getting such an understanding as the male has,"
      she will come to love that masculine principle in herself and
      become masculine in her character. Then she will be discontented
      with her own sphere of duties and unfitted to render home and
      domestic life happy.

824   MAKER, Mrs. O.S. "The Ladies' Loyal League." Continental
      Monthly 4 (July):51-56.
          Regrets that some women do not realize or object to the
      fact that woman's duties are not identical to man's and become

filled with indignation and "restless tumult" over their "supposed wrongs." Insists that women and men must not interfere
with the duties of one another. Describes the work of the
Ladies' Loyal League in "fostering a healthy, intelligent
patriotism, in the social and domestic circles of our land."

825   "The Rights of Women." Godey's Lady's Book 67
       (September):229.
       Believes that the Creator has assigned different spheres of
action to the two sexes and that there is enough work for each in
its own department. Woman should keep to her own sphere and
adorn it, "not, like the comet, daunting and perplexing other
systems, but as the pure star, which is the first to light the
day, and the last to leave it."

1865

826   HALE, SARAH JOSEPHA. "Editors' Table." Godey's Lady's Book
       70 (March):278.
       Wishes woman not to "wound the delicacy of her mind, or
derogate from her womanly dignity of fame" by mounting rostrums,
taking office, or engaging in inappropriate professions. Woman
should influence as a mother and be educated for her home duties.
"We would not change the stations of the sexes, or give to women
the work and offices of men. But fit them for their own work."

827   HALE, SARAH JOSEPHA. "Editors' Table: Diminutions of the
       English Language." Godey's Lady's Book 70 (May):464.
       Proposes the adoption of more titles and professions ending
in "ess" so that women "will not usurp the man's title." Notable
are professoress, scholaress, teacheress, Americaness, president-
ess, paintress.

828   HARLAND, MARION. "A Christmas Talk with Mothers." Godey's
       Lady's Book 71 (November):391-402.
       Is critical over complaints that the large family is a
curse. Believes that "amidst the wild clamor of woman's rights,"
woman is best who rears strong, good sons and gentle, noble
daughters in the role "appointed her by the Wise Parent of all."

1868

829   "Woman's Arithmetic." Harper's Bazar 1 (18 January):190.
       Alleges that women have no idea of the value of money
except in small sums. Thus they can spend hundreds of dollars
for a dress or shawl without a moment's hesitation but "will
higgle about the difference of a cent in the price of a dozen
eggs."

830   "Mr. Thom. White's Little Sermon." Putnam's 11 (March):
       354-62.
            Marriage is becoming more and more rare because woman is
       complaining and dissatisfied. She demands everything and does
       nothing. She is not man's partner. All she wants is to spend
       money. In truth her right is to be a loyal wife and a loving
       mother. Woman is not intended to be the same or act in the same
       sphere or do the same work as man, despite what "mannish women
       and womanish men" are now saying. That is subverting the laws of
       her own being. Woman cannot do man's work because "she is a
       perpetual invalid . . . that is one great fact of her existence
       which cannot be ignored, and it settles the question, if nothing
       else did it, of her inability to compete with man." Insists that
       there is no "world's work" which woman can perform.

831   "Woman and the World, from an English Point of View." Every
       Saturday 5 (9 May):588-90.
            Deplores the change in British women. Says that woman has
       bought her freedom by sacrificing womanliness and modesty, "by
       flattering the wooer's base preferences before marriage, by en-
       couraging his baser selfishness afterwards," by hounding her
       husband at his club, and by having only a couple of children.
       Her reward is that "the old world of home and domestic tenderness
       and parental self-sacrifice lies in ruins at her feet." Today's
       woman is stripped of all that is womanly.

832   "Modern Mothers." Eclectic Magazine 70 (June):741-43.
            Believes that modern women are disinclined to be mothers
       and will not or cannot nurse their children. Says maternity is
       looked upon as a kind of degradation. Points out that "this wild
       revolt against nature, and specially this abhorrence of mater-
       nity, is carried to a still greater extent by American women, with
       grave national consequences resulting." Reprinted from the
       Saturday Review (London) 25 (29 February):268-69.

833   "Ideal Women." Eclectic Magazine 71 (July):844-48.
            Although there is a great variety of ideal women, all wish
       to please men and mold their lives in harmony with theirs. No
       society can tolerate independence in its members. "Hence the
       defiant attitude which women have lately assumed, and their
       indifference to the wishes and remonstrances of men, cannot lead
       to any good results whatever." Such women neglect their homes
       and are full of "vague restlessness" and "fierce extravagance."
       Pleads with modern women to return to the lost ideal "and become
       again what we once loved and what we all regret." Reprinted from
       the Saturday Review (London) 68 (9 May):609-10.

834   "Ideal Women." New Eclectic 2 (July):343-47.
            See 833. Reprinted from the Saturday Review (London) 68
       (9 May):609-10.

835   "Feminine Affectations." Harper's Bazar 1 (25 July):
       617-18.

Opposes two sorts of "affected" women: the intense womanly woman, who is self-conscious, attitudinizing, gets her own way, and imposes her will on others; and the mannish woman, "affected in her breadth and roughness," which he calls "a mere assumption of virile fashions utterly inharmonious to the whole being, physical and mental, of a woman."

1869

836   FROTHINGHAM, O.B. "Is There Such a Thing as Sex?" Nation 8 (4 February):87-88.
Says yes, "the fact of sex is comprehensive, complete and exhaustive." Men and women are essentially and radically unlike, distinct in bodily form and feature, mentally and morally. "They neither think, feel, wish, purpose, will, nor act alike." Insists that both cannot occupy the same sphere or reach the same standard.

837   "Women's Literature." Harper's Bazar 2 (6 February):94.
Deplores women's love of sensationalism in literature. Says "this dread of dullness is one of the most foolish things about women, and one of the causes, inter alia, why their conversation is so often not worth listening to." Accuses women of gossiping because they cannot converse. Faults women for thinking that their social value lies in prettiness and in the amount of personal admiration they can gain.

1870

838   "The Exclusiveness of Women." Every Saturday 9 (19 March):179.
No matter that woman legally has no rights; the "moral reality" is that she rules her husband, manipulates him, sails around him. Finds that woman, "being more exclusive, more jealous, more arbitrary and narrower than he, is able to impose her own will and code on him, and to make him accept her will unconditionally." Faults women for being exclusive, jealous of other women, inhospitable to their husbands' friends and family, all of which makes domestic life boring. Reprinted from the Saturday Review (London) 29 (19 February):242-43.

839   CONANT, WILLIAM C. "Sex in Nature and Society." Baptist Quarterly 4 (April):176-97.
A long discussion basically supporting separate and distinct spheres. Denies that men have oppressed women. Rather, the relation of the sexes is as Nature intended. The family must have a head and a name. If women were to be independent, it would practically abolish the family name. Describes those who would reform women as "perhaps the most irreligious school of reformers the world has ever seen, profane persons." Entreats women to know their calling and resist temptation to step out of their proper sphere.

840   "Woman and Government." Christian Union 2 (July):17-18.
          "[Woman] is destined by her very nature to live for the
most part in a sphere of personal relations." Therefore, she is
not suited to dealing with politics, the community, the general
rather than the individual and particular. "The very things that
make her what she is, as wife, or sister, or mother--sensibility,
affection, warm, deep feeling, quick and tender sympathy--will
constantly tend to warp her judgment, to make her lose sight of
the general for the sake of some individual case or object that
has taken a deep hold upon her." Alleges that even those who
support woman suffrage realize that it will "introduce them into
a sphere of duties whose publicity would be very distasteful."

841   GODKIN, E.L. "Another Delicate Subject." Nation 11
          (14 July):21-23.
          Against Woodhull, the editor argues in favor of the double
standard, saying that "the degree of guilt depends upon the
degree of temptation," which is strong in men, weak in women.
Insists that woman's chastity preserves the family.

842   "Womanliness." Southern Magazine 7 (October):451-55.
          Fears that among advanced women, womanliness is shunned,
maternity a bore, children shunted aside. Women are becoming
hard, fierce, and self-asserting; they are no longer tender and
modest, and are taking up men's professions. Urges a return to
womanliness. Reprinted from the Saturday Review (London) 30 (6
August):166-68.

                                    1871

843   LINTON, E. LYNN. "The Modern Revolt." Eclectic Magazine 76
          (February):196-203.
          Finds in the revolt against maternity, "which is so marked
a social feature in America," the saddest part of the modern
women's revolt. Argues that if women are poorly educated, it is
the fault of women, particularly the mothers who educated them.
Of all the duties special to women--motherhood, housekeeping,
cooking, fashion, etc.--none have been brought to perfection.
Then how could they take on more? Actually, it is just that
"women crave public applause, an audience, excitement, notoriety,
more than mere work." This is due solely to personal ambition.
Reprinted from Macmillan's Magazine (London) 23 (December
1870):142-49.

844   SANTLEY, HERBERT. "Marriage." Lippincott's 8 (October):
          395-403.
          Describes marriage as decreasing. Among the reasons cited
are "the defective training of women," which causes them to be
unreasonable, "blinded to the beauties of the world of thought,"
prejudiced, "acting from vague, crude impulses," and capable of
little beyond providing humanity with poorly trained offspring

and inflicting themselves upon "an unhappy and outraged family."
Deplores "the neglect to inform [women] of their nature as ani-
mals and their functions as mothers of the race."

1872

845   TAYLOR, M.F. "Marriage and Divorce." Southern Magazine 11
      (October):447-52.
            Says woman's claim to her rights is misdirected. Wants her
      to "have a more wholesome restraint upon matrimonial dissolu-
      tions, and better social rules." Predicts that she will then
      again "find great contentment, peace and happiness around the
      fireside and in the family circle."

1873

846   PORTER, D.G. "The Liberal Education of Girls." Christian
      Quarterly 5 (July):306-29.
            Says our girls are not well educated; have become weak, in
      poor health, frivolous. Woman's true role is to be a helper to
      man in a private capacity. Women are sickly because they have
      stepped outside the home—woman's constitution needs the quiet of
      home, daily practice of domestic industry, not severe labor or
      listless idleness. It is woman's misguided ambition that leads
      her to clamor for political rights. Calls upon women to dismiss
      their servants and to engage in the useful and honorable duties
      of domestic life. The youngest girl should be disciplined in the
      common, useful, and necessary employments of domestic life, not
      in school. "Too many subjects enfeeble the body, belittle the
      mind, and pervert the moral sense!"

1874

847   "Wives at Discount." Harper's Bazar 7 (31 January):74.
            Finds that there are so many more women than men, espe-
      cially at watering places, that eight maidens cling to one man.
      Says it is unnatural that men are declining to marry and blames
      women, who are antagonistic toward men. Warns "advanced" women
      that "there can be no true progress for them save in the company
      of, not in opposition to, men."

1876

848   SHERWIN, JOHN C. Sermons on the Family Relations. Chicago:
      Lakeside Publishing Co., 95 pp.
            Worries that if women are granted the opportunity to strug-
      gle "in stormy debates and in violent civil strifes," they will
      be robbed of their power over man and made rougher. Then "the

more tender and lovely feelings of the soul" will be smothered and woman will become weak. Claims that "it is a mistake to suppose that woman will have more influence by appearing in the sterner qualities and labors of man."

1877

849   "Women of the Southern Confederacy." Southern Review, n.s. 21 (April):333-62.
      In writing of women of the southern confederacy, states that he will show care in writing of the living, "for it is the poorest compliment that can be paid a woman to drag her from modest retirement into the glare of public notice." Believes no high type of woman would willingly bring heself before the public. Implicitly criticizes northern women who do otherwise.

1880

850   WELLS, KATE GANNETT. "The Transitional American Woman." Atlantic 46 (December):817-23.
      The face of the modern woman today "is stamped with restlessness, wandering purpose, and self-consciousness." She no longer enjoys cooking for her family; affection for the home is waning. "Instead of grace, there has come in many women an affectation of mannishness, as is shown in hats, jackets, long strides, and a healthful swinging of the arms in walking." Woman has become more selfish. "Formerly, to be a good housekeeper, an anxious mother, and obedient wife, was the ne plus ultra of female endeavor,--to be all this for others' sakes. Now, it is to be more than one is, for one's own sake." The article has a notably querulous tone throughout.

1881

851   NEWTON, R. HEBER. Womanhood: Lectures on Woman's Work in the World. New York: Putnam's Sons, 315 pp.
      A series of lectures given to young women in the winter of 1878-79. Asserts that "many foolish and some dangerous things have been said and done by those who claim to champion the woman's movement." Says that new movements are often characterized by erratic action. Observes that "eccentric and by no means lovable people have pushed to the forefront of this 'cause,'" including long-haired men and short-haired women. Even so, they cannot push woman out of her proper sphere, the home.

852   Rockford Seminary Thirtieth Commencement: Essays of Graduating Class, 22 June 1881. DeKalb, Ill.: "News" Steam Press, 39 pp.

Of seventeen class members, only Kate Tanner was antifeminist. In "'Too Many Gates to Swing On,'" she worries that women "are constantly distracted by the outcries of women who protest against womanhood and wildly strain to throw off their most lovable characteristics. They want power, political power, and yet the world is entirely what their home influence has made it." Asserts that women are needed at home, not in public assemblies. In her address Jane Addams favored wider opportunities for women.

853   RUSKIN, JOHN. Pearls for Young Ladies: Collected and Arranged by Mrs. Louisa C. Tuthill. New York: J. Wiley & Sons, 247 pp.
      Standard conservative antifeminist opinions—much from Ruskin's Sesame and Lilies (see 865).

1882

854   GRIFFLIN, WALTER T. The Homes of Our Country; or, The Centers of Moral and Religious Influence; The Crystals of Society; the Nuclei of National Character. New York: Union Publishing House, 640 pp.
      Conceives that man might take on housework and "woman might be instigated to contend for the palm of science, to pour forth eloquence in senates, or to 'wade through fields of slaughter to the throne.'" But recoils in horror at the thought: "Revoltings of the soul would attend this violence to nature, this abuse of physical and intellectual energy, while the beauty of social order would be defaced, and the fountains of earth's felicity broken up." Insists on the doctrine of separate spheres.

1883

855   GOODWIN, HENRY MARTYN. The Seven Pillars of Womanhood: An Address Delivered before the Young Ladies of the Soronian Society in Olivet College, 19 June 1883. Chicago: Jameson & Morse, 22 pp.
      Grants that woman may compete with man "at the polls, on the platform, at the bar and in the pulpit," but asserts that "it will be at the sacrifice of that nameless power and influence, more persuasive than words or reasoning, which she wields with such queenly sway, and which is all the more powerful because of its gentle and unobtrusive and unasserting manner." Deplores these days of "bold aggressiveness and loud self-assertion" which crowd out womanly gentleness and modesty.

856   "Dr. Dix on the Woman Question: Editorial." Popular Science Monthly 23 (May):120-23.
      Quotes and summarizes Dr. Dix's lenten lectures. Woman is different from man and has a different sphere. Whatever unfits

woman for her proper duties or makes her despise domesticity,
"whatever now acts on her high-wrought nature, her ambition, her
self-love, to turn her steps away from the homelife, and inflate
her with visions of a career in the public places outside . . .
is working against the best interests, the hope, the happiness of
the human race." Editor agrees with Dix, says the women's movement is against the home and wants women to compete with men.
Complains that women's colleges all violate the "fundamental law
of progressive education," that it should fit the student for
life. Wants women trained for domestic life.

1884

857   DIKE, SAMUEL W. "Some Aspects of the Divorce Question."
      Princeton Review, n.s. 13 (March):169-90.
         Cautions against individualism, which he says is ruining
      the family, causing an increase in divorce, making woman forget
      her condition and lose her capacity for maternity. Sees "a
      voluntary refusal" of the responsibility of maternity on the
      grounds of individuality.

1886

858   TALMADGE, THOMAS DE WITT. The Marriage Ring: A Series of
      Sermons on the Duties of the Husband and Wife, and on the
      Domestic Circle. New York: J.S. Ogilvie, 204 pp.
         Warns women against becoming "dizzied and disturbed by the
      talk of those who think the home circle too insignificant for a
      woman's career, and who want to get you out on platforms and in
      conspicuous enterprises."

859   MISTER, JAMES F. "Law of Married Women." American Law Review
      20 (May-June):359-65.
         Discusses the history of modern legislation regarding mar-
      ried women and considers proposed changes. Approves of married
      women controlling and owning their own property but cautions
      against their being able to enter into transactions dealing with
      this property without their husband's consent. She needs his
      practical experience and guidance. Approves the policy of keep-
      ing strife out of the family circle and preserving "an asylum
      where human energies may be recuperated," and feels it is unwise
      to circumvent "the restraints which God and nature and wisdom
      impose and experience and observation sanction. . . . It may be
      seriously questioned whether any officious interference of the
      law into the family household, except for protection from vio-
      lence (however well intended), ever operated beneficially."

860   CRAIK, DINAH M. "Concerning Men." Forum 4 (September):38-48.
        Absolute equality between men and women is impossible.
Nature is against it; "every girl's education, mental, moral,
physical, ought to be primarily with a view to wifehood and
motherhood, the highest and happiest destiny to which any woman
can attain." Physically and mentally woman's powers are limited.
Most of the article is about women, because men and women are
inextricably mixed. Reprinted from Cornhill (London) 9
(October):368-77. Condensed and reprinted in Eclectic Magazine
109 (December):738-44 (see 175).

1888

861   POMEROY, HIRAM STERLING, M.D. The Ethics of Marriage. New
        York and London: Funk & Wagnalls, 197 pp.
        A treatise against abortion. Says he feels sympathy with
efforts by true and earnest women for the advancement of women
but believes that "many of those who have been connected with the
Woman's Rights Movement, and, at least, some of the advocates of
higher education for women, have been to blame for disseminating
opinions and theories which, indirectly at least, have aided and
abetted the sin against maternity." Some feminists think that
maternity is "a sort of low-grade drudgery which properly may be
left to those who lack the will and the ability necessary to
carry them into a higher sphere." The highest role for woman is
motherhood—everything else she undertakes is caused by social
imbalance and imperfection.

862   DIX, Rev. Dr. MORGAN. "Is Marriage a Failure?" Cosmopolitan
        6 (November):95.
        Marriage is a failure, and it is woman's fault "by her
luxury, her extravagance, her addiction to the pleasures of the
world, her recklessness of duty, her irresponsibility."

1889

863   "Manly Women." Eclectic Magazine 113 (August):213-15.
        Says women are imitating men—shooting, betting on races,
using slang, frequenting music-halls, etc.—for two reasons:
first, because of "curiosity, which is their hereditary legacy
handed down from Mother Eve," and second, because it is the
fashion. This is a mistake, for by doing so women are losing
their charms of gentleness and modesty and losing the respect of
true gentlemen. Reprinted from the Saturday Review (London) 67
(22 June):756-57.

864   OSWALD, FELIX L., M.D. "Sexual Characteristics." Open Court
       3 (5 September):1812-14; (7 November):1922-25.
           Alleges that the reason women have endured oppression and
       injustice over the ages is that they are naturally conservative.
       "Their proper constitution qualifies them to receive and to
       preserve, rather than to originate." Women could fill many
       public positions but they cannot be expected to initiate the move
       to remove barriers. "Innovation is foreign to their natural
       sphere of function." Finds the sexes differ mentally in kind
       rather than in degree, on women's side talent, imitation, and
       adaptation, on men's genius and origination. Foresees a division
       of labor based on sexual characteristics--to men the creative
       thought and food-winning, to women administration and communica-
       tion, care and education of the young, and homemaking.

                                  1890

865   RUSKIN, JOHN. Sesame and Lilies: Three Lectures. Rev. and
       enlarged ed. New York: W.L. Allison Co., 244 pp.
           Upholding the separate spheres: woman private, man public
       doctrines.

866   JEUNE, Mrs. "Women of To-Day, Yesterday, and To-Morrow."
       Eclectic Magazine 114 (February):177-85.
           Insists that women have become unsexed by political speak-
       ing and that Satan has been incarnated in the Primrose League to
       drag women from their pedestals. The unnatural platform life
       will lead to hysteria, nervous exhaustion, heart weakness, and
       sickly children. Women should stick to their proper role and
       sphere, "not encroach on ground fitted only for stronger wills
       and rougher natures." Woman "is, and always must be, physically
       and intellectually inferior to the man." Reprinted from National
       Review (London).

867   BODINGTON, ALICE. "The Marriage Question from a Scientific
       Standpoint." Eclectic Magazine 114 (April):488-93.
           Argues that our existing social relations rest upon funda-
       mental differences between men and women, the most important of
       which is "the subordination of women to men," which has its roots
       in women's inferior strength and capacity of both mind and body.
       Denies the possibility of equality or the need for change. Re-
       printed from Westminster Review (London) 133 (February):172-80.

868   ALLEN, GRANT. "Woman's Intuition." Forum 9 (May):333-40.
           Alleges that the goal of women's rightists is "to turn
       women, if possible, into feeble, second-rate copies of men." But
       despite all that "lady lecturers and anti-feminine old maids can
       do to unsex their sisters," men will continue to marry womanly
       women, not "recalcitrant mannish women." Assures that women will
       be protected against the enemies of womanliness in their own sex

by men. Claims that it is "a vulgar, material view" which "en-
deavors to exhalt the harder mannish qualities at the expense of
the softer, purer, and finer womanish ones." Says woman's highest intellectual [sic] quality is intuition, a variety of
instinct.

869   KENEALY, ARABELLA, M.D. "The Talent of Motherhood." Review
      of Reviews 2 (December):593.
           Insists that the essential, crucial test of womanhood is
      motherhood. Her education and training should fit her for this
      function. "The best mother is the best woman." Drawing on her
      medical practice, compares the baby of a woman who undertook to
      develop her mind and body vigorously (a modern woman) with the
      baby of a delicate, modest, shrinking woman and finds the first
      child "stunted and ill-developed, with a narrow bulging forehead,
      sunken cunning eyes, and sensual mouth," with inferior intellect
      and "a marked deficiency of moral perception." The second child
      was beautiful, sturdy, intelligent, precocious, steady, loving
      and generous. The woman's rights extremist, taking a backward
      step in evolution, has blunted her child's power. Condensed and
      reprinted from National Review (London) 16:446ff. Reprinted in
      871.

                                1891

870   LINTON, E. LYNN. "The Revolt against Matrimony." Forum 10
      (January):585-95.
           Says it is [English] women, with their unrest, rampant
      individualism, and impatience of discipline, who are advocating
      facility of divorce and laxity of sexual relations. This con-
      firms what everyone predicted, that moral evil follows when women
      move out of the home. Warns that were they given political
      power, they would give preference to the individual at the ex-
      pense of the community and moral standards.

871   KENEALY, ARABELLA, M.D. "The Talent of Motherhood."
      Eclectic Magazine 116 (February):189-97.
           Reprint of 869.

872   DODGE, MARY ABIGAIL [Gail Hamilton]. "Woman's Place in the
      Republic." Home-maker 7 (November):628-30.
           Believes that woman's place is by man's side. She should
      do her work, not man's. "If, being a woman, she does not discern
      her work, but desires man's work, she is not woman at her best."

873   LINTON, E. LYNN. "The Wild Women as Social Insurgents."
      Eclectic Magazine 117 (November):667-73.
           In obliterating sex distinctions the wild woman destroys
      the finer distinctions of civilization. She smokes with men,
      engages in sports and shooting--all unwomanly activities. She
      also opens up a shop and tries to make money, even with no
      economic need. Wild women make spectacles of themselves on the

stage, rant from the platform, advertise themselves unabashedly, bet, breed horses, advocate free love, and mock maternity and domestic duties. Urges wild women to "cast off their ugly travesty and become what modesty and virtue designed them to be." Reprinted from Nineteenth Century (London) 30 (October):596-605.

1892

874   [BEING A FAMILIAR LETTER FROM A WOMAN OF QUALITY]. "Morals, Manners, and Female Emancipation." Eclectic Magazine 119 (December):777-82.
        In a homey style, lays all deterioration in manners and morals to women. Judges the emancipation of women as graceless, even vulgarly and violently rude. "We have in this determination to square shoulders with men . . . the secret of the degradation of manners in good society." Reprinted from Blackwood's Edinburgh Magazine 152 (October):463-70.

1893

875   CONWAY, KATHERINE E. "Woman Has No Vocation to Public Life." Catholic World 57 (August):681-84.
        Part of a roundtable conference entitled "The Woman Question among Catholics," on the woman question, two of three essays of which were antifeminist. Is amazed to hear the woman question raised among Catholic women. Asserts that the Catholic woman is the normal woman, and that is why Catholic women are indifferent to woman suffrage and disinclined to organize into women's congresses, etc.

876   DONNELLY, ELEANOR C. "The Home is Woman's Sphere." Catholic World 57 (August):677-81.
        In conference entitled "The Woman Question among Catholics." Opposes women going out of the home to jostle with men, dress and talk like men, force themselves into man's occupations, and criminally neglect their own duties. Warns that "all that is gentle, attractive, womanly withers under the hot sun of publicity and notoriety."

877   "Woman's Kingdom." Godey's Lady's Book 127 (September): 372-74.
        The clear-headed, rational, educated woman knows the folly of the kind of iconoclasm advocated by the woman's rights agitator. She knows there is "a line of demarcation beyond which the reflecting woman feels intuitively that she should not venture." Admits that there may be attractions in a public life for ambitious women, but "the innately refined woman feels an instinctive repugnance to passing out of her own sphere."

<u>1894</u>

878   HOLDEN, MARTHA EVERTS [Amber]. <u>A</u> <u>String</u> <u>of</u> <u>Amber</u> <u>Beads</u>.
      Chicago: C.H. Kerr, 139 pp.
            Insists that nothing is harder on the nerves or more dis-
      agreeable than a mannish woman. "With a strident voice and a
      swaggering walk, and a clattering tongue, she takes her course
      through the world like a cat-bird through an orchard." Dislikes
      a "coarse-tongued man" but can find no language strong enough to
      denounce a woman of "slangy speech, and vulgar jests, and harsh
      diatribes." Closes with a wonderful metaphor: "On the principle
      that a strawberry is quicker to spoil than a pumpkin, it takes
      less to render a woman obnoxious than to make a man unfit for
      decent company."

879   "Editorial: The Bachelor Girl." <u>Godey's</u> <u>Lady's</u> <u>Book</u> 128
      (May):626-27.
            The bachelor girl lives as independently as a man and
      dresses, smokes, wears her hair short, and takes care of herself.
      Is rather mild toward the type but disapproves of her "swagger."

880   BISLAND, ELIZABETH. "The Cry of Women." <u>North</u> <u>American</u> 158
      (June):757-59.
            Observes the bitter clamor about woman's condition to be
      growing. Will allow woman to "run the race, paint, write, teach,
      speak, as her talents dictate," so long as she remembers that her
      real work is bearing and rearing children. Then "such outbursts
      of restless passion and discontent as have of late defaced
      [woman's] writings will be changed from a cry into a song."

881   WALSH, WILLIAM S. "The Conceited Sex." <u>North</u> <u>American</u> 159
      (September):369-73.
            Says both sexes are vain but woman is also untruthful,
      insincere, and willfully distorts facts. She forfeits her own
      health and comfort with her cosmetics and clothing; she also
      jeopardizes the higher evolution of the race and may bring forth
      criminals, all because she wants to attract man and triumph over
      him. In her excesses, she is becoming tinged with masculinity.
      Faults contemporary woman for sacrificing her health and impair-
      ing her powers of maternity for the sake of fashion. Finds
      advanced woman to be "as conceited and self confident as can be."
      She is ready to take on anything man does but her shrill self-
      assertiveness betrays her consciousness of weakness and
      infirmity.

882   "Character Note--The New Woman." <u>Eclectic</u> <u>Magazine</u> 123
      (November):685-87.
            Parades Novissima forth in all her repulsiveness--unbounded
      self-satisfaction, aggressive air of independence, long stride,
      sallow skin, large nose, unblushing, critical, wishing to prove
      "that women's mission is something higher than the bearing of

children and the bringing them up." But, according to the
author, "she has failed."

883   WINSTON, Mrs. ELLA W.   "A Fallacy of the W.C.T.U." American
      Journal of Politics 5 (November):479-86.
           Asks why the W.C.T.U. has accomplished so little. Is it
      because women do not have the vote, as Frances Willard insists?
      No, it is because mothers are not doing their jobs that there is
      so much intemperance. Claims that the remedy is not woman suf-
      frage but better-trained mothers and better homes.

                                   1895

884   EDSON, CYRUS, M.D.   "Concerning Nagging Women." North
      American 160 (January):29-37.
           States that nagging causes all sorts of trouble, both to
      the nagger and those she nags. Nagging takes blood away from the
      stomach and sends it to the brain, so naggers are almost always
      thin. Believes it might not be a bad idea for the husband to
      beat the nagging wife, "for physical fear of a whipping might be
      sufficient to make her control herself." See also 889.

885   MALLON, Mrs. ISABEL ALLDERDICE [Ruth Ashmore].   "The Restless-
      ness of the Age." Ladies' Home Journal 12 (January):16.
           Warns the young woman against following "the footsteps of
      the so-called advanced woman of to-day" because she will be "a
      nervous, fretful, irritable woman, dreaded by society at large
      and a continual source of unhappiness in your home." Has no
      sympathy with the advanced woman. The best channel for woman's
      influence is setting a good example in the home.

886   TRASK, KATRINA.   "Motherhood and Citizenship: Woman's Wisest
      Policy." Forum 18 (January):609-15.
           Warns women that evolution is to be preferred over revolu-
      tion. It is the fault of mothers if men repress and degrade
      women. Women should so educate their sons that when they are
      grown, they will grant suffrage to women; this is better than
      antagonizing men now. Women must be patient and wait and do
      their job of motherhood well.

887   BOYESEN, HJALMAR HJORTH.   "The Matrimonial Puzzle." North
      American 160 (February):203-9.
           States that marriage is a mess because women want to be
      men's equals and still want men to be chivalrous. If women want
      equality and independence, they must forgo marriage, for there is
      no equality in matrimony.

888   PARKHURST, CHARLES H., D.D.   "'Andromaniacs.'" Ladies' Home
      Journal 12 (February):15.

Warns woman against mannishness, which he calls "andromania." Deplores any minimizing of the distinctions between
masculinity and femininity.

889   EDSON, CYRUS, M.D.   "Nagging Women—A Reply."   North American
      160 (April):440-45.
          In response to complaints from readers over his earlier
      article on nagging women (see 884), asserts that women cannot
      take criticism.

890   PARKHURST, CHARLES H., D.D.   "The True Mission of Woman."
      Ladies' Home Journal 12 (April):15.
          States that woman's primary sphere is the home. Blames
      "domestic laxity and miscellaneousness" for "a good deal of the
      world's current mischief."

891   BISLAND, ELIZABETH.   "Modern Woman and Marriage."   North
      American 160 (June):753-55.
          Describes modern women who denounce marriage as a failure
      as a "blatant and empty-headed crew . . . crowing hens . . . the
      half-baked, shrieking sisterhood." Warns that it is women who
      have created marriage—men are naturally brutes—and that chil-
      dren will suffer if "that fair temple of life called marriage" is
      destroyed.

892   EASTMAN, MARY J.   "The Woman Question: Retrogressive Path-
      ways." American Magazine of Civics 7 (July):31-36.
          Disagrees with Frances Willard, who would so purify the
      world that it becomes homelike and all women can go about in it.
      Says women must stay in the home to make it a real retreat; they
      cannot go out into the world and have a home.

893   GRANT, ROBERT.   "The Art of Living: The Case of Woman."
      Scribner's Magazine 18 (October):465-76.
          Says woman's emancipation is all right but should not go
      too far—that is, not to her becoming a bank president, merchant,
      judge, banker, or member of Congress. "What is to become of the
      eternal feminine in the pow-wow, bustle, and materializing rush
      and competition of active business life?" Says woman's physical
      and moral nature will prevent her from throwing off her domestic
      ties and duties. Wants to be convinced that women are earnest-
      minded before giving them the vote. Likes the old Eve left in
      her.

                                1896

894   LEEKE, REBECCA L.   "The New Lady."   Century 29 (January):
      476-77.
          Compares unfavorably the "new lady," who is loyal to her
      womanhood, "the type of everything that is strong and sensible
      and intellectual and noble and pure in womanhood," with the woman

of the new school, "the advanced woman," who makes pretentious claims of equality, opposes and is in conflict with man, and causes men to cease being courteous and protecting of ladies. The new lady will emerge when the dust settles.

895   HAWEIS, Mrs. "The Soft Sex." Eclectic Magazine 126
       (April):505-9.
            Believes the new modern indulgences will spoil women and make them too soft. It was better for woman's character to have to obey father and husband. Finds ugly perils in the new paths. "Revolt against received opinion and regular habits, the destruc- tion of standards, the loss of the old piety without new ballast to replace it, all sorts of discomfort and mischief--well, we have seen a little of it in the Revolt of the Daughters, and it was not pretty." Reprinted from Good Words (London) 37:37-40.

896   "On Being a Woman." Living Age 211 (3 October):62-64.
            Insists that it is pointless for women to try to change their lot, for the destiny of woman is decided by the facts of nature, so complaints are neither useful nor dignified. Counsels that "as the state of life of being a woman is quite unalterable women may be content to make the best of its limitations." Reprinted from the Spectator (London) 77 (29 August):269-70.

897   "Shakspere [sic] and the New Woman." Catholic World 64
       (November):158-69.
            Woman is rebelling against "her most necessary ally. . . . She is perhaps incited to such a rebellion by a few discontented petticoated demagogues." Within her own sphere woman is "a thing of beauty . . . outside of it she is a foreign excrescence ugly to behold." In regard to women in men's dress, points out that Shakespeare's characters put it on "only on account of extreme exigency," blushing with maidenly shame.

                              1897

898   MAYHEW, WILLIAM H. "Marriage and Chastity." New-Church
       Review 4 (January):70-88.
            Says marriage is the natural condition of life. In mar- riage woman has a foreordained role. Certain "practical diffi- culties" have made marriage not always possible (local excess of women over men, large numbers of unhappy marriages bringing marriage into disrepute, and so on), but "these are abnormal conditions--disorderly conditions." We should not draw our prin- ciples of action from what is abnormal and disorderly. "There is no occasion for throwing down the true ideal of womanly life and womanly use because it is not immediately attainable by all."

899   FITZPATRICK, F.W. "Woman and Domestic Architecture." Midland
       Monthly 10 (June):558-65.

Says woman's influence in architecture has not been bene-
ficial. Declares that woman insists willfully on a certain style
and will look until she finds an architect who will build it.
Woman knows less about architecture than anything else; "her will
and her whims must reign supreme," and she forces the public "to
look upon absurdities and freaks in buildings." Calls upon
magazines to educate women to good taste and for women to use
their influence for better buildings.

900   MOODY, HELEN WATTERSON. "The College Woman." Review of
      Reviews 16 (August):194-95.
         Reprint of 901.

901   MOODY, HELEN WATTERSON. "The Unquiet Sex: Women's Clubs."
      Scribner's Magazine 22 (October):486-91.
         Worries about the eagerness, insistence, and extremism of
      some women to advances in education, technology, and politics,
      "the wonder and wide opportunities of this century." Sees this
      restless activity as hectic rather than natural and as showing
      "an eagerness of disease" rather than of health. Says many women
      today "would gladly exchange all the privileges of 'emancipation'
      for the exemptions of a lesser liberty." Believes women's clubs
      should be for recreation, not improvement.

                              1898

902   GIRVIN, ERNEST A. Domestic Duels; or, Evening Talks on the
      Woman Question. Conversations Relating to the Domestic, So-
      cial, Industrial, Historical and Political Phases of the Sub-
      ject. San Francisco: E.D. Bronson & Co., 277 pp.
         Argues that the respective spheres of man and woman are
      "immutably fixed by laws far beyond human control, and when
      either of the sexes in any society persistently violates these
      laws, or oversteps the narrow limits which they define, the whole
      social fabric inevitably crumbles into chaos." Book proposes to
      warn American women of their peril and point them back to the old
      paths of happiness and safety. Done in the form of a narrative
      about Mr. and Mrs. Notion containing lectures on why women should
      do housework, bear many children, accept psychic and physiolog-
      ical differences between the sexes, eschew professional careers,
      and not vote.

903   MOODY, HELEN WATTERSON. "The Unquiet Sex: The Case of
      Maria." Scribner's Magazine 23 (February):234-42.
         Says that women are by nature home-makers. Yet the task is
      becoming so taxing these days that many are moving into apart-
      ments and hotels. Faults women for trying to gain "a superficial
      knowledge of many things" and to become the political peers of
      men when they should have been reforming their own area, the

home. Then they will not lose servants. Says that until women
can organize the home, they do not deserve suffrage.

904   MABIE, HAMILTON W. "Recent Comments on Men, Women, and Man-
       ners." Book Buyer 16 (May):344-45.
           Praises Helen Moody's antifeminist series in Scribner's,
       1897-98, for having "the quality of good talk; the talk of a man
       [sic] who knows the drawingrooms, the clubs, the places of
       resort, and who has not only observed, but thought."

905   PECK, HARRY THURSTON. "The Woman of Fascination."
       Cosmopolitan 26 (November):71-83.
           A fascinating woman never has a large hand, and "a really
       large nose in a woman is fatal. . . . Stout women are never
       fascinating." Blue eyes are never fascinating, nor is a small
       mouth. "Very few women can walk well. They waddle. But the
       woman of fascination will move easily and swiftly along, gliding
       rather than walking--an embodiment of the poetry of motion." The
       fascinating woman does not have a powerful mind, "is never what
       is called 'an educated woman,' than which there is nothing more
       repellent to a sane and world-taught mind. . . . Learning,
       'education,' have never yet sat gracefully upon a woman. They
       make her pedantic, self-assertive, pragmatical and bigoted." The
       fascinating woman is, on the contrary, "accomplished."

                                    1899

906   [BOK, EDWARD]. "The Rush of American Women." Ladies' Home
       Journal 16 (January):14.
           Believes that housekeeping is a profession rightfully leav-
       ing little spare time for women to be involved in women's clubs
       and organizations. It is a "fatal idea" that women must do
       something outside the home. No happy wife or true mother ever
       complains about the narrowness of the home. In contrast, women
       on the platform or using a pen "hysterically and frantically
       demanding an expansion of woman's opportunities" have barren
       homes. Calls the platform woman "a blot upon American womanhood"
       and warns, "no woman in a happy American home can ever afford to
       listen to these parasites of her sex."

                                    1900

907   AN AMERICAN MOTHER. "What the American Girl Has Lost."
       Ladies' Home Journal 17 (May):17.
           Asserts that the modern girl has lost the strength of
       repose, has lost her health because her nerves are ruined, has
       lost all sense of fitting personal modesty, and "has deliberately
       chosen to make herself familiar with that class of prurient sub-
       jects formerly left to the knowledge of men."

908   "Words from Ruskin for Women." Current Literature 28
       (May):145.
            Quotations from Sesame and Lilies.

909   BIRNEY, Mrs. THEODORE. "The Twentieth-Century Girl: What We
       Expect of Her." Harper's Bazar 33 (26 May):224-27.
            States that our ideal modern girl realizes that parenthood
       is above all vocations. She prepares herself for it by getting
       exercise but developing "no special set of muscles at the expense
       of the nervous force which in a woman should be so carefully
       conserved." She can earn her living but would not leave her
       comfortable home simply for the sake of "a mistaken independence,
       or a desire for a so-called career." Wholly traditional, subtly
       antifeminist.

910   [TOPICS OF THE TIMES]. "Women of Leisure." Century 60
       (August):632-33.
            The woman of leisure "is becoming rare to the point of
       impressing one as an exotic." This is too bad. Where are those
       pauses for renewal and refreshment, those quiet centers where one
       is soothed? Men have toiled that women may be "endowed with all
       the beauties and gentle graces which he himself has missed. They
       represent beneficently to his imagination all manner of noble and
       lovely things." Holds up European women, who are able voluntar-
       ily to efface their personality--quiescent women, serene women.

911   [A GRANDMOTHER]. "A Solution of the Domestic Problem."
       Living Age 227 (24 November):492-97.
            Asserts that women will have better servants when they stop
       speaking on platforms, riding bicycles, getting educated, and
       instead look well to the ways of their households. Reprinted from
       Macmillan's Magazine (London) 82:448ff. Reprinted in 914.

912   DELAND, MARGARET. "Studies of Great Women: Cornelia."
       Harper's Bazar 33 (22 December):2153-56.
            Finds that the feminine ideal of selflessness which
       Cornelia embodies is subtly and surely changing. Women have more
       occupations open to them, but they are complicating industrial
       life by entering trades and professions. They are also losing
       that "loveliness in living" which was part of femininity. Yet
       that "almost always aesthetically objectional person . . . the
       'New Woman,'" does not seem to care. She would rather be "stren-
       uous, useful, generally wholesome" than feminine. Opposes woman
       suffrage because it may "double the present ignorant and uncon-
       scious vote." Deplores the raising of individualism over duty.

913   UNITE, PLEASAUNCE. "Disillusioned Daughters." Living Age 227
       (29 December):801-7.
            Suggests that women are restless because they have turned
       away from sewing, embroidery, clear-starching, and ironing--
       beautiful domestic pursuits. Believes women need domestic manual
       labor. Urges that we "restore to domestic pursuits the honor

that was theirs in the eighteenth century." Reprinted from
Fortnightly Review (London) 74 (November):850-57.

1901

914   [A GRANDMOTHER]. "A Solution of the Domestic Problem."
       Eclectic Magazine 136 (January):47-52.
            Reprinted from Macmillan's Magazine (London) 82:448ff.
       Reprint of 911.

915   "Woman and Lynch Law." Harper's Bazar 34 (2 March):589.
            Editorial that criticizes Carrie Nation and her lawless
       hatchet: they are "lynching the saloon." Allows that the saloon
       may be guilty but finds Mrs. Nation and her ax "a deplorable
       spectacle."

916   FINCK, HENRY T. "The Influence of Beauty on Love."
       Cosmopolitan 30 (April):589-98.
            Beauty is beyond all doubt of the feminine gender. It is
       woman's duty to attain it. Here is her future, not in competi-
       tion with man. It is a fatal error for woman to try to become
       independent of man. "She should make him her slave, ask him to
       emancipate her from all outdoor labor, to let her grow up, with
       her children, like a flower in his garden, so that he may have
       beauty for beauty's sake."

917   FINCK, HENRY T. "'Only a Girl.'" Independent 53 (9 May):
       1061-64.
            Urges women and girls to be glad they are female, the
       superior sex. Condemns "mannish women."

918   AN AMERICAN MOTHER. "What of the Woman Herself?" Ladies'
       Home Journal 18 (June):10.
            Alleges that the nineteenth century has infected American
       women with "an unhealthy craving for public work and public
       applause." Says that women who must earn their support deserve
       God's and man's respect, but that too many women rush into the
       marketplace just for notoriety. Meanwhile, the white American
       race is becoming extinct. The nineteenth century dragged women
       from their natural base, but they are nervous and restless rather
       than content. But notes that some are returning to the home.

919   "In Defence of the Husband's Hour." Harper's Bazar 35
       (June):184-86.
            Advises women to keep their husbands happy in the evening,
       not to talk to them but rather let them smoke their cigars. Keep
       love warm in its nest by keeping out discord and disagreement and
       bar the door against "selfish demands."

920   PYKE, RAFFORD. "What Men Like in Women." Cosmopolitan 31
       (October):609-13.

Says men like grace and daintiness in women--"awkwardness
. . . is very hard to overlook." Men like women to be responsive
but loathe the cheap Bohemian woman who wishes a false comradery
with men and is really seeking the vulgar and salacious in conversations with them. Alleges that women differ from men in mind
and in body. Man wants woman's mind to complement his. He likes
her to be absolutely dependent upon him.

921   GREGORY, ELIOT. "Our Foolish Virgins." Century 41
      (November):3-15.
            A nasty catalog of the types of young New York women of the
      day: young vagrants allowed to run wild by their parents, who
      spend their time shopping, going to tea, playing bridge, visiting
      bachelor painters in their studios, being photographed--"encour-
      aged to shirk both cares and responsibilities and pass days and
      evenings in idleness." He wants the American girl to be fault-
      less, "not a disheveled sportswoman, weather-beaten and ill kept;
      not an adventurous navigator, square of jaw and unchangeable of
      face; not a household tyrant, versed before her time in the
      sinister lore of the world; not a tramp saint or an idle goddess,
      but a gentle, home-loving maid."

                              1902

922   POWELL, LEWIS. The Twentieth Century Home Builder: Being a
      Treatise on the Home, and Woman as the Builder of Home.
      Nashville, Tenn.: Publishing House of the M.E. Church, South,
      47 pp.
            Says that home is "the true sphere of woman's influence.
      This is her realm by divine appointment." She does not belong on
      thrones as a rule, nor "in legislative halls, not in short hair
      and meager dresses, but at home!"

923   HARLAND, MARION. "The Family versus the 'Solitude of Self.'"
      Independent 54 (23 January):202-7.
            Says men have given women all the rights they have asked
      for, for which we should honor them. Someone should start a
      man's rights movement. Bemoans woman's reluctance to have chil-
      dren. Alleges that methods for avoiding childbirth "are respon-
      sible for more pain and more chronic invalidism than the natural
      process of bringing children into the world according to God's
      appointment." Says the "least desirable" elements will continue
      to reproduce and calls upon "patriotic . . . large-minded women"
      to match them.

924   FRANCIS, HENRY WALDORF. "Marriage and Dress." Arena 27
      (March):292-96.
            Why aren't young men marrying? Because they cannot afford
      to. Too many women are taking their jobs, and all the women want
      is to buy fine clothing. Women become ever more "imbued with the

love of dress. . . . A majority of women think of little else
than dress." Well, it is their fault if no man will marry them!

925   HART, LAVINIA. "Motherhood." Cosmopolitan 32 (March):463-74.
       A paean for motherhood as woman's highest ambition. "If
the women who yearn to accomplish something would cease straining
their eyes toward the distant horizon for a life-work and look to
the field in which they stand, we might have more of them [sic]."
It is because they cannot get away from "the natural feminine
instinct to 'meddle' that women of strong character look for work
outside the home."

926   PYKE, RAFFORD. "Husbands and Wives." Cosmopolitan 32
       (April):611-15.
       Women's widening interests have affected not only her will-
ingness to marry but also her success in marriage. Believes
that marriage "is now becoming far more difficult because of the
tendency to discourage a woman who marries from merging her
separate individuality in her husband's."

927   WINCESTER, BOYD. "New Woman." Arena 27 (April):367-73.
       Allows that woman should be educated, possess legal and
social rights, and have the right to her own development. "However, every one who cherishes the slightest regard for the rare
virtues and qualities of sweet womanhood must resent and abhor
the too manifest tendency of modern social, industrial, and
educational innovations to unsex and abase our young women. . . .
Thought is masculine; sentiment is feminine."

928   PYKE, RAFFORD. "The Woman's Side." Cosmopolitan 33
       (July):323-28.
       Sees three distinct and different groups of married women,
some happy, some indifferent, some unhappy. Alleges that those
restless, neurotic, intense women who denounce man as a tyrant
and are most prominent in "prating" about their rights are of the
last class. They cry against marriage and against man-made laws
when in fact their real problem is that they were mismated.
Explains feminism as purely "physiological."

929   CRANE, ALICE ROLLINS. "Desirable Reforms in Motherhood."
       Arena 28 (November):499-505.
       Modern women make terrible mothers. Cites as examples the
"female lecturer"--"there can be no question of the crime attach-
ing to the skirts of women--who are mothers, but devoid of moth-
erliness--constantly to be seen on public platforms professing to
be intensely interested in reforms." Also criticizes fashionable
women and the slovenly, slatternly mother. "All the wickedness
of the human race can be traced to incompetent motherhood."

930   "The Woman's Fault." Harper's Bazar 36 (November):1021.
       Faults individualism in women because it breaks up family
relations. If a marriage is unhappy, it is almost always the

woman's fault. Woman must subordinate her individual will to the
common good.

1903

931   BOYESEN, HJALMAR HJORTH. "The American Bride." Cosmopolitan
        34 (February):373-82.
            Today's women are full of unrest and undefined longing, but
        underneath the aspiration for education, suffrage, and a part in
        the active affairs of life is the ultimate saving desire for the
        commonplace--a home, husband, and children. "There is something
        pathetic in the ill-disguised yearning of women who have been
        caught up in the cog-wheels of a nation's destiny, or thrust
        into public view by fame, for the quiet home and conventional
        life they might have had."

932   PECK, HARRY THURSTON. "What a Father Can Do for His
        Daughter." Cosmopolitan 34 (February):460-64.
            A father can rescue his daughter from the female world:
        "From close association with a father, the young girl quite
        unconsciously acquires something of the largeness of the man's
        nature and loses something of the pettiness and narrowness of the
        woman's."

933   BISLAND, MARGARET. "The Curse of Eve." North American 17
        (July):111-22.
            Blames the falling white birthrate on "the over-education
        and abnormal public activities so ardently encouraged among our
        women since the close of the Civil War." Says any emancipation
        of women beyond domesticity is an unmixed evil. Women are denied
        an equal share in man's intellectual and physical career as an
        inexorable law of nature--"a law that never fails to deprive
        intellectually developed woman of her fecundity." Says any ten-
        dency to pull women out of the home increases the divorce rate
        and decreases the birthrate. Wants to reassert the motherhood
        ideal.

934   CHRISMAN, OSCAR. "Education for the Home." Arena 30
        (October):401-9.
            Education must take into consideration the difference be-
        tween women and men. In man self-preservation is strongest; in
        woman race-preservation is strongest. Man reasons; woman loves.
        Women may receive the same education as men, but they should also
        be educated for their "natural profession of maternity." It will
        solve the national divorce problem when woman is educated in
        college for the profession of homemaking and maternity. "One can
        hardly conceive of the pleasures and profits to mankind that will
        come when women become specialists in homemaking."

<u>1904</u>

935   BOK, EDWARD. "The Ratio of Real Mothers." <u>Ladies' Home</u>
      <u>Journal</u> 21 (January):16.
           Says women are not such good mothers as they used to be.
      Blames them for dissipating their energies in diverse channels to
      the neglect of their children. Women should stay at home.

936   AN ALUMNA. "Alumna's Children." <u>Popular Science Monthly</u> 65
      (May):45-51.
           Alleges that college women have fewer children because of
      physical weakness based in arrested development in girlhood—"to
      their unwise manner of work and to untimely nervous strain in our
      grammar and high schools." Totally impressionistic.

937   PYKE, RAFFORD. "The Pursuit of Man." <u>Cosmopolitan</u> 37
      (October):691-94.
           The sex-instinct is "the one marvelous and terrible posses-
      sion of woman, and to it, in spite of custom, in spite of theory,
      in spite of everything, she is dedicated for all time." There-
      fore, it is she who pursues, not man—she who has the mating
      instinct. It is a law of nature: "Man is really more detached
      than woman. His moral and physical fastidiousness is actually
      greater, and were hers not less than his, the purposes of life
      would be frustrated." It is all part of nature's plan. That is
      why marriage is woman's career.

938   PYKE, RAFFORD. "Strength in Women's Features." <u>Cosmopolitan</u>
      38 (November):111-14.
           Deplores the development of "mannish" traits in women. "So
      many women single out for imitation the qualities which may be
      necessary to a man, but which in a woman are not only quite
      unnecessary but wholly odious. . . . Each sex has its own gifts,
      its own weapons, its own resources, and each should be content
      with what it has and should give over borrowing from the other."
      Says the woman suffrage movement has failed because it has been
      in the hands of "brawling, noisy, homeless shriekers, who are
      always holding 'congresses' and denouncing the tyrant man, and
      who have been making a holy show of themselves for fifty years."
      Finds one Carrie Nation enough. Devolves into physiognomy—how
      to read a woman's face and hands for her character.

939   HARRIS, Mrs. L.H. "Reflections upon Old Bachelors in New
      England." <u>Independent</u> 57 (29 December):1492-94.
           Berates men for not marrying and commiserates with single
      women. Says "there is nothing more pathetic or reproachful in
      American life than the increasing numbers of delicate women who
      have been forced to declare themselves the industrial and intel-
      lectual equals of men." Finds it unmanly of men to suggest that
      women can take care of themselves. A peculiar way of blaming men
      for feminism.

1905

940   CLEVELAND, GROVER. "Woman's Mission and Woman's Clubs."
      Ladies' Home Journal 22 (May):3-4.
      Is appalled by the "restlessness and discontent" of the
woman suffrage movement which is undermining the character of our
wives and mothers. Finds "this particular movement . . . so
aggressive, and so extreme in its insistence, that those whom it
has fully enlisted may well be considered as incorrigible." Is
concerned about the organized club movement as it shows women to
be discontented with their home life. Fears that some women's
clubs are "harmful in a way that directly menaces the integrity
of our homes and the benign disposition and character of our
wifehood and motherhood." Believes "it should be boldly declared
that the best and safest club for a woman to patronize is her
home." Reminds women of their "Divinely appointed path."

941   ROOSEVELT, THEODORE. "The American Woman as a Mother."
      Ladies' Home Journal 22 (July):3-4.
      Describes the primary duty of woman to be a wife, mother,
helpmeet. Worries about the nation if woman loses her sense of
duty, sinks in "vapid self-indulgence" or becomes so twisted that
"she prefers a sterile pseudo-intellectuality" to her duty and
self-sacrifice. Deplores the modern tendency to small families
and easy divorce.

942   GIBBONS, Cardinal JAMES. "Pure Womanhood." Cosmopolitan 39
      (September):559-61.
      Denies that restricting woman to the "gentler avocations of
life" fetters her aspirations. Rather, it secures to her "those
supereminent rights that cannot fail to endow her with a sacred
influence in her own proper sphere. As soon as woman entrenches
upon the domain of man, she is apt to find that the reverence
once accorded her is wholly or in part withdrawn. To debar her
from such pursuits, is not to degrade her." Women belong at
home, educating their children, especially in religious
instruction.

1906

943   HARRIS, Mrs. L.H. "The Single Woman's Problem: Why the
      'Problem' Exists." American Monthly Magazine 62 (August):
      426-27.
      Part of a series of responses to an earlier article. Be-
lieves that the problem of the single woman exists because about
twenty-five years ago women decided to become independent. As a
result, they have made married women discontent with their lot,
have lowered the wage scale, and have caused antagonism between
the sexes. But "it is better to be a good mother than to be a
great artist or a great musician or a great anything else."
Counsels women to go back to the natural order of things; marry.

It is only "the monumental stupidity of women" that drives them
to compete with men rather than have power over them.

1907

944   HARRIS, Mrs. L.H. "Superwoman." Independent 62
       (21 February):426-28.
           Argues that the superwoman is the antithesis of the
       "advanced" woman. The latter suggests agitation, masculinity,
       antagonism; she is not woman enough. The women's righters are
       not superwoman either; in fact, they impede her arrival. Super-
       woman is beautiful, motherly, emotional.

945   "A Clergyman's Opinion of Women." Independent 63 (22 August):
       427-32.
           States that women's reasoning processes lack logic; women
       are vague, can think of only one thing at a time, have poor
       memories and unstable moods. But cautions that it is foolhardy
       for women to ignore their femininity. "This so-called 'business
       woman' is an anomaly; the woman who 'mingles in politics' is a
       monstrosity; the woman who boasts of her cleverness in doing
       'men's work' is an absurdity; the woman whose conceit is in her
       masculinity errs in vision and stumbles in judgment." What we
       want to emphasize is differences between the sexes, not equality.

946   ROGERS, Mrs. ANNA A. "Why American Marriages Fail." Atlantic
       100 (September):289-98.
           Blames high divorce rate on woman: (1) on her "failure to
       realize that marriage is her work in the world. (2) Her growing
       individualism. (3) Her lost art of giving, replaced by a highly
       developed receptive faculty." American women are spoiled, ego-
       centric, idle, and extravagant. Reprinted in 947.

947   "Is Woman to Blame for the Present Marital Unrest?" Current
       Literature 43 (November):535-37.
           Summary of 946.

1908

948   ABBOTT, LYMAN. The Home Builder. New York: Houghton
       Mifflin, 128 pp.
           Abbott's home builder is no feminist; in fact, she laughs
       at those who would reform her traditional life. She wishes to be
       exempt from jury duty, military service, and suffrage. "She has
       too much pride in her father, her brothers, her husbands, and
       her sons, to accept the Pharisaic boast that women are so supe-
       rior to men that their votes would purify all public life of its
       pollution." She wants influence, not power.

949   ELIOT, CHARLES W. "The Normal American Woman." Ladies' Home
       Journal 25 (January):15.
           Insists that exceptional women who follow a male profession
       contribute much less to the real progress and development of
       mankind than normal women who marry and bring up five or six
       children.

950   ROGERS, Mrs. ANNA A. "Why American Mothers Fail." Atlantic
       101 (March):289-97.
           Women should set their hearts and minds to mothering.
       "Women fret themselves and others for the right to vote, and they
       do not see that their son's vote, their brother's, their
       friend's, is verily their own." There is plenty of work for
       women.

951   SAUNDERS, LUCY M. "Divorce or Devotion: The Wife Must
       Decide." Appleton's Magazine 11 (April):472-75.
           Woman is responsible for the outcome of the marriage con-
       tract into which she has entered. Woman must keep herself on a
       pedestal and furnish her husband with an ideal to work for. If
       her husband looks elsewhere, it is her fault.

952   CORBIN, AMY FOSTER. "The American Wife: A Woman's Criti-
       cism." Appleton's Magazine 11 (May):597-601.
           Faults American women for thinking only of themselves.
       "The American vampire is the wife." Says that even if woman
       suffrage were granted, woman's "surest way to power lies in her
       influence with her husband." A good wife can uplift, a bad wife
       ruin a man.

953   HALL, G. STANLEY. "From Generation to Generation." American
       Monthly Magazine 66 (July):249-54.
           Worries that the cultured classes are tending to celibacy
       or to late marriages with very small families. "Is there any-
       where one normal woman of thirty-five or forty, even though she
       be a feminist, who would not in her heart of hearts prefer a
       husband, home, and above all, children of her own to any or
       everything else the world has to offer?"

954   SHOLL, ANNA MC CLURE. "Are the Days of Chivalry Dead?"
       Appleton's Magazine 12 (October):456-58.
           Predicts that "when the pendulum has swung to its limit in
       the direction of women's newly acquired privileges," there is
       likely to be a reaction, signs of which are not wanting, in favor
       of the world-old ideas. Then women will return to the fireside,
       but bringing with them riper experience and broader sympathies.
       Chivalry is not dead.

955   MACPHAIL, Dr. ANDREW. "The American Woman." Living Age 259
       (31 October): 297-302; (7 November):371-74.
           Insists that men and women are complementary to one an-
       other. Believes that "in so far as the woman acquires the qual-
       ities and characteristics of the man she becomes to that extent

futile." Seems to think that the American woman is particularly
unfeminine, idle, luxury-loving. Says she is failing in motherhood as she pursues her "rights." But she has lost her influence. Predicts that the feminine woman will win out. Reprinted
from the Spectator (London) 101 (3 October):497-98 and
(10 October):537-38.

1909

956   ROGERS, ANNA A. Why American Marriages Fail, and Other
      Papers. Boston and New York: Houghton Mifflin, 213 pp.
         Claims that American women are spoiled, extremely idle, and
      extravagant, to the detriment of their marriages. Women do not
      need to vote; they just need to get their husbands and sons to
      vote properly.

957   VORSE, MARY HEATON. "The Inconsequential American Woman."
      Appleton's Magazine 13 (January):66-71.
         American women are the most indulged and petted women in
      the world but do nothing but waste and spend. American women owe
      men for women's colleges, money to spend, freedom from work--
      these are proofs of the generosity and chivalry of American men.
      American women do not help their husbands as foreign women do.
      They should take more interest in their husbands' work.

958   MEYER, ANNIE NATHAN. "The Problem Before Women." Appleton's
      Magazine 13 (February):194-97.
         Finds an analogy in the situations of blacks and women.
      For both the problem is to find the best work to do without
      repudiating the past. Cites Booker T. Washington's work training
      blacks, especially for domestic and manual work. Says women need
      the same kind of wise training to take up old duties in a new way
      and to be led back to the home.

959   HOFFMAN, FREDERICK L. "The Decline in the Birth Rate." North
      American 189 (May):675-87.
         Notes that the birthrate of native-born of native stock is
      declining dramatically and says it is caused by deliberate
      actions by women. Immoral doctrines are being spread in peri-
      odicals, including a statement by Ida H. Harper that women know
      how to and will regulate the size of their families. Calls this
      "monstrous advice of a deliberate crime, . . . a gospel of self-
      ishness and immorality." Insists that "the duty of maternity may
      impose heavy burdens and responsibilities, but it is one which no
      normally married woman can shirk, save at the risk of bodily and
      moral ruin."

960   BIRGE, PAUL F. "Differences of Sex." Harper's Weekly 53
      (3 July):6.

Argues that differences based on sex pervade the whole being and are both physical and psychological. Insists that woman's task is exerting personal influence in the home. Opposes woman suffrage.

961   JONES, ELLIS O. "Are Women Human?" Lippincott's 84 (August):204.
Clever dialogue between the Paradoxical Person and the Old-Fashioned Person, the gist of which is that women used to be just human beings with things to think about, like children and pies, but now they have become Women, "a something which cannot forget that she is a Woman, and which, therefore, is somehow the irreconcilable enemy of something else, called a Man." Asserts that until the latter part of the nineteenth century, "women were never heard of in history."

1910

962   LATIMER, CAROLINE WORMELEY, M.D. Girl and Woman: A Book for Mothers and Daughters. New York: D. Appleton, 331 pp.
Insists that men and women should stay in their separate spheres, which are different and complementary. Women should not receive an identical education with men because it might teach them to despise motherhood. It might also lead to physical and mental disabilities.

963   KRETSCHMAR, ELLA MORRIS. "Home-making and Health." Good Housekeeping 50 (February):151-53.
Believes that women's pace is getting too frantic, causing them to become neurasthenic and anemic and marriages to suffer. There is too much club activity. Suffrage will not help, it will only "double political and economic confusion." Woman should go back to the home. "The 'limelight,' to woman, is blighting at best, leaves her broken physically, and mentally wretched." Woman is queen in her home.

964   [ABBOTT, LYMAN]. "A One-Sided Argument." Outlook 94 (9 April):787.
Denies that women are discriminated against by the laws of New York State regarding dissolution of marriage. The laws are framed to contribute to the solidarity of the family, by which woman and man become one. Opposes any individuality in marriage or any unwillingness on the part of woman to merge her identity in marriage.

965   ABBOTT, LYMAN. "In the Family--the Hebrew Ideal." Outlook 95 (9 July):522-26.
Believes that women and men complement rather than duplicate each other. Finds that "a masculine woman and a feminine

man are equally abhorrent to nature; they are abnormal specimens
of the race." Calls advocates of the women's movement pagans.

966   HILLIS, Mrs. NEWELL DWIGHT. "Some Failures of American
       Women." Outlook 95 (16 July):571-75.
       Blames women for the rise in divorce--too little to do,
too much prosperity, too little preparation of our girls for
homemaking.

                              1911

967   SALEEBY, CALEB WILLIAMS, M.D. Woman and Womanhood: A Search
       for Principles. New York and London: M. Kennerley, 398 pp.
       Advances "Eugenic Feminism," which means that the best
women must become mothers. "Women can compete successfully with
men only at the cost of complete womanhood," which is too great a
cost.

968   SALEEBY, C[ALEB] W[ILLIAMS], M.D. "The Purpose of Womanhood."
       Forum 45 (January):44-50.
       Believes it an error to suggest that there are no differ-
ences between women and men. This doctrine of sex-identity is
advocated either by unmanly men or masculine women--"palpably
aberrant and unfeminine women." The purpose of woman is
motherhood.

                              1912

969   TARBELL, IDA M. The Business of Being a Woman. New York:
       Macmillan, 242 pp.
       Insists that woman's business is to be a wife and mother,
to be conservative. In contrast, the uneasy woman, the feminist,
wants to imitate man and his activities--work, clothing, smoking.
In striving to be like man, woman has become cold, hard, repel-
lent. She has sacrificed her womanly endowment. Calls the woman
at the front of the woman's movement "a tragic figure," restless,
blindly struggling, frantic.

970   TARBELL, IDA M. "The Uneasy Woman." American Monthly
       Magazine 73 (January):259-62.
       A chapter from The Business of Being a Woman (969). Women
are blaming men for their troubles.

971   HARRIS, Mrs. L.H. "Moving Pictures of English and American
       Women." Independent 72 (4 April):715-18.
       Presents unflattering portraits of both English and Amer-
ican women. Says men are getting tired of the spoiled American
woman and are less respectful and courteous to her. She in turn

tries to reinstate herself through the woman's movement, demanding better protection in laws, equal suffrage, etc. Says the American woman blames man for her condition when actually women are to blame.

972   "Is Woman Making a Man of Herself?" Current Literature 52
       (June):682-84.
              Summary of 970.

973   BOK, EDWARD. "The Job That Was Too Big." Ladies' Home
       Journal 29 (July):3.
              Asserts that many "platform women" can talk in public with ease but cannot talk with one small child in their home. Insists that "it was not the smallness of her task, but its greatness, its appalling greatness that drove her from her home to the platform . . . crying for a wider sphere." Says her job in the home was too big for her.

974   STRINGER, ARTHUR. "The Renaissance of Woman." Collier's 49
       (27 July):20-21.
              After being protected by man for centuries, woman is now reentering industrial life, which is causing her reproductive powers to diminish and her character gradually to become defeminized. But woman "cannot rise above the cold logic of biology." She must be a mother first. She must not "denature her womanhood by elbowing a way into work. . . . For when woman refines herself beyond the nobilities of this animal instinct and obligation, she merely refines herself and her nation out of existence."

975   ANDERSON, HARRIET. "Woman." Atlantic 110 (August):177-83.
              Women do not need rights—they have duties. Everything in woman's life should contribute to making her a mother.

                                  1913

976   CORBIN, CAROLINE F. Woman's Moral Duty in the Home. Bulletin
       no. 20. Chicago: Illinois Association Opposed to Woman Suffrage, 4 pp.
              Insists that if women do not do their work in the first ten years of their children's lives, the children may be ruined. "Such a child finds himself, at the arrival of puberty, in the possession of self-acquired or very possibly actually inculcated knowledge which may lead him directly to habits of immorality, and even to the door of the brothel." Insists that "no power of suffrage in the hands of women will reach the lives of children who have been neglected in the home years of their existence."

977   HARTLEY, C[ATHERINE] GASQUOINE. The Truth about Women. New
       York: Dodd, Mead & Co., 404 pp.

Opposes the woman's movement as "a wastage of the force of womanhood," which should be spent in the service of the race, not in individuality. Motherhood is the truth about woman.

978   Matrimony and the Building of Homes. Bulletin no. 16.
      Chicago: Illinois Association Opposed to Woman Suffrage,
      6 pp.
          Argues that matrimony and the building of homes are the panacea for today's social ills. They teach self-sacrifice, patient bearing of crosses, duty. There is a finer and higher work for woman to do than the work of politics--shaping her children morally.

979   The Mission of Mothers. Bulletin no. 18. Chicago: Illinois
      Association Opposed to Woman Suffrage, 4 pp.
          Traditional arguments.

980   A World Without God. Bulletin no. 19. Chicago: Illinois
      Association Opposed to Woman Suffrage, 4 pp.
          Argues that if women are to keep improving the race from generation to generation by caring for children, men must do their part by supplying the homes and doing the world's work. "Study and investigation prove that the original division of the labor of the sexes as ordained by the Maker of the world, is amply justified, even in this latter day, as opposed to the man-made schemes of Socialism."

981   "Ellen Key's Attack on 'Amaternal' Feminism." Current Opinion
      54 (February):138-39.
          Summarizes Key's book, The Woman Movement, now translated into English. Key opposes a feminism which does not exalt maternity, specifically that of Schreiner and Gilman.

982   MARTIN, EDWARD S. "Editorial on the Woman Question." Ladies'
      Home Journal 30 (March):25.
          Is extremely critical of Mrs. O.H.P. Belmont, who he says is typical of a kind of woman who has not found herself and so is restless and agitated. Prefers simple, tranquil, motherly women with an inner governor.

983   "The Restless Woman." Collier's 51 (16 August):13.
          The restless woman has "temporarily lost sight of her goal." Women need to return to their homes and the old forms, for "when woman ceases to express essential womanhood, when she ceases to express the mothering instinct, she becomes a disturber of the world's work, a slightly exotic deflector of man's efficiency, a troublesome sex machine. Only in motherhood is woman able to win her own center of quiet and man's belief in her."

984   BOK, EDWARD W. "One Reason for the Saloon." Ladies' Home
      Journal 30 (October):6.

Alleges that one of the reasons the saloon exists is that women are incompetent cooks. Believes that if women cook men's food better and become better housekeepers, they will render an important service to the cause of temperance.

985   CARTLAND, ETHEL WADSWORTH. "Childless Americans." Outlook 105 (15 November):585-88.
Deplores the refusal of women to have children or the tendency to have only one or two. Intellectual and artistic women are singled out for censure, as is the educated woman, because "with education for woman has come also the knowledge of how she may remain childless."

1914

986   BOK, EDWARD. "A Woman's Idea of the Woman's Part." Ladies' Home Journal 31 (May):5.
Praises Mrs. George Goethals, wife of the builder of the Panama Canal, who hurried back to his side to support him. Calls her sentiment "old fashioned, but in these screeching days of sex-equality doctrines it is fine to hear this old-fashioned conception of a wife's part so well expressed by a woman of large vision." The relative place of man and woman—man as worker, she by his side being protected—will not change.

987   ELIOT, CHARLES W. "Woman That Will Survive: A Message to American Mothers." Delineator 85 (August):5.
Insists that no professional, political, economic, or social gains can compensate women for the loss of their most important function, motherhood. Some exceptional women may follow men's professions and take part in public discussion and activities, but they will have less happy and serviceable lives than their happily married, child-bearing contemporaries. All women should be prepared in youth for maternity. All other training should be subordinated to this main function. "The ultimate woman is, then, the vigorous, nursing mother of a family."

1915

988   SMALL, ALBION W. "The Bonds of Nationality." American Journal of Sociology 20 (March):629-83.
A long fragmentary essay that grew out of a graduate course. Section 4, "A Coherent Family Type," exalts the social value of loyalty within a family and deplores those who would fragment it. Believes "the most dangerous enemy to the coherence of the family of the economic middle class in the United States is the comparative freedom and desire to pursue individual interests." Blames feminism, pointing out that "the social gains of women in the United States have been at the expense of a regrettable amount of detraction of the family," alleging that

feminists have disparaged and ridiculed the role of woman as
homemaker. "Sarcasm, invective, scorn, conscious and unconscious
misrepresentation have been so liberally employed in the femi-
nistic movement that it has been a mighty factor in creating the
present unrest in the middle-class American family."

989   "Birth Control: A Symposium." Harper's Weekly 61
       (2 October):331.
           R.C. Brannon, M.D., asserts that preventing large families
       has caused "an increase in insanity, tuberculosis, Bright's dis-
       ease, diabetes, and cancer."

                              1916

990   RICHARDSON, ANNA STEESE.   "Easy Alimony." McClure's 46
       (March):16-18, 55-57.
           Describes numerous examples of marriage, and all the women
       are bad; they follow the route of easy marriage, easy divorce,
       easy alimony. Mocks feminists, who say that "the modern woman
       wants economic independence. Does freedom with alimony spell
       economic independence?" Suggests decreasing the scale of alimony
       after the first year, with the expectation that by the end of the
       third year woman would be self-supporting or remarried. Wants to
       prevent women being rich and lazy on alimony. Seems to have used
       a very small sample.

                              1917

991   ELIOT, CHARLES W.   "The Small Family: Its Causes and Conse-
       quences." Delineator 90 (March):14, 40.
           Deplores the ever-shrinking American family and the disin-
       clination of American women to bear many children. One of his
       chief targets is long-term employment for women. Feels astonish-
       ment and dismay that normal woman would prefer any life to that
       of a mother of a good-sized family. Promotes motherhood as
       intellectually satisfying, lofty, tender, with deep and lasting
       joys. Warns that "relentless Nature will wipe out in a few score
       years any race whose women fail it in this respect."

                              1920

992   ABBOTT, LYMAN.   "Has Woman Renounced Her Job?" Outlook 124
       (11 February):233.
           Finds some women today think of motherhood only as an
       avocation. The country is tending to anarchy because women are
       not doing their jobs as mothers. But they will come around.
       Most women are still homemakers and mothers and wives.

993   HARRIS, CORRA. "That 'Secret' Marriage." Independent 102
       (5 June):311, 342.
          Faults Fannie Hurst's secret marriage, just recently re-
       vealed, saying that this is not a good example for other young
       women. Complains that Hurst "is petting herself, making an
       exception of herself because she is a professional woman with a
       career to keep." Concludes: "Nobody's career is so important as
       one marriage well made."

                              1921

994   "Courtship after Marriage." Atlantic 128 (November):649-54.
          Attributes the failure of men and women to marry to several
       causes: puritanism, romanticism, and feminism. Charges feminism
       with "bewildering society regarding the relations of the sexes."
       Says women are revolting against nature and seeing the home and
       family as, at best, an evil necessity. Says feminists are lower-
       ing women morally to the level of men. "It is to be hoped, and
       in fact is to be expected, that after this exaggerated movement
       of protest by the Feminists has spent its force, we shall have a
       return to a sane and natural attitude toward the marriage rela-
       tion and all that it implies in obligations and ultimate
       contentment."

Education of Girls and Women

The initial response to women's attempt to improve their education was positive so long as the instruction was directed at the traditional accomplishments. When feminists increasingly insisted on an education equal to men's, opponents became more vocal, focusing in particular on the undesirability of coeducation. Here, however, the sides cannot be neatly drawn. Generally people who favored coeducation were attempting to improve women's lives and can be considered feminists. They were usually moderates. On either side there were opponents to coeducation and supporters of single-sex education. Feminists like M. Carey Thomas who opposed coeducation argued—and some still maintain—that young women needed their own colleges where they could see and study under women scholars, where they would be assured positions of power, and where they would not be distracted by social life.

Some antifeminists opposed coeducation because they alleged that women lowered standards in formerly male colleges, that they lowered the "tone," distracted men, diluted scholarship, etc. When women took all the prizes, it was because they were not creative intellectually, just good students. Other antifeminists opposed coeducation because they did not want women educated like men. Rather, they wanted women to be educated for homemaking in all-women's colleges; domestic science was to be the answer here. Many articles and books point to the low marriage rate for women in women's colleges and predict that native-born stock will soon die out altogether.

To sum up, the reader will find antifeminists who support and others who oppose coeducation and therefore oppose or support women's colleges. What they all share is a fear that education will make women less womanly, less domestic, "unsex" them, and make them independent.

1837

995   Y., B. "Thoughts on the Happiness of Woman as Connected with the Cultivation of Her Mind." [Godey's] Lady's Book 15 (November):204-6.

Allows that woman may learn but warns that she should take
care never to outshine man, for "he will not bear that woman
shall be his equal, much less his superior." Weaker in frame,
she must always be dependent upon man and should therefore strive
to please him.

1850

996   FISHER, Rev. SAMUEL W. "Female Education." Godey's
      Lady's Book 40 (April):279-81.
           Favors female education but separate spheres. Says woman
      always loses when she leaves her sphere for man's. She becomes
      no longer a woman but not quite a man. Woman should shun "the
      labors of the field, the pulpit, the rostrum, the court-room" and
      maintain the domestic life.

1852

997   PALMER, RAY. Address on the Education of Women, Delivered at
      the Anniversary of the Pittsfield Young Ladies' Institute, 30
      September 1852. Albany: Gray, Sprague & Co., 31 pp.
           Warns against letting woman "jostle the coarser sex in the
      scramble for wealth, honor and position." Does not want her
      raising her voice in debate. Says it would transform her into
      "an Amazon" and she would lose feminine instincts. Wants woman
      educated for her sphere.

1857

998   LIPSCOMB, A.A. "Education of American Women." Harper's
      Magazine 15 (November):776-83.
           States that woman should be educated for the private
      sphere, not the public sphere--that would violate and outrage her
      constitution.

1860

999   "Errors in Female Training." Eclectic Magazine 51
      (September):62-67.
           Argues that present-day education is making girls and young
      women manlike, destroying feminine graces. In defense of women's
      rights some have gone too far, allowing women to claim equality
      with men, "intermeddle with all knowledge," and become self-
      sufficient. This may gratify women's vanity, but it will ruin
      their modesty and self-abnegation, which should be the crowning
      virtues of the sex. Finds in modern female education "a courting
      of publicity, a striving after bold effects, a fostering of
      independence, a nurturing of self-conceit, a developing of undue

self-reliance" which produces "forwardness of character, bois-
terousness of manner, audacity of mien, and curtness of speech."
Reprinted from Eclectic Review (London) 4 (July):71-78.

1861

1000   HALE, SARAH JOSEPHA. "Editors' Table: Vassar Female Col-
        lege." Godey's Lady's Book 61 (October):347-48.
            Applauds the proposed curriculum as appropriate to woman's
        sphere. Is relieved that they are not yielding to those who
        would urge women into employments which "the economy of Provi-
        dence has allotted to man." Believes that restricted occupation
        exalts rather than degrades woman.

1863

1001   "The Education of Women." Godey's Lady's Book 66
        (January):40.
            Does not favor equal education for women and men. Finds
        there must be qualities special to the sexes and so there should
        be education special to them also.

1002   "Education of the Female Sex." American Journal of Education
        13 (June):232-42.
            Aphorisms on woman's education; all of the traditional
        arguments from the Bible forward.

1003   [GERMAN AUTHORITIES]. "Suggestions on Female Education."
        American Journal of Education 13 (September):495-502.
            More snippets from antifeminist authorities (see 1002), all
        insisting that woman's education must be entirely different from
        man's.

1865

1004   SPALDING, J.R. "Female Education as It Is and as It Should
        Be." Hours at Home 2 (November):80-88.
            Believes that each sex should be educated according to its
        special qualities and needs. Women have modesty, tenderness, and
        grace; if they lose them they are unsexed. Woman's intellect
        should be expanded but not stimulated unnaturally so as to make
        the intellect the central seat of her life and turn her into what
        "every body has heard of and nobody loves, 'a strong-minded
        female.'"

1867

1005   S. "Punishment of Girls in School—And Boys." Monthly
        Religious Magazine 37 (January):68-71.

Says girls are docile, gentle, etc., when good but when the
fine elements of girlish character are inverted, "they induce to
a refinement of wiles and subtleties and depravities which leave
the boys and men a good way in the distance." Therefore, little
girls must be punished equally with boys when they misbehave.

1870

1006   ALLEN, W.F. "The Sexes in Colleges." Nation 10
       (3 March):134-35.
       Objects to coeducation because college offers so much free-
dom to the student that a woman is in moral danger. Also doubts
that most girls "can do, without breaking down physically, the
intellectual work which their more robust brothers can safely
undertake."

1871

1007   Beauty Is Power. Reprinted from London ed. New York: G.W.
       Carleton, 310 pp.
       Says a "true college" education for women would unfit them
for women's duties and sphere. Calls the plan to establish a
woman's college in England a "foolish project."

1008   "Women in the Colleges: Editorial." Scribner's Monthly 2
       (September):546-47.
       Finds coeducation safe and good but opposes dispensing with
single-sex colleges because "men are not women, women are not
men, and for their differing spheres of life and labor they need
a widely different training." Asserts that "the claiming of
places for women in young men's colleges as a right, and the
denunciation of their exclusion as a wrong to woman, are the
special functions of fanatics and fools."

1009   "College Doors Opening." Every Saturday 11 (14 October):363.
       Describes coeducation in the best eastern colleges as an
experiment of uncertain outcome involving morals as well as
education. Asserts that women and men are not alike "either in
intellectual desire or in intellectual capacity."

1873

1010   CLARKE, EDWARD H., M.D. Sex in Education; or, A Fair Chance
       for the Girls. Boston: J.R. Osgood, 181 pp.
       One of the seminal books in nineteenth-century antifem-
inism. Argues that girls can be as well educated as boys but at
great physical cost: "neuralgia, uterine disease, hysteria, and
other derangements of the nervous system." Alleges that the

muscles and brain cannot function at the same time, so if a girl overworks her brain in puberty, her reproductive system will become diseased, even destroyed. Gives many clinical examples from his practice. Coeducation is his special target because it has produced the evils he describes. Insists that "identical education of the two sexes is a crime before God and humanity, that physiology protests against, and that experience weeps over." Would have girls study less than boys, and allow them more time for rest.

1011   GODKIN, E.L. "The 'Coeducation' Question." *Nation* 16
        (22 May):349-50.
            Says that coeducation, like suffrage, is based on Mill's argument that sex is merely a physical accident with no effect on character, nervous force, or mental or moral constitution. Disagrees with that position, upholding rather "the common notion" that "the first great step in civilization was the separation of the sexes, and the allotment to them of different duties and spheres, and the creation of a set of conventions for the preservation of female modesty and the protection of the family."

1012   PORTER, D.G. "Collegiate Education for Girls." *Christian
        Quarterly* 5 (October):433-58.
            Responding to a suggestion that woman be educated for homemaking in college, writes that woman's education should be liberal rather than special. But he does not favor equal education. "There is, doubtless, a practical difference of texture between her brain and his, corresponding to that which distinguishes the two systems generally." Man's brain is firm and tough, woman's sensitive and delicate. Man's "grows stronger and firmer by exercise," whereas woman's "would be irritated and enfeebled by the same process continued to a similar extent." Warns against sacrificing the woman to the scholar. Complains that too many liberally educated women do not marry. The young woman can accomplish only two thirds the intellectual labor of her male counterpart. Women can never keep pace with men intellectually; they are not adapted to do independent thinking or pioneer work.

1013   ELIOT, CHARLES W. "Clarke's Sex in Education." *Nation* 17
        (13 November):324-25.
            A favorble review of 1010.

1014   SEARS, E.H. "The Co-education of the Sexes." *Monthly
        Religious Magazine* 50 (December):567-68.
            More notice and approval of Clarke's *Sex in Education* (see 1010).

1015   "'Sex in Education.'" *Monthly Religious Magazine* 50
        (December):552-59.

A review, with long excerpts, of Clarke's Sex in Education
(see 1010). Finds him substantially correct.

1874

1016   TYLER, Rev. WILLIAM SEYMOUR. The Higher Education of Women.
        An Address. Mt. Holyoke Seminary, 3 July 1873. Northampton,
        Mass.: Bridgman & Childs, 31 pp.
           Opposes coeducation. Expects both it and woman suffrage to
        fail "because women themselves, women generally--the truest,
        purest and best of the sex, for the most part, do not wish for
        the right of suffrage." They know they will lose more than they
        gain. Their good sense and right feeling will tell them that
        influence is better. The same true, pure, good women do not wish
        for coeducation. Predicts that coeducation will "inevitably
        either break down the health and constitution of woman, or change
        the curriculum and lower the standard of college education,"
        because woman is physically incapable of enduring the same educa-
        tion as man. Prefers that women be educated at home or in a
        homelike setting to protect their purity.

1017   TYLER, WILLIAM S. "The Higher Education of Women."
        Scribner's Monthly 7 (February):456-62.
           Summary of 1016.

1018   "Clarke's Sex in Education." Old and New 9 (March):379-83.
           An approving review of Clarke's Sex in Education (see
        1010).

1019   MAUDSLEY, HENRY, M.D. "Sex in Mind and in Education."
        Popular Science Monthly 5 (June):198-215.
           States that there is a limited amount of energy in every
        human. If a young woman expends it in mental activity, she will
        injure herself physically. Nature intends a different course for
        women than for men and so woman should have a different educa-
        tion. Asserts, "there is sex in mind, and there should be sex in
        education." Then summarizes Clarke's book, and mentions both
        Nathan Allen and S. Weir Mitchell. Says improper education
        unsexes woman intellectually, morally, and physically. Asserts
        that "the main reason of woman's position lies in her nature,"
        for she is "more or less sick and unfit for work" one week a
        month during the best years of her life. Reprinted from
        Fortnightly (London) 21 (April):466-83.

1020   GODKIN, E.L. "The Replies to Dr. Clarke." Nation 18
        (25 June):408-9.
           Continues to support and advance Clarke's warnings about
        coeducation and women's education.

1878

1021   MARSH, ROBERT WINTHROP. "The Higher Education of Women."
        Potter's American Monthly 10 (January):1-15.
           Supports higher education for women but opposes woman's
        "committing the grave mistake, of trying to make herself like a
        man, and of aping his special talents and pursuits." Woman
        should allay prejudice by keeping within her sphere. Remainder
        of article describes Mt. Holyoke at length, Smith, Vassar, and
        others.

1882

1022   PATTERSON, C. STUART. "Coeducation in the University of
        Pennsylvania." American 5 (21 October):24-25.
           Repeats the stereotypes about what women and men are and
        then worries about what will occur following removal of the
        safeguards that have been placed around women "to keep them
        unspotted from the world." Says "there are facts of history,
        works of genius, and laws of physiology, which all intelligent
        men and women know, and which all men and all women ought to
        know, and which modest men and women cannot mutually discuss.
        . . . [There are] subjects to which no modest woman can . . .
        listen without a blush."

1883

1023   "The Back-down of Dr. Dix: Editorial." Popular Science
        Monthly 23 (July):409-11.
           Deplores Dr. Dix's stand on women's education. Dix had
        chaired the committee that investigated the admission of women to
        Columbia and had recommended that women be admitted if they
        provided their own accommodations. Editor opposes woman receiv-
        ing the same education as man—she needs an education to fit her
        for the home.

1024   CLOUSTON, T.S., M.D. "Female Education from a Medical Point
        of View." Popular Science Monthly 24 (December):214-28;
        (January 1884):319-34.
           A lecture delivered at the Philosophical Institution of
        Edinburgh in November 1882. Presents a physiological view of
        education. Health is to be preferred over intellectual education
        in women. "Why should we spoil a good mother by making an ordi-
        nary grammarian?" Argues that the mothers of great men were not
        well educated. Wants girls to conserve their energy, which is
        limited, and grow fat, which is spare power for the future.
        Wrong methods of education can cause anemia, stunted growth,
        thinness, nervousness, headaches and neuralgia, excessive use of
        stimulants, hysteria, inflammation of the brain, and insanity.
        Education must not endanger the race.

1884

1025   MAUDSLEY, HENRY, M.D. Sex in Mind and in Education.
        Syracuse, N.Y.: C.W. Bardeen, 34 pp.
            Repeats much of Clarke's argument (see 1010). Says there
        is sex in mind and in education. Women must be educated for
        their foreordained work as wives and mothers. Opposes coeduca-
        tion because it fosters harmful competition in girls. It also
        causes imperfectly developed reproductive systems: "The main
        reason of woman's position lies in her nature."

1886

1026   D'ALFONSO, NICOLO. "Problem of Education for Women."
        Education 6 (February):360-68; (March):420-28.
            Believes that because of their physical organization, women
        are "permanently subject to nervous irritability, extremely im-
        pressionable and mobile, even in their adult state." The ex-
        ternal world fascinates them irresistibly, and they are incapable
        of stability, constancy, and firm purpose. Warns that all this
        is permanent: "there is no educative force that can completely
        and constantly change her psychological state." Woman's special
        mission is therefore education within the private sphere. Trans-
        lated by Victoria Champlin.

1027   "The Higher Education of Women." Academy (Syracuse) 1
        (June):297-99.
            Reports on an article by Mrs. E. Lynn Linton in Fortnightly
        Review (London) 46 (October):498-510. Linton believes that by
        expending energy in obtaining a higher education, women unfit
        themselves physically for maternity. Further, those women whose
        desire and ambition to compete with men requires a higher educa-
        tion must remain celibate. Also believes that because women are
        more individualized than men, they are more disorganized. Thus
        they do not take into account the general good, only their own.
        In America this may result in "the painless extinction of man."
        Academy editor agrees with Linton, adding that the present gen-
        eration is inclined to think more of its rights than of its
        duties.

1028   LINTON, E. LYNN. "The Higher Education of Women." Eclectic
        Magazine 107 (December):812-20.
            Opposes higher education of women because of the expense,
        because of its deleterious effect on women (it makes them arro-
        gant, pretentious, vain), and because it ruins them for preg-
        nancy, lactation, and child-rearing. Girls should study always
        with quietness and self-control, always under restrictions
        bounded by their sex and its future possible function. Or if
        they go in for intense study, they should dedicate themselves as
        Vestals of Knowledge, never to marry and have children. Re-
        printed from Fortnightly Review (London) 46 (October):498-510.

1029   LINTON, MRS. E. LYNN. "The Higher Education of Women."
        Popular Science Monthly 30 (December):168-80.
        Reprinted from Fortnightly Review. Reprinted in 1028.

                                1887

1030   "Education and Co-education." Critic 11 (20 August):85-86.
        Women who marry and have children must not and indeed
        cannot do anything else "if they understand their own responsi-
        bility." Thus higher education for women conflicts with woman's
        natural vocation. Is totally opposed to coeducation because "it
        is liable to tint the manners and talk of the girls with a
        freedom and slanginess caught from the boys, rather than to teach
        the latter good behavior. . . . Between the sexes the familiar-
        ity of classroom and college community has nothing to recommend
        it." Has grave doubts about the wisdom of educating women in
        college.

1031   MARBURY, ELIZABETH. "Education of Women." Education 8
        (December):235-39.
        Claims that there is sex in the mind, that there are
        "strongly marked mental differences between the sexes." Women are
        receptive, men originative. If women and men should be educated
        identically, the world might lose its variety of thought.

                                1889

1032   MAGNUS, Lady KATE. "The Higher Education of Women." Eclectic
        Magazine 112 (February):246-50.
        Wonders whether higher education for women is "justified
        from the aesthetic, or the ethical, or the economic standpoint."
        Asks, "Is it needful, is it admirable, this hopelessly, heedfully
        unattractive departure from traditional womanhood?" Believes the
        modern tendencies are fostering selfishness and one-sidedness in
        women. Lays the alarming surplus of women to women's arguing
        with, competing with, rivaling man but not attracting him. Coun-
        sels that marriage is the most demanding and most bestowing of
        all professions open to women. Reprinted from National Review
        (London) 12:663ff.

1033   GOODELL, WILLIAM, M.D., and MITCHELL, S. WEIR, M.D. "Co-
        Education and the Higher Education of Women: A Symposium."
        Medical News 55 (14 December):667-73.
        Goodell thinks that "prolonged confinement, prolonged
        brain-work, and prolonged intellectual rivalry are . . .
        injurious to physical and sexual development" in women. Finds
        ill health commonly associated with brilliant scholarship. Op-
        poses coeducation. Mitchell believes that study is "sexually
        incapacitative" for many young women. Thinks coeducation is

"abominable," "absurd," and "foolish." Not all respondents opposed coeducation.

1891

1034   LE BON, GUSTAVE. "The Education of Women and Its Effects."
        Educational Review 1 (January):101-3.
            Likens women intellectually to barbarian and half-civilized
        peoples. Finds in both groups an inability to reason, lack of
        reflectiveness, lack of critical spirit, inability to associate
        ideas or discover affinities or differences, inability to hold to
        opinions, a tendency to generalize from particulars, want of
        precision, and impulsive character. Women have a powerful memory
        which makes them superficially good students, but they lack
        imagination and reason confusedly. Warns that education is also
        physically damaging to women. Counsels that women must receive a
        much less rigorous education than men, with little memorization
        of dates and battles and with the goal of producing good wives
        and mothers. Reprinted from Revue scientifique.

1893

1035   SINCLAIR, JANE COOPER. "Co-education in the West." North
        American 157 (October):509-11.
            Says doubts are beginning to arise in the West over the
        system of coeducation. Young women are allowed to be too inde-
        pendent, and young men become too familiar. The setting is too
        exciting and the strain too great for many young women. Favors
        separate education.

1894

1036   GORREN, ALINE. "Womanliness as a Profession." Scribner's
        Magazine 15 (May):610-15.
            Says questions are arising about higher education for
        woman. Women are losing their womanly quality. Education is
        causing a strain, making them "incapable of fulfilling adequately
        the essential functions of womanhood, of gaining or giving happi-
        ness as wife or mother." Does not want educated woman to be
        freed from the emotional, womanly side of life. Reprinted in
        1037.

1037   GORREN, ALINE. "Is the Representative American Woman Womanly?"
        Review of Reviews 9 (June):708.
            Reprinted from 1036.

1895

1038   PARKHURST, CHARLES H., D.D.   "College Training for Women."
        Ladies' Home Journal 12 (May):15.
             Wants higher education for women to foster among its stu-
        dents a tendency to become homemakers. Opposes coeducation or
        male education or male teachers for women.

1896

1039   BROWN, HELEN DAWES.   "How Shall We Educate Our Girls?"
        Outlook 53 (7 March):431-32.
             Reading, writing, beautiful speech, a little music, being
        agreeable--these are the basics. Wants the girl's education
        directed to fitting her for the home. Argues that "the best
        organization in the world is the home. Whatever in the education
        of girls draws them away from that is an injury to civilization."

1040   WHIBLEY, CHARLES.   "Women and University Degrees." Review of
        Reviews 13 (April):479.
             Is protesting against "the encroachment of women" at
        Cambridge. Says this will cause the degradation of learning, for
        "women are the sworn enemies of Greek and Latin" and would side
        with the Philistines. Editor of Review of Reviews obviously does
        not agree with Whibley, calling his article a "shriek of male
        hysterics." Reprinted from Nineteenth Century (London) 41:531-
        37.

1897

1041   BOUGHEY, A.H.F.   "The Universities and the Education of
        Women." Eclectic Magazine 129 (July):19-25.
             Women want Oxford, Cambridge, and Dublin to grant them
        degrees as well as an education. Argues that degrees for women
        are unnecessary. Worse, women will not be satisfied to stop here
        but will ask for more. Worries about tendencies to abolish all
        distinctions of sex in matters of education, for intellectual
        powers of men and women are different. Rather than opening up
        male universities to women, a university should be established
        for women. Reprinted from New Review (London) 16:502ff.

1042   MOODY, HELEN WATTERSON.   "The Unquiet Sex: The Woman
        Collegian." Scribner's Magazine 22 (August):150-56.
             Blames higher education for women, especially single-sex
        institutions, for women's dissatisfaction with their life and
        work. Says women should be educated to be wives and mothers,
        housewives, cooks--"the natural and simple division of labor is
        the one that assigns to women the duties and activities that
        centre in the home." Cannot understand why any woman should
        complain about this division of labor.

1898

1043   "Women at Oxford and Cambridge." Living Age 216
       (22 January):219-33.
            Argues that admitting women to Oxford and Cambridge would
       greatly injure the universities, women, and the coming generation
       of youth. Deplores American coeducation for fostering women
       taking over teaching, crowding out men, operating public librar-
       ies, and generally lowering the level of teaching. England
       should emulate Germany in educating only a few exceptional women.
       There are two sexes because it was intended that each have its
       work to do, so they should also be educated differently and
       separately. Blames the woman's movement for "extreme laxity in
       divorce, for the institution of female clergy and . . . many
       other aberrations." Deplores women wearing men's clothes, playing
       their games, and smoking. Reprinted from Quarterly Review
       (London) 186 (October 1897):529-51.

1899

1044   GODDARD, ASA E. "Some Reflections on the Present Education of
       Women." New-Church Review 6 (January):101-13.
            Feels that in some of the present tendencies of modern
       education "there is something radically wrong, decidedly un-New-
       Church." Wants us to look higher and determine what is best for
       each sex and then plan education accordingly. Because woman will
       have care of children, she should in her education develop those
       qualities of purity, love, self-sacrifice, and hope. She should
       hold up high ideals for the race. Even thinks "each sex requires
       a nourishment which is not required by the other, and that this
       depends upon their different uses." Not sameness but harmony is
       called for.

1045   PECK, HARRY THURSTON. "The Overtaught Woman." Cosmopolitan
       26 (January):329-36.
            Foresees problems if women are permitted access to higher
       education, allowed to specialize, to become investigators, and to
       seek distinction in fields that require single-minded devotion.
       Alleges that the great specialist is less exacting of women than
       of men, so that he lowers his standards for women and then his
       work suffers a distinct deterioration. He has been betrayed by
       chivalry. Thus both women and scholars are damaged by women
       pursuing higher education.

1046   "Concerning Woman's Education." Outlook 61 (11 March):581-83.
            Argues for a different education for women than for men,
       preparing them for the home rather than competition with men.
       Deplores "that pseudo-progressiveness which, under the guise of
       developing a 'new woman,' would make an effeminate man."

1047   GOUCHER, JOHN FRANKLIN, et al.   "The Advisable Differences
        between the Education of Women and That of Young Men."   School
        Review 7 (December):577-99.
            Says the education of women and men should be different
        because women and men are different.   "The highest function of
        womanhood is motherhood."   Anything else is exceptional and "non-
        adjusted."   In discussion, William C. Collar says colleges demand
        an amount of work dangerous to the health and beauty of women.
        Professor William T. Sedgwick of M.I.T. is in favor of single-sex
        institutions and of education for women that takes into account
        their physiological weaknesses.   Professor Charles W. Eliot says,
        "function should ultimately determine education."   Since the
        functions of men and women are different, their education should
        be different.

                                1900

1048   WRIGHT, THEODORE F.   "The Collegiate Education of Women."   New-
        Church Review 7 (January):112-16.
            Says the result of giving women education identical to that
        of men is to create "mannish young women, ambitious to excel in
        everything but as matrons of families--a life which they abhor."
        This product simply justifies the criticisms of those who think
        that college education disqualifies young women for their best
        life.   Quotes with favor the inaugural address of Caroline
        Hazard, new president of Wellesley, with whose views of feminine
        education he agrees (and which M. Carey Thomas rejected in organ-
        izing and later serving as president of Bryn Mawr College).

1049   MITCHELL, S. WEIR, M.D.   "When the College Is Hurtful to a
        Girl."   Ladies' Home Journal 17 (June):14.
            Wants all girls to be trained in housework before they go
        to college.   Insists most cannot and should not try to keep up
        with men.   Competition with men is perilous.   Asserts that those
        who overvalue learning are ill-dressed: "I never saw a profes-
        sional woman who had not lost some charm.   There comes a little
        hardness, less thought as to how prettily to do or say things;
        affected plainness of dress; something goes."   Speaks from the
        sad experience of seeing the health of ambitious women wrecked.
        Warns those about to "sail the seas of success" that the seas are
        treacherous.   From an address delivered in 1896 to the students
        of Radcliffe College (see 208).

1050   AN AMERICAN MOTHER.   "Is a College Education the Best for Our
        Girls?"   Ladies' Home Journal 17 (July):15.
            Argues against college education for young women because it
        does not fit them for their life's work.

1901

1051   SETON, WILLIAM. "The Higher Education of Woman and
        Posterity." Catholic World 73 (May):147-49.
            Favors woman's education and other improvements so long as
        woman has the wisdom to stay what God has made her, man's help-
        mate and best beloved. But worries that "coming perhaps with
        woman's emancipation is a tendency to make the future woman more
        manlike, and the future man more womanly. . . . Now this con-
        vergence of characters, this approximation of the sexes, would,
        if long continued, seriously endanger the progressive evolution
        of the race. It might lead to retrogressive development and--
        except through a miracle--to final extinction." Woman's nervous
        system would degenerate. Let woman study astronomy if she will;
        once she has a baby, "she will find more delight in its twinkling
        eyes than in all the planets of the solar system."

1052   "The American Woman." Independent 53 (6 June):1334-36.
            Editorial that expresses worry that American universities
        are becoming feminine. Wants universities to be of a more dis-
        tinctly masculine nature. Opposes coeducation because it "fos-
        ters the predominance of the feminine." Refers to Münsterberg's
        article in the International Monthly (see 248).

1053   "The Educated Mother." Independent 53 (5 December):2911-12.
            Editorial that argues that everyone is talking about the
        falling birthrate and blaming the educated woman. Editor agrees.
        Says education of woman "must be vain and unprofitable in its
        results unless it can be made strenuous enough to overcome any
        recently acquired reluctance to be the sturdy mother of a stal-
        wart race."

1902

1054   CURTIS, W.A. "Coeducation in Colleges: A Man's View."
        Outlook 72 (13 December):887-90.
            Alleges that men oppose women's attending college with them
        because woman has become "not his ally, his helpmeet, his wife,
        but his competitor, his rival," and has cheated him of herself.
        She halves his income and doubles those seeking employment.
        Marriage is decreasing, the social evil is increasing, family
        life is passing away. "In just such measure as woman has in-
        creasingly driven man out of his wonted employments, in such
        degree has our national courtesy departed, in such degree has the
        opposition to coeducation grown."

1903

1055   VAN DE WARKER, ELY, M.D. Woman's Unfitness for Higher Coedu-
        cation. New York: Grafton Press, 225 pp.

Asserts that coeducation is the result of women raising money to force colleges to admit women (Michigan, Johns Hopkins, Rochester, and Cornell are cited) rather than the result of public necessity and demand. Argues "that the demand for it, and the money which purchased for it a place, came from the women who were exploiting the equal suffragist movement." Argues that coeducation makes impossible demands upon women physiologically (cites Clarke, entry 1010) and ruins women for maternity. Coeducation is causing the colonial strain to die out. Coeducation is unfair to women because it does not educate them for their lives as women. It also promotes too much socializing between the sexes and leads to a moral breakdown and sexual depravity.

1056   GOVE, AARON, et al. "Coeducation in High Schools." National Education Association Proceedings 1903:297-300.
The superintendent of schools in Denver believes that boys and girls should not receive identical education; instead; girls should go to school with boys until noon and then girls should go home to engage in home duties. This will allow boys to prepare for college or business and girls to prepare for their life duties. Is supported in discussion by the superintendent of Boston schools and others, but opposed by several others.

1057   HALL, G. STANLEY, et al. "Coeducation in the High School." National Education Association Proceedings 1903:446-60.
Asserts that men and women are completely different and should be--with progress in civilization they diverge and draw apart. Schools should "push distinctions to the uttermost, to make boys more manly and girls more womanly." Opposes the feminization of education. Says coeducation diminishes the mystique of the other sex, which leads to fewer marriages. Says "man-made methods" are not the best for woman because "she is a generic being, nearer to the race." Emphasizes that "coeducation in the middle teens tends to sexual precocity." Discussants were both pro and con.

1058   FINCK, HENRY T. "Why Coeducation Is Losing Ground." Independent 55 (5 February):301-5; (12 February):361-66.
Asserts that coeducation leads to early engagement and marriage and to flirtation, which interferes with study. When girls mingle with boys, they become "bold-faced, free and easy." Prefers "sympathy, amiability, and winsomeness" to the "ostentatious independence and aggressiveness which co-education tends to breed in women." Deplores intellectual competition between the sexes. Women, who are intellectually precocious, take all the prizes, thus discouraging our boys, but lack "mental muscularity." Wants women trained to be wives and mothers and urges that textbooks be "feminized"--made descriptive, sentimental, and moral. Opposes making scholars or intellectuals of women.

1059   BOK, EDWARD. "The College and the Stove." Ladies' Home
        Journal 20 (April):16.
            Says a girl's intellectual achievements do not matter if
        she is "lacking in the womanly instinct that makes for a just
        appreciation of domestic science." Regrets that so much of
        woman's higher education is useless. Wants domestic education
        taught in every girls' college, and the college to be more
        friendly to the stove.

1060   GIGLINGER, GEORGE. "Divorce and Its Effects on Society."
        Catholic World 78 (October):92-98.
            Blames rise in divorce rate on, among other things, coedu-
        cation, "because it sets aside the laws of nature, which require
        a different training for the girl from that of the boy, according
        to the different natures and different callings in life."

1061   MARTIN, EDWARD S. "Girls and Their Education." Harper's
        Bazar 37 (December):1134-41.
            Believes girls should be educated to be wives, not wage
        earners. Finds marriage and wage-earning to be "imperfectly
        compatible occupations," so educate the girl for her primary
        function of wife and mother and only incidentally to earn her
        keep.

                                    1904

1062   HALL, G. STANLEY. "Coeducation." National Education Associa-
        tion Proceedings 1904:538-42.
            Wants girls to glory in and emphasize the ebb and flow of
        their menstrual cycle, not repress it as the feminists would have
        them do. Believes "there is something wrong with the girl in the
        middle 'teens' who is not gushy, sentimental, romantic at least
        at times." Does not want girls to be thoughtful and regular in
        their conduct and life. Worries that in coeducation, "perhaps
        familiarity relaxes sexual tonicity--one of the most precious of
        all educative influences." Argues that "mental strain in early
        womanhood is a cause of imperfect mammary function, which is the
        first stage of the slow evolution of sterility."

1063   "Are There Too Many Women Teachers?" Educational Review 28
        (June):98-102.
            Summarizing a pamphlet issued by the Male Teachers' Asso-
        ciation of New York City. Worry that the existence of so many
        unmarried female teachers "is diminishing the extent, power, and
        influence of the home," that female teachers are ruining their
        physical well-being. They insist that "the differentiation of
        the sexes indicates a differentiation of vocation." Boys need
        contact with virile men if they are to become manly men. Women
        as teachers are followers, unable to initiate or reason. Women
        teachers feminize the course and methods of study. The group
        wants all boys from age ten on to be taught by men.

1064   VAN DE WARKER, ELY, M.D. "Is the Education of Women with Men
       a Failure?" Harper's Weekly 48 (20 August):1288-89.
            Asserts that money for coeducation has been raised by
       suffragists as part of a plot. Coeducation is a hybrid that does
       not take woman's needs into account. The equal-suffragists first
       unsex women and then coeducate. Asserts that woman's place as a
       medical doctor is determined by her sex; she should be a women's
       specialist. Author's main argument is with coeducation, not
       higher education for women.

1065   "Co-Education." Current Literature 37 (September):273.
            Quotes articles in Popular Science Monthly, Medical Record
       (2 July 1904), and by G. Stanley Hall as raising serious ques-
       tions about coeducation. Medical Record says higher education
       elevates the intellectual over the emotional, to the detriment of
       woman's natural vocation. Hall says "mental strain in early
       womanhood is the first stage in the evolution of sterility."

                              1905

1066   SMITH, A. LAPTHORN, M.D. "Higher Education of Women and Race
       Suicide." Popular Science Monthly 66 (March):466-73.
            Argues that the higher education of women is extinguishing
       the race--it develops woman's brain at the expense of her body.
       Asserts that an extraordinarily developed brain unfits woman for
       wifehood and motherhood. Alleges chemical reasons (phosphates).
       Educated women marry later and have fewer or no children. Al-
       leges increase in "child-murders" (infanticide? abortion?). All
       this adds up to race suicide caused by the higher education of
       women.

1067   CLEVELAND, ALFRED A. "The Predominance of Female Teachers."
       Pedagogical Seminary 12 (September):289-303.
            Asserts that the predominance of female teachers is not
       good. Says women should predominate at the lower grades, men at
       the higher grades, especially for boys. Contrasts qualities of
       male and female teachers: men have broader scope and make their
       pupils work harder. Women pay more attention to mechanics,
       drill, and details. Women "inspire more personal devotion but
       less of ambition." Concludes that women's present preponderance
       in education "is detrimental to the best interests of our
       schools."

                              1906

1068   HALL, G. STANLEY. "The Question of Coeducation." Munsey's 34
       (February):588-92.
            Sees two dangers in coeducation: first, the feminization
       of education is leading to the progressive extinction of the male
       teacher. Second, it is bad because the sexes are different in

                              241

bodily construction, organs, biological and physiological functions. "Education should push sex distinctions to their uttermost, make boys more manly and girls more womanly." Blames
coeducation for inducing a love of freedom in woman, sending her
out into the office and shop, and striving for intellectual
careers. Insists that women develop their brains at the expense
of reproduction. "Over-activity of the brain during the critical
period of the middle and later teens will interfere with the full
development of mammary power" and lead to race suicide.

1069   FELTER, WILLIAM L. "The Education of Women." Educational
        Review 31 (April):351-63.
            Warns that if we force the same education on woman as on
man, we unsex her and make her mannish. Woman's education should
prepare her for her normal occupation of wife and mother, not
aiming at "the choice few who are unusually gifted." Lists the
usual physical and mental differences, citing particularly
woman's lack of creative endeavor: she has a good memory but no
originality. The course of study for girls in secondary schools
and colleges should aim to cultivate health. Worries that
college-educated women are shunning motherhood and argues that
"girls should not be trained primarily to independence and self-
support" but rather should be imbued with altruism.

1070   ARMSTRONG, J.E. "Limited Segregation." School Review 14
        (December):726-38.
            This principal of Englewood High School, Chicago, argues
that nature has different intentions for boys and girls; thus
they should be educated separately in their teens. "Is a crea-
ture endowed by nature with marvelous intuitions [woman] to have
these powers crippled by a course in higher mathematics or other
forms of logic?" Sees his role as assisting boys and girls in
their early teens "to differentiate in their characteristics, so
that each shall be better prepared for the higher complementary
relations of life."

                                1907

1071   SHIELDS, THOMAS EDWARD. The Education of Our Girls. New
        York: Benziger Brothers, 299 pp.
            Presents a dialogue among educators to demonstrate that
coeducation is wrong because it tries to make men and women
duplicates rather than allies. Women should be educated for only
two vocations: wife and mother or religious. The feminist
educators in the group come off the worst.

1072   MC BRYDE, JOHN M., Jr. "Womanly Education for Woman."
        Sewanee Review 15 (October):467-84.
            This member of the Sweet Briar Institute wants southern
colleges to revert to the type of woman idealized in the Old

South. Quotes Thomas Nelson Page's <u>Social</u> <u>Life</u> <u>in</u> <u>Old</u> <u>Virginia</u>
<u>Before</u> <u>the</u> <u>War</u> (1897). Wants domesticity taught with less atten-
tion to physical and intellectual stimulation. Seeks to "check
this growing spirit of restiveness" in young women. Says "women
should bear in mind that they form, or ought to form, the conservative, restraining, purifying, ennobling element in our society."

1073   "An Opportunity for Modern Feminism." <u>Review</u> <u>of</u> <u>Reviews</u> 36
        (November):627-28.
        Summary and quotations from an article by Professor P.J.
Blok in the Dutch review <u>Onze</u> <u>Eeuw</u>, in which he condemns coeducation and casts doubt on woman's scientific ability. Women can
collate data but cannot attain to scientific truth. "The feminine mind is by nature partisan, strongly inclined in the direction of this or that solution, not scientifically independent."
Asserts that the real opportunity for feminism is in investigat-
ing the differences between the two sexes, not in trying to make
them similar.

                              1908

1074   HALL, G. STANLEY. "Feminization in School and Home." <u>World's</u>
        <u>Work</u> 16 (May):10237-44.
        Observes that the teaching force is overwhelmingly female,
with the result that punishment is banished and replaced by
sentiment. Alleges that boys need an occasional thrashing, or
else they will become obstinate, willful, and neurotic. Believes
if you flog the boy, he will not beat his wife as an adult. Boys
are becoming rowdy because of the feminization of the schools.
Anything that makes for identity of the sexes is degenerative.
They should be kept separate in education.

1075   ELIOT, CHARLES WILLIAM. "Higher Education for Women."
        <u>Harper's</u> <u>Bazar</u> 42 (June):519-22.
        Believes that higher education for women should prepare
them to be mothers of large families, which is "the normal occupation of women." Higher education should perfect family and
civic life. Argues that "it is not the chief happiness or the
chief end of women, as a whole, to enter . . . new occupations,
or to pursue them through life."

1076   AN OCCASIONAL CORRESPONDENT. "A Year Amongst Americans."
        <u>Living</u> <u>Age</u> 258 (11 July):75-80.
        Says coeducation in America is permanently damaging adoles-
cent boys by causing them to become effeminate. The main cause
is the female teacher. Asserts that even with good will on his
part, cannot find in coeducation "any promise of adequate correc-
tion of the tendency to prefer the easy to the hard course even
when the hard happens to be the right course." States further
that the same thing is seen "not only in politics, but equally,

and with equally disastrous effects, in other phases of American
life." Reprinted from the Times (London).

1077   HALL, G. STANLEY. "The Awkward Age." Appleton's Magazine 12
        (August):149-56.
              Mainly on adolescent boys; about one page concerned with
        girls. Argues that girls' activity must be restricted for four
        or five years in adolescence to avoid arresting "mammary, uter-
        ine, and pelvic development." Cautions that "it is a strange but
        portentous fact that just these most vital of womanly functions
        surrender more readily than do others the energy they need."
        Parents must be careful because the system can be depleted with-
        out any outward manifestation and then the girl will go through
        life defective or abnormal. The "purely intellectual" aspects of
        school should be minimized for girls.

1078   HALL, G. STANLEY. "The Kind of Women Colleges Produce."
        Appleton's Magazine 12 (September):313-19.
              Criticizes women's colleges for preparing women for "glori-
        fied spinsterhood" rather than motherhood. Finds "bookishness
        and grinding study" to be "utterly unnatural for girls in the
        teens and early twenties." Sees grave consequences if women
        overwork in these years. Opposes allowing girls to study ethics
        or aesthetics or to become introspective. The best study for
        women is child-bearing and child-rearing.

1079   HOWARD, WILLIAM LEE, M.D. "Helpless Youths and Useless Men."
        American Monthly Magazine 67 (November):51-56.
              Women teachers are destroying male students. "Every boy
        should be taken away from feminine influence at fourteen years of
        age." The sexes must be separated in high school and boys taught
        by virile men. Out with fancy textbooks, foreign languages,
        English grammar, poetry, cultivation, and female teachers.

                                   1909

1080   HALL, G. STANLEY. "The Budding Girl." Appleton's Magazine
        13 (January):47-54.
              Wants the adolescent girl to remain naive, spontaneous, and
        natural. Much of the article is spent describing and relating
        conversations with girls he knows, showing their interest in
        clothing and adornment, relations with other girls, quixotic
        study habits, and intellectual interests, all supporting Hall's
        notions about adolescent girls already described. Exclaims:
        "How all the cant about equality and identity flees in the face
        of common sense!"

                                   1910

1081   HUTT, Mrs. W.N. "The Education of Women for Home-making."
        National Education Association Proceedings 1910:122-32.

Declares this is the age of women, not "of the so-called
new woman with her fads and fancies, her mannish ways, her
aggressive manners, boldly asserting her so-called rights and
demanding the franchise." Wants to advance "the real woman" who
has "the trained brain and heart and hand, the maker of the home
and the helper and inspiration of mankind." Says girls and women
must be fitted for this role through training.

1911

1082   MÜNSTERBERG, HUGO. "Is Co-education Wise for Girls?" Ladies'
        Home Journal 28 (15 May):16, 32.
            Opposes coeducation in high school and college. Wants
        women educated to be the guardian of American culture. Coedu-
        cation either neutralizes sexual attraction, leading to race
        suicide, or reinforces it, distracting women from their studies.
        It is also poor practice pedagogically to mix "two such unlike
        groups of pupils" as girls and boys.

1912

1083   PARTRIDGE, G.E. Genetic Philosophy of Education. New York:
        Sturgis & Walton, 401 pp.
            An "epitome" of the published writings of G. Stanley Hall
        by a former lecturer at Clark University. In his chapter on "The
        Education of Girls," insists that boys and girls must be differ-
        ently educated and warns that "excessive intellectualism incul-
        cates wrong ideals about life, and leads the girl away from the
        simple plain life of home, and the ideals of motherhood and
        wifehood, without which she is certain to be neither morally nor
        physically a complete woman." Opposes coeducation in high school
        and thinks that "the current ideal of the woman's college is a
        violation of the biological." Wants manners, feelings, senti-
        ment, religion, refinement, and the personal taught and stressed.

1084   BARDEEN, C.W. "The Monopolizing Woman Teacher." Educational
        Review 43 (January):17-40.
            Expresses concern over the monopoly that women are gaining
        in the teaching profession because women are at their zenith as
        teachers at twenty-eight. Teaching is too draining on them.
        They insist on teaching when they should be in bed those one or
        two days a month. "This sex limitation draws upon the woman's
        capital, and while she may endure it three or four years without
        apparent loss of vigor, in the end it often produces a nervous
        wreck." Women are also impossible between forty and fifty.
        Furthermore, women are subject to coarse suggestions and sexual
        harassment. This soils them and produces in them an unhealthy
        contempt for man. Teachers of long experience become unattrac-
        tively aggressive. Women who do not marry are failures.

1914

1085   CHADWICK, Admiral F.E. "The Woman Peril in American Educa-
        tion." Educational Review 47 (February):109-19.
            Deplores the fact that the American boy has been under
        female tutelage for generations. This has had an evil effect on
        masculine character. It is "most unreasonable and illogical"
        that the training of our future leaders should be entrusted to
        women. What we have produced is "a feminized manhood, emotional,
        illogical, non-combative against public evils." Insists that "no
        woman, whatever her ability, is able to bring up properly a man
        child." Holds up Prussia as a positive example of masculine
        training. The boy under female tutelage, in contrast, "goes
        through life a maimed man."

1086   PASSANO, LEONARD M. "The Woman Peril in American Education."
        Educational Review 48 (September):184-86.
            Agrees with Admiral Chadwick (see 1085) that it is bad for
        boys to be taught by women after about age thirteen.

1915

1087   PASSANO, LEONARD M. "The Woman Peril: A Reply." Educational
        Review 49 (April):407-9.
            Continues to insist that male teachers should teach boys.
        Male teachers are worth more than female because they are phys-
        ically more fit, usually better trained, more rational and less
        emotional than women; they also have "more stability of character
        and a higher sense of truth and justice." Warns that with fem-
        inism comes "a lowering of the manners and habits of the better
        women to the level of the worst."

1088   JOHNSON, ROSWELL H., and STUTZMANN, BERTHA J. "Wellesley's
        Birth-Rate." Journal of Heredity 6 (June):250-53.
            Bemoan what they see as "the extraordinary inadequacy of
        the reproductivity" of Wellesley graduates, especially honor or
        Phi Beta Kappa graduates. Believe that "separate colleges for
        women, in the United States, are from the viewpoint of the
        eugenist an historic blunder." Criticize the continuance of
        separate colleges for women, now that coeducation is accepted,
        and berate them for not introducing domestic education and child-
        care into the curriculum, calling this "ill-adjusted education."
        Urge parents to send their daughters to coeducational schools and
        benefactors to insist that colleges for women teach domestic
        science or do without their donations.

1089   "College Girls as Wives and Mothers." Literary Digest 51
        (17 July):107-8.
            Condensation and reprint of 1088.

1917

1090   "Brains versus Beauty." School Review 25 (March):219.
        Responding to a complaint that some high school principals
select their female teachers on the basis of beauty and appearance rather than experience, ability, and brains, the editor
supports this practice, stating that a homely, unkempt woman has
no place in the classroom. "She may have several degrees and
dangle with a black string about her neck a Phi Beta Kappa key,
but she has not womanly brains. Qualities of personal untidiness
are consummate proof that she has not woman's supreme qualifica-
tion, lovable, womanly attractiveness, best summed up in the term
'wholesomeness.'"

1918

1091   MAUDSLEY, Dr. HENRY. "Sex in Mind and Education." Educational
        Review 55 (May):427-39; 56 (September):158-68.
        Believes that women are marked out by nature for a very
different course in life than men and that it is physiologically
unwise for them to try to run the same course as men. Insists
that there is sex in mind as well as in body. Thus there should
be sex in education. Women become men's intellectual equals at
the cost of the next generation and of their own health. Draws
on Clarke's Sex in Education (see 1010), Dr. Nathan Allen (1019),
and S. Weir Mitchell; mocks J.S. Mill. Reprinted from Fortnightly Review (London) of April 1874 (21:466-83) and given wide
circulation by C.W. Bardeen in his Series of School Room Classics.

1919

1092   ABERNETHY, JULIAN W. "The Anomaly of Coeducation." School
        and Society 9 (1 March):259-62.
        Opposes coeducation. Says "there are certain natural in-
congruities and repugnancies connected with coeducation in college that can not be denied or remedied." Injecting women into
colleges causes "resentment among alumni and students, becoming
at times an active hostility amounting almost to rebellion."
Says students are justified in complaining that "coeducation
breaks up the unity of college life and makes against college
spirit and enthusiasm." Young men also resent the fact that
women win all the honors and prizes.

1920

1093   PHILLIPS, R. LE CLERC. "Women of Mark and Their Education."
        Bookman 51 (May):328-31.

Higher education for women has not yet succeeded in producing either intellectual or personal genius in them. "If these
facilities do not, cannot, and are not intended to foster unusual
literary and other abilities in women, then the feminists are on
false ground in ascribing women's comparative lack of artistic
and literary achievement to defective education in the past.
Some other reason must be found, for the higher education has not
been in operation quite long enough to have produced some thing
worth producing in the way of women of mark." The implication is
that women are intellectually inferior and that education cannot
remedy this lack.

Women's Intellect and Character

This section covers ground similar to the previous one on education, but here the focus is specifically the quality of woman's mind, her intellectual ability, and her character. She is found deficient in all three. Intellectually, women are imitative, not original; parasites; synthetic, not analytical; quick, intuitive, dreamy, emotional, conservative, childish, more primitive than man, and incapable of abstract thought. Several writers state that there have been no women of genius (see especially 1126) and that women have never accomplished anything equal to men. Women are urged to channel their limited, finite energy into maternity, not intellect. Early in the twentieth century one writer urged that a woman not attempt to drive a car because she cannot think of two things at once (see 1149).

Much of this deficiency is attributed to women's smaller and weaker brain. Late in the nineteenth century pseudoscience is enlisted to prove that women's brains are lighter in weight and color, less convoluted, and indelibly stamped "female." The occipital lobes, seat of emotion, are more highly developed in women than in men. Men's brains get more oxygen and so are more efficient and effective. Feminists spent much time trying to prove that women's brains were not inferior by measuring and weighing skulls and brains, providing ratios, charts, etc.

Women are either angels or devils. Bad women are hopeless and female criminals worse than male. Women do not like other women; they are also intolerant, undisciplined, lack humor, and exhibit greater and less uniformity of character than men; further, they are both predictable and unpredictable, lack a sense of honor and loyalty, are less moral, and do not pay their bills. This section has a depressingly contemporary sound.

1841

1094 RAUCH, Rev. FRIEDRICH AUGUST. _Psychology; or, A View of the Human Soul._ 2d ed. New York: M.W. Dodd, 401 pp.
This book by the late president of Marshall College in Pennsylvania was used as a college text. Discusses the qualities

of mind produced by sexual difference. Women and men differ
physically, psychologically, and mentally. Women's thinking
rests on feeling; they are not productive, only imitative.
Woman's highest happiness is to be a mother.

1846

1095   FERGUSON, FERGUS. Views, Respecting the Comparative Strength,
        Distinctive Features, and Proper Cultivation, of the Minds of
        the Sexes: Being a Lecture Delivered before the Eclectic
        Society of Wesleyan Seminary, 5 March 1846. Marshall: Bunce
        & Fox, 20 pp.
             Finds "an innate, inborn, and irradicable difference in the
        minds, the temperaments, and the propensities of the sexes."
        Each sex is fitted for an appropriate sphere. Should woman be
        educated as a man, she would become coarser and less refined than
        a man: "It is a common remark that a woman, once given to a vice
        of any kind, carries that vice to a greater excess than man; and
        she is, consequently, more exposed if she swerve from a correct
        course." Says ambition is the last thing to be desired in a
        woman's character.

1854

1096   "Woman in France: Madame de Sablé." Eclectic Magazine 33
        (December):433-47.
             Insists that woman has not yet contributed any new form to
        art, any discovery in science, or any deep-searching inquiry in
        philosophy because her small brain and "her physical conditions
        refuse to support the energy required for spontaneous activity."
        Reprinted from Westminster Review (London) 62 (October):448-73.

1857

1097   HALE, SARAH JOSEPHA. "Editors' Table." Godey's Lady's Book
        54 (March):177-78.
             Argues that genius does have sex. No matter how women try
        to stamp out their femininity--on the rostrum, in writing--it
        will shine through.

1858

1098   BUCKLE, HENRY THOMAS. "The Influence of Women on the Progress
        of Knowledge." Eclectic Magazine 44 (June):190-201.
             Agrees that no woman has made a discovery sufficiently
        important to mark an epoch in the annals of the human mind, but
        women have been influential because they have encouraged in men
        deductive habits of thought, thereby rendering "an immense though

unconscious service to the progress of knowledge." Does not
argue for educating women better; rather, wants women's influence
to increase. Reprinted from Fraser's Magazine (London) 57
(April):395-407.

1859

1099   "Woman in Extremes and Varieties of Character." Eclectic
       Magazine 46 (January):84-92.
          Places women in extremes, either "mere stocking-darners,
       and domestic nonentities" or "strong-minded 'rights of women
       folks,' (a very objectionable class)," who neglect their house-
       holds to pursue social and intellectual questions. Generally
       women are either better or worse than men. Female drunkards
       cannot be reformed; cruel women are diabolical. "Such women
       stand out like finger-posts on a sunny shore, indicating where
       the treacherous quicksands lie, and proving the female character
       to be capable of great enormities." Reprinted from Tait's
       Edinburgh Magazine.

1860

1100   "The Intellect of Women." Living Age 64 (21 January):184-86.
          Offers as the greatest argument against the equality of
       intellect in women and men that women have not achieved the
       height and variety of men's accomplishments. Women have other
       talents--for pleasing, patience; for detecting small frauds in
       the household; enthusiasm; unargumentative suggestiveness.
       Asserts that British women need no improvements. They are the
       best they can be already. Reprinted from the Saturday Review
       (London) 9 (8 October 1859):417-18.

1861

1101   RAUMER, KARL VON. "Education of Girls." American Journal of
       Education 10 (March):227-64; (June):613-48.
          Warns against young women trying to become as well educated
       as young men, which "only an entirely unwomanly young woman"
       would attempt. But such would be impossible because women do not
       have the mental faculties of men. If the young woman becomes
       "thoroughly learned," she is "deficient in delicate womanly cul-
       ture." The girl must become accustomed to interruption in any
       activity for "services of love" to younger children or parents.
       Girls must be kept from hearing, reading, singing, or playing
       anything ugly or bad. Translated from the German (source unknown).

1864

1102   "Women's Friendships." Eclectic Magazine 63 (December):403-5.
       Women are not good friends with women because they lack
variety. They are too much alike ever to be great friends.
Reprinted from the Saturday Review (London) 18 (6 August):176-77.

1868

1103   "Weak Sisters." Every Saturday 6 (7 November):593-95.
       Finds women always go to extremes and are either saints or
sinners: "they carry a principle to its outside limit." Is
relieved that the weak sister and her theories do not rule the
world but worries that strong-minded women are taking over.
Finds that "the revolt of our women against undue slavery goes
very near to a revolt against due and wise submission." Reprinted from the Saturday Review (London) 26 (10 October):484-85.

1869

1104   HENSHAW, SARAH E. "Are We Inferior?" Galaxy 7 (January):
       125-31.
       Believes that man's mind moves analytically, woman's syn-
thetically, so masculine understanding must lead the way. It all
goes back to Eve, the first woman, who "mistook her own perceptions, threw her mental powers into confusion, brought discredit
upon them, and bewildered her originally unerring insight."
Since then, men, with their slower but surer understanding, have
taken precedence.

1105   BY AN OLD BACHELOR. "Feminine Amenities." Every Saturday 7
       (2 January):29-30.
       Says women are always more or less antagonistic to one
another, cannot combine, do not support each other, and feel
contempt for each other's intellect--that is why woman's emancipation is not succeeding. Presents a particularly negative portrait of women's relations with women. Reprinted from the
Saturday Review (London) 26 (5 December 1868):743-44.

1870

1106   REED, JAMES. Man and Woman, Equal but Unlike. Boston:
       Nichols & Noyes, 78 pp.
       Insists that women should be discouraged and restrained
from doing work that calls for "exercise of the reasoning faculties,--for judgment and intellectual effort"--because this is
outside their sphere.

1107   "The Education and Influence of Women." <u>Southern Rev</u>___.
        8 (October):406-19.
            Says that woman is inferior to man physically and lacks the
        strength of body and the energy of will to develop her mind.
        Woman's will is stronger than man's in suffering, but he is the
        discoverer, the doer, the producer of works of genius and art.
        In the race of genius, "woman is the Atalanta, who turns aside to
        pick up the golden apple while man pressed right on to the goal
        before him, and so wins the prize." Points out that the world is
        prejudiced against learned women. Insists that "man's intellec-
        tual superiority is established by the word and the providence of
        God. . . . Intellect is masculine." Gives women some consola-
        tion, though--man may be the superior animal and the superior
        intelligence but woman is the superior being.

1871

1108   "The Intolerance of Women." <u>Every</u> <u>Saturday</u> 10 (3 June):522.
            Finds women intolerant, especially of each other. Explains
        this by pointing out that women have been excluded from the real
        business of life and have not been forced to emancipate them-
        selves from the caprices of individuality. Believes that men
        would give women the vote and allow them wider work opportunities
        if they thought this would enlarge women's minds, but finds in
        "the narrowness and folly of some of the champions of 'Woman's
        Rights' . . . the real obstacles to their cause." Warns against
        adding women's intolerance to the world's government.

1109   "The Politics of Women." <u>Lippincott's</u> 8 (August):168-74.
            Provides a catalog of female faults, among them the asser-
        tion that "humor is a very rare quality in woman." Charges women
        with being small in small things, although they do hang together
        in times of calamity.

1873

1110   SPENCER, HERBERT. "Psychology of the Sexes." <u>Popular</u> <u>Science</u>
        <u>Monthly</u> 4 (November):30-38.
            Alleges that woman can with extraordinary effort surpass
        men intellectually but by decreasing her maternal functions so
        that she is no longer feminine. Woman arrests her development
        earlier than man to preserve her energy for reproduction. Thus
        she does not attain the same power of abstract reasoning and
        sentiment of justice--the latest products of evolution--as man.
        Woman has different parental instincts than man, another evidence
        of mental specialization. In a Social Darwinian manner alleges
        that traits developed in woman to ensure her survival.

1874

1111   CLARKE, EDWARD H. The Building of a Brain. Boston: J.R.
        Osgood, 153 pp.
            Repeats his arguments in Sex in Education (see 1010), with
        support from many medical doctors, columnists, etc.--includes
        numerous excerpts and testimonials. Men's and women's brains are
        different and should remain so. "Progress is impossible without
        accepting and respecting the difference of sex."

1875

1112   VAN DE WARKER, ELY, M.D. "Sexual Cerebration." Popular
        Science Monthly 7 (July):287-301.
            Finds that the brains of woman and man are different.
        Woman will not do man's work in a man's way. Woman has gentle-
        ness of mind, which causes her character to be mobile and plia-
        ble, to avoid harshness and fixity of thought. She has maternal
        emotion, his is paternal. "Mentally men and women define two
        opposite types of mind."

1876

1113   GODKIN, E.L. "The Political Morality of Women." Nation 22
        (30 March):205-6.
            Asserts that men and women have different moral codes
        because they experience society differently. Finds it natural
        that "the mere difference in pursuits and interests of the two
        sexes should create a difference in their respective moral
        outlook."

1879

1114   BROOKS, W.K. "The Conditions of Women from a Zoological Point
        of View." Popular Science Monthly 15 (June):145-55;
        (July):347-56.
            The male organism is the variable organism, the female the
        conservative. The female keeps all that has been gained during
        the past history of the race, while the male is the originating
        element in the process of evolution. If the past furnishes no
        guide, then we must look to the judgments of men. Women have
        greater uniformity of character than men, and are more predict-
        able by other women. Women persuade and influence, men convince
        or move by argument. Higher education must address itself to
        these differences and increase them for the benefit of the race.

1880

1115   BENNETT, A. HUGHES, M.D. "Hygiene in the Higher Education
        Women." Popular Science Monthly 16 (February):519-30.
            Warns that, as a rule, women break down when they attempt
        "severe and prolonged mental exertion, more especially if it is
        associated with anxiety and physical fatigue." Woman's sexual
        system has a profound influence on her physical nature. Her
        nervous system is smaller and more unstable than man's. "Trif-
        ling nervous ailments are almost universal in women." Woman's
        brain is smaller and lighter than man's and of "inferior anatom-
        ical construction" and therefore "less capable of such high and
        extended mental powers" than man's. Opposes encouraging women to
        follow learned professions. Marriage and motherhood are the best
        condition for women. Reprinted from Sanitary Record (London).

1116   HARDAKER, Miss M.A. "The Ethics of Sex." North American 131
        (July):62-74.
            Alleges that men reason, and their thinking is a better
        quality than women's. Women's brain activity is merely emotional
        and dreamy. Woman is excluded from political activity because of
        "her defective reasoning powers" and "her incapacity for judging
        of general interests." She has a small brain, which limits her
        field of activity. "Small brains cannot give birth to great
        thoughts." Therefore, man is "permanent master in the domain of
        intellect." Finds the claim of women to intellectual equality
        with men "childish." Surprisingly, favors woman suffrage because
        it would increase the disposition of women to reason and think
        independently. But sees a greater danger in opening the way for
        women to pursue public office. Let them just vote.

1881

1117   DELAUNEY, G. "Equality and Inequality in Sex." Popular
        Science Monthly 20 (December):184-92.
            Says the female surpasses the male in certain inferior
        species only. The supremacy of the male is the highest evolu-
        tionary state. Cites the traditional stereotypes—men have
        better blood, are more muscular and taller, and have heavier
        skeletons and larger chests; women have flat feet. Man's brain
        is larger, more developed in the frontal lobe, the seat of intel-
        lectual faculties, whereas in woman the occipital lobes, seat of
        the sentiments, are more voluminous. Woman's virtues are shown
        to be flawed; for example, women are acknowledged to be more
        charitable, but their charity is "often narrow and intolerant,
        and exercised for the sake of proselytism." From the standpoint
        of evolution, women are always about a century behind men. Many
        "scientific" experts quoted.

1882

"Science and the Woman Question."
hly 20 (March):577-84.
ic evidence to prove the physiological
brain, body, food assimilation, and
thinking in an hour because his brain
ition, woman's energy is diverted to
away from the brain. Asserts that "the necessary
outcome of an absolute intellectual equality of the sexes would
be the extinction of the human race."

1883

1119   HAMMOND, WILLIAM A.   "Women in Politics."   North American 137
        (August):137-46.
            Asserts that "grave anatomical and physiological reasons"
        demand that the movement for woman suffrage be arrested.   Woman's
        brain is smaller.   Man's brain is shaped differently than hers,
        is more convoluted, and the gray matter thicker and heavier.
        Woman's brain is "a brain from which emotion rather than intel-
        lect is evolved."   It cannot reason abstractly or exactly; it is
        imitative, not originating.   "No great idea, no great invention,
        no great discovery in science or art, no great poetical, dramatic
        or musical composition, has ever yet emanated from a woman's
        brain."   Woman is likened to a package of dynamite, "perfectly
        harmless till some one disturbs the equilibrium of its parti-
        cles," and then an unpredictable power.

1887

1120   ROMANES, GEORGE J.   "Mental Differences of Men and Women."
        Popular Science Monthly 31 (July):383-401.
            Says that the brain of woman is smaller than man's and
        also, quoting Sir J. Crichton Browne, is shallower and receives
        less blood, resulting in absence of originality in her intellec-
        tual work.   A woman's information is also less wide, deep, and
        thorough than man's.   Woman's judgment is below man's--more
        superficial, less impartial, more emotional.   On the plus side,
        woman's senses are more refined and their perception quicker.
        Woman is more emotional, has less restraint, likes emotional
        excitement, and lacks willpower.   Reprinted from Nineteenth
        Century (London) 21 (May):654-72.

1888

1121   ROMANES, GEORGE J.   "Concerning Women."   Forum 4 (January):
        509-18.

Argues that woman's intellectual powers are less than man's on the evidence that women have not accomplished anything. Warns that strong-minded women are mistaking the best interests of women. But nature will always take care that such aberrations are rare.

1122   FLEMING, GEORGE. "On a Certain Deficiency in Women."
       Eclectic Magazine 111 (September):387-92.
       Finds that feminine minds rarely have a capacity for serious thinking—"the mind of the average woman appears to be absolutely deficient in the power of coherent impersonal thought." Voluntary solitude is offered as the solution, but he exhibits little understanding of the difficulty of women's achieving that. Reprinted from University Review (London).

1890

1123   HARLAND, MARION. "The Truth about Female Criminals." North American 150 (January):138-40.
       Asserts that wicked women, who are more wicked than wicked men because they must climb higher walls than men to become wicked, play on public sympathy with tears, hysteria, and cajolery to get lighter sentences. Says the truth is that bad women are very bad and should receive no mercy.

1124   "The Effect of the New Careers on Women's Happiness." Living Age 186 (19 July):190-92.
       Grants that women have intellectual capacity but warns that moving into new spheres may bring unhappiness, burdensome work, and more. Doubts that "the work of intellectual mill-horse [will] suit the tenderer and more sensitive natures of women." Insists that they will become even more exhausted than men by "the more mechanical departments of high intellectual toil." Their independence will become irksome to them, but they will be excluded "from the exercise of that happy and gentle vigilance for the well-being of others for which their nature appears specially to fit them." Reprinted from the Spectator (London) 64 (21 June):862-63.

1891

1125   MAYO, Mrs. I.F. "Are Women Worse Than Men?" Review of Reviews 3 (February):155.
       Insists that women are worse than men. They are "distinctly inferior . . . in very many important elements of human character." They "blind themselves to their own wickedness by using innocent terms to describe plain sins." Provides a long list of woman's faults. Reprinted from Leisure Hour (London).

1126   SEAWELL, MOLLY ELLIOTT. "On the Absence of the Creative
        Faculty in Women." Critic 19 (28 November):292-94.
             Finds women utterly lacking in creativity. The arts and
        sciences, as well as civilization, are due to man. "It would
        scarcely be overstating the case to say that all men possess
        genius in some form, and no women ever possessed it in any form."
        A literary woman may be accorded a lofty place in her own time
        but not by posterity. Women's literature lacks universality and
        immortality. This failure to create is perfectly overwhelming in
        other areas: music, painting, manufacturing, and inventing.
        Asserts that, left to themselves, women "would have remained in
        utter barbarism, owing to their inability to create anything
        whatever." The woman who imagines that she has an intellectual
        mission becomes "inevitably ridiculous." Article received many
        rebuttals.

1894

1127   BROWER, EDITH. "Is the Musical Idea Masculine?" Atlantic 73
        (March):332-39.
             Queries why women have not been musical geniuses? Alleges
        that "because woman, as the lesser man, is comparatively defi-
        cient in active emotional force, she cannot . . . produce that
        which, at its best, is the highest and strongest of all modes of
        emotional expression." In explaining this belief, maintains that
        what passes for emotion in women is actually nervous excitabil-
        ity. Woman's finer, frailer nervous system would go to pieces if
        her emotions were excessively powerful, whereas man is strong
        enough for strong emotion. Finds woman deficient not only in
        emotions but also in imagination and in dealing with the ab-
        stract. All these lacks keep women from composing great music.

1128   SCHUYLER, WILLIAM. "The Emancipation of Woman from Woman."
        Open Court 8 (16 August):4186-89.
             Alleges that woman needs emancipation from women, not from
        man. Uses examples of fashion, housekeeping (snooping by women),
        and conversation (gossip). Women cannot be just to one another
        or get along with one another in clubs.

1129   "Women: According to Hall Caine." Review of Reviews 10
        (November):551.
             According to Hall Caine, woman is fundamentally and natur-
        ally inferior to man--"it is a pathetic tragedy based on natural
        law." Reprinted from Young Woman (London).

1897

1130   BROWNING, OSCAR. "Universities and the Higher Education of
        Women." Forum 24 (October):225-33.

Reports that after twenty years' experience in education, has never seen woman's work to equal man's. There is always a "fundamental difference" in their written work. Believes that women are not mentally equal to men and that they should not be educated as men or with men.

1898

1131   DAVIDSON, THOMAS. "The Ideal Training of the American Girl."
       Forum 25 (June):471-80.
       Believes that women "belong to a more primitive type of humanity than men." They react "half-instinctively," clinging to "old habits, customs, and fashions." Women are rarely inventors, even in their own sphere. Argues that educating girls the same as boys would lead to "monstrous uniformity." Alleges that the advocates of women's rights really want "men's rights" for women. "But such passion and advocacy are, it seems to be, only evidences of crudity and want of culture."

1899

1132   M., D.S. "Women Artists." Living Age 220 (18 March):730-32.
       Admits that in other fields women have accomplished something, but in the arts of music and design, they have been "little more than parasites." Believes that women lack "the originating inventive power of design." Woman imitates because she is docile, but she does not originate. Reprinted from the Saturday Review (London) 87 (4 February):138-39.

1133   THOMAS, WILLIAM I. "Sex in Primitive Morality." American Journal of Sociology 4 (May):774-87.
       Since "the bulk of morality turns upon food rather than sex relations . . . it is to be expected that morality, and immorality as well, will be found primarily to a greater degree functions of the motor male disposition." Woman copies male morality rather than establishing her own, for she has feeble motor power.

1134   "Women and Science." Living Age 221 (10 June):727-30.
       Women have ability in exact sciences but "deficiency of imagination as well as of creative force." They have produced no first-rate poets or composers. "They can think along a groove, so to speak, better than men" and draw conclusions rapidly and accurately. "They cannot create, by natural law, but they can search and draw from their searching accurate deduction." Reprinted from the Spectator (London) 82 (25 March):409-10. Reprinted in Eclectic Magazine 133 (July):144-46.

1900

1135   HUNEKER, JAMES. "The Girl Who Plays Chopin." Harper's Bazar
       33 (23 June):466-68.
            Finds that most women play Chopin abominably because they
       are deficient in brain weight and in nervous and spiritual pow-
       ers. But then most men play him abominably too. Women should
       stick to healthy, sweet-souled Mozart, etc. "American girls
       require fresh air and sunlight in their art, so if finical crit-
       ics write that women cannot play Chopin, let them console them-
       selves--have they not the bicycle?" See also 1144.

1136   HARRELL, H. "Women as Criminals." Arena 24 (July):108-12.
            Citing the Italian criminologist and physician Lombroso
       (The Female Offender, partial English translation 1895), says
       that the cerebral cortex is less active in women than men, with
       the result that genius is more common in men than women and few
       women are born with criminal tendencies, "but when these are
       present the criminality is more intense and depraved in them than
       in the male delinquents." Women criminals are often motivated by
       vengeance and are excessively obstinate in denying their crimes.

1137   HUNEKER, JAMES. "Women and Music." Harper's Bazar 33
       (22 September):1306-8.
            Believes that women cannot interpret all composers with
       equal success; women lack big tonal effects because they are
       weaker and because of the "muscular conformation of woman's
       arm"--she has no triceps muscles. Allows that women may play any
       piano music, and play it well, but not remarkably well. Finds
       their playing often charming but questions whether it is "ever
       great, spiritual, moving art." See also 1144.

1901

1138   BOK, EDWARD. "Women as 'Poor Pay.'" Ladies' Home Journal 18
       (June):14.
            Asserts that women are notoriously slow to pay their bills.
       Says it is because they are thoughtless and do not realize the
       moral responsibility attached to every debt they contract. It is
       these failings that make him impatient with "higher education"
       for girls. Says the education of our girls lacks practicality.
       "If girls had less of a smattering of high-sounding knowledge,
       and were better grounded in the practical lessons of living, it
       would be infinitely better for their future happiness."

1139   WILCOX, ELLA WHEELER. "Insight." Cosmopolitan 31 (June):
       208-11.
            Briefly describes, and accepts the conclusions of, recent
       literature from Europe attesting to the inferiority of woman's
       brain as compared with man's; charges woman with lacking concen-
       tration, system, and patience to make her great. Woman is dis-
       tracted by details and concerned about appearance. Blames men

for making women discontent with their lot by sneering at or
pitying them. Woman would never have tried to be superior in the
mental realm had men given her appreciation and admiration.
Concludes: "All this talk of equality and inequality of the
sexes is senseless."

1140 DICKSON, EDITH. "Woman and the Essay." Dial 31
      (1 November):309-10.
        Women cannot produce critical essays because they are more
self-conscious and more conventional than men. They either atti-
tudinize or repress themselves. They are too familiar with their
reading public. They are partisan rather than disinterested.
They are not tolerant. They lack literary style. They go to
extremes: if lightness is wanted, they become flippant; trying
for profundity, they are labored; attempts at conversational tone
become triviality. Women are not willing to exercise patience in
writing, so "they are never artists in the use of words."

1141 FINCK, HENRY T. "Evolution of Sex in Mind." Independent 53
      (26 December):3059-64.
        Calls "the most extraordinary foible of the woman suffra-
gists" their failure to realize that sexual traits of the mind
are altered by education, employment, and environment. If women
persist in doing men's work, in the course of a generation or two
they will become mannish and unsexed. Women are either better or
worse, never equals, of men. When women become mannish, men
degenerate in the other direction, becoming loathsomely and un-
naturally effeminate. Only in the savage state do men and women
resemble each other. The so-called New Woman is actually "a very
old-fashioned, primitive and crab-like sort of woman." The
bloomer costume's worst fault was that it affected the minds of
the bloomers long after they removed the hideous dress.

1902

1142 PYKE, RAFFORD. "What Women Like in Women." Cosmopolitan 34
      (November):35-40.
        Woman's character makes her take everything personally and
concretely. She is incapable of abstract thought or of acting on
principle. Although women feel a solidarity with their sex,
doubts "whether friendship in its very highest sense can ever
exist between two women" because they can never give each other
unhesitating confidence and unswerving loyalty. Women by nature
cannot trust each other. Nor do they understand honor and loyalty because "with a woman everything is viewed from an intensely
personal point of view. . . . The truth is . . . that women au
fond are always traitors to their own sex."

1904

1143   BACHELOR, ANTONY. Wanted--A Wife. New York: D.V. Wein,
        292 pp.
            Says woman's weaker body prevents her from attaining equal-
        ity with man in intellectual and moral life. The feminine brain
        does not equal the masculine brain. Women can learn but not be
        original or synthetic. Asserts that the woman's movement has led
        to loss of woman's peculiar charms--modesty and chastity--and
        increase of vanity and pride. Deplores women in sports.

1144   HUNEKER, JAMES G. Overtones: A Book of Temperaments. New
        York: Charles Scribner's Sons, 335 pp.
            His chapter on "The Eternal Feminine" is a reworking and
        amplification of his earlier essays on women playing Chopin and
        interpreting music (see 1135 and 1137). Most women play Chopin
        mechanically. Women cannot play all composers with equal suc-
        cess. Women lack interpretative power--they lack muscles. Cites
        Laura Marholm [Hansson] with approval (see 207). Believes wom-
        an's role in music is to be the inspirer of all art.

1145   MEYER, ANNIE NATHAN. Woman's Assumption of Sex Superiority.
        N.p., 7 pp.
            Reprinted from 1146. Reprinted in 556.

1146   MEYER, ANNIE NATHAN. "Woman's Assumption of Sex Superiority."
        North American 178 (January):103-9.
            Questions whether women have purified and ennobled American
        public life. Argues that although woman's education has improved
        over the past few years, her character has not similarly devel-
        oped. Finds "a grave danger to the moral force of womanhood in
        woman's increasing participation in organized effort, in public
        life." Blames women on platforms for gaining applause too eas-
        ily, shirking the unapplauded, unknown, quiet work. Finds bit-
        terness, contempt, and hostility toward man in speeches at
        woman's conventions. Reprinted in 556 and 1145.

1905

1147   ELLIS, HAVELOCK. "The Mental Differences of Women and Men."
        Independent 58 (23 February):409-13.
            Says the sexes are fundamentally equal but mentally di-
        verse. Finds "both mischievous and useless" the efforts of
        pioneers of the women's movement to treat women and men as iden-
        tical. "Women will always be different from men, mentally as well
        as physically," and should be. This is what makes men and women
        charming to one another: "We cannot change them, and we need not
        wish to."

1908

1148   VORSE, MARY HEATON. "Have Women a Sense of Honor?"
       Appleton's Magazine 11 (March):316-20.
            Asserts that women's sense of honor is not as good as
       men's. "I think that there is a code among men which does not
       exist--certainly to the same extent--among women, and where men
       break this code they are discredited as a woman is not." Women
       snoop in friends' drawers, read others' letters, betray trusts,
       perjure themselves, use feminine appeal and influence, pump their
       servants, listen at keyholes and on telephones, etc.

1909

1149   ROLLINS, MONTGOMERY. "Women and Motor Cars." Outlook 92
       (7 August):859-60.
            Insists that women should not be licensed to drive gasoline
       cars. Says that "the natural training of woman is not in the
       direction to allow her properly to manipulate an automobile in
       case of emergencies. She is not trained to think of two things
       at once." Women are also not strong enough to drive cars. Fur-
       ther, they will fail to observe traffic laws, preferring to
       assume that man will give them the right of way. Finally, they
       are naturally hysterical and will not know how to behave should an
       accident threaten.

1915

1150   TOMLINSON, MAY. "Womankind." Forum 53 (February):237-43.
            Believes that woman will have to rid herself of many de-
       fects before she can be equal to man. Among her faults are
       "unreason, self-will, jealousy, envy, spite." Woman needs more
       discipline, not more freedom. If women will earnestly set about
       making themselves over, they will find woman suffrage of little
       importance.

1916

1151   NESBIT, E[DITH]. "Slaves of the Spider." Living Age 288
       (26 February):571-73.
            Insists that women's rights will never be taken seriously
       as long as women follow fashion. Women's shops, women's pages,
       and fashion papers prove that "the great mass of women are not as
       yet fitted for the use of power and responsibility; and, what is
       more, . . . they do not really desire these." Says "we cannot
       shut our eyes to the fact that woman in the lump is silly."
       Reprinted from the Westminster Gazette (London).

Women's Work, Professional Employment, and Creativity

Notions about the kinds of work women can and should do are based
in part on received ideas about women's place and also about their
intellectual and physical abilities. Work relating to women's domestic activities--teaching school, needlework, nursing children and
other women, and domestic service--is generally allowable as long as
marriage and motherhood are the eventual professions. Some would
allow women to be physicians to women and children, but others oppose
the very idea of women as doctors (see 1159, for example). Again and
again women are admonished not to do men's work.

Much concern is expressed over women going into factories and
industry. Writers insist that such work does physical damage, im-
pairs women's ability to bear healthy children, and threatens their
chastity. Other forms of work closed to women include journalism,
engineering, literature, music, painting, architecture, and sculp-
ture. Many writers flatly insist that women have never created anything first-rate.

Many fears are revealed: women will not marry if they have paid
work, they will not want or be able to bear children, and they will
sap men's ambition by lowering men's wages. Some writers support the
practice of paying women less than men for the same work because men
must support families. Many allege that men have more to offer as
workers--strength, larger brains, and worldly experience.

By the end of the century, with women increasingly moving into
business, articles examine the quality of their work and often find
it lacking. Several women describe how their personal life suffered or
even was destroyed by their working. All uphold a rigid concept of
the division of labor.

1851

1152   HALE, SARAH JOSEPHA.   "Editors' Table."   Godey's Lady's Book
        42 (January):65-66.

Argues that women are not able to compete with men because
they do not have mechanical or inventive ability. Opposes those
who would place women in the workshop to compete with men. "The
true woman cannot work with materials of earth, build up cities,
mould marble forms, or discover new mechanical inventions to aid
physical improvement." But she has a higher and holier vocation,
namely, to work with human materials: "Her orders of architecture are formed in the soul."

1853

1153   HALE, SARAH JOSEPHA. "Editors' Table." Godey's Lady's Book
        47 (July):84-85.
        Holds "no Amazonian theories of woman's capacity to do
man's work." Women have no place in hard outdoor work or in
mercantile pursuits. Women may be helpers and may work indoors
if economically necessary--mentions type-setting and waiting on
the table. Praises Mr. Godey for employing eighty-eight female
operatives on the Lady's Book.

1855

1154   "Editors' Table: Lady Physicians." Godey's Lady's Book 50
        (March):175.
        Favors female physicians (for women and children) but dis-
approves of "ladies in the pulpit, or in trousers, or delivering
lectures, except certain lectures, which are womanly things
enough, and, in most instances, highly called for." Reprinted
from the Philadelphia Saturday Evening Mail, a weekly paper
edited by George R. Graham.

1155   HALE, SARAH JOSEPHA. "Editors' Table: Employments for Young
        Women." Godey's Lady's Book 50 (April):367-68.
        Favors limited types of employment for young women that can
be usefully continued after marriage. Among these are school-
keeping, needlework, and artificial flower-making--"all pleasant,
quiet, home employments." In contrast, clerkships, storekeeping,
type-setting, and factory work "unfit the woman for the wife and
mother." Believes we have enough to do without "encroaching on
man's work."

1860

1156   "Queen Bees or Working Bees?" Living Age 64 (21 January):
        181-83.
        Critique of an essay by Bessie Rayner Parkes, English
feminist. Reviewer disagrees with her, saying that rather than
educate women on the assumption that they will not marry, "the

greatest of social and political duties is to encourage marriage." It is dangerous for women to be independent. Marriage
is woman's profession, and if she fails to attain it, she has
failed in business. It is better for men, women, the state, and
society that women not be taught to be useful and therefore be
"independent of the chances of life. We do not want our women to
be androgynous." Reprinted from the Saturday Review (London) 9
(12 November 1859):575-76.

1863

1157   "Lady Diplomatists." Eclectic Magazine 58 (January):61-69.
        Women have been used as ambassadors, but usually after
becoming the widow of an ambassador. Women are not fit to govern. They cannot carry out strict justice but instead are arbitrary, precipitous, ruled by their hearts, and influenced by
favorites rather than merit. But women are compensated for
their inability to govern by their influence over their husbands.
Warns that women must not be granted a place in the political
affairs of the state or they will become estranged from their
family. Reprinted from St. James's Magazine (London) 5 (November
1862):467-79.

1158   "A Tilt at the Woman's Question." Harper's Magazine 26
        (February):350-56.
        Lauds women's accomplishments in the home and approves
women's education, but wants women to remain in the home.
"Seeing what they have done for this nation, as mothers and
wives, let no one think that as artists, in professions, or in
the daily drudgery of business life they can do a better work."

1864

1159   CROLY, JANE CUNNINGHAM [Jennie June]. Jennie Juneiana: Talks
        on Women's Topics. Boston: Lee & Shepard, 240 pp.
        Opposes women doctors in a chapter entitled "Lady Doctors,"
exclaiming, "Lady doctors! from such the Lord deliver us! The
increase of deaths among women would be frightful. There is a
natural viciousness among women towards each other which is
totally incompatible with strict justice, and especially mercy.
They would purge, and blister, and drug, without feeling the
first softening influence from the milk of human kindness within
their breasts."

1160   "Literary Women." Living Age 81 (25 June):609-10.
        Asserts that literary work would interfere with domestic
duties. Observes that "literary work has a tendency to wear off
some of the delicate bloom which is perhaps the finest part of a
woman's natural character." For a woman to become a great

writer, she must undergo a defeminizing process--George Sand is a
prime example, a beacon that points to the direction that literary women are going. Says women are also debarred from great
achievements in literature by a lack of education and no development of critical facilities. Women have a mission as grand as
writing--keeping alive for men certain ideals. Reprinted from
the London Review.

1867

1161   WALLACE, S.E. "Another Weak-Minded Woman: A Confession."
        Harper's Magazine 35 (November):792-96.
            Cautions women against attempting to write literature. It
        is better to have reared fine sons and daughters than to have
        written "Aurora Leigh" or to have translated the Inferno. Women
        should "avoid women looking for 'spheres' and 'missions.'"
        Argues that the real reason women are unhappy is that "nearly all
        women write is feverish and morbid." The fact that man was
        created first means "the colors of his life are deepest, the
        currents of his being strongest." There will never be a female
        Shakespeare or Milton. No woman's hand will "write grand ora-
        torios or create beauty like the Apollo." Even when women vote
        or hold office, they will never be men.

1868

1162   HALE, SARAH JOSEPHA. "Editors' Table: Domestic Service."
        Godey's Lady's Book 77 (August):174.
            Quotes Gail Hamilton, who says that the cure for low wages
        is for women to go into domestic service. Blames women them-
        selves for low wages, because they do poor work: "They are equal
        only to the coarse, common pay, and there are such multitudes of
        them that their employer has everything his own way."

1869

1163   SPENCER, EDWARD. "Women Artists." Southern Review, n.s. 5
        (April):299-322.
            Can find no woman artist who has risen above mediocrity--
        pleasing performances, that is all. Alleges that this is due to
        lack of true artistic insight rather than lack of opportunity.
        This deficiency is true in all the arts--drama, poetry, acting,
        and love-literature: "Her art-work is almost invariably petty,
        inadequate, mean." Alleges that woman's true sphere is that of
        affections, and that if she rises intellectually to an abnormal
        degree, she sinks morally. But it is best that she remain in her
        affectional sphere and let her artistic faculties remain in
        abeyance to her domestic nature, "half-breeched spasmodists" to
        the contrary.

1164   SPENCER, EDWARD. "Women Artists." New Eclectic 4 (June):
       641-57.
          Reprinted from 1163.

1871

1165   E. "Women's Work: What a Woman Says About It." Monthly
       Religious Magazine 46 (September):280-82.
          Notes that women may sometimes succeed in work where men
       have failed, but "in the everlasting fitness of things, there is
       work fitted for men and work fitted for women." Woman's work is
       in the home. Women's education should train them for domestic
       work, and if they must earn money, let it be with their hands.
       "No woman who understands any branch of work required in a family
       ever needs to starve or be unhappy."

1872

1166   HALE, SARAH JOSEPHA. "Editors' Table: Shall Women Do the
       Work of Men?" Godey's Lady's Book 84 (February):190.
          Quotes an article by the Reverend John O. Mens in The True
       Woman that asserts that letting women do the work of men would be
       "a step back into barbarism." Mens also opposes woman suffrage as
       another intrusion by women into men's civil life.

1167   HUTCHINSON, NELLY MACKAY. "Woman and Journalism." Galaxy 13
       (April):499-503.
          Finds limited opportunities for women in journalism. Women
       could never succeed as managing editor, first, because it is
       physically impossible, and, second, because of their nature and
       social position. Nor could women be leader-writers. They can be
       book reviewers, but first they must conquer two serious faults:
       "gush and unevenness." Faults female journalists for being slov-
       enly and spiteful, defects that "are the result of that almost
       universal want of American women--the want of a keen, exact habit
       of reasoning."

1874

1168   "Who Shall Earn?" Harper's Bazar 7 (13 June):378.
          Says only women who must find employment should work.
       Women would earn more if their fields were not crowded by those
       who seek employment only because of restless ambition. Sometimes
       well-to-do daughters work because they want better clothing. Let
       such restless women educate themselves and improve their culture,
       rather than getting a job.

1875

1169   AMES, AZEL, Jr., M.D. Sex in Industry: A Plea for the
       Working-Girl. Boston: J.R. Osgood, 158 pp.
            Opposes women working in industry because it harms them
       physically, and leads to moral delinquency and insanity. "Woman
       . . . holds in industry a position inconsistent and incompatible
       with the coeval possession of her true plane." Suggests banning
       woman from certain employments and curtailing her hours in oth-
       ers. Invokes pseudoscientific evidence: "The weight of evidence
       that may be presumed to be worthy of confidence and consideration
       would seem to leave no doubt that the normal, the God-appointed
       work of woman, wherein lie her full equality, her peerage, her
       glory, and her power, is that of the home and the mother, the
       rearer, the trainer, the blessing of man."

1876

1170   RHODES, ALBERT. "Woman's Occupations." Galaxy 21
       (January):45-55.
            Generally favors wider employment opportunities for women
       but objects to feminists' putting themselves forward in public.
       Does not want women to "abandon that purity and unobtrusiveness
       of manner which is the natural attribute of their sex." Let
       women maintain modesty of demeanor and dress and shun "forward
       manners, massive chains and bracelets, and robes of glaring
       color," all of which true men abominate.

1879

1171   "Women's Mistakes about Work." Lippincott's 24 (August):
       236-43.
            Alleges that women seldom rise to great excellence in what
       they undertake when they leave their own special domain because
       they will not plod, they will not consent to severe study and
       really hard, sustained effort. Uses art as an example of woman's
       superficial labor, although it is visible in other areas also.
       Says too many women refuse to do "the work that lies just ready
       for their hands--the commonplace, every-day duty that stands
       waiting to be ennobled by their skilled and cultivated perfor-
       mance of it."

1882

1172   ELLIOTT, CHARLES W. "Woman's Work and Woman's Wages." North
       American 135 (August):146-61.
            Asserts that when woman enters the labor market in competi-
       tion with man, she drags down and cheapens his labor. Enlarging

woman's sphere into the factory or mill is evil. If women compete with men in brain-work, they reduce men's wages. Further,
woman's knee is badly constructed for standing and her wider
pelvis makes standing tiring. Doubts that it is "progress" for
women to "unsex" themselves and compete with men, to ruin their
health and temper, to crush the great function of their being.
Insists flatly, "She cannot be a man, and she cannot do the man's
work."

1883

1173   "Progress and the Home: Editorial." Popular Science Monthly
       23 (July):412-16.
          Opposes Emily Blackwell's recent article on industrial
       position of women. Insists that the division of labor between
       the sexes is fundamental to society. There must be no rivalry or
       competition. Warns that "the precipitation of woman into the
       outer world of conflicts, where the strongest have their way,
       would involve a dissolution of human society, and is not even
       possible as an experiment." Bemoans anything which threatens the
       home or woman's place in it.

1884

1174   CROCKER, Hon. GEORGE G. Argument at the Hearing before the
       Committee on Woman Suffrage, 29 January 1884. N.p., 8 pp.
          Questions whether women have prospered in private business.
       If so, then perhaps they would do well in the administration of
       public affairs. But alleges that they have done poorly or noth-
       ing as lawyers, ministers, doctors, and in business. Finds that
       "women go into the medical profession in greater numbers than
       into any other, but their success there is lamentably marred by a
       large percentage of humbug and immorality." Believes woman suf-
       frage is wrong and would do harm.

1175   LONSDALE, MARGARET. "Platform Women." Eclectic Magazine 102
       (May):642-47.
          Insists that teaching, influencing, and literature are ac-
       ceptable women's work, but is against women on the public plat-
       form. Asserts that there are serious intellectual drawbacks to
       women as public orators: they are one-sided. There are also
       physical drawbacks in the strain. Warns that "in self-assertion
       we lose respect." Women who exhibit themselves upon platforms
       unconsciously lower the standard of womanhood in the world's
       eyes. Platform women become hardened, antagonistic, talked-
       about, and mocked. It is not worth it. Reprinted from
       Nineteenth Century (London) 15 (March):409-15.

<u>1886</u>

1176   BLAKE, LILLIE DEVEREAUX, and DENSLOW, VAN BUREN.   "Are Women
       Fairly Paid?"   <u>Forum</u> 2 (October):201-11.
            In the form of a dialogue. Blake says women are fairly
       paid. Denslow gives several antifeminist reasons why they are
       not: Flattery is the proper wage of women, but it gets men in
       trouble. Female clerks get paid less than male because women
       prefer to buy from male clerks and so they are worth more to the
       employer. Female teachers are paid less than male because they
       are transient workers. Women are constitutional invalids and are
       unfit for work at least one sixth of their lives. Believes that
       "society fails in the degree that woman works for wages at all,
       and succeeds only as she is rescued from such a fate."

<u>1889</u>

1177   HARLAND, MARION. "The Incapacity of Business Women." <u>North
       American</u> 149 (December):707-12.
            Declares that men conduct all branches of business more
       successfully and systematically than women. Arraigns saleswomen,
       female stenographers, and female typists, insisting that, phys-
       ical disabilities aside, women "<u>do not work as men do</u>."

<u>1890</u>

1178   COOPER, H.C. "Light or Shadow?" <u>North American</u> 151
       (July):127-28.
            Disagrees with George Parsons Lathrop, who urged audacity
       in female novelists. Says the word "is a strong one, and repul-
       sive to the instinctive delicacy of every true woman." Thinks it
       would be at a fearful cost to both women and the world for women
       to have to step over their delicacy and modesty to rise as
       novelists.

1179   HARLAND, MARION. "Domestic Infelicity of Literary Women."
       <u>Arena</u> 2 (August):313-20.
            Agrees that it is difficult to be a literary woman and a
       homemaker. Seems to be siding with feminist position but in
       closing says that the higher duty outranks the lower and then
       equates "the higher duty" with housework. "Another may write
       your story, or poem, or essay. Nobody else in all the universe
       can mother your boy, or be your girls' guide and best friend."

<u>1891</u>

1180   PIKE, G. HOLDEN. "Journalism as a Profession for Women."
       <u>Review of Reviews</u> 3 (May):390-91.

Does not like the idea of young women being reporters,
saying it would be unseemly for an unprotected girl to travel
about London or another city in the evening. Girl reporters
become bold, encroach on men's province, and lose feminine
graces. There are other jobs for women on newspapers besides
reporting. Reprinted from Girl's Own Paper (London).

1181   HALE, EDWARD EVERETT. "The Work of Women." Cosmopolitan 11
       (September):632-35.
       Questions whether "thoughtful, conscientious and intelli-
gent women [are] really sure that they wish to cut loose from all
the traditions of the school of chivalry?" If women are part of
the general working force, they can expect no deference, which is
the difference between savage lands and civilized ones. Women
lower wages. Women waste time in meetings, whereas "really
efficient men hate the machinery of public meetings."

1892

1182   HENDERSON, C.R. "Woman's Work for Wages." Science 20
       (30 September):190.
       This recorder and assistant professor of social science at
the University of Chicago finds grave perils in enlarging woman's
sphere to allow her to work in industry. Girls are taking the
places of men at lower wages. Marriages are decreasing, as is
the birth rate. Opposes unions' supporting unlimited work for
women. Says that, fortunately, most women are not in the work
force for long.

1893

1183   GOSSE, E[DMUND] W. "The Poetry of Women." Critic 22
       (21 January):37-38.
       Excerpt from a lecture at Newnham College. States that
"the artistic nature is not strongly developed in [woman]. She
has energy, imagination, sentiment, invention; but she has not
the artistic impulse." He then praises Christina Rossetti as
"the solitary woman-poet of the Anglo-Saxon race who cultivates
poetry as one of the fine arts."

1184   HARLAND, MARION. "Counting-Room and Cradle." North American
       157 (September):334-40.
       Says women's missions of motherhood and homemaking are
"untransferable." "Men may write her books or paint her pictures" but they cannot bring children into the world. Faults
women for suggesting to their sisters that they should work as
men, for which women are bodily unfit. Woman cannot play the man
on the job and "be every woman to home, spouse and children." She
thereby unsexes herself.

1185   HAYNE, J.L. "The Doom of the Man Clerk." Review of Reviews 8
        (October):459-60.
              Argues that young women are pushing young men out of jobs,
        that more than half the young women who work do not need to and
        take places properly belonging to men. Young women should be at
        home. Then young men would marry them. Otherwise the country
        will fill with bachelors and spinsters. Reprinted from the
        Canadian Magazine (Toronto).

1186   KREBS, T.L. "Women as Musicians." Sewanee Review 2
        (November):76-87.
              Asserts that women have not excelled as productive musi-
        cians because women do not exercise reason. Rather, they are
        dominated by emotions and intuitions; they are instinctive and
        intuitive. Woman's "nature is opposed to the cold reasoning and
        the solution of profound musical problems, such as must be en-
        countered by the successful composer." Woman inspires and in-
        fluences music rather than writing it. Women also cannot be good
        critics of music because they feel intuitively, respond emotion-
        ally, and thus "are frequently led astray in their judgments."

                                    1894

1187   FERRERO, GUILLAUME. "The Problem of Woman, from a Bio-
        Sociological Point of View." Monist 4 (January):261-74.
              Says it is a natural law that man must labor and struggle
        to live and woman should not. Calls female labor "a pathological
        phenomenon." When mothers work, the mortality rate among mothers
        and children is higher. She should therefore be exempted from
        labor on physiological grounds as well as because we wish her to
        be beautiful and attractive. The working woman grows ugly and
        loses her grace. Says suffrage is entirely useless to woman--she
        should stay out of the arena of political strife.

1188   FERRERO, GUILLAUME. "Why Women Ought Not To Work." Review of
        Reviews 9 (April):475-76.
              Reprint of 1187.

1189   MATHEWS, FANNIE AYMAR. "Women and Amateur Acting." North
        American 159 (December):759-60.
              Declares that amateur actresses have no talent or inspira-
        tion; they just want notoriety. Labels it a very demoralizing,
        unwomanly pastime and says it has produced all over the country
        "a clique of young women . . . whose style is bizarre, whose
        manners are meretricious and unwomanly" and whose atmosphere, she
        implies, is that of the brothel.

                                    1895

1190   HARTMANN, EDWARD VON. The Sexes Compared and Other Essays.
        Translated by A. Kenner. New York: Macmillan & Co., 164 pp.

Says those who are "clamoring for the equalisation of the sexes" are "faddists." Women are totally unfit for public business by their sentimental nature. Women cannot work either physically or mentally as hard as men. Opposes training women for occupations because it makes them shun marriage.

1191   A BUSINESS WOMAN. "Women in the Business World." Outlook 51
       (11 May):778.
       Finds that women block their own advancement in the business world by their many faults. Blames "the inherent faults of the sex" for differences in the wages of women and men. Says women lack a sense of honor, take jobs for which they are not trained or suited, take short cuts, are frequently irresponsible and troublesome, are dishonorable in the use of time, and use ill health as an excuse. Their lack of balance and of the recognition of the fitness of things is their greatest handicap.

1192   OWENS, MARTHA J. "How Many Women Are Going into Business."
       Chautauquan 21 (June):337-40.
       After a seemingly feminist opening, in which she asserts that "a woman has just as much natural, moral, and legal right to engage in business as a man," turns to serious questions that must be settled in regard to women in business life. The business woman must either leave all prospect of matrimony behind her or be regarded as merely a temporary worker. Concludes that "woman can never be in the business world what man is." She is handicapped by the maternal instinct, so that she will always yearn for the hearthstone. Her greatest achievement will always be as wife and mother.

1193   ROGERS, ALICE, M.D. "The Literary Life of Woman—Does It
       Interfere with Her Domestic Life?" Outlook 52 (26 October):
       666-67.
       Finds that professional or public life interferes with woman's domestic life: "Not that such a woman has no knowledge of domestic duties or no capacity for doing them, but simply that she cannot combine the two." Asserts that the average woman who undertakes a domestic life must give all her time, thought, and energy to the job: "She will have other outlets, of course, but they must be subsidiary."

1194   "Orchestral Women." Scientific American 73 (23 November):327.
       Says woman may be able to perform a solo but she cannot stand the strain of four or five hours of daily rehearsal followed by public performances. Thus she can never compete with male musicians or become a serious orchestra performer. Reprinted from the Musical Courier (South Africa).

1896

1195   BOK, EDWARD. "When Work Fits Woman." _Ladies' Home Journal_ 13
        (February):14.
            Opposes entry of women into large mercantile and manufac-
        turing establishments. If woman must work, let her be a domes-
        tic. This mad race on the part of girls to go into the business
        world is contributing to the degeneracy of young womanhood.

1196   "Literary Ladies." _Eclectic Magazine_ 127 (October):466-69.
            Quotes several misogynistic statements like those of Dr.
        Johnson, as well as Dickens, "Literary Ladies," and Edward
        Fitzgerald. Hopes in time that literary ladies will soften along
        the lines of Ruskin's "Queen's Gardens." Reprinted from _Temple
        Bar_ (London) 108 (August):576-81.

1897

1197   BUCKLER, G.G. "'The Lesser Man.'" _North American_ 165
        (September):295-308.
            States that physical differences between the sexes predes-
        tine them to different kinds of work. Women have never achieved
        on a par with men--"Looking impartially at history, we cannot
        claim that the widespread mental and artistic activity of women
        has in a single instance achieved anything absolutely first-rate,
        whether as creation or as discovery." This will always maintain;
        woman's achievement will not equal man's.

1198   JARVIS, STINSON. "The Truly Artistic Woman." _Arena_ 18
        (December):813-19.
            A cautionary tale--artistic women have no common sense, are
        immoral, and make poor wives: "Such a person is not to be neces-
        sarily regarded as intended for the somewhat straitening cares of
        wifehood, but rather as a gift to the world as a whole, who may
        be expected to adopt an uncontrolled width and freedom in every-
        thing pertaining to her existence."

1898

1199   WHITING, ELEANOR. "Woman's Work and Wages." _Lippincott's_ 61
        (May):670-77.
            Believes that it is not to the best interests of either the
        average woman or society for woman to become "a direct wage-
        earner." Matrimony is woman's profession and has been for thou-
        sands of years. Says women are paid less than men because they
        cannot do as much or as good or as varied work as they. Some-
        times working women undercut the wages of working men, and this
        harms the family life of the entire nation. Finds "the smallness
        of wages and the hardships of competition that women are forced
        to endure a blessed safeguard to civilization, and to woman

herself." The world needs the love, romance, tender relations, beauty, grace, and loveliness "brought to it by the spiritual influence of good women."

1200 WHITING, ELEANOR. "Business or the Home for Woman?" <u>Living Age</u> 217 (14 May):482-84.
      Condensed and reprinted from 1199.

1899

1201 BACHE, DALLAS, M.D. "The Place of the Female Nurse in the Army." <u>Journal</u> <u>of</u> <u>the</u> <u>Military</u> <u>Service</u> <u>Institution</u> 25 (November):309.
      This assistant surgeon general of the U.S. Army objects to women serving as nurses in division hospitals or on hospital trains or boats. Observes that men can be soldiers as well as nurses; women cannot. Cites problems arising from the need for separate housing, meals, and toilet facilities. Sees in this innovation "much expense, idleness, risk of friction, and a certain disquiet about immorality . . . without commensurate gain." Wants to restrict women's nursing work in the army to permanent and sedentary hospitals in time of war and to larger hospitals not fused with army posts in times of peace so as to "permit of the discreet accommodation of these women."

1900

1202 BOK, EDWARD. "The Return of the Business Woman." <u>Ladies'</u> <u>Home</u> <u>Journal</u> 17 (March):16.
      Asserts that women cannot take the strain of business employment: "they are not physically constituted to stand the strain of the peculiar work which business demands." They have not the endurance nor the productive value of men. God never intended woman for the rougher life planned out for man. The business world is foreign soil for woman: the home is her natural sphere. Women have hurt businesses and have been hurt by them, filling our rest cures, sanitariums, and hospitals to the doors. But women are returning to the home and "their natural and right-ful feminine work."

1203 "Woman as a Financier." <u>Harper's</u> <u>Bazar</u> 33 (17 March):245.
      Believes that women should stay out of business. They cannot change business but business can change them. "As the conservor of the morals of society, woman has much to fear from business and nothing to hope." Woman should practice moral influence. "The business of woman in the world is with the hearts, not with the moneybags, of humanity."

1204 "Women and their Work: The Truth." <u>Harper's</u> <u>Bazar</u> 33 (24 March):250.

Declares that Nature has destined woman for home work.
Finds the role of wife and mother the noblest end of woman.
Points out that woman's health has been damaged by business, so
woman becomes "a victim, not a triumph, of modern theories of
industrial progression for the sex." Believes she should work in
the home because "household industry is more tolerant of the
physical deficiency of woman labor."

1205   "Women and Work." Harper's Bazar 33 (31 March):274.
Compares the human experience of wage-earning to a recent
experiment with spiders. Spiders were bred to spin silk and
thereby replace the silkworm. The female spiders did the most
spinning after producing their young but--alas!--they ate the
males. Similarly, a Massachusetts Bureau of Labor Statistics
study has shown that when a man is assisted by his wife or
children in earning the family living, he does not earn as much
as other laborers. When he is assisted by both, he earns the
least. That means that "the earning capacity of the woman or
child is exercised at the expense of the industrial greatness of
the man." Faults the woman worker for undermining her husband's
strength. "She has yet to consume him quite," but all should
heed the lesson of the spider.

1206   AN AMERICAN MOTHER. "The American Woman in the Market-Place."
Ladies' Home Journal 17 (April):19.
Objects to women taking work from the hands of men; it is
allowable only if they are forced by necessity to support themselves. Despairs that women belittle their own work, the family,
marriage, and motherhood. Working women who marry soon divorce,
and there are countless childless homes. Woman should do her
work, not enter the male marketplace.

1207   FINCK, HENRY T. "Is Gallantry an Insult to Women?"
Independent 52 (12 April):881-83.
Warns women that "after they have gobbled up all that the
men have hitherto claimed as their own and, by lowering prices
with their competition, have doubled the difficulty of supporting
a family," the men will not continue to be courteous to them.
Women want privileges but, he asserts, "they are dancing on a
volcano." If women persist in working and thinking like men, all
those special feminine qualities that make men gallantly adore
them will be destroyed. Believes that "they would thus lose
infinitely more than they will ever gain by succeeding with their
present aspirations."

1208   HARRISON, Mrs. BURTON. "Home Life as a Profession." Harper's
Bazar 33 (19 May):148-50.
Bewails the fact that so many girl graduates want careers
instead of marriages. Urges them to make home life the supreme
center of life. "No reward of intellectual supremacy, no winning
of money on her own account, no plaudits of lookers-on bestowed
upon her achievements of brain and energy" could make up to her

the loss of that "simple elemental experience, old as the world,
apportioned to Eve's daughters all alike!"

1209   "Mother's Labor Problem." Harper's Bazar 33 (11 August):961.
        Counsels mothers not to go to work to support the family
because children will suffer.

1210   RANDALL, E.A. "The Artistic Impulse in Man and Woman." Arena
        24 (October):414-20.
        Women are less creative than men because they are passive
by nature or cultivation. Women began the first of arts or
crafts, "but, after this artistic impulse passed beyond the
rudiments, we find it in the hands of the men." Women play
music; men make it. "In imitative art, women succeed much better
than men. . . . China painting and decorative art in general are
the speciality of woman, who excels in the minor, personal artistic impulses, and in this way gives vent to her restricted life."

1901

1211   BOK, EDWARD. "Is the Newspaper Office the Place for a Girl?"
        Ladies' Home Journal 18 (February):18.
        Reports asking fifty of the leading newspaper women whether
the newspaper office is the place for a girl. Of the forty-two
who answered, three said yes, thirty-nine said no: they would
not want their daughter to work in a daily newspaper office.
Wrote fifty editors with the same question; thirty replied, all
emphatically negative.

1212   "Literature and Women." Current Literature 30 (April):477-78.
        Advocates a limited sphere for the woman writer--"to reveal
Nature in a feminine guise, becomingly and nobly transformed by
passing through the alembic of womanhood." Women write their
best instinctively and emotionally. They must do womanly, not
manly, work. "Let women write or inspire; the issue will be one,
provided they follow the guidance of their hearts." Condensed
and reprinted from Macmillan's Magazine (London) 83 (November
1900):29-34.

1213   FINCK, HENRY T. "Employments Unsuitable for Women."
        Independent 53 (11 April):834-37.
        Women should work away from the home only if compelled to
support themselves. Criticizes reformers who are trying to con-
vince women that they should be independent and self-supporting.
Says factory work endangers female chastity and woman's health.
Would ban as unwomanly "all employments which make women bold,
fierce, muscular, brawny in body or mind."

1902

1214   FLOWER, ELLIOTT. "Are Women to Blame?" _Arena_ 27 (June):
        635-39.
            Why does there exist a prejudice against female clerks and
        stenographers when previously there was a great demand for them?
        It is the women's fault. They are not willing to relinquish
        those privileges to which they have become accustomed. They take
        all their sick leave, take longer than men to begin work and
        longer to get ready to quit, "prink" on the job, arrive to work
        late, and weep when reprimanded.

1903

1215   WADLIN, HORACE GREELEY. _Extract from an Address Delivered in_
        1903 before the Massachusetts Federation of Women's Clubs.
        Boston: Massachusetts Association Opposed to the Further
        Extension of Suffrage to Women, 2 pp.
            Insists that women do not get the same wages as men because
        they do not do the same work. They also look forward to marriage
        rather than advancement.

1904

1216   THOMPSON, FLORA MC DONALD. "The Truth about Women in
        Industry." _North American_ 178 (May):751-60.
            The woman worker is "a frightful failure." Calls her "an
        object of charity," "an economic pervert," and "a social menace."
        She increases the cost of production and diminishes its effi-
        ciency. She reduces man's wage but not his responsibilities.
        She leaves the home and undermines her health, injuring her
        reproductive organs and causing deteriorating health in future
        generations. Argues that it is better for a family to suffer
        want than for a man to become dependent on his wife's earnings.
        Reprinted in _Review of Reviews_ 29 (June):753-54, and in _Current_
        Literature (see 1219).

1217   "Is the Woman Worker a Frightful Failure?" _Harper's Weekly_ 48
        (21 May):785-86.
            Summarizes Flora McDonald Thompson's article (see 1216) and
        writes in strong support of it, saying that women's working has
        been an economic failure with "mischievous physiological conse-
        quences," injuring woman's reproductive organs.

1218   "Should Wives Be Wage-Earners?" _Gunton's Magazine_ 27
        (July):25-33.
            Asserts that it is essential that the wife devote her time
        and energy to the home "if the husband is to have any social
        pride in his domestic and social status." Wives are wage-earners

only at the crude levels of social life; in an advancing society, they can remain at home.

1219   C., S.A. "Women as Wage-earners." Current Literature 37
        (September):240-42.
            Condensation and reprint of 1216.

1905

1220   GOMPERS, SAMUEL. "Should the Wife Contribute to the Family
        Support? My Answer Is Emphatically 'No!'" Woman's Home
        Companion 32 (September):16.
            Opposes wives working because they would leave their homes
        and children "unprotected and uncared for during the working
        hours." Contends that "the wife or mother, attending to the
        duties of the home, makes the greatest contribution to the sup-
        port of the family." Gompers was the only male respondent among
        four (S.B. Anthony, Ella Wheeler Wilcox, and Ida M. Tarbell) and
        the only one who opposed wives' working.

1906

1221   RICHARDSON, DOROTHY. "Difficulties and Dangers of Working
        Women." Annals of the American Academy of Political Science
        27 (May-June):624-26.
            Foresees grave dangers for the working woman, with her
        delicate and complicated nervous organization. Finds most female
        wage-earners to be unhealthy. Also finds them unable and unfit
        to sustain effort in their work. Does not think women will ever
        develop equal industrial abilities--"as potential mothers they
        are functionally limited mentally and physically."

1222   DALE, ALAN. "Why Women Are Greater Actors than Men."
        Cosmopolitan 41 (September):517-24.
            Women are innate actors: "the art of simulation is dis-
        tinctly feminine rather than masculine." The best female actors
        are mothers; only then do they realize their life's mission.
        "For, after all, it is her mission--isn't it?--in spite of all
        the twaddle and the woman's rights nonsense that is dinned into
        our ears, day by day, by cold, metallic non-mothers." Man should
        not envy woman her superiority in acting because man has the real
        creativity and work: he is the sculptor, painter, novelist,
        playwright, builder, architect, lawyer, journalist. Acting, with
        its pretense, is woman's art, and she excels at it unless she
        decides to become "emancipated" and unwomanly.

1907

1223   BOK, EDWARD. "In an Editorial Way." Ladies' Home Journal 24
        (January):5-6.

Declares that women are going into business in decreasing
numbers. Despite fifty years of agitation and exploitation of
the "wrongs of women," women are returning home, letting their
common sense reassert itself, returning to being wives and mothers. The real business woman is the woman in the home.

1908

1224   "Women and Work." Living Age 256 (8 February):372–75.
       Observes that women are displacing men and lowering wages.
Says that women enter the labor market thoughtlessly and with
indifference. Yet in a rather contradictory conclusion, urges
legal protection of women workers. Reprinted from the Saturday
Review (London) 104 (28 December 1907):787–88.

1225   DREWS, KARL. "Women Engineers: The Obstacles in Their Way."
       Scientific American Supplement 65 (7 March):147–48.
       Argues that women are not becoming engineers because they
are bodily and mentally weak. Women are not creative. They also
lack highly developed spatial perception. See 1226.

1226   "Woman's Inferiority to Man in the Light of Engineering
       Science." Current Literature 44 (May):553–54.
       Summary of an article by Dr. Karl Drews in Berlin Umschau.
According to Drews, women are deficient in creative capacity and
are too weak physically to become engineers. "The essentials of
engineering science seem to bring out the truth that the real
quality of woman is limitation." A female engineer in any scientific sense is a contradiction in terms as women cannot use
mathematics to solve problems and women are strictly unscientific. "A woman of genius has never existed, because genius is
universality, and the quality of woman, as already stated, is
limitation. Genius is, therefore, masculinity in its highest
form. Engineering is so stupendous because it can not be brought
down to woman."

1227   NEWELL, MARY O'CONNOR. "The Failure of the Professional
       Woman." Appleton's Magazine 12 (July):98–104.
       Believes that to succeed in business a woman must be "de-
sexed" and act and think like a man. Points out that women have
failed to make good in business and the professions. Blames the
failure on the fact that "woman will not pay the price of success." Finds women will not work hard enough long enough, are
temperamentally unsuited for competition, unable to be dispas-
sionate, and without a sense of abstract justice. They wait to
be liberated by marriage, their ultimate career.

1909

1228   A SUCCESSFUL BUSINESS WOMAN. "Why I Will Not Let My Daughter
       Go into Business." Ladies' Home Journal 26 (September):16.

The wife and mother of four relates how she took a job in
business when her husband could not settle down and earn enough.
She became successful. He stopped working altogether and began
living off of her. She was setting a terrible example for her
sons, so she got a divorce. He remarried and another woman made
a man of him. Bemoans her entry into business.

1911

1229   "Phrases of the Feminine Fictionist." Living Age 269
        (20 May):509-10.
            Mocks the diction, descriptions, and characters of women's
        fiction. Reprinted from the Saturday Review (London).

1230   BOK, EDWARD. "Has Her Work Been Taken Away?" Ladies' Home
        Journal 28 (September):5.
            Denies that women's work is diminishing and that therefore
        she must go out into the world of affairs. Women have plenty of
        work to do in the home and rearing children. Reminds "female
        agitators" who harp on "the declining character of man" that if
        men are deteriorating, it is because mothers are not doing a good
        job.

1231   BOK, EDWARD. "When a Woman Has a Choice." Ladies' Home
        Journal 28 (September):5.
            Insists that a woman must choose between a life of love and
        home and family and an independent life with a career. She
        cannot have both. Women should stop complaining that they have
        no choice--they do, they choose to marry or not.

1912

1232   TARBELL, IDA M. "Making a Man of Herself." American Monthly
        Magazine 73 (February):427-30.
            Women are invading men's world by adopting masculine ways
        like smoking and wearing mannish suits and boots. But although
        women are not reaching the top rank in men's fields, they still
        become cold, self-centered, intensely personal--repellent.

1913

1233   TARBELL, IDA M. "Excerpts from The Business of Being a
        Woman." Ladies' Home Journal 30 (January):24.
            States that women who succeed in business or the profes-
        sions become cold and repellent. Nature and society are antag-
        onistic toward the militant woman because her career is wasteful
        and has cost her loveliness. Wants woman to develop "the work
        Nature and society laid upon her into a profession dignified,
        beautiful and satisfying."

1234   MARTIN, EDWARD S.   "Editorial on Woman's Part in the Future."
       Ladies' Home Journal 30 (February):21.
           Accuses President Thomas of Bryn Mawr of overvaluing inde-
       pendence for women and the wage-earning, untrammeled career and
       of undervaluing "the career that goes with marriage and domestic
       life."

1235   BOK, EDWARD.   "The Woman Who Really Holds a Man."   Ladies'
       Home Journal 30 (March):6.
           Opposes the right of wives to earn wages after marriage
       because it creates "domestic chaos."   Warns that a working wife
       "may lead to a bank account, but it is the hearthstone woman who
       holds a man."

1236   "Woman in Industry a Racial Evil."   Literary Digest 46
       (12 April):826-27.
           According to the Medical Record (New York), "the wholesale
       employment of women is an unmitigated evil."   Such women are
       refusing to undertake the duties of motherhood and home, which is
       causing the race as a whole to suffer.

1237   MARTIN, EDWARD S.   "The Economic Independence of Women."
       Ladies' Home Journal 30 (May):25.
           Says married women who are mothers cannot succeed also in
       the world of work, and faults feminists for suggesting they can.
       Praises Ellen Key for following the right path.   Finds that
       "altogether too many of the active suffragists present as their
       credentials for the work of rearranging human life the glaring
       evidences of their failure to live it successfully as it is."
       Women who have made a mess of their life should not present
       themselves as examples for other women.   But all they want to do
       is make a great noise, not convince people.

1238   KEIR, D.R. MALCOLM.   "Women in Industry."   Popular Science
       Monthly 83 (October):375-80.
           Opposes women working in industry and stores because it is
       decreasing women's fertility and harming the next generation.
       Working women are subject to a whole host of ills: pelvic dis-
       orders, constipation, scanty menstruation, miscarriage and still-
       birth, overworked kidneys, hysteria, anemia, sterility, a
       stunting of mentality, an inordinate craving for excitement,
       nervous exhaustion, sleeplessness, loss of appetite, and malnu-
       trition.   Women should be legally prevented from working in
       industry.

                                  1914

1239   MONAHAN, MICHAEL.   "The American Peril."   Forum 51 (June):
       878-82.
           Warns that Americans are "suffering from too much woman-
       ism."   Cites Admiral Chadwick (see 1085).   Asserts that we are

"living under a Gynarchy and the symbol of government is a Powder-
puff!" Blames the work of women in journalism, magazines, etc.,
for churning out silly, mediocre stuff of interest to women.
Modesty and restraint have disappeared and standards declined
with a rise of women in journalism. In catering to women, pub-
lishers "have brought this period of petticoat supremacy and
petticoat inferiority to our doors." Criticizes women journalists for turning the theater into a brothel, for spotlighting the
suffragette, who is a libel on American young womanhood, and for
touting equality of the sexes, that "monstrous inversion."

1240   MARTIN, JOHN. "The Married Teacher." New Republic 1
        (19 December):23.
        This letter from a member of the New York Board of Educa-
tion asserts that married women teachers are inefficient and
habitual absentees.

                            1915

1241   AUBREY, H.M. "Liberty and License." Forum 53 (April):449-54.
        Finds that as women have gone out into the men's world to
work, they have become indifferent to female chastity, adopting
instead the male standard. This is causing divorce to increase
enormously and to be less stigmatized than in the past. Believes
these trends to be undesirable.

1242   HODGSON, ELIZABETH. "Equal Salaries for Men and Women
        Teachers." Education 35 (May):571-77.
        Opposes equal pay for teachers because the male teacher is
usually married and therefore a more complete human being who
contributes more to society, knows more about society, etc. Also
argues that we need more male teachers, especially for boys, and
so must pay them more. We also need male teachers to teach "aggressive citizenship." Describes women teachers as less valuable
than men because they "renounce normal destiny, have few ties
that knit them into the community, and often fade and shrink
because the social currents do not flow through their veins."

                            1916

1243   MARTIN, JOHN. "The Four Ages of Woman." Survey 35
        (26 February):629-31; (4 March):668-70; (11 March):695-96;
        (18 March):720-22; (25 March):750-51.
        Opposes allowing women to work in any area or occupation--
"natural law bars women from eminence in industrial life. And
nature will not be gainsaid." Opposes married women and mothers
working outside the home. Mocks and misconstrues feminists
throughout. Over against feminism would place humanism. Based
on his book, Feminism: Its Fallacies and Follies (see 324).

                            285

1244   KIRKLAND, WINIFRED.   "The Woman Who Writes."   Atlantic 118
        (July):46-54.
            Denies that women have as much vitality as men or that
        "woman's brain is the equal of man's in originality, in concen-
        tration, or in power of sustained effort. . . . I can't do so
        much work, or do it so well, as a man." Says she feels embar-
        rassed and not ladylike when forced to admit that she is a
        writer.

                                  1917

1245   DAMPIER, Lady CATHERINE DURNING.   The Upbringing of Daughters.
        London and New York: Longmans, Green, 250 pp.
            Opposes women training for and entering the professions.
        Says that "from the biological, and . . . also from the psycho-
        logical, standpoint, there is only one reasonable purpose that
        should animate a woman, which is the desire to become the mother
        of children."

                                  1918

1246   A MERE MASCULINITY.   "This Feminism Business."   Woman's Home
        Companion 45 (April):12, 68-70.
            Says he believes in women in business, although "to be
        perfectly frank, it hasn't pushed business very far ahead, as the
        world counts progress." Also alleges that women do not have big
        jobs because they do not take them. Repeats traditional ideas
        about woman's and man's natures. Denies that there is much
        unequal pay for equal work--men are usually "delivering something
        in the job that a woman can't deliver." Argues that "women
        simply cannot work as hard as many days a month as men. Decent
        men, in business, recognize that fact and make allowance for it."
        Women are in business only temporarily, and that is as it should
        be. Finally, worries that feminism means no children. His brand
        would protect mothers and children and homes, not destroy them.

                                  1919

1247   WILKINSON, MARGUERITE.   "Are Women Safe for Democracy? Two
        Minutes [sic] Interview with Charles M. Schwab." Touchstone 4
        (February):357-61, 432.
            The prowoman interviewer talks briefly with Schwab, of the
        U.S. Shipping Board and powerful business leader, who believes
        that "the average woman has the greatest economic opportunity in
        her own home . . . in the wise use of her husband's wages." He
        states further that "the present conditions that throw thousands
        of women out of their homes and into industry are abnormal and
        will not last." Rest of article refutes Schwab's position.

1248   "Women Tramway-Conductors Are Not an Unalloyed Blessing."
       Literary Digest 62 (30 August):80-82.
            Presents many complaints about women tramway conductors in
       Great Britain, among them rudeness, lateness, breakdowns of equip-
       ment, and pilfered funds. On the other hand, women are better
       than men at clerical work, although not at superintending cler-
       ical work. See responses from women working in banks, mostly
       positive, in Literary Digest 66 (17 July 1920):116-211. Quota-
       tions and summary from the Freeman's Journal (Dublin).

                              1920

1249   HARTLEY, CATHERINE GASQUOINE. Women's Wild Oats: Essays on
       the Refixing of Moral Standards. New York: Frederick A.
       Stokes, 238 pp.
            Deplores the movement of women into new occupations and
       activities brought about by the war, calling it "a confusion of
       values [that] has led women astray." Would bring society back to
       "a disciplined freedom; to a recognition of their own needs and
       the needs of others."

1250   "Woman's Place Not in the Bank." Literary Digest 64
       (13 March):141-43.
            Summary and excerpts from an article in the Commercial and
       Financial Chronicle arguing that "it is better for women them-
       selves and for the community in general that hereafter women
       leave the banking business to men." The Chronicle article in-
       sists that the best women have functions in the community and
       especially in child-bearing and child-rearing which make employ-
       ment unwise.

1251   NORMAN, HENRY. "The Feminine Failure in Business." Forum 63
       (April):455-61.
            Declares that women have been "notoriously unsuccessful" in
       business. This is because they attend to details but cannot rise
       above personal appeals to abstractions. Alleges that "the ulti-
       mate goal of the average woman in business is the hymeneal al-
       tar." Women may work hard but are inferior in "originality,
       initiative and inventiveness." There are both physical and men-
       tal barriers to woman's succeeding in business. "Woman in busi-
       ness has not proved herself man's equal, and to just that extent
       she is a failure."

                              1921

1252   HERGESHEIMER, JOSEPH. "The Feminine Nuisance in American
       Literature." Yale Review 10 (July):716-25.

Says American literature "is being strangled with a petticoat." If we leave all questions of aesthetics to women, we get
a dull, emasculate, cheap literature.

1253   "Farewell to the Woman Conductor." Literary Digest 70
        (2 July):26.
        Points out that women are more expensive to employ than men
because they require separate quarters; therefore, they would
have to be paid less than men. Women are also handicapped in
physical strength. Women will hereafter work in the stations and
offices rather than on the cars, according to an editorial writer
in the Electric Railway Journal (New York).

Women and Religion

Early in the nineteenth century, some women sought to have a more active role within the church, especially to speak in public. Much of this was in connection with the abolition movement. Materials in this section interpret the Bible strictly, citing St. Paul, a favorite of all antifeminists, and insist on women being silent, modest, and subordinate to men. Eve is cited as an example against women pursuing an active role.

In some of these selections there is an interesting undercurrent of rivalry between Protestants and Roman Catholics, each group insisting that women fare better under its aegis. By the beginning of the twentieth century, some Protestant women were seeking ever wider and more professional activities, including ministry, which are opposed in some of the later articles. Catholic women maintained a more conservative posture throughout. Feminism is seen by all as a threat to women's piety.

1822

1254   C., A.B. "Is It Proper for Women To Be Employed as Public Teachers of Religion?" Christian Spectator 4 (June):291-92.
       Quotes Scripture in considering men's commission and authority in the world. Finds that no woman was ever commissioned by God to be a preacher and that none served in the ministry of John the Baptist, Jesus, or the early church. Therefore, women should not be employed as public teachers of religion.

1837

1255   STEARNS, JONATHAN FRENCH. Female Influence, and the True Christian Mode of Its Exercise: A Discourse Delivered in the First Presbyterian Church in Newburyport, 30 July 1837. Newburyport, Mass.: John G. Tilton, 24 pp.
       Opposes women leaving their Bible-appointed sphere to speak in public, call themselves independent, or fancy an equality with

men. This is not an amiable or becoming course of action. "For,
if an effeminate man is always despised, no less so, as nature
herself teaches, must be a masculine woman." Is particularly
concerned that Christian women are beginning to suggest that
women may speak in public. This would lead to society breaking
up and becoming "a chaos of disjointed and unsightly elements."

1838

1256   "Influence of Christian Mothers." Christian Review 3 (March):
        20-34.
            Woman's ministry is silent and unobtrusive, not in the
        public notice. She lives and labors in obscurity. But she must
        not pine for a more extended field of action. Holds up for
        emulation as an "illustration of the benefits which a single
        pious female may bestow upon the world" the example of the mother
        of John Newton, whose prayers and instructions converted her son,
        even though she died when he was seven. Newton was an abandoned
        youth but then recovered to live "a life of piety and useful-
        ness." Goes on to discuss Newton's career, forgetting mothers
        altogether.

1839

1257   DEERFIELD ASSOCIATION. Address to the Churches Connected with
        the Deerfield Association. Concord, N.H.: Christian Panoply
        Office, 16 pp.
            States that there is no warrant for women to serve as
        leaders or teachers in "preaching, exhorting or praying in pro-
        miscuous public, religious assemblies." Further finds it "dis-
        gusting" for women "to take a leading part in the discussions,
        business and bustle of public assemblies." Asserts that the
        loveliness of woman depends on modesty of demeanor and retirement
        from the noisy world, so that man protects and shields her. In
        addition, the domestic duties of women are incompatible with
        public activities. The word of God forbids woman taking equal
        standing with man in public teaching or leading public worship.
        Each sex must stay in its proper sphere.

1855

1258   HUNTINGTON, F.D. "The Christian Woman." Monthly Religious
        Magazine 14 (December):301-10.
            Asserts that woman can realize her proper mission only as
        she is inspired by the Christian faith. Says Christianity "con-
        centrates the aimless and restless purposes of woman on the one
        grand object of a personal acceptance with God."

1867

1259   HARBAUGH, H. "The Christian Idea of Almsgiving." Mercersburg
        Review 14 (April):165-210.
             After a long discussion on almsgiving and philanthropy,
        including a discussion of the office of deacon, turns to the
        office of deaconess and a consideration of the ministry of women.
        Says women in Christianity go forth as women, not as some "modern
        reformatory socialistic systems" would have them go, as men.

1260   KNOWLTON, STEPHEN. "The Silence of Women in the Churches."
        Congregational Quarterly 9 (October):329-34.
             Insists that women should keep silent in church because
        they were made second, made for man, made by God to be subordi-
        nate. "It is the proprieties of her subordinate relation that
        require a woman to keep silence in the house of God." For a
        woman to speak she usurps man's authority and subverts God's
        order. Soon all other subordination would be lost. She tried
        taking the lead once and fell: "She made a little speech once
        that was the world's undoing; now let her keep silent."

1868

1261   DUREN, CHARLES. "Woman's Place in Religious Meetings."
        Congregational Review 8 (January):22-29.
             Woman's place is settled by Scripture and reasons given for
        it. Eve, who was formed second, transgressed. Woman "is not a
        safe teacher, because at first she was deceived, and led man into
        sin and she would be very likely to lead others again into error
        and sin." Therefore, woman must be subject to man, not usurp
        authority over him. She may speak in small social gatherings,
        but she must not be assuming. She is saved through child-
        bearing.

1869

1262   MUNNELL, THOMAS. "Woman's Work in the Church." Christian
        Quarterly 1 (October):508-23.
             Woman can do any work a Christian ought to do except pulpit
        preaching. It is a principle of division of labor. "The Lord
        does not love 'manly women,' nor 'womanly men.' They both alike
        are 'abomination unto the Lord.'" No man fit to be a husband
        desires a strong-minded woman for a wife. A woman who assumes
        the place of man must renounce her special privileges.

1870

1263   ROSS, A. HASTINGS. "The Silence of Women in the Churches."
        Bibliotheca Sacra 27 (April):336-59.

Demonstrates by reference to Scripture that "a limitation
of some sort has been placed by the Creator upon the sphere of
woman." Says women must continue to remain silent in church--
"silence in the churches is a part of woman's obedience or subjection, announced in the curse uttered at the gate of Eden by
God upon woman. This reason . . . is as permanent and extensive
as the race itself." Woman was the transgressor. Woman must not
preach or even ask questions in church. Nor prophesy. Keep
silent! See objections considered in 1265.

1264 CADY, D.R. "The Biblical Position of Woman." Congregational
      Quarterly 12 (July):370-77.
      Woman was created with a special reference to man--to be
his helpmeet. The two are complements, "so unlike they cannot be
compared. . . . A masculine woman is a monster; a feminine man a
'lusus naturae' beneath contempt." Woman is secondary, shrinking
from rude contact and strife, unfit for leadership and public
station. "However desirous we may be, and ought to be, to en-
large the sphere and develop the powers of woman for the good of
the race and the glory of God, yet it is safe to work, only in
the line, and within the limits of the revealed Word. We do not
know the mischiefs which may follow if we transcend them."

1265 ROSS, A. HASTINGS. "The Silence of Women in the Churches--
      Objections Considered." Bibliotheca Sacra 27 (October):
      740-59.
      In answering objections to his April article (1263), argues
that these rules of silence are "universal and perpetual." Sees
infidelity threatening those churches that set aside God's word.
There is plenty for woman to do without seeking another forbidden
fruit.

1872

1266 "How the Church Understands and Upholds the Rights of Women."
      Catholic World 15 (April-July):78-91, 255-69, 366-80, 487.
      Protestantism "has suffacted woman's highest aspirations
for three hundred years. . . . No nation of antiquity, save the
Jews, had any respect for the female sex," beyond considering all
women possessions of husbands and fathers. Only the Roman Catholic Church "has marked out a noble margin for women's genius."
Series proceeds to look at woman's role in the age of martyrdom,
of fathers of the church, in Middle Ages. Women should continue
their mission within the church.

1873

1267 STEVENSON, J.M. "Woman's Place in Assemblies for Public Wor-
      ship." Presbyterian Quarterly 2 (January):42-59.

Woman was created subordinate to man, and after the fall
this subjection of woman's will to man's was increased "expressly
on account of her priority in sin." Using Scripture proves that
woman is not meant by God to perform public ministry. Changes in
woman's condition and education still do not change the essential
relations of the sexes. It would be a shame for woman to usurp
authority over man--according to Scripture, it would be "uncomely, indecorous" for woman to pass out of her fitting sphere
and assume the position where the stronger and sterner should
stand.

1874

1268   FINK, R.A. "Women in the Church." Lutheran Quarterly 4
       (April):220-33.
       Declares that women are excluded from fulfilling pastoral
offices in the church because they lack a "robust constitution,"
"strength of body," and "physical adaptation to the work" which
are required. They have delicate frames. Thinks that "those
women give the best proof of their piety and zeal who cheerfully
obey the precepts of inspiration, though excluded from public
teaching." They can still be useful to the church, as mothers.
In fact, no mother should dare ever be away from home, as a
minister often must be.

1269   MOORE, AUGUSTA. "May Woman Speak in Meeting?" Congregational
       Quarterly 16 (April):279-84.
       Women have plenty of work to do without being called on to
speak or pray in meeting. In fact, Christ was a good and true
friend to woman but he wanted "to hear [her voice] where agitation and excitement did not shake it into a mutter, worry it into
a whine, nor hoist it into a screech." Insists that "the representative, the model woman, was never made for public efforts."
Further, "not one woman in ten can control her voice." When
woman speaks in public, she make her baby colicky.

1270   [SMALLEY, J.C.]. "A Word for Women, by One of Themselves."
       Catholic World 19 (May):277-80.
       Calls for a feminine Catholic literature, saying that the
Holy Catholic Church will protect such literary women from "fa-
naticism" and from "the mistakes of the so-called 'strong-minded.'"

1271   "Speaking or Babbling." Congregational Quarterly 16
       (October):576-87.
       Disagrees with suggestion that the prohibition against women
speaking in church was mistranslated and actually was against
babbling. Says proper definition of word is to speak. Therefore, women are not to speak in church.

1880

1272   LATHBURY, BERTHA.   "Agnosticism and Women."   Living Age 145
        (1 May):302-7.
              States that agnosticism is growing among women as among
        men.   Discusses some of the dire consequences, repeating all the
        while the usual cliches--women are more restless and excitable,
        their brains are more easily deranged.   Predicts that agnosticism
        will lead to euthanasia, the end of charity to the poor and sick,
        the termination of education for the ignorant, etc.   Illogical
        argument.   Woman's place is in the home.   Reprinted from Nine-
        teenth Century (London) 7 (April):619-27.

1882

1273   CORT, Rev. CYRUS.   "Woman Preaching Viewed in the Light of
        God's Word and Church History."   Reformed Quarterly 29
        (January):123-30.
              Agrees with the Presbyterian Church's pronouncement in
        1832--meetings of pious women by themselves for conversation and
        prayer are acceptable but let women not exhort or teach in public
        promiscuous assembly.   Says "women preaching and praying in pro-
        miscuous assemblies is a modern and unscriptural innovation and a
        perversion of Apostalic and Christian usages."   Warns that "it
        can only be injurious in its ultimate results."   Quotes St. Paul,
        Calvin, other religious groups in support.   Says sensible, pious,
        orthodox women understand this position and their role in the
        church.

1883

1274   HARRIS, Rev. Dr. J. ANDREWS.   "Where is Woman's Place?   Three
        Views of Dr. Dix's 'Calling of a Christian Woman.'"   American
        6 (14 April):6-8.
              Two respondents are prowoman, but the Reverend Harris
        supports Dr. Dix in limiting woman's role in the church.

1885

1275   SPALDING, J.L.   "Has Christianity Benefited Woman?"   North
        American 140 (May):399-410.
              Says that under Christianity woman becomes the equal of
        man.   Denies that the church's making man the head of the family
        is unjust, citing tried and true clichés as to why he should be
        in charge.   E.C. Stanton had taken the opposite view in the same
        issue (pp. 389-99).

1276   PATTON, W.W.   "Skepticism and Woman."   New Englander 44
        (July):453-71.

Insists that woman is honored only under Christianity.
Points out that "the loud-mouthed agitators for woman's rights
are never found on heathen shores." They let missionaries do
that work while they "remain amid the comforts and privileges of
Christian lands, to argue in behalf of their peculiar ideas and
methods of human progress." There have been women skeptics over
the years because it has been fashionable in some circles, and
women are impressionable; masculine-minded educated women often
assert pseudo-independence and think they have a mission "to
enlighten the world on the deep questions now mooted in philosophy and religion." But happily "such unbelievers are exceptions
to their sex."

1888

1277   WILLMARTH, JAMES W. "Woman's Work in the Church." Baptist
       Quarterly Review 10 (October):466-88.
          Women must work according to the will of God, not according
       to human judgment and self-will. Turn to Scriptures. "Disregard
       of natural instincts will be sure to produce abnormal and perni-
       cious monstrosities." Further, "the project of 'female suffrage'
       and the practice of female political activity are anti-Biblical
       . . . part of the infidel and anarchical outcome of the French
       Revolution."

1889

1278   TERRELL, A.P. "Should the Sisters Pray and Speak in Public?"
       Christian Quarterly Review 8 (July):335-60.
          Abominates "the whole modern heresy of 'Woman's Rights.'"
       A female politician makes his flesh crawl. Woman suffrage is
       "nauseating." Disapproves of women in the pulpit, on the lecture
       rostrum, even conducting prayer meeting or leading in prayer for
       mixed audiences. Insists that "the plain meaning of God's word
       is against this whole thing." Examines religious teaching and
       practice, as well as Scripture, to prove his point.

1892

1279   MOODY, W.S., Jr. "The Turning of the Worm." Harper's Weekly
       36 (31 December):1270.
          Insists that women are going too far "vigorously pretending
       to be as good as men." They even wear "nearly all kinds of men's
       clothing." But the worm has turned. Recounts an incident where
       women tried to infiltrate a men's choir and wear surplices and
       caps. The bishop forbade the women "to enter the chancel or even
       to sit in the church unless they took their things off," saying
       that "vestments were for men, not for women." The bishop allowed
       that women might wear men's garments in the street if they chose

but not in church. He would let men and women sing together but
the women could not sit in the chancel.

1895

1280   EASTON, Rev. PETER Z. Does Woman Represent God? An Inquiry
       into the True Character of the Movement for the Emancipation
       of Woman. New York: Fleming H. Revell, 19 pp.
           Argues that the doctrine of woman's rights is not in ac-
       cordance with the word of God. Woman does not represent God.
       Further, woman's rights is anti-Christian and worse, devilish--
       "it is the last, final, and complete embodiment of Satanic malice
       and malignity." Insists that "emancipated woman, trampling under
       foot the laws of God in nature and revelation, so far from being
       a purifying and refining element in society, is herself an incar-
       nate demon, with nothing womanly about her but the name, a crea-
       ture of unbounded lust and merciless cruelty, a combination of
       Messalina and Lady Macbeth."

1900

1281   AN AMERICAN MOTHER. "Have Women Robbed Men of Their Reli-
       gion?" Ladies' Home Journal 17 (February):17.
           Declares that modern woman spends too much time outside the
       home and so does not teach her family religion.

1903

1282   NEVE, J.L. "Shall Women Preach in the Congregation? An
       Exegetical Treatise." Lutheran Quarterly 33 (July):409-13.
           Insists that a careful exegesis will always show that Paul
       forbids women to preach in the church. "True Christian tact will
       always easily finds what a woman can do without breaking in upon
       that ground rule of creation which Paul . . . has re-established."

1283   SEEBACH, MARGARET R. "Shall Women Preach?" Lutheran
       Quarterly 33 (October):579-83.
           Partially disagrees with Neve (July 1903). Believes that
       women should do anything other laymen [sic] do--teach in Sunday
       schools, pray in prayer-meetings, conduct mid-week services. But
       women cannot be trained for the ministry because it would require
       their celibacy--it is impossible for woman to combine home duties
       with a profession. Further, woman's mind is different from
       man's--she cannot ordinarily argue logically. Fears that a woman
       could not win and hold men to the church. Finally, worries that
       public speaking would be a dangerous intoxicant for any woman who
       had the taste for it, leading to spiritual dilettantism. "The
       very sensationalism of doing a thing so new would be a positive
       injury to a sensitive mind." Accept teachings of St. Paul.

1905

1284 FLETCHER, MARGARET. "Come o'er and Help Us." Catholic World
      82 (December):311-16.
         Calls for a new Catholic woman "to atone for the untold
      evil women have wrought."

1907

1285 "Are We Threatened by a Feminine Christianity?" Current
      Literature 42 (April):420-22.
         Feminine influence is seriously menacing modern Christian-
      ity, according to the views of President Benjamin I. Wheeler of
      the University of California, Captain Mahan at West Point, and
      the Reverend Carl Delos Case, in a new book, The Masculine in
      Religion. Women are more suggestible and emotional than men;
      they usurp the place of masculine will and intellect in the
      church. Case says we need a revival of "muscular Christianity."

1914

1286 "The Feminist Revolution as a Religious Catastrophe." Current
      Opinion 57 (July):43-44.
         Cites Owen Johnson, author of The Salamander, who sees the
      roots of feminism in religious agnosticism. "Women are losing
      their faith and losing the discipline and self-restraint that
      were the product of that faith."

1916

1287 "Fear That Feminists May Capture Pulpits in the Church of
      England." Current Opinion 61 (October):255.
         British feminists are seeking to have women allowed to
      preach in church, but churchmen are appalled. They see a femi-
      nist conspiracy and fear feminist outrages.

1917

1288 GOUDGE, HENRY LEIGHTON, et al. The Place of Women in the
      Church. Milwaukee: Young Churchman Co., 204 pp.
         Various writers uphold Paul's view of women's role in the
      church, praise women's work as deaconesses, deny women's ordina-
      tion, but praise the medical ministry of women. Of particular
      interest is an article by Lady Henry Somerset, "The Claim of the
      Priesthood for Women," in which she deplores the "clamour" and
      "pitiful discontent" of women who demand to be ordained as
      priests; insists that woman's place is at the hearth and her true
      role is mother.

1918

1289   PEEBLES, Rev. ISAAC LOCKHART. Are Men and Women Equal? The
        Question Answered. Nashville, Tenn.: M.E. Church Publishing
        Hosue, 23 pp.
            Insists that men and women are not equal. Man has a
        larger skull, brain, heart, etc. Woman was created to be a helper
        and not an equal. Scripture quoted extensively. If women did as
        Paul instructed, they would have no time for "wine and card
        parties, ball games, worldly clubs, and godless amusements. In-
        deed, they would have no time for even the present-day woman's
        rights." Urges women to spend their time and money "instructing
        one another in the great duties of home life." Then "there would
        be an end to the restlessness, dissatisfaction, unhappiness,
        gadding about, home rupture, divorces, home murders, and loss of
        souls of this day." Urges women not to be dissatisfied with
        their home sphere but to live "the Bible life."

1920

1290   "Woman's Progress Toward the Pulpit." Literary Digest 67
        (23 October):34.
            A balanced report with one notable antifeminist comment by
        the Reverend Euclid Philips in the Presbyterian arguing against
        women in the pulpit, saying that women have a mission in the
        church but it is not in the pulpit. "Let not, he urges, 'the
        Presbyterian Church become an institution of women and weak
        men.'"

Women's Bodies

This section focuses on women's bodies, the exercise women take, and the clothing they wear. American women very early sought to modify their clothing for comfort and ease of movement and were quickly rebuked and called Amazons, viragos, and unsexed. In this section we can see why dress reform as an early program of the feminists was a complete failure. Once again the Bible is used, this time to prove that woman in "man's" dress is indecent. Opposition to dress reform had two main peaks, the first in the early 1850s, when through the Lily Amelia Bloomer fostered interest in the bloomer, and the second in the 1890s, when women began more widely to adopt a bloomer-type costume for bicycle-riding and sports.

Closely allied to change in dress is wider physical activity. This too is opposed because it will destroy women's grace, make them mannish and coarse, and physically unfit them for their duties as women, especially child-bearing. Women should be delicate and graceful, not physically strong. As Dr. Arabella Kenealy stated, "any extreme of muscle-power in a woman [is] in itself evidence of disease" (1318). She and others allege that physically active women get all sorts of diseases and pass them on to their children and grandchildren.

A final aspect is the assertion that women and men have completely different bodies. Writers argue that as we ascend the evolutionary scale, these differences increase. Many focus especially on the brain, alleging that women's and men's brains are entirely different in structure and function (see especially 1307). Some articles here have application to women's education. The reader will also find in that section and in the section on women's intellect and character material on women's brains.

1783

1291 A Treatise on Dress. New Haven: Thomas & Samuel Green, 32 pp.
   Observes that women are wearing superfluous, dangerous, forbidden garments and ornaments. They do this because they are

haughty and proud and lack proper modesty, meekness, and humble-
ness of mind. "The [Scriptural] command is exceedingly plain,
and nothing but pride of heart, or a haughty disposition to adorn
yourselves with those forbidden things, can keep you from understanding that they are forbidden."

1797

1292   WRIGHT, GEORGE.   The Lady's Miscellany.   Boston: William T.
       Clapp, 225 pp.
       Warns women against approaching the masculine in their
attire, for it will destroy their grace and softness.   Says that
Addison criticized such a transformation in his lady, and the
present age needs such a censor.   Particularly objects to riding
habits which conceal woman's charms, "her figure, her manner, and
her graces."   Says they "wholly unsex her, and give her the
unpleasing air of an Amazon, or a virago."

1848

1293   [NEVIN, JOHN W.]   "'Women's Rights.'"   American Whig Review 8
       (October):367-81.
       Foresees the impossibility of transsexual organ trans-
plants.   "Both anatomically and physiologically considered, the
whole body is made to participate in the sexual character.   Man
and woman are so completely different in their whole organization
that . . . no single part of the one could be properly substi-
tuted for the corresponding part of the other."   Woman who for-
sakes her own character and sphere unsexes herself and becomes
coarse.   "Such an 'emancipation,' made general in any community,
would involve the overthrow ultimately of all taste and refinement, the downfall of all morality and civilization."   It would
also be the end of marriage.

1859

1294   HALE, SARAH JOSEPHA.   "Editors' Table: Costume vs. Criti-
       cism."   Godey's Lady's Book 58 (March):271-72.
       Reports she has been condemned by a medical doctor in New
York State for the kinds of fashions she displays in the Lady's
Book but mocks the dress reformers (with illustrations)--"we
would dissuade any of our friends from wearing such a costume."
Alleges that the strongest women wear close-fitting clothing,
that changing fashions brings improvements to the race, and that
the most morally refined nations are those where the dress of
woman and man is most distinct.

1860

1295   GARDNER, AUGUSTUS K., M.D.   "Physical Decline of American
        Woman." Knickerbocker Magazine 55 (January):37-52.
              Blames fast dances like the polka which jar the frame for
        injuring the health of American women. Also believes that women
        begin abusing themselves at boarding schools and become feeble,
        pale, waxen-faced, nervous, and generally good for nothing.
        Charges widespread infanticide, saying in horror, "Each indi-
        vidual claims for herself whether or not to have children."
        Calls this "arrant laziness, sheer, craven, culpable cowardice"
        and "a dastardly shirking of duty." Asserts that abortions are
        ruining women's health and warns that anyone guilty of this crime
        suffers for many years after in consequence. Opposes taking
        "precautionary measures against conception," saying they cause
        "local congestions, nervous afflictions, and debilities."

1296   L., Mrs. M. "Dress: How to Adorn the Person." Godey's
        Lady's Book 60 (March):230-32.
              Attests that such is the power of Godey's that "if the
        'Bloomer Costume' were to appear in the Lady's Book on the first
        of the month, we should see it in Chestnut Street or Broadway
        within a week after." But hopes that this costume will not gain
        Godey's approval and support. "We do not admire the dress; it is
        unfeminine, and therefore to be avoided."

1297   "Well-Dressed." Godey's Lady's Book 61 (November):433-35.
              Declares that dress affects manners and vice versa. Be-
        lieves no knight would ever have borne arms in defense of a woman
        in the bloomer costume. Warns that dressing imitative woman in
        such a way would make her more like a man: "put her into the
        wide-awake [a hat], the short skirt, the jacket, into the pockets
        of which she is very apt to thrust her hands, you will generally
        find her sayings curt, and her laugh loud."

1869

1298   BENSON, EUGENE. "About Dress and Women." New Eclectic 4
        (May):601-4.
              Quips that "man legislates, woman ornates." Says she ar-
        ranges but does not invent. "With the exception of Miss Anthony
        and a few of her scattered and noisy sisters," woman "shuns
        abstractions. Instead of trying to remake our laws, she remakes
        her costume."

1871

1299   MITCHELL, S. WEIR, M.D. Wear and Tear or Hints for the Over-
        worked. Philadelphia: J.B. Lippincott & Co., 59 pp.

States that young women should have their brains only
lightly tasked until age seventeen at least. Better to abandon
school than lose health. Asserts that today's American woman is
"physically unfit for her duties as woman."

1872

1300   LOGAN, OLIVE SIKES. Get Thee Behind Me, Satan! A Home-born
        Book of Home-truths. New York: Adams, Victor & Co., 298 pp.
        Thinks the suffragists erred twenty-five years ago when
they "associated that movement with eccentric notions of dress."
Calls the bloomer costume "stiff, hard-lined, cast-iron." "Yes,
the woman-suffrage women made a vital mistake in joining on to a
movement which related specially to the social and intellectual
status of woman a side issue . . . such a comparatively trivial
matter as the cut of her clothing." Frankly, she is glad young
women care about dress and appearance.

1873

1301   "The Reform in Dress." Harper's Bazar 6 (13 September):578.
        Allows that dress reform is desirable but denies that it
can be brought about by "gatherings, or public speeches, or loud-
mouthed iterations of the assertion that the present is something
altogether indecent and abominable." Alleges that the bloomer
reform produced little but Dr. Walker. Asserts that women have
an instinct for the beautiful and a love of adornment which
cannot be stopped.

1879

1302   LE CONTE, Professor JOSEPH. "The Genesis of Sex." Popular
        Science Monthly 16 (December):167-79.
        Lecture delivered to a class in comparative physiology at
the University of California in 1877. Provides a scientific
discussion of the development of male and female from asexuality
through bisexuality to unisexuality (separation of the sexes in
different individuals). Warns that "that form of woman's rights
which would assimilate as much as possible the two sexes is certainly in direct conflict with the law of evolution which we have
been tracing."

1880

1303   SWISSHELM, JANE GREY. Half a Century. 2d ed. Chicago:
        Jansen, McClung & Co., 363 pp.
        Deplores the involvement of feminists in dress reform.
"The women themselves, leaders of the malcontents, promulgated

and pressed their claim to bifurcated garments, and the whole
tide of popular discussion was turned into that ridiculous channel." Calls the women's rights movement "madness" and says it
brought out hordes of publicity seekers. Clearly opposes woman
suffrage.

1888

1304   TALMADGE, THOMAS DE WITT. Woman: Her Power and Privilege:
       A Series of Sermons. New York: J.S. Ogilvie, 200 pp.
       Cites Deuteronomy 22:5, says bloomerism in this country
years ago seemed about to break down this divine law "but there
was enough of good in American society to beat back the inde-
cency." Abhors womanish men and finds masculine women equally
repugnant. Describes them as copying man's stalking gait and
striding down the street, wishing they could smoke cigarettes
("and some of them do"), talking boisterously, and roaring with
laughter. "Withal there is an assumed rugosity of apparel."
Pleads: "O woman, stay a woman! You also belong to a very
respectable sex. Do not try to cross over. If you do you will
be a failure as a woman and only a nondescript of a man."

1890

1305   "Modern Mannish Maidens." Eclectic Magazine 114 (April):
       449-58.
       Worries that too much physical exercise "may bring to the
female form [a] masculine and uncomely aspect." Deplores women's
taking up certain games like cricket, hockey, football, boxing,
and even rounders. Women should avoid all games involving violent running, because in them "the movement is constrained and
awkward--may we say it without disrespect? a kind of precipitate
waddle with neither grace, nor dignity." Why are women becoming
mannish? As "the redundant sex" they must jostle for popularity,
and this gives them notoriety. Women are also taking up smoking.
But "we desire to see women remain women, and not aspire to be
poor imitations of men." Reprinted from Blackwood's Edinburgh
Magazine 147 (February):252-64.

1306   COPE, EDWARD D. "The Material Relations of Sex in Society."
       Monist 1 (October):38-47.
       Asserts that woman's disadvantages are of natural origin
and cannot be overcome. She has inferior muscular strength and
is incompetent for active work during menstruation and child-
bearing. She is also mentally disabled, having "inferior power
of mental co-ordination and . . . greater emotional sensibility,
which interferes more or less with rational action." She is
helped and protected by man, but "any system which looks to a
career for women independent of man, such as man pursues, is
abnormal and injurious to her interests."

1892

1307   BROWNE, Sir JAMES CRICHTON.   "Sex in Education." Educational
        Review 4 (September):164-78.
            Alleges that men's brains differ from women's in structure
        and function. Men's brains weigh more than women's. The parie-
        tal lobes are larger in men, occipital lobes larger in women.
        Brains of women are more symmetrical and have fewer convolutions;
        women's brains get more blood but it is of a poorer quality.
        More blood goes to the anterior region of the male brain (voli-
        tion, cognition, and ideomotor processes), and to posterior re-
        gion of female brain (sensory functions). Says overpressure in
        female education affects women's brain, causing it to consume
        itself and bringing nervous disturbances, insomnia, anaemia, and
        general delicacy, anorexia scholastica. Reprinted from Lancet
        (London).

1308   LAWRENCE, GEORGE H.   "The Goddess of Fashion." Godey's Lady's
        Book 125 (December):655-57.
            Calls the dress reformer a "gynecocratic crank" who would
        have woman masquerading in the bloomer costume, whereas women
        have a special prerogative to keep in touch with the latest
        fashions. Indeed, it is a quality of woman's mind that she must
        feed her appetite for the beautiful in the form of finery or
        decoration. This is woman's outlet for her sense of beauty.

1893

1309   LAWRENCE, GEORGE H.   "The Dress Reformer." Godey's Lady's
        Book 126 (January):115-17.
            Calls dress reformers a "peculiar bundle of feminine idio-
        syncrasies." Hopes dress "deformers" will abandon "as a lamen-
        table failure all their tasteless and tiresome reformatory
        schemes." Accuses them of wanting to destroy the "tasteful and
        the beautiful" in woman's dress, forgetting that it is woman's
        special prerogative "to look pretty, sweet and charming" and to
        adorn herself. Defends passing fashion and fads as gratifying
        woman's "insatiate appetite for ever changing moods and fancies."
        Assumes that the dress reformer, a "strong-minded female of
        mannish tendency," dresses in her "roomy and clownish apparel"
        because she is physically unattractive. The average woman knows
        "to be out of fashion is to be out of the world."

1310   MILLER, GEORGE, M.D.   "Female Brains and Girls' Schools: A
        Discussion." Eclectic Magazine 120 (March):355-61.
            A discussion in play form among four male and two female
        characters in which the Medical Knight repeats the traditional
        arguments about woman's brain, etc. A Medical Lady attempts to
        refute his arguments, but he has the first and last word. Hard
        to tell whose side author is on, but he makes the Lady Doctor

look foolish. Reprinted from Gentlemen's Magazine (London) 50
(January):31-41.

1311   "The Individual Significance of Clothes." Godey's Lady's Book
        126 (June):783-86.
             Asserts that "dress is one of the most beneficient results
        of civilization. . . . Nothing is so true an index to a woman's
        character as her clothes." Warns that women who put on masculine
        garments lose something of their womanly charm. Cautions that
        men do not like masculinity in woman's dress. Asserts that women
        ought to study dress as diligently and as painstakingly as any
        fine art.

1312   EDSON, CYRUS, M.D. "American Life and Physical Deteriora-
        tion." North American 157 (October):440-51.
             This commissioner of health of the State and City of New
        York finds that an increasingly large proportion of American
        women are unable to perform their functions as mothers. Says
        girls' studies seriously impair their physical health. Also
        reports that "a very large number of American women now refuse to
        bear children," implying use of abortions ("criminal opera-
        tions"). Those who bear one or two children become invalids.
        The system of education must be changed. Strong influence of
        Clarke notable (see 1010), although he is not mentioned.

1313   "Cui Bono?" Godey's Lady's Book 127 (November):629-30.
             Rails against dress reform and the dress reformer. Finds
        the reform dress ridiculous, ugly, and "uniformly sexless."
        Doubts it is more healthful and comfortable and asserts that "it
        were a brave woman indeed who would voluntarily conceal her
        shapeliness beneath a loose blouse and 'bloomers.'" Compares
        dress reformers to rabid anarchists. Argues that the corset is
        practically indispensable to women.

1895

1314   "At the Parting of the Ways: A Conversation." Atlantic 76
        (November):691-95.
             In this dialogue between "alumna" and "alumnus," he insists
        that women cannot match men athletically. In men we admire
        force, in women grace. "A sinewy, muscular woman is an anomaly,
        pretty sure to offend the nearer she reaches the likeness of
        man." "Alumnus" has the last word.

1897

1315   THOMAS, WILLIAM I. "On a Difference in the Metabolism of the
        Sexes." American Journal of Sociology 3 (July):31-63.
             Women and men have different metabolisms: women are closer
        to plant life, store energy, are anabolic; men are closer to

animal life, consume energy, and are katabolic. Examines a great
body of morphological, physiological, ethnological, and demo-
graphic data to demonstrate that women are nearer to the plant
process than men. Among his proofs is the fact that woman's
brain is smaller than man's most pronouncedly during her period
of reproduction. She converts her surplus energy into offspring.
The allotment of tasks results from these different energy levels.

1898

1316   Etiquette for Americans by a Woman of Fashion. Chicago:
        Herbert S. Stone, 273 pp.
            Takes a dim view of women bicycling, saying that "exclusive
        women must ride bicycles only in the country." Disapproves of
        women smoking or modifying their dress: "The women who chew gum,
        wear yachting caps, bloomers, and bend their backs over handle-
        bars are quite outside the pale of etiquette."

1899

1317   THOMAS, WILLIAM I. "Sex in Primitive Industry." American
        Journal of Sociology 4 (January):474-88.
            The somatological differences shown to exist between man
        and woman are reflected in the labors of primitive society: man
        is engaged in activities requiring strength, violence, speed,
        craft, and foresight; woman is involved in slow, unspasmodic,
        routine, stationary activities. Attention of woman is directed
        to the vegetable environment.

1318   KENEALY, ARABELLA, L.R.C.P. "Woman as an Athlete." Living
        Age 221 (6 May):363-70.
            Asserts that woman has gained in physical strength at the
        expense of her womanly faculties. She used to glide; now she
        strides. She has lost soft flesh and gained joints. "Her move-
        ments are muscular and less womanly. Where they had been quiet
        and graceful, now they are abrupt and direct. Her voice is
        louder, her tones are assertive. She says everything--leaves
        nothing to the imagination." Regards "any extreme of muscle-
        power in a woman as in itself evidence of disease." Also asserts
        that the athletic woman is squandering the birthright of her
        future offspring by developing her muscles. Reprinted from Nine-
        teenth Century (London) 45 (April):636-45. Reprinted in 1319.
        See 1320 for rejoinder.

1319   KENEALY, ARABELLA, M.D. "Woman as an Athlete." Eclectic
        Magazine 132 (June):875-82.
            Reprinted from Nineteenth Century (London). Reprint of
        1318.

1320   KENEALY, ARABELLA, L.R.C.P.   "Woman as an Athlete: A Rejoin-
       der." Living Age 222 (22 July):201-13.
            Repeats her argument (see 1318) that there is finite energy
       in women and that one can have either delicacy or muscularity in
       women, not both. Recommends the rest cure for athletic women.
       Says children of robust women "are, in every instance, inferior--
       if not always physically, certainly in mental quality or in human
       charm--to those of the more womanly type." Uses the example of
       working class women and children for proof. Also insists that
       robust women get cancer, gout, tuberculosis, lunacy, epilepsy,
       and every species of neurosis more often than womanly women.
       Reprinted from Nineteenth Century (London) 45 (June):915-29.
       Reprinted in 1321.

1321   KENEALY, ARABELLA, M.D.   "Woman as an Athlete: A Rejoinder."
       Eclectic Magazine 133 (September):357-69.
            Reprinted from Nineteenth Century (London).   Reprint of
       1320.

                                    1900

1322   W., T.P. "The Redundancy of Spinster Gentlewomen." Living
       Age 227 (1 December):529-44.
            Says that because there is a redundancy of women and a
       decline of marriage, young women are brought into increased
       competition for men. Those who fail affect an air of indepen-
       dence and indifference to the male sex and become exaggeratedly
       athletic. Blames, among other things, "an unnatural preponder-
       ance of the sheer masculine in her blood." This "silly assimila-
       tion of male manners and male sports" is more pronounced among
       less attractive women and leads to "hardening and roughening the
       feminine exterior . . . a strident voice, a self-assertive man-
       ner, a brusque and abrupt address of malekind, and a general
       lapse of attractiveness." Women must give up these male manners.
       Cites Dr. Arabella Kenealy. Reprinted from Scottish Review
       (Paisley, Scotland) 36:88ff. Reprinted in 1324.

1323   "A Plea for Long Skirts." Harper's Bazar 33 (8 December):
       2066.
            An editorial comment. Would prefer women to be lovely
       rather than wear the more hygienic shorter skirts. Asserts that
       "a short-skirted woman on the street, except in a deluge of rain,
       is a blow to one's ideals. The older the woman the greater the
       blow." Wants women to retain their mystery and charm with long
       skirts.

                                    1901

1324   W., T.P. "The Redundancy of Spinster Gentlewomen." Eclectic
       Magazine 136 (January):77-92.

                                    307

Reprinted from <u>Scottish</u> <u>Review</u> (Paisley, Scotland) 36:88ff.
Reprint of 1322.

1906

1325   BOK, EDWARD. "Are Girls Overdoing Athletics?" <u>Ladies'</u> <u>Home</u>
       <u>Journal</u> 23 (May):16.
       Believes that "misdirected physical exercises" are injuring
girls and making for "future invalidism." No woman can attempt
pole-vaulting, high jumping, or broad jumping without injuring
herself. Insists that "girls between fourteen and sixteen years
of age should do no physical work except walking and swimming and
such household labor as does not involve straining or lifting."
Finds undue excitement particularly dangerous in causing "too
great a strain on the developing nervous system."

1907

1326   BOK, EDWARD. "Death's New Clutch on Woman." <u>Ladies'</u> <u>Home</u>
       <u>Journal</u> 24 (October):8.
       Finds that women are suffering more than ever from cases of
"nerves" because they are trying to carry more that their loads
as women. Our grandmothers "were content to be women, wives and
mothers, and not voters and reformers besides." When woman
ventures outside her sphere, then "the rebellious nerves in-
stantly and rightly cry out, 'Thus far shalt thou go, but no
farther.'"

1911

1327   HARLAND, MARION. "Women, First--Please!" <u>Independent</u> 70
       (12 January):75-79.
       Applauds the practice of men giving seats to women, of
which she was reminded by a sign in an elevated railway station
in Boston. Warns that if women are not treated carefully, they
will become mannish. This can happen also because of too much
physical exercise. Women can never become men, only indifferent
copies.

1328   BOK, EDWARD. "When Women Ape Men." <u>Ladies'</u> <u>Home</u> <u>Journal</u> 28
       (15 March):5.
       Is shocked by a store's offering for sale "mannish" apparel
for women. Says it is all right for women to have qualities like
courage, endurance, and self-reliance, which one normally looks
for in men, and for men to be patient, sympathetic, and tender
when necessary, "but a womanish man or a mannish woman is a
caricature." Insists that "what God has made separate and different it is folly for woman and man to try to reshape in one
mould."

308

1912

1329   [ABBOTT, LYMAN].   "The Enemy at the Gate."   <u>Outlook</u> 100
        (6 April):767-68.
        Editor suggests some remedies for the evils described in
Max Schlapp's article in the same issue (see 1330), among them
that "the forces that are driving women into the keen competition
of industrialism and away from the home should be studied and
should be resisted." Worries that the coming generation is being
injured by the burdens being placed on women's weak shoulders.
Girls should be trained to see that motherhood is their highest
calling and that competition with men is not an enlargement of
woman's sphere.

1330   SCHLAPP, MAX G., M.D.   "The Enemy at the Gate."   <u>Outlook</u> 100
        (6 April):782-88.
        Asserts that the tension of modern life is causing the
family to break up and criminals and imbeciles to be born in
every grade of life. Women are becoming abnormally active,
demanding the vote, "breaking up meetings, storming and insulting
public men in the streets, throwing stones, and smashing windows." Finds these conditions "only an evidence of a nervous
distress that has become universal." Women are shunning child-
bearing and the birthrate is dropping. Worse, the number of
defectives born is growing alarmingly. This is because women are
no longer quiescent. When women act like men, they use up energy
faster than it can be stored, and "in extreme cases the natural
function will cease." Better to save her energy for her
offspring.

1331   SCHLAPP, Dr. MAX G.   "Our Perilous Waste of Vitality."
        <u>Literary Digest</u> 44 (27 April):878-79.
        Condensation and reprint of 1330.

Index

Index

Index

Index

Index

Index